THE CASE OF GEORGE PELL

Melissa Davey has been *Guardian Australia*'s Melbourne bureau chief for several years. She has been nominated for three Walkley Awards and two Quill Awards, and has won two New York Festival awards for *The Reckoning,* a podcast series she collaborated on with David Marr and Miles Martignoni. She has also won awards from medical bodies for her work reporting on rheumatic heart disease in Aboriginal children, and for her investigation into the brutality of gynaecologist Emil Shawky Gayed. The latter triggered a government inquiry and saw her win a Walkley in 2019.

Melissa frequently appears on BBC World News, and on commercial radio in Australia and overseas.

melissaldavey.com
@MelissaLDavey

THE
CASE OF
GEORGE
PELL

reckoning with
child sexual abuse by clergy

MELISSA DAVEY

SCRIBE
Melbourne • London

Scribe Publications
2 John St, Clerkenwell, London, WC1N 2ES, United Kingdom
18–20 Edward St, Brunswick, Victoria 3056, Australia
3754 Pleasant Ave, Suite 100, Minneapolis, Minnesota 55409, USA

Published by Scribe 2020

Typeset in 12/17 pt Adobe Garamond Pro by the publishers

Printed and bound in the UK by CPI Group (UK) Ltd, Croydon
CR0 4YY

Scribe Publications is committed to the sustainable use of natural
resources and the use of paper products made responsibly from those
resources.

9781912854707 (UK edition)
9781925849684 (US edition)
9781925938159 (ebook)

A catalogue record for this book is available from the British Library.

scribepublications.co.uk
scribepublications.com
scribepublications.com.au

*I dedicate this book to all those who were ignored,
disbelieved, or threatened by people with the power to do
something, but who instead chose to be complicit.*

Contents

One	Committal	1
Two	Royal commission	23
Three	Mistrial: part I	71
Four	Mistrial: part II	96
Five	The evidence ends	144
Six	Hung	157
Seven	The missing witness	197
Eight	Retrial: part I	208
Nine	Retrial: part II	244
Ten	Martyr	276
Eleven	Appeal	298
Twelve	Acquittal	320
Thirteen	Victims	351
Fourteen	Perpetrators	365

Author's note 391
Acknowledgements 395
Appendix A: Joint trials or separate trials? 399
Appendix B: Jury trials or judge-only trials? 403
Index 409

CHAPTER ONE

Committal

'Accountability of the hierarchy means criminal accountability
for the crime of concealment. We don't have one criminal
conviction in Australia against members of the hierarchy of the
Catholic Church who have taken part in concealing abuse that
occurred. And those who are overseas enjoy impunity.'

– Dr Judy Courtin, lawyer

It was the middle of the night in Rome on 29 June 2017, six months
before Australia's Royal Commission into Institutional Responses
to Child Sexual Abuse was due to deliver its final report, when
detectives from Victoria Police's Taskforce SANO served a summons
on Cardinal George Pell's legal representatives in Melbourne. He
was charged with historical child sexual abuse offences, and was
ordered to appear in court in Melbourne on 26 July that same year.
Victoria Police's deputy commissioner, Shane Patton, only said that
there were multiple complainants. It was not clear what had been
alleged, what the specific charges were, or how many charges there
were.

There had been talk of the police investigation and potential
charges for months, ever since Melbourne-based reporter Lucie
Morris-Marr broke the story for News Corp of a police probe into
allegations against Pell. In July 2016, I had also spoken to a man,
Les Tyack, who told me he saw Pell 'very clearly' exposing himself

to three young boys at Torquay Life Saving Club in the summer of 1986 or 1987. I asked Tyack if he had told any of his friends about the incident at the time. He named two friends and gave me their phone numbers. I called those people immediately after getting off the phone to Tyack, before he could warn them that I might ring, and both men verified his story.

Tyack told me that when he walked into the change rooms, Pell was there, and he was facing three young boys while towelling his back.

'Then I went to have a shower and he was still standing there when I got out, this time with the towel draped over his shoulder and full-frontal facing the boys,' Tyack said.

Tyack said the boys appeared to be about eight to 10 years old, and were about two to three metres in front of Pell on the bench along the opposite wall to the entrance.

Tyack said the boys were dressed by the time he got out of the shower, and he told them to gather their belongings and leave the room. He said he then spoke to Pell.

'I said, "I know what you're up to. Get dressed and piss off, and don't come back to the surf club. If I see you here again, I'll call the police."'

He said he never saw Pell again.

'I'd seen him in the surf club two or three weeks prior to the incident, and I didn't know who he was. I was talking to a couple of surf club members and I said, "Who's that guy?," and they said, "That's George Pell," expecting me to know who he was and that he was a bishop. That's why I didn't tell the police at the time, because I thought who's going to believe me over a bishop of the Church? But it was something I did mention to mates early in the piece.'

At the same time, two former St Alipius students alleged to journalist Louise Milligan on the ABC's *7.30 Report* that Pell had repeatedly touched their genitals while swimming with them at the

Eureka pool in Ballarat in 1978–79. Pell was episcopal vicar for education in the Ballarat diocese at the time.

In October 2016, news broke that Pell had been interviewed in Rome by police about allegations against him. So in mid-2017, while the news of charges being laid was not surprising, it was still sensational. At the time, Pell was the treasurer of the Vatican and the Holy See, a position that placed him as one of the top men in charge after the Pope. He was once believed to be in the running to replace Pope Francis. Once charges were laid against him, Pell became the highest-ranking Catholic official in the world to be facing trial over historical sexual-offence allegations. There had been rumours, until then, that charges might be laid at any moment, or that perhaps the case would be dropped at any moment, on the grounds that the offences were too historical and the evidence too weak. The media had been playing a waiting game.

At a televised press conference held in the hours after the news of the charges being laid broke, Pell vehemently denied what he was being accused of.

'There has been relentless character assassination for months,' he said, adding that he was 'looking forward finally to having my day in court. I am innocent of these charges, they are false.'

'The whole idea of sexual abuse is abhorrent to me,' he continued. 'I've kept Pope Francis, the Holy Father, regularly informed during these long months and have spoken to him on a number of occasions in the last week, most recently a day or so ago.

'All along I have been completely consistent and clear in my total rejection of these allegations. News of these charges strengthens my resolve, and court proceedings now offer an opportunity to clear my name and return back to work.'

A statement from the Vatican said that the Holy See respected the Australian justice system, but added:

At the same time, it is important to recall that Cardinal Pell has openly and repeatedly condemned as immoral and intolerable the acts of abuse committed against minors; has cooperated in the past with Australian authorities (for example, in his depositions before the royal commission); has supported the Pontifical Commission for the Protection of Minors; and finally, as a diocesan bishop in Australia, has introduced systems and procedures both for the protection of minors and to provide assistance to victims of abuse.

On 5 March 2018, day one of the committal hearing of Pell, I had no inkling that this case was about to consume the next couple of years, at least, of my life. I was a mid-level reporter, one face in a media pack that included reporters from around the globe who had descended on the Magistrates Court on William Street in Melbourne. They were all vying for a seat in the committal hearing and hoping to learn more about what the cardinal was being accused of having done. Meanwhile, governments around the world were holding inquiries into institutional child sexual abuse.

I could not know then that one year later I'd be receiving emails, messages on social media, and phone calls from people wanting to know more about the case, demanding answers. I did not fathom that I'd receive emails from staunch Catholics, from priests, who would write their own expansive takes on the case based on hearsay or research after the fact, demanding I read their work. When I did not respond, they would email again, reminding me that I had not read their arguments for Pell's innocence, and demanding I do so. I would be accused of bias for simply having been at court and having reported on what was said. I would burn out. I would receive calls throughout the day and night from international media wanting to interview me about what had unfolded. My mental health and stamina began to seriously deteriorate.

But on that day, 5 March 2018, I was simply at work, covering a story of international interest, as I had done for other topics and major events many times before.

A committal hearing is not a trial. Rather, it's an opportunity, from the defence team's perspective, to test the Crown's witnesses to see if they stick to the evidence in their statements, and to explore evidence beyond that contained in their statements to ensure there will be no nasty surprises in the presence of a jury in a later trial. Sometimes, the committal is an opportunity to have serious, indictable charges against their client dismissed on the basis of weak evidence. Mostly, though, it is an opportunity for the defence to learn more about witnesses and the evidence being relied on by prosecutors, so that if the case does go to trial, they can better prepare.

A senior detective in Victoria Police told me, 'Some use it to identify weak aspects of the evidence for later exploitation in the presence of a jury. Very rarely, the committal hearing can result in the total capitulation of a Crown case, to the extent that the case may be dismissed, but this is rarely the case, due to committal rules.

'At a committal, the evidence of the Crown case must be taken "at its highest". The question is not whether the accused person is guilty beyond reasonable doubt, but rather whether a jury, properly instructed, considering all of the evidence "taken at its highest", could – not would – be satisfied of the accused's guilt beyond reasonable doubt. So matters of credibility and reliability of a witness play a far less significant role in a committal, as they are matters in the realm of jury consideration.'

From the prosecution's perspective, a committal hearing is a chance to test the evidence to see if their case has a good chance of succeeding at trial. (In Australia, whether this is a judge-only trial or one heard before a jury depends on the state or territory.) A prosecutor represents the state, territory, or federal government, and acts to uphold the laws of those governments. From the public's perspective, the committal process can prevent abuses of power; it's a means of holding prosecutors to account when they charge people with serious crimes to ensure their investigations have been rigorous enough to justify doing so. It can ensure they aren't acting based on spurious or selfish political interests. Going to trial is also expensive and laborious. It is not in the public interest for a trial to be held that has little to no chance of succeeding, when those resources could be spent prosecuting elsewhere.

It is not unusual for a person charged with serious criminal offences not to give evidence at committal, since anything they say can be used as evidence in a resulting trial. Because there is no jury, witnesses can be put through the wringer by legal counsel in a way that can feel more adversarial than at a trial. Of course, there are rules in a committal hearing; it's not a case of 'anything goes' in terms of questions that can be asked of witnesses. But defence barristers especially may test the witnesses and the boundaries of the court rules to see, at best, if they can get the prosecution to capitulate, and the case to fail or be withdrawn. More usually, if prosecution or defence counsel sense uncertainty or weakness, or something to exploit, they know where to focus their attack in any trial that might follow. Similarly, if a witness is credible and comes across as honest, defence barristers may start preparing their client for the possibility of plea talks.

I spoke about these matters with Peter O'Brien, a criminal defence lawyer in New South Wales who represented many victims at the child sexual abuse royal commission, and who works for defendants and complainants in the criminal justice system. He told me that committals don't always involve a lengthy hearing, and are often quick and administrative.

'The committal process has changed a lot over the last 20 years, and in some instances it is almost perfunctory, where there is no real set of proceedings other than an adjournment to the higher court,' he said. 'There are higher tests in Victoria and New South Wales to demonstrate it's in the interest of justice for complainants in sexual assault matters to give evidence at committal.'

The role of the magistrate is to listen to all of the evidence and to rule on whether the prosecution's case is capable of satisfying a jury beyond reasonable doubt on any or all of the offences a defendant has been charged with. The magistrate will dismiss some or all of the charges if the evidence does not meet this test. This does not mean the defendant is innocent – that's not what a magistrate is ruling on. Clearly, if a defendant pleads guilty, cases are generally more straightforward; that plea is noted, along with any statement given by the defendant, and the case is sent to the County or Supreme Court for sentencing. Charges may also be dropped by prosecutors for various reasons during or prior to a committal hearing; perhaps a witness has become unwell, has died, or has dramatically changed their report.

Pell's case was extraordinary, not only because he was the world's most senior Catholic cleric to be facing child sexual abuse charges. The prospect that he might go on to face trial, and that this would occur in Victoria – a state where a judge-only trial was not an option – meant there was a risk that reporting on the committal hearing might prejudice any potential jurors if Pell was ultimately committed to stand trial. It meant that while journalists could be present in the court to report on the committal proceedings, we could not report the specific charges he was facing, or even report the overall number of charges. Not only that, but we were not told what the charges were. We, of course, learned about some of them as we sat in the court, but we were learning on the fly, little able to prepare, and seriously restricted in how we could report on the various witnesses who gave evidence, in case we also revealed the names of victims or the charges Pell faced. Witnesses in sexual assault cases are protected in Victoria – publishing identifying details is illegal.

The only expression we were allowed to use to report the charges at the time was that Pell had been charged with 'historical sexual assault offences', due to a strict suppression order issued by the court to prevent disclosure of certain information in the case. Suppression orders are not at all unusual in sexual assault cases: they protect both the alleged victim and the defendant, and also protect against the risk of jurors being prejudiced by details in media reports. Suppression orders are rarely permanent, and are usually lifted once the legal process in complete.

There was already commentary about whether someone as senior as Pell could receive a fair trial, even with a suppression order in place. Ahead of the committal, I spoke to an international legal expert, Professor Gideon Boas, a barrister and professor of law at La Trobe University, who told me, 'Just because Pell happens to be a very senior member of the Catholic Church, it does not mean he will not receive fair and impartial treatment, or that a court wouldn't be capable of delivering a verdict based on the evidence placed before them in the same way it does in many high-profile cases.

'We often see cases where a well-known person is charged with serious offences and yet they receive a fair trial. I also think most of the reporting on Pell has been fair, balanced, and factual, and the fact is we have a system in place whereby people, no matter who they are or what they're charged with, are entitled to a fair trial.'

In a statement, the Catholic archdiocese of Melbourne reiterated that Pell was entitled to a fair trial. Pell had 'been a friend and brother priest' of the Melbourne archbishop, Denis Hart, for more than 50 years, the statement said.

'The Archbishop is conscious of the Cardinal's many good works which have been acknowledged both nationally and internationally,' the archdiocese said. 'It is important all in society recognise that the presumption of innocence applies.'

Conservative commentators and politicians who said they were worried about Pell receiving a fair trial nevertheless weighed in on the case publicly. Former prime minister Tony Abbott told Fairfax media that 'the George Pell I have known is a very fine man indeed'. The Archbishop of Hobart, Julian Porteous, told *The Mercury* newspaper in Tasmania that he was 'shocked and disappointed' that Pell had been charged.

'The possibility of a fair trial is compromised,' Porteous insisted. 'I don't know how a jury could proceed with a trial where [there is] so much media out there.'

Early on, there was a blow to the prosecution's case. On 2 March 2018, three days before the committal hearing, prosecutors withdrew one of the multiple charges against Pell because the accuser had died of cancer on 6 January 2018. Details of the charge that was dropped could not be reported at the time because of the impending committal hearing and the potential for prejudice.

The accuser was Damian Dignan, who, in March 2016, along with two other boys, had alleged on the ABC's *7.30* program that he had been molested by Pell. Dignan said his abuse had occurred at a swimming pool in Ballarat. Australian media at the time could only report that a charge had been dropped after an accuser had died, although some media did name Dignan. Other news organisations felt that even naming Dignan was a risk, because if members of the public had seen the *7.30* episode, they might recall the accusations and make assumptions about the charges Pell faced. This would be a problem if they were then selected for the jury. The difference in coverage revealed that even lawyers acting for media companies were grappling with the suppression order and what it meant. The fierce debate about whether the trial could be fair, combined with the risk of breaching a court-ordered suppression order, meant that most media organisations were justifiably terrified of breaching the order; however, some pushed boundaries more than others.

Police formed a wall on either side of the footpath along William Street, flanking Pell on both sides as he walked up to the court on the first day, where reporters from dozens of news outlets from around the world were waiting. Outside the court, people held up placards that read, 'No trial by media' and 'The truth will set you free'.

When Pell entered the courtroom shortly after 9.00 am, a woman called out, 'Hello, Father.' Lawyers dealt largely with administrative and preliminary matters before closing the court to the media and the public just before 10.30 am, because the alleged victims were to give evidence.

It was my first introduction to Pell's defence barrister, Robert Richter, renowned in legal circles for his theatrical interrogation style, his meticulous attention to detail, and his ability to uncover evidence that detectives had missed. Mostly, he was known for representing some of Victoria's most notorious gangland figures, and successfully. He was an interesting choice for Pell: Richter is a progressive atheist; Pell, a conservative Catholic. But Pell chose the best, not the most Catholic, when it came to his personal affairs, including his case. Richter, like Pell, is in his seventies. Unlike Pell, Richter is slim, his black barrister robes draping his body. Once a heavy smoker, he could at times be seen pacing outside the court, vaping. He sports a squared grey beard and black, round-framed spectacles, and speaks with pomp and flair.

On day one, the court heard that the alleged victims, known as complainants, would have support staff next to them while they gave evidence in a remote-witness facility. Prosecutors also asked for permission for a witness support dog to be allowed in the facility, which was described in the court as 'a relatively new initiative'.

Richter responded, 'I always thought dogs were there for children and very old people, but if they want a dog ...' To which the magistrate presiding over the committal, Belinda Wallington, swiftly replied, 'They're also for vulnerable people.'

Richter replied, 'Well, whatever comfort the dog can give, we don't object to the dog.' Richter, tongue in cheek, asked for Pell to be allowed a priest as a support person, owing to his age and a medical condition. In the end, Pell had to make do with his loyal supporter and friend Katrina Lee, the executive advisor for the Archdiocese of Sydney. She sat in the court with him most days, one row behind him, one seat to his left. Pell sat in the front row.

The next two weeks were a blur of witnesses being called to the stand, peppered with questions that reporters – with no knowledge of the charges Pell was facing, or of who was accusing him of what, and when – struggled to relate to the broader picture. Wallington's decision as to whether to order Pell to stand trial would largely hinge on evidence that neither the media nor the public were privy to. The complainants were cross-examined in the first week and a half of the hearing, which was held behind closed doors. This is not unusual in cases involving sexual-offence allegations, as it serves to prevent alleged victims from being put on public display. But with much of the hearing closed to media, and details of the charges unable to be reported for legal reasons, journalists were forced to omit details and explanations from their reports. What was left to report, then and now, was Richter's cross-examination of witnesses who were not the accusers.

Perhaps the most telling example of Richter's style of defending came when he called for the magistrate, Her Honour Belinda Wallington, to stand down. Wallington is highly experienced in sexual assault cases – and at the time of Pell's committal, she was the supervising magistrate for sexual offences. She was unlikely to be swayed by Richter's descriptions of one witness as a 'nutter', or of others as being unreliable because of time they had spent in psychiatric wards. And she was utterly unmoved when Richter accused her of bias towards prosecutors and told her she should disqualify herself from hearing the case. Wallington calmly responded, 'Your application is refused.' The case continued, and Richter moved on. None of the legal counsel looked surprised. This was just Richter at work.

On 14 March, once all of the complainants had given evidence and been cross-examined, the media were allowed to return to the court. We learned over the next two weeks that there had been further setbacks to the prosecution case. Another witness had withdrawn from the case, citing serious illness. Another made a fresh statement to police, which meant that his previous statement needed to be withdrawn and his allegations considered separately as part of a new investigation. Details of these statements and victims, and their allegations, were not given to the media.

What followed in the committal hearing was evidence from a series of witnesses who were never called when the case ultimately went to trial. This included family members of the victim whose complaint that Pell had sexually abused him and his friend when they were both 13-year-old boys in Melbourne's St Patrick's Cathedral choir would ultimately lead to Pell being unanimously convicted by a jury some nine months later.

The father of the choirboy who said he and a fellow choirboy were abused by Pell at St Patrick's gave evidence, and can only be identified as 'S' in order to protect his son's identity. His son had reported the alleged offending to police as an adult. S and other family members of the boys did not give evidence during the subsequent trial because their evidence was hearsay – that is, they had not been direct witnesses of the alleged offences, and had learned of the alleged abuse too long after it first occurred. Generally, with some exceptions, hearsay evidence is prohibited. So these witnesses were dropped by the time of the trial, and the jurors never heard what they had to say.

In the committal hearing, the court learned that S had been interviewed by police in 2015. He told them that, 'looking back, things make a lot of sense to me now' in relation to his son. He told the court he got the general impression his son was happy and enjoying singing in the St Patrick's Cathedral choir in 1996, when he was 13 years old. But things then changed.

'In 1997 I just got the impression he wasn't really settled there,' he told the court. 'I got the impression he was bullied.' In his twenties, his son went on to have 'a pretty rough time of it' in relation to abusing alcohol, S said.

'The only thing I can say is I was assessing his state of mind as a father, and he just seemed to me to be not settled or happy with himself, content,' S told the court.

Richter told the court that S never mentioned Pell by name when he gave a statement to police in 2015 about what he knew about allegations his son had been sexually offended against while in the St Patrick's Cathedral choir. In his statement, S mentioned only notorious paedophile Gerald Ridsdale and 'priests', but never named Pell, Richter told the court. S replied that this was because his son did not want to talk about the allegations involving Pell, and could not bring himself to tell him about it. His son asked his older brother to tell S about the allegations for him. Richter put it to S that an allegation involving Pell was 'an invention of yours since July 2015 when you made your statement' to police. 'You've just made that up after you've made your statement, right?' Richter said. 'Between July 2015 and today, you made that up.'

S responded, 'That is an insult. No.'

The choirboy's sister and brother also gave evidence at committal.

The sister, identified only as 'H', said her brother had told her a bishop had exposed himself to him while he was a choirboy, and that the culprit was 'fucking George Pell'.

Richter accused H of making up the part about Pell being named by her brother. H denied making it up. Her brother was crying when he made the disclosure, H said. When she raised the conversation with her brother again at a later date to see if he was okay, he refused to talk about it further, she said.

Richter pressed her on why she didn't try to get more details about the allegation from her brother. 'Don't you care?' he asked her.

'Of course I do,' she replied. 'It was [my brother's] private pain and it's not for me to know unless he wants me to know. I was very concerned about the allegation, but I could see it was very embarrassing and hurtful for [him] … I didn't want to continue to probe him.' She said her brother also told her in the car that what had happened to him 'has fucked me up, you have no idea how much it has fucked me up', and that Pell 'pulled his dick out'. Her brother went to police to make a formal statement in 2015, the court heard.

Asked to elaborate on the disclosure her brother made to her, H told the court, 'We were coming home from my grandmother's eightieth birthday. We were in the back of the car. We'd both had quite a bit to drink. My younger brother was in the front of the car with his girlfriend. [My brother] said something along the lines of, "You don't know what's happened to me. He exposed himself to me." I said, "Who, what, why?" And he said, "A bishop." And then he said that it was George Pell.'

Richter: You came from a good Catholic family, yes?

H: Yes.

Richter: And you said to him, 'What, do you mean George Pell, he was the archbishop, not the bishop,' didn't you?

H: No. I was raised a Catholic, but I wasn't a strict Catholic by any means, and I didn't know the ins and outs of positions and people within the Church.

Richter: Are you seriously telling this court that you had no idea about the distinction between an archbishop and a bishop?

H: I am telling you that, yes.

When Wallington asked Richter why this mattered, he responded that he was 'testing her credibility on not knowing the difference between an archbishop and a bishop'. At the time of the alleged offending, Pell was the Archbishop of Melbourne, and not a bishop.

Richter then put it to H, 'You were pretty drunk, weren't you?'

H: Yes.

Richter: This is an exchange between two drunken people after a lengthy session of drinking, right?

Again, Wallington intervened. 'Well, hold on,' she told Richter. 'It wasn't a lengthy session. They were at a party, and they ...'

Richter interrupted her. 'They were both drunk.'

Later, as the committal hearing came to a close, Richter would tell Wallington that he was well aware of his interrogative and confronting cross-examination style, saying, 'Whilst I have to confess to cross-examining witnesses sometimes with some, what might be considered, brutality, it was necessary from time to time in order to try and expose perjury, and so while I confess for the manner, I do not apologise for the content.'

As well as hearing from family members of the choirboy, the court heard that several men alleged Pell had sexually offended against them while playing games with them as children at a swimming pool in Ballarat in the 1970s. One of the men also alleged he was sexually offended against in the pool change room. The court heard from their family members, too.

The sister of one of the alleged pool victims said her brother had accused Pell of abusing him at the Eureka pool in Ballarat in the 1970s, and had told her that 'George put his hand and fingers up their backside'.

'And into his anus?' Richter asked.

'No, he didn't say that,' she replied.

The alleged pool victim's other sister also gave evidence, telling the court that in around 2012 or 2013, her brother 'made the comment that when being in the pool and being thrown up high, that was an opportunity for the accused [Pell] to place his finger up your [the victim's] bum'.

Richter asked, 'That denotes penetration, is that right? Did your brother ever claim that he had had his anus penetrated?'

She responded, 'Not to my knowledge, no.'

Throughout the committal, Pell sat each day in courtroom 22 in the same seat, head bowed, sometimes taking notes, always dressed in the same outfit: black pants, black shirt, and a beige jacket. At one point, someone left an Easter egg on his chair in the front row.

One of the more distressing allegations that was revealed during the committal came from a man who said that, when he was a child, Pell would take him from the boys' home where he was a ward of the state and rape him. One of these alleged rapes occurred during a screening in Ballarat of the film *Close Encounters of the Third Kind*. A former cinema usher and projector operator of the theatre, John Bourke, was asked by Richter whether he had ever noticed Pell attend a screening of the film, and he said he had not.

'If a child was heard to scream out on the balcony, an usher would have heard, yes?' Richter put to him.

Bourke responded that, yes, an usher would have investigated.

Bourke was asked if he ever noticed blood on the seats of the theatre. He said he had not, although he added that that was something a cleaner more likely would have identified and cleaned.

When Wallington delivered her decision on 1 May 2018 as to whether Pell would face trial, journalists learned that Pell had been facing 26 charges, but we still could not report this. Seven of those charges had been dropped or withdrawn before or during the committal hearing, we learned.

Wallington threw out eight charges relating to the man who said that he had been raped as a boy by Pell at the cinema and other locations. Wallington found the witness was not credible. The offences were alleged to have occurred over a 12-month period from September 1978, when the complainant said he was removed by nuns and by Pell from the St Joseph's boys' home and taken to various locations and raped, including at the movie theatre. But records showed to the court revealed that the complainant did not live at the boys' home during this time. His foster mother also gave evidence that the complainant did not live in the boys' home during that time, but lived with her.

'He [the complainant] could not reconcile the differences,' Wallington found as she delivered her decision. 'In this case the inconsistencies must be examined as a fundamental defect in evidence.' She said this had damaged the complainant's reliability. 'I find [his] evidence as a whole is not of sufficient weight for a jury to convict,' she said.

Charge 15 related to a complainant identified only as 'MB'. MB moved to Ballarat with his family as a child. On 27 July 2016, he watched a program about Cardinal Pell on the ABC's *7.30*, and a few days later he contacted ABC journalist Louise Milligan to say that he had information about Cardinal Pell offending at the Eureka pool in Ballarat. He told her he had sent an email to *The Sydney*

Morning Herald saying he had seen something at the pool, but that she was the first person he had spoken to. Milligan took notes of their conversations and later wrote about his experiences in her book on Pell. MB said that when he was a child and swam in the pool, 'Pell slid his hands around the front of my groin. It was a gentle touch or a caress of my penis and testicles from the front. Again this was done so that no one could see what he was doing, always under the water.'

Wallington found that MB had demonstrated a poor memory during the committal hearing, not just of the alleged abuse 40 years earlier, 'but also of two years ago when he gave his statement and even of his answers given shortly before in his evidence'. MB's lack of recall was often a non-responsive way of avoiding answering the questions, Wallington found.

> When clarity was sought, he said variously, 'Just whatever, mate, whatever', or 'I'll leave it up to you. Whatever you think works' and 'No comment.' To the question, do you recall what you said a minute ago, he responded, 'I can't recall.' The Crown in their submissions concede that MB's behaviour in cross-examination can be seen as being uncooperative with the process. MB was an unsatisfactory witness. It is difficult to see how a jury could convict on the evidence of a man who has said on his affirmation that he cannot recall what he said one minute ago. Even allowing for the stresses of giving evidence, the overall effect of MB's evidence is that the only matter upon which he is able to be certain is his allegation. His evidence is crucial to proof of the charge. In my view this is one of those rare cases where the witness demonstrated such a cavalier attitude towards giving his evidence that a jury could put no weight on it. The accused is discharged on charge 15.

Wallington ordered that Pell stand trial on charge 16, an indecent assault alleged against a victim identified only as 'PC'. PC had lived at the St Joseph's boys' home in Ballarat from the time he was a baby. PC told police that Pell would come to the home in the summer to use the pool, and that children would climb up on him in the pool. He alleged Pell put his hands up inside his shorts and put his finger in his anus.

'It hurt a lot [according to PC], and it happened a number of times over the years,' Wallington noted. 'In my view, the allegation that it happened on multiple occasions weakens the hypothesis of an accident. I am satisfied that the evidence of PC is sufficient weight upon which a jury could convict, and the accused is committed for trial on charge 16.'

Charge 17 involved a complainant identified as 'LT', who also attended the Eureka pool regularly as a boy and said he would often see Pell there. He described Pell as 'a magnet' to all the male children there, and said Pell would throw the boys around in the pool. On a day at either the end of grade five or six, LT joined the throwing game for the first and only time. He said Pell put one of his hands on his left arm and placed the other onto his right buttock over his shorts, and that it felt like one of Pell's fingers touched his testicles. He said he felt very uncomfortable, and didn't get back into the pool after that when Pell was there. But under cross-examination by Richter, it was put to LT that the touching could have been an accident, to which he replied, 'I do not know, I don't know.'

'These concessions are fatal to the prosecution case,' Wallington said.

Another complainant, 'AS', described a day when his family went water-skiing at Lake Boga in the summer of 1975, when he was 10 years old. Pell visited the lake, and AS said he would stand on Pell's shoulders to balance before jumping into the lake. He said Pell kept sliding his hands up higher and higher until his fingers were digging into his groin area. He also said that when he slipped down the front of Pell's body, Pell had an erect penis. His evidence had similarities to the complainant identified as 'PC', who said that on three occasions in a swimming pool, Pell 'stuck his finger in my arse, through my togs which made me let go and fall off him. His finger didn't go into my anus, just between my bum cheeks.' Meanwhile, complainant LT said that while playing a throwing game in the pool with Pell he 'felt his other hand reach up and hold my crotch area. The hand on my crotch would cover my penis and testicles and would also cover my anus area. On half of these occasions he would also place his hands under the shorts and underpants I was wearing. His fingers would touch my penis and testicles on these occasions.'

Wallington found the totality of the evidence of PC, LT, and AS meant that a jury might convict on two possible charges, and she ordered Pell to stand trial on those charges.

Charges 20 to 26 related to the complainant who said that Pell had sexually assaulted him and his friend at St Patrick's Cathedral when they were 13-year-old boys. Wallington ordered Pell to face trial on those charges, too. In total, Pell was committed to face trial on 10 charges: seven relating to offences against two choirboys that occurred at St Patrick's Cathedral in the 1990s, and three relating to offending that occurred in swimming pools in Ballarat in the 1970s.

'You may plead guilty or not guilty,' Wallington told Pell. 'It is your right to plead not guilty to all of the charges or some of them. Whatever you say will be recorded and may be given in evidence if you appear before a judge. Do you plead guilty or not guilty?'

Pell stood up and declared he was 'not guilty'. He would maintain his innocence throughout the trial.

Because the charges that Wallington ordered be heard before a jury related to two different locations and two different periods of time, they were separated into two trials. (For a brief discussion of the arguments for joint or separate trials, see Appendix A.) The charges relating to St Patrick's Cathedral would be heard in August 2018, and the charges relating to the Ballarat swimming pools would be heard in November 2018. It was decided that the first case, which became known by those in the court as 'the Cathedral trial', would be heard before the chief judge of the County Court, Peter Kidd.

It was official. Pell would be facing a jury.

During directions hearings before Pell's Cathedral trial, it was decided that the evidence of certain witnesses in the committal hearing was inadmissible under the *Evidence Act*, and so those witnesses would not be called during the trial. This included the evidence from the complainant's family members. Chief Judge Kidd also ordered that a suppression order be placed on the case. Because there would be two trials – the Cathedral trial and the Swimmers' trial – the suppression order could not be lifted until both trials were complete, because jurors selected for the second trial risked being prejudiced by the outcome of the first. This type of suppression order is not at all unusual in cases where a defendant faces multiple trials. The suppression order in Pell's case prohibited reporting about any part of the trials in any state or territory in Australia, including on any website or in any media accessible from Australia.

Suppression orders are not meant to be a catch-all that prevents every detail from a trial from ever being leaked. But they are a mechanism to mitigate any damage and to keep information that is published prior to a trial as minimal as possible. In Pell's case, both the prosecution and the defence wanted the suppression order in place, and no media organisations opposed the move. Journalists were only allowed to report, going forward, that Pell had been charged with multiple historical sexual assault offences and would stand trial. We could not report the dates of the trial, or the fact that the trial was underway once it started.

So, with a near blanket suppression order in place, journalists prepared to enter the trial of the most powerful Catholic figure in the world ever to have been charged with child sexual abuse, knowing we would not be able to report a word about it for months on end.

CHAPTER TWO

Royal commission

'Such high status also meant that complete and unsupervised
access to children was unquestioned. Indeed, in a number of
cases we heard that parents were delighted if attention was
shown to their child by a religious member of their faith.'
– Justice Jennifer Coate, Royal Commission into Institutional
Responses to Child Sexual Abuse

Cardinal Pell's committal hearing and subsequent order to stand
trial followed one of the most thorough and comprehensive
investigations into child sexual abuse in the world. On 13 August
2014, reporters from newsrooms throughout the state of Victoria,
Australia, attended a briefing by the Royal Commission into
Institutional Responses to Child Sexual Abuse. The chair of the
commission, Justice Peter McClellan, was at this intimate and
entirely off-the-record media briefing. He gave no exclusive media
interviews throughout the commission's work, and has not done any
since it ended.

McClellan's desire to meet with reporters and to provide
them with a background overview of the commission's work
spoke to the seriousness with which the commission was taking
its task and the gravity of what was unfolding. By that point, the
commission – which formally opened on 3 April 2013 – had heard
hundreds of stories of child sexual abuse from throughout Australia.

Barely one year into its five-year-long inquiry, it had already held more than 1,800 private sessions with child sexual abuse survivors, along with 15 public hearings. During hearings in Sydney, it had heard from victims who felt they had been failed by the Catholic Church's 'Towards Healing' protocol, officially called 'Towards Healing: principles and procedures in responding to complaints of abuse against personnel of the Catholic Church in Australia protocol'. This was the Catholic Church's internal method of responding to, addressing, and resolving allegations made by child sexual abuse victims. The Church also used the protocol to assess how much risk an abuser in their ranks posed to children, and to decide whether victims were telling the truth.

Towards Healing, described by the Church in protocol documents as a 'just and compassionate' initiative, applied to the Catholic Church in every state and territory in Australia except Melbourne. There, the Catholic Church had its own protocol, called 'The Melbourne Response', established in 1996 by the then Archbishop of Melbourne, George Pell. It has since been widely reported that the Australian Catholic Bishops' Conference had expected Pell to adopt the Towards Healing protocol in Melbourne, and was displeased that he established a scheme of his own. A difference between the schemes was that Towards Healing did not officially place a cap on payments to survivors of abuse. Pell accepted during evidence he later gave before the royal commission that introducing the Melbourne Response meant that Towards Healing was not a national, unified protocol. The Melbourne Response also initially capped payments to survivors at $50,000. It later increased this to $75,000 in the face of complaints and lobbying from victims that the initial amount was grossly unjust and inadequate.

The first and only time I met and questioned McClellan was at this informal and off-the-record media briefing ahead of the royal commission's hearings into the Melbourne Response. Current and former members of the Catholic archdiocese of Melbourne were about to be interrogated as to how they and those who ran the scheme had responded to allegations of child sexual abuse. It also marked the commission's first public hearings in Victoria. Pell, who was by this stage Australia's most senior Catholic, having been made a cardinal by the Pope in 2003, was on the commission's list of people to interrogate.

The briefing went for about one hour, and about a dozen journalists from throughout Victoria attended. McClellan insisted we call him by his first name – I would later learn he also insisted that survivors he heard from in private sessions do the same – and as we peppered him with questions, he mentioned that child sexual abuse was so pervasive that the commission could investigate around 1,000 institutions if it wanted to. But it had a budget and a deadline, so about 70 institutions – the most egregious offenders – would fall under its gaze. This included not only religious institutions such as the Catholic Church, but private and state-run institutions, including schools, orphanages, and sports clubs.

I could not appreciate then that this was the beginning for me of what would turn into more than half a decade of reporting on child sexual abuse, including, eventually, the trial of Cardinal George Pell, who at that point I knew very little about. In 2014, I was relatively new to the news organisation *Guardian Australia*; I had moved to Melbourne from Sydney just a couple of weeks before the briefing with McClellan. *Guardian Australia* was preparing to cover the Victorian state election, and I was also planning to cover the inquest into the death of 11-year-old Luke Batty, who had been beaten and stabbed to death by his father in public on a cricket oval in Victoria. My attention was firmly on state politics and the issue of family violence, which had become a key Victorian election issue, largely driven by the Batty case and the advocacy work of his mother, Rosie Batty. I would soon learn of the similarities between family violence and child sexual abuse: the difficulties that victims face in coming forward, the shame, the responses from children to being abused, the lack of accountability, and the abuse of power.

The royal commission had been announced on 12 November 2012 by the then prime minister, Julia Gillard. It came as historical child-abuse allegations were increasingly being revealed in Australia and in other countries, notably the US and Ireland. One of the final triggers for the Australian inquiry was an open letter by Peter Fox, a senior New South Wales police investigator, that was published in *The Newcastle Herald* accusing the Catholic Church in Australia of covering for paedophiles and other abusers, and of hindering police investigations.

'The allegations that have come to light recently about child sexual abuse have been heartbreaking,' Gillard told reporters as she announced the royal commission from Parliament House in Canberra. 'These are insidious, evil acts to which no child should be subject. There have been too many revelations of adults who have averted their eyes from this evil.'

Few knew more or were more vocal about this wilful ignorance than Anthony and Chrissie Foster. Their experiences with the Catholic Church are tragic, and their fight for justice is the subject of Chrissie's memoir, *Hell on the Way to Heaven*, published in 2010 in collaboration with journalist Paul Kennedy. The Fosters were instrumental in exposing the injustices of the Melbourne Response, and in pushing for a royal commission. They were among those to give evidence to the royal commission at its public hearings, during private sessions, and at roundtable meetings. The Fosters firmly believe that if Pell had responded to child sexual abuse appropriately when he was the Archbishop of Melbourne, one of their daughters,

Emma, would still be alive, and the other, Katie, would not be permanently disabled, requiring 24-hour care.

Emma and Katie were sexually abused at their Catholic primary school, Sacred Heart in Oakleigh, Victoria, by the notorious paedophile priest Father Kevin O'Donnell. O'Donnell's serial abuse of the Foster girls began in the late 1980s and continued into the early 1990s, and it had a brutal and lasting effect on their entire family. Emma disclosed her abuse in March 1996 and Katie in November 1997, and their parents watched in horror as their daughters' lives slowly disintegrated due to the trauma. Emma died of a drug overdose in 2008, when she was just 26 – a suicide following years of self-harm and depression. Katie suffered from severe depression, and turned to drinking at hazardous levels to try to escape the trauma of her abuse. In 1999, when she was 15, she was hit by a speeding car after walking in front of it following an alcohol binge. She spent a year in hospital, now uses a wheelchair, and has permanent brain injuries. O'Donnell would later be exposed as one of Australia's most notorious paedophiles. He raped boys and girls as young as five years old, and Emma was just a preschooler when O'Donnell began to abuse her.

After Emma disclosed her abuse by O'Donnell, the Fosters arranged to meet with Pell in his capacity as archbishop and as the architect of the Melbourne Response. That private meeting was held in February 1997. At the time, Katie was yet to disclose her abuse, but O'Donnell was a known and convicted sexual abuser of children.

The Fosters wanted Pell to strip O'Donnell of his priest's title and to respond with understanding and compassion to Emma's abuse. They also wanted to question Pell over his appointment of psychiatrrist Professor Richard Ball to manage the counselling arm of the Melbourne Response, known as Carelink. Ball had supported O'Donnell in his sentencing hearings in 1995. O'Donnell had been charged with 49 child-sex offences and jailed for 39 months, but was released on parole the following year. In fact, Ball wrote helpful psychiatric reports about many of the Catholic Church's accused priests at their trials in Victoria, helping their defence teams to obtain lighter sentences. Subsequently, O'Donnell died in 1997 a free man, and was buried a priest.

The Fosters wanted to know why Pell thought it was appropriate to employ Ball to look after the psychiatric needs of victims when he had at the same time helped defend their abusers in court. Given that O'Donnell was by now known to be a frequently offending paedophile, they believed Pell would respond to the abuse of their daughters with, at the very least, concern. However, Chrissie Foster said she soon realised this would not be the case. When they told Pell of the horrific self-harm and eating disorders that had ravaged their daughter as a result of her abuse, Foster recalls Pell saying, 'I hope you can substantiate what you're saying in court,' and 'It's all gossip until its proven in court.'

'This is what he jumped down our throats with. It was obscene. We wanted him to look into it, or remove O'Donnell's title, but no. He wouldn't have a word of it. It was … just such arrogance.'

Pell also insisted to the Fosters that Ball was the best man available for the Carelink job.

In the same meeting, the Fosters showed Pell a graphic A4 print of Emma's slashed wrists to demonstrate the extent of her self-harm. It seemed to have little effect. As the child sexual abuse crisis facing Australia worsened, with more survivors coming forward and more allegations of cover-ups being made, Pell was asked in 2002 to do an interview with the TV program *60 Minutes*. By this time, he was the Archbishop of Sydney, and when journalist Richard Carleton asked him about the meeting with the Fosters in 1997 and the image of Emma's trauma they had confronted him with, Pell denied having ever seen the photo.

In 2012, the Victorian government held a parliamentary Inquiry into the Handling of Child Abuse by Religious and other Non-government Organisations, and Chrissie Foster gave evidence. A transcript of that evidence shows she told the inquiry that Pell was the first person to whom she had shown the image of her bloodied daughter. At the same time, he was handed a photo of Emma receiving her confirmation certificate from Pell two years earlier.

'I held my breath, hopeful that we could reach this man on a deeper level and he could offer us some sympathy, or a display of surprise perhaps, something, anything,' Foster told the inquiry. 'Archbishop Pell, however, peered at it for a moment and with an unchanged expression said casually, "Mm, she's changed, hasn't she?" He handed the picture back to us. We couldn't believe his response. He was the first person we'd shown the image to. It was too distressing for anyone we knew to see. But it did not disturb the archbishop. Not a grimace or a frown.'

Foster told me she was nonetheless surprised when allegations were first made in 2002 that Pell had committed sexual abuse offences himself, while a seminarian, against a 12-year-old altar boy at a youth camp on Phillip Island in 1961. Pell denied the allegations, and stood down while they were investigated by former Supreme Court judge Alec Southwell. In October 2002, Southwell published his findings, saying he had not been able to verify the complaint, given the lack of corroborative evidence and some concerns about the complainant's credibility, as he had a criminal record for violence and drug-related offences. However, Southwell could not establish that the offending did not happen either. Pell claimed the finding as a vindication of his innocence and as a victory. His clerical career flourished. He returned to his position as Archbishop of Sydney, and in 2003 the Pope appointed him as a cardinal, escalating him to the position of Australia's most senior Catholic.

Although she had experienced Pell's coldness firsthand, the

allegations that he had abused a child were a shock to her, Foster said. 'I never would have dreamt he would do those things. But then I thought to myself, *It all makes sense now, his attitude towards us in the meeting.*'

The Fosters' experience with Pell during their private meeting with him in 1997 to talk about their daughter's abuse was part of what compelled them, along with other survivors and advocates, to push for a royal commission. 'He was the head honcho in Melbourne, the man in charge, and he had the power and authority to intervene and remove priests, and yet he didn't give a damn about our children, to the point he's telling us it's gossip and to prove it in court,' Foster said. 'What the hell?

'Three days after this meeting, it ate away at me and it hit me: *Oh, I understand.* I realised he knew we had no proof and that's why he kept shoving it down our throats to go to court. He knew we couldn't. That was his bullying. It was just disgusting to go there with the rape of our child, and by then she's been anorexic for a year, in and out of psych units, cutting her wrists and herself, and all he can say is, "Go prove it in court."

'What sort of attitude is that? He was crushing us by getting us to prove it. What proof could we have, what proof does a child have? Do they take a camera with them? Of course not. It was his [O'Donnell's] word against her word, and Pell knew it. If Pell had been nice to us that day, if he had said, "Oh my goodness, we do our best to get rid of paedophiles, but every now and then one gets through and I'm sorry, we'll do our best to look into it," then we would have backed down.'

But Pell did not say that, and so the Fosters did not back down. They would go on to dedicate many more years of their lives to fighting for justice for their daughters and other victims, and to expose the callousness they had experienced through Pell's Melbourne Response scheme.

'Pell created the monster, which was us, Anthony and me. That was his doing,' Chrissie says.

In August 1998, Emma received a written apology from Pell about her abuse, and his Melbourne Response scheme offered her $50,000. This was the maximum amount of compensation offered through the scheme to victims at that time. Emma and her parents did not immediately sign up to the offer, and began to consider other options, including taking independent legal action. More than one year later, in November 1997, as Emma and her parents were still considering their options, they learned that Katie had also been abused by O'Donnell. Chrissie discovered a suicide note that Katie had written disclosing the abuse. They began the process of applying for compensation through the Melbourne Response once again, this time for Katie. They also made an application to the scheme for compensation from the Church for themselves – the abuse of two of their daughters and their high-needs psychiatric care had drastically changed their lives and drained their resources. While the Church accepted that Emma and Katie had been abused, they rejected the application for redress for their parents.

On 18 August 2018, when she gave evidence to the child sexual abuse royal commission in Melbourne, Chrissie Foster described what had happened to Katie on 28 May 1999. 'Katie was crossing a road while she was under the influence of alcohol. Katie was hit by a car and the impact stopped her heart and caused a number of bleeds and swelling to her brain. Katie was in a comatose state for about four months and remained in hospital for almost one year. The accident left her with permanent brain damage. For the rest of her life Katie will require 24-hour care. While it remained a priority for us to continue working towards bringing a case against the Catholic Church, we were faced with many challenges and adjustments to our lives following Katie's accident. On 26 May 2000 Katie left hospital and returned home to us.'

By then, the Fosters had decided to reject the Church's compensation offer. Under the Melbourne Response terms and conditions, accepting redress required signing a deed of release forgoing their right to take legal action. Victims were also routinely told by the Church that if they chose not to accept an offer through the Melbourne Response and instead pursued legal action, their claims would be 'strenuously defended' by the Church. For many, even a scant offer of compensation through the Melbourne Response was better than the prospect of facing off against the Church and its powerful lawyers and supporters in a court.

Nonetheless, the Fosters chose legal action. In the face of overwhelming evidence, the Church settled with the Fosters in 2005 for $750,000. This was on the condition that they make no further compensation claims against the Church, and not disclose the conditions of the settlement. By this point, the Fosters had been in an almost decade-long legal process. They agreed to the settlement. But the settlement did not stop them from fighting for a royal commission.

'We wanted an inquiry that would be all-encompassing,' Chrissie says. 'This abuse was happening Australia-wide, and we wanted the truth to come out. Because this crime has been happening in the Church for centuries, and they'd gotten away with it. A lot of us believed this had to stop and be exposed. A royal commission was the big picture.' The Fosters knew that if the commissioners ordered Church officials and indeed themselves to give evidence, the Church could not hide behind deeds of settlements. Over the years, prime ministers from both sides of politics – John Howard, Tony Abbott, and Kevin Rudd – had rejected calls for a royal commission. It took Julia Gillard, an atheist, to make it happen.

Chrissie still remembers the moment when, on 12 November 2012, the announcement came, broadcast live on television.

'Anthony and I were at Tonimbuk, a small farming area in Gippsland [Victoria], and we were gardening. Anthony got a text, and he took out his phone and the text said, "Congratulations on the inquiry".' At first, the Fosters thought the text was referring to the Victorian government's Inquiry into the Handling of Child Sexual Abuse by Religious and Other Non-government Organisations. But this didn't make sense, since that inquiry had been announced seven months earlier.

'About 15 seconds later, Anthony and I stopped and just looked at each other,' Chrissie recalls. 'We both ran down to the house, and as I got to the kitchen I saw my phone on the table.' She saw a missed call from Paul Kennedy, the journalist who had helped her to write her book and who was well aware of the Fosters' campaign for a royal commission. 'I thought, *Surely not.*'

They turned on the television, which was tuned into the ABC.

'And there was Julia Gillard on the screen talking about a royal commission. We were overjoyed, jumping around and cheering, and we had a big hug. It was just astounding. A lot of us had been asking for this for a long time.'

They knew that Pell would be put under pressure to face the commission, because he'd had numerous high-profile roles in Australia, including as Archbishop of Sydney and of Melbourne; he had, for a time, he lived and worked with men who would turn out to be Australia's most notorious paedophiles; and he was the architect of the scheme that dealt with victims such as their own daughters. Questions that they and many others had about how the Melbourne Response was run, who it was run by, the so-called independence of those who ran it, and who in the clergy knew about abuse but covered it up or failed to act might finally be answered.

This royal commission would also be my first in-depth encounter with Pell, and the first time I had deeply interrogated the issues of child sexual abuse. I had not lived in Victoria during the parliamentary inquiry; the Southwell report was before my time. I had not read the book about Pell, titled *The Prince*, written by my *Guardian Australia* colleague David Marr. I grew up with no religion. I never went to Sunday school, and had never attended a mass. I had never read the Bible. I had nothing against the Church in general, but no investment in it either. My family were never religious, although, like many children, I was baptised – in my case, due to pressure from my father's extended family.

My dad remembers, 'You moved your head away from the priest every time he tried to put the water on you … you were not going to let that priest put that water on your head.' I guess that means I never was truly baptised. I consider myself an atheist, and have none of the Catholic guilt so many people describe. I went to public non-religious schools in Perth, Western Australia, where I grew up.

The only time I had really engaged with Pell as a journalist was close to midnight on 11 February 2013, when Pope Benedict resigned. I was working the night shift at *The Sydney Morning Herald* at the time, and the chief of staff wanted me to try to get Pell on the phone for a comment. I was not able to, although his press office did send a statement. I would come to the story of the royal commission with no strong biases towards or against Pell, no anger, no sense that this man was himself responsible for committing any crime. I was facing a steep learning curve. Perhaps that's why McClellan's comment in the media briefing that the commission, if it had the time and resources, could investigate 1,000 institutions, stuck with me. Just how pervasive was institutional child sexual abuse? And for it to have been so endemic for so long, how many people had known, but failed to act?

The first time I spoke to the Fosters was on 17 August 2014, when I had a conversation with Anthony ahead of the royal commission's hearing into the Melbourne Response. It was the first time I had looked into the scheme and understood the concerns about it. Anthony told me that when it came to the way the Church handled paedophiles and victims, reform would not come easily, and that was why the royal commission was important.

'It's something that has to be forced upon them through public opinion,' he said.

Under Australian legislation, royal commissioners have considerable powers of discovery and cross-examination, and royal commissions are for the most part considered a prestigious form of inquiry. This Royal Commission into Institutional Responses to Child Sexual Abuse, also known as the 'child sexual abuse royal commission', was a public reckoning with state, private, and religious institutions, once unaccountable and untouchable, and it was widely covered by the media. Major hearings, such as when Pell gave evidence, were streamed on television by the ABC, and all of the public hearings were live-streamed over the web.

There was an aspect of Pell's first royal commission appearance that struck me. This was the man who had designed and implemented the Melbourne Response, and who had taken up the role of Archbishop of Sydney five years later, in 2001, becoming one of those responsible for the running of the Towards Healing protocol there. By the mid-1990s, well into Pell's time in senior positions within the Catholic Church in Australia, child sexual abuse was a known and pressing problem that senior Catholics from around the world – all the way up to the Vatican – were discussing how to address. Pell was privy to these discussions. By the time of his 2014 appearance before the child sexual abuse royal commission in Australia, Pell was a cardinal who was soon to depart for Rome to take up a senior position as head of the Vatican's Secretariat for the Economy, essentially putting him in charge of the Vatican's finances and close to the Pope.

And yet Pell seemed to have come to the royal commission utterly underprepared and unequipped to answer basic questions about child sexual abuse, including its prevalence and impact. This stood out to me because Pell must have known that all eyes would be on him, and he would also have known the matters he would be questioned about. His appearance before the commission would have warranted weeks of preparation, given the gravity of the subject and its impact on thousands of survivors.

When presented by the commission with figures about what was then known about the prevalence of child sexual abuse within Catholic institutions, Pell seemed keen to point out that abuse was much more common within families – something the commissioners were aware of. Their task was to investigate institutional abuse, and in this instance Pell was there to help them understand how abuse had been and was being addressed by senior figures within the Catholic Church. Pell could not have been expected to have had every statistic about abuse or every aspect of his response to it at the front of his mind. However, he would have known that survivors would be looking towards him for answers, compassion, understanding, and evidence that, whatever had occurred in the past, the Catholic Church now understood its failures and the facts of child sexual abuse and its impact. But the only data fresh in Pell's mind by the time he appeared before the commission for the first time in Sydney seemed to be reports from the media, rather than any peer-reviewed literature or academic data, and he had a flimsy grasp, at best, of what he had read, often saying he could not recall answers off the top of his head.

The chair, McClellan, reminded Pell that he had on occasions expressed concern that the numbers cited about the prevalence of child sexual abuse in the Catholic Church might be exaggerated.

Pell responded, 'What I probably did say was that they were taken out of context and not compared to the very significant number of offences that occur in other institutions and the overwhelming majority of such offences which occur outside institutions.'

Counsel assisting the royal commission, Gail Furness, then asked Pell – given his extensive involvement in Towards Healing and the Melbourne Response – what he had done to understand the prevalence of child sexual abuse within the Catholic Church specifically.

'Oh, I've studied and talked and thought about it for years,' Pell said. 'I've met quite a number of victims. I've attended public meetings with victims. I've tried to read the literature.'

Furness: Cardinal, you say 'the very significant number of offences and the overwhelming majority of such offences which occur outside institutions'. What data do you point to support that evidence?'

Pell: Well, there was a recent press report on this, and I don't think it's contested anywhere, that about 80 per cent of these offences are committed outside institutions. I'd have to – I couldn't pull up chapter and verse. But within the last few months, there was a press report saying that 55 per cent of the offences of paedophilia occurred in so-called blended families and 45 per cent occurred with natural parents. That's quite wrong, but that was the way the report was written, because the sample of natural parents was eight or nine times as great as the sample for the blended parents. So in other – I think United States – statistics, it's four or five times, I might be wrong on that, the rate of natural families as distinct from blended families. I think, according to this survey, it would have been eight or nine times, but that did not appear in the press reports.

Furness: Are you referring to the press reports of a published data or survey, are you?

Pell: Yes, yes.

Furness: Not the actual published data or survey itself?

Pell: I'm referring to the press reports, and I'm – I might have got

my secretary to actually get hold of the report, and if there was –
I can't remember that directly, but from somewhere reliable, I got
accurate information about the size of the samples.

Furness: So somewhere reliable, but you can't tell us where that
is at the moment?

Pell: Not with absolute certainty, but I think that I would have
got my secretary to access the actual report which was the basis
for the press account.

Furness: Can you help us with the title of the report?

Pell: No, I can't, but I can get that to you later today.

Furness then reminded Pell that the royal commission had asked
Catholic Church Insurance, the Church's Professional Standards
Office, and the Archdiocese of Sydney to hand over all of the data
they had in relation to allegations of child sexual abuse committed
by priests within the archdiocese. Furness told Pell that the data
the commission had obtained from that process revealed that 55
ordained clerics within the archdiocese had been the subject of
a claim of child sexual abuse since March 2001, when Pell was
appointed as Archbishop of Sydney.

Pell responded that the statistics were inaccurate.

Furness continued that 842 priests had held an appointment in
the Sydney archdiocese since 1952, and, assuming that the figure
of 55 priests was accurate, 6.5 per cent of clerics who had held an
appointment since 1952 had been the subject of a complaint of child
sexual abuse on or after the time that Pell became archbishop.

Furness added that since abuse is under-reported, and since
they had only interrogated data on complaints made since Pell was
appointed Archbishop of Sydney, it was safe to assume this was a
conservative estimate of the rate of abuse within the Archdiocese of
Sydney.

Pell responded, 'I'm not sure of the logic of that, because I know when our stats nationally were being put together, I believe the figure was around 4 or 5 per cent historically. I'm aware also that the Sydney archdiocese has had fewer of these crimes than some other areas, so I would be surprised – it's not impossible, but I would be surprised if we were, in the Sydney archdiocese, 2 per cent higher than the national average, if the national average is 4 or 5 per cent.'

The royal commission would go on to find that of the 6,875 survivors it had interviewed in private sessions, 58.6 per cent had been abused in a religious institution. The largest proportion of these – a total of 2,489 survivors interviewed by commissioners – were abused in Catholic institutions. This meant that 61.8 per cent of all survivors interviewed who had been abused in a religious institution had been abused within a Catholic institution.

'As of 31 July 2017, we had made 2,252 referrals to police, and police had laid charges in a number of cases. Of those 2,252 referrals, 1,229 related to child sexual abuse in religious institutions,' the final report of the royal commission stated.

'The perpetrators of child sexual abuse we heard about in private sessions held various positions in religious institutions, but most held positions of leadership or authority. 24.8 per cent (1,000 survivors) told us about abuse in places of worship or during religious activities. In several of the religious institutions we examined, the central factor, underpinning and linked to all other factors, was the status of people in religious ministry. Within religious institutions there was often an inability to conceive that a person in religious ministry was capable of sexually abusing a child.'

Many survivors interviewed by the royal commission reported having been abused in places of worship or related locations, such as in a confessional or a priest's residence in seminaries, and during religious activities.

'Compared with perpetrators of child sexual abuse in the wider community, research suggests that Catholic clergy perpetrators are an atypical group. They tend to begin offending later in life and to be better educated, less antisocial and more likely to have male than female victims,' the commission found.

'We heard that personality factors that may be associated with clergy and religious perpetrators include narcissism, dependency, cognitive rigidity and fear of intimacy.'

On 18 August 2014 at Melbourne's County Court, the child sexual abuse royal commission began its hearings into the Melbourne Response, the first formal and external review of the scheme since it began in 1996. There would be further public hearings in Melbourne over the coming years, interrogating abuse within the Catholic Church in Victoria. But case study 16 was to focus on the Melbourne Response alone, including the experiences of child sexual abuse victims who had sought redress from the Church through the scheme.

The commission heard that the Melbourne Response had three key components: a panel of independent commissioners who investigated allegations of sexual abuse; a free counselling and professional support service known as Carelink; and a compensation panel that made recommendations to the Archdiocese of Melbourne about ex gratia compensation payments to victims.

Under its powers of discovery, the commission asked the Archdiocese of Melbourne to hand over all of its data on the Melbourne Response from when it began in October 1996 through to 31 March 2014. These documents revealed that 351 complaints of child sexual abuse had been made to the Melbourne Response during that period. Of these complaints, 326 were upheld by an independent commissioner, nine were not upheld, and the remainder were, as of the date of the royal commission hearings, undetermined – in some cases because the complainant had died or had chosen to pursue action through the courts. Of the 326 complaints upheld, six were subsequently settled outside the Melbourne Response. Eighty per cent of the complaints related to child sexual abuse allegations from 1950 to 1980. Sacred Heart Primary School and the Sacred Heart Parish, both in Oakleigh (where the Fosters' daughters were abused), were the two institutions within the Melbourne archdiocese subject to the largest numbers of complaints.

Chrissie Foster was the first witness to give evidence to the commission during this public hearing, at which Pell was due to give evidence for a second time – this time via a video-link from Rome. As she read her statement to the commission, her husband, Anthony, took over when it became too much. In the courtroom, with their evidence live-streamed on the ABC and over the internet, they recounted in meticulous detail their daughters' tragic stories. Abuse survivors and advocates filled the courtroom seats, some of them weeping as the Fosters gave their evidence. Emma had visited doctors, specialists, and pathology services 906 times in the 10 years from 2005, plus she had at least 75 outpatient psychology appointments and more than 52 admissions into hospital, detox, and rehabilitation clinics.

'Despite all this professional help and our love for her, our Emma sadly never recovered from the sexual abuse she suffered,' Chrissie told the commissioners. 'Her life continued to spiral out of control, and in January 2008 she took her own life. Katie has never recovered from being hit by a car while binge drinking to escape the memories of her sexual assault. She will always require 24-hour care.' Their eldest daughter, Aimee, had also suffered as she witnessed the disintegration of her sisters' lives, Foster said. On 15 July 2008, Anthony gave an interview to the ABC's *Lateline* program and spoke of Emma's death. In response to the interview, Bishop Anthony Fisher described the Fosters as 'dwelling crankily on old wounds'.

'Emma had died only six months earlier,' Chrissie told the

commissioners. 'We lived with the pain of our wounds daily, and still do. We found these comments to be very hurtful.'

Her statement went on to say that according to the Archdiocese of Melbourne, the three stages of the Melbourne Response were intended to be independent of one another.

'This is not reflective of our experience with the Melbourne Response,' she said. 'The Independent Commissioner's role is to determine whether an assault has occurred, yet we were faced with a situation where the Independent Commissioner requested to speak with Emma, we assumed in relation to accepting the offer of $50,000. We found this to demonstrate a lack of independence. Having experienced both the Melbourne Response and the legal system as a means of gaining compensation, our view is that the legal system is a far superior option than engaging in the Melbourne Response. We would like to see changes to the legal system to allow victims to receive full and just compensation for what has happened to them.'

On the same day, the commissioners also heard from Paul Hersbach, who told of horrific abuse suffered by his father, his uncle, and himself at the hands of Father Victor Rubeo, who had abused boys and girls over three decades as he worked in dioceses throughout Victoria.

'Both my father and his twin brother were groomed and sexually abused by Father Rubeo, and neither twin knew of each other's abuse until later in life,' Hersbach told the commission.

He described how Rubeo ingratiated himself into the family, attending family milestones and holidays, and, after coming over for dinner on Sundays, would stay the night. He also opened the family's mail, paid bills, and bought groceries.

Rubeo had the family stay with him at his presbytery in East Brighton for six months while a new house was being built for them. 'He took over the running of the family and behaved like he was in charge,' Hersbach said.

It wasn't until Hersbach was 16 that his father told him he had been sexually abused by Rubeo as a child.

In 1996, Rubeo pleaded guilty to two counts of indecent assault against Hersbach's father and uncle. In 2010, fresh charges were laid against him, but he died on 16 December 2011, the same day he was due in court for his committal.

Hersbach did not go into detail about his own sexual abuse, and said it had taken him a while after his father's revelation to accept that he, too, was a victim. 'Of all those things Rubeo did to me, the worst was robbing a young boy of his father,' he said.

'For 16 years he inserted himself between us by behaving and making decisions as though he was my father. This was far worse than any physical abuse could ever have been, and it breaks my heart he took this away from us.'

Hersbach had claimed assistance through the Melbourne Response, and told the court he had met the Melbourne Response's independent commissioner, Peter O'Callaghan QC, one-on-one in his chambers. 'He said words in effect, "Look, I'm obliged to say go to the cops if you want, but based on what you told me, I don't think anything is going to happen."' O'Callaghan had been hand-picked by Pell for the role, which saw him assess the legitimacy of complaints of abuse, and decide whether victims should be compensated.

Hersbach said he had accepted the advice from O'Callaghan at the time, but in retrospect felt it was inappropriate.

This meeting was followed by a letter from O'Callaghan which said, 'With respect to the unsurprising haziness of your memory there would not appear to be much point in your taking the matter to the police. However, that is a matter for you.'

He had never been encouraged to seek independent legal advice or go to the police. 'I felt there was no room in the process for compassion, debate, or for me, the victim,' Hersbach said.

He was ultimately given a payout of $17,500, although he had no idea how the Church had arrived at that figure. It had taken him a year to bring himself to sign the deed of release.

'My feelings have changed in the last five years towards the deed of release I signed,' he told the commission. 'Now it causes me angst – the Church has taken so much from me over years.

'I want the Church to acknowledge that the deed of release adds to victims' burden, and for those victims that desire it, I want the Church to release the victims from obligations under the deeds.

'And I want the Church to acknowledge the value of payments grossly undervalues the impact of sexual abuse on victims.'

When it was his turn to give evidence to the commission, O'Callaghan said that the Melbourne Response was based on 'natural justice', and that when he was assessing an abuse claim he would take on a role similar to a magistrate in a criminal case. Except that O'Callaghan was considering victims under the Church's own canon law, not criminal or civil law.

He told the commissioners that he was not attempting to discourage victims from going to police, but rather, if he held a 'reasonable opinion' that victims might have difficulty in proving their case to the police, he 'thought it appropriate' to say so. Victims were also told that if they went to the police, they would no longer be eligible for compensation through the Melbourne Response.

Four days after the evidence given by the Fosters and Rubeo, Pell appeared before the royal commission. By this time, he had taken up the senior position of financial controller of the Vatican, and so he made his appearance via video-link at 4.00 pm Australian Eastern Standard Time, which was 8.00 am in Rome. Pell's evidence went for more than two-and-a-half hours, and was marred by technical difficulties. But it was enough time for survivors packed into Melbourne's County Court to get perhaps the strongest sense since the commission began its hearings of the way Pell had viewed and responded to child sexual abuse through the Melbourne Response.

Pell told the commissioners that he introduced the scheme in 1996 because dozens of sexual abuse complaints had come to the attention of the Church, putting it under great pressure. It was also the reason he appointed O'Callaghan to investigate the claims, he said. Pell added, however, that the claims from some victim-advocacy groups neeed to be viewed with with some scepticism.

Counsel assisting, Gail Furness, asked, 'Was there any work that you did or you instructed to be done to come to a view as to how many complainants there may be out there who wished to come forward to the independent commissioner?'

Pell replied, 'I was aware of a report in the newspapers, and of course through my eventual meetings at groups of survivors and victims, that was brought home to me very clearly, and there were groups such as Broken Rites that were very active.

'Well, with some of those groups I took what they said with a grain of salt. But nonetheless there was evidence something needed to be done to deal with the suffering.'

He also said he had not watched the evidence given by Hersbach earlier in the week.

'Did you view his evidence, Cardinal?' Hersbach's lawyer, Sean Cash, asked him.

'No, I didn't. I have a job here in Rome,' Pell replied, to gasps and shocked laughter from the public gallery.

As Furness questioned Pell about the Melbourne Response, he revealed that he did not believe compensation to be the main point or 'arm' of the response, because he did not believe that was what victims wanted.

'My primary concern was to try to help the victims, and I regarded the other arms of the Melbourne Response as being more important than this particular arm because many victims then and probably now did not have money as their primary concern.'

Furness responded, 'If it was the case that money was not a concern of yours and affordability of the scheme was not a concern of yours, why place a cap at all?'

Pell responded, 'I didn't say it was not a concern of mine. I said it was not my prime concern. I have an obligation or had an obligation as archbishop to take care of the resources of the archdiocese. But I was quite clear that we provide what was regarded as appropriate by these very significant figures who were working on the Compensation Panel, and I don't recall any request from them to vary the cap at least during my time.

'I would also suggest that it would be useful to compare that amount that Melbourne offered and is offering with what other agencies, government-sponsored agencies, offer, and I repeat that I, myself, have never been a fan of caps.'

Furness put it to Pell that the government, through the victims-of-crime legislation, offered payments to victims even though the government itself was not responsible for those crimes. She said that any suggestion that the Melbourne Response was therefore similar to or superior to any other compensation schemes available at the time was misleading.

It was then that Pell made a strange analogy that drew further gasps from the room in Melbourne, despite prefacing it by saying he would give a 'non-controversial' example to illustrate his point:

> To some extent, the Church situation does resemble that of the government. If there is a series, for example, of trucks carrying merchandise around the country, if in fact these are improperly serviced or the drivers are pushed to work for too long, obviously there is a culpability somewhere in the authority chain.
>
> If in fact the driver of such a truck picks up some lady and then molests her, I don't think it's appropriate, because it is

contrary to the policy, for the ownership, the leadership of that company to be held responsible. Similarly with the Church and the head of any other organisation. If there has been – every precaution has been taken, no warning has been given, it's I think not appropriate for legal culpability to be foisted upon the authority figure.

The royal commission chair, Justice Peter McClellan, did not let these comments pass.

McClellan: When a priest, through the act of the parish or in any other way, gains access to a child who comes to the Church with a parent's [permission] … that is quite different to the relationship between the truck driver and the casual passenger, isn't it?

Pell: Yes, I would certainly concede that.

Anthony Foster later described Pell's comments as 'ludicrous'. 'It was an invalid analogy,' he said. 'Above all, the Church should be a moral leader.'

Pell was questioned comprehensively by Furness about his appointment of Ball as the manager of the Melbourne Response's counselling program, Carelink. Ball was the psychiatrist responsible for both listening to and counselling victims as well as perpetrators, which the Fosters and others said was a clear conflict of interest. On rare occasions, victims who came through Carelink were also then referred on to Ball's private practice for continuing treatment. He would also sometimes provide evidence for the Church about perpetrators in court cases.

When Pell was asked about Ball's 'double role' in supporting victims and perpetrators, he responded, 'I'm not sure to what extent I was aware of that double role in precisely that way at that time.'

Later in his evidence, Pell told Furness, 'Given that his role was oversight and supervision, and given that no person was obliged to go to him for counselling ... I thought his role as leader of this service was appropriate, given his distinguished record, given his high level of competence and high level of appointment.'

Furness asked Pell if he had considered the appointment of Ball from the perspective of a victim or complainant. How would they feel confiding in a person known for providing treatment to priests and providing them with evidence in court on behalf of the Church?

Pell responded that it was certainly something he very carefully considered, and he said that the Fosters as well as families of other victims made their concerns known to him. Nonetheless, Pell said, the archdiocese 'did not feel that it compromised his professional integrity, and we moved of course to assuage, not completely, these concerns by repeating that nobody had to go to Professor Ball'.

Furness pressed him on this belief, and the following exchange occurred:

Furness: Well, it wasn't a question of his professional integrity, was it? It was a question of how victims perceived his position as the public face of clinical services being provided to victims of Church abuse in the archdiocese? It's not about him; it's about them?

Pell: And we considered their argumentation, their point of view very, very carefully, took advice, but at that stage we did not share it, did not share their views.

Furness: So how did you take their views into account?

Pell: By listening to them, by asking advice on their views, by discussing the matter with Professor Ball, by asking what were the comparable professional standards in this area, was what he was doing unique or was it something that was not uncommon in the psychology profession.

This comment from Pell struck me as odd, but it was not interrogated further by Furness. I was curious as to what evidence there was that it was 'not uncommon' at the time for psychiatrists to have both victims and their perpetrators as clients. I phoned a former Australian mental health commissioner and eminent psychiatrist, Professor Ian Hickie, for clarification. Hickie said it was true that professional attitudes in psychiatry had changed and improved over time, and were different in the 1990s, when Pell was archbishop. But even by the 1990s, Hickie said, psychiatry as a field was aware of the increased community focus on child sexual abuse, and psychiatrists by then believed that taking on multiple roles, including the dual treatment of victims and the assessment of the victims' perpetrators, was problematic. 'This issue about intrinsic conflicts is longstanding in psychiatry,' Hickie told me.

Furness did press Pell on why the views of victims towards Ball did not outweigh those of Pell's:

Furness: You didn't understand, Cardinal, that it wasn't about Professor Ball and his views; it was actually about the victims and their views?

Pell: I think that is an overstatement and somewhat misleading. It very much also concerned Professor Ball because there was an implicit criticism of his integrity.

Furness: So you saw it in terms of Professor Ball's integrity rather than the perceptions of victims; is that right?

Pell: Could I repeat that that is exactly what I have not said. I have said that the considerations, the point of view of the victims, was very carefully considered, as well as the position of Dr Ball.

Furness: And ultimately the victims' concerns were rejected?

Pell: And the views of the victims' advocates on the suitability of Professor Ball for this role, we stated we did not share them.

What the royal commission did was highlight the way that the Catholic Church as an institution, along with senior figures within it, perceived child sexual abuse. Victims stretched the truth, the Church believed. Catholic institutions, rather than victims and advocates or the justice system, should get the final say on who was heard and trusted, those in power believed. And, as the royal commission would go on to find, the Catholic Church heard the concerns of people like the Fosters, but then promptly dismissed them.

Another arm of the royal commission's inquiry significant to Pell was case study 28, which examined the responses of the Catholic Church authorities in Ballarat to allegations of child sexual abuse. The commission's final report on Ballarat is available to the public online, as are the final reports on all of the commission's case studies.

However, until May 2020, around 100 pages of the case study's findings were unavailable. Entire sections were blacked out, redacted. Most of those sections related to the commission's findings about Pell.

Between Pell's second appearance before the royal commission in August 2014 and his third and final appearance in March 2016 for the Ballarat hearings, Pell had more questions to answer than about how the Archdiocese of Melbourne had responded to and investigated allegations of child sexual abuse within its institutions during the period he had served as auxiliary bishop.

The Ballarat-focused hearings heard evidence that while he was an assistant priest at Ballarat East from 1973 to 1983, Pell allegedly was involved in moving paedophile priest Gerald Ridsdale, a friend of his at the time, between parishes. Pell also worked at the parish during a period when several Catholic priests were later found to have assaulted young boys, the commission heard, raising questions about how, given his senior position, Pell could not have known about this.

One of Ridsdale's victims was his own nephew, David Ridsdale, and he gave evidence at the first of the commission's Ballarat hearings. He alleged that he told Pell about the abuse he had endured, but that Pell encouraged him to keep quiet. Pell denied the allegations via a statement from Rome.

Australia's most notorious paedophile, Gerald Ridsdale, committed about 180 offences against children as young as four between the 1960s and the 1980s, including while working as a school chaplain at St Alipius boys' school in Ballarat. He is now in prison, having pleaded guilty to new historical offences as recently as April 2020.

Pell, who supported Ridsdale during his first court appearance for child-sex offences in 1993, has always denied knowing of any child abuse occurring in Ballarat while he worked there as a priest and with a clerical group called the College of Consultors during the 1970s and 1980s. Pell also spent time living with Ridsdale in 1973, but has said he had no idea he was a paedophile. Ridsdale held 16 appointments within the Church during his 29 years as a priest. He was moved from parish to parish, from role to role, as the Church had a policy of moving abusers around once the accusations against them became too strong in any one particular parish. This meant that the abusers became someone else's problem.

The commission heard that Pell was involved in a consultors' decision to move Ridsdale from the Mortlake parish in Ballarat to Sydney in 1982. Pell had previously denied having moved Ridsdale out of the parish, and said he would never condone any decision to move a priest if he knew he had abused children.

Pell was due to fly into Victoria from Rome in December 2015 to face the commission in person and respond to their questions around these allegations. Ballarat, an inland town 100 kilometres north-west of Melbourne, is still reeling from the impact of historical child sexual abuse today. Following the allegations that emerged during the royal commission's hearings, abuse survivors in Ballarat, a town of about 100,000 people, made their presence known. They and their supporters began to tie thousands of colourful ribbons to the fences surrounding Catholic schools and churches in the town; although they have at times been cut down by Catholic clergy, the ribbons always return. The commission heard evidence from the Ballarat Survivors Group that at least 45 victims of child sexual abuse at the hands of clergy had taken their own lives in the town. There have been many more since then.

In its final report into Ballarat, the commission found:

> This case study exposed a catastrophic failure in the leadership of the Diocese and ultimately in the structure and culture of the Church over decades to effectively respond to the sexual abuse of children by its priests.
>
> That failure led to the suffering and often irreparable harm to children, their families and the wider community. That harm could have been avoided if the Church had acted in the interests of children rather than in its own interests.

Other notorious paedophiles operated in the Catholic parishes of the small town. The commission interrogated all reports of abuse relating to Ballarat received by Catholic Church authorities between 1 January 1980 and 28 February 2015. They found that 140 people made a claim of child sexual abuse against priests and other clergy in Ballarat, and that, because abuse was under-reported, the actual number would have been much higher. Ninety per cent of the claims made were against seven priests, with the highest number of complaints – 78 – being against Ridsdale.

When I walked through the town in the lead-up to Pell's appearance, I asked residents how the revelations had affected the community. One resident told me, 'When you walk through the town and see the ribbons, it reflects the sadness, but also that there's just a lot of support in the community for the victims.'

The commission found there could be 'no doubt' that Bishop Ronald Mulkearns, the then bishop of Ballarat, 'knew or strongly suspected that these priests had sexually abused children in the diocese'. Mulkearns managed the diocese from 1971, during a time when numerous notorious paedophiles – including Ridsdale, Robert Best, and Edward Dowlan – were abusing children. Their combined victims ran into the hundreds.

The commissioners were satisfied that 'by late 1975 Ridsdale had admitted to Bishop Mulkearns that he had offended against children and that Bishop Mulkearns knew that Ridsdale's conduct was known to the police in Bendigo and it's likely he knew of the general talk in the community about Ridsdale'.

Despite being aware of allegations about Ridsdale, Mulkearns did nothing when a 14-year-old boy, Paul Levey, was sent to live with Ridsdale in the Mortlake presbytery in 1982 for more than six months. Levey gave evidence to the commission that he slept in Ridsdale's bedroom and that he was sexually abused frequently.

'[Mulkearns] knew that the boy's mother was concerned about the situation and sought his assistance, but he ignored her,' the royal commission found. 'By this time, Bishop Mulkearns knew of Ridsdale's admission of offending against boys. It is inconceivable that it would not have occurred to him that Ridsdale should not have had a boy living with him and that the boy was, at least, at risk of sexual abuse by Ridsdale.

'Bishop Mulkearns' response to Mr Levey living with Ridsdale in the Mortlake presbytery demonstrated a total absence of concern for the welfare of that boy. Bishop Mulkearns deliberately left Mr Levey in danger.'

At the time, Pell was a member of the College of Consultors of the Ballarat diocese, a group of senior priests who advised Mulkearns on the appointment of priests. In July 1977, Pell took part in a consultors' meeting that sent Ridsdale on to a parish in Edenhope, in western Victoria.

Ballarat was anxious for Pell's return to the town to answer questions from the commission about the way the diocese responded to these paedophiles and what he knew about Ridsdale. After the evidence from survivors was heard, Pell confirmed to the royal commission that he would fly from Italy to Australia to attend the Ballarat hearings, and said he was horrified by the allegations against him. While a royal commission does not have the authority to summon people from overseas to appear before it, Pell wrote to the commission in May 2015, saying he would be prepared to fly to Australia to give evidence. The commission took him up on the offer.

In November 2015, weeks before Pell was due to appear, the commission announced it would have to move Pell's appearance to Melbourne's County Court due to the high level of public interest in his evidence – the small Ballarat courthouse would simply not be able to accommodate everyone.

And then, on 11 December 2015, days before he was due in Australia to give evidence, Pell's legal counsel, Allan Myers QC, told the commission that Pell was too unwell to travel. Myers made an application for Pell to give evidence via video-link from Rome instead, as he had done the previous time he gave evidence.

Myers told the commission chair, Justice Peter McClellan, that Pell 'deeply regrets this and has been preparing himself for this duty for some time'.

McClellan refused the request.

He said that, given there were complex matters that Pell was due to give evidence on, and that there had been technical problems when Pell previously appeared before the commission via video-link, he would defer Pell's evidence until February 2016, when further hearings into abuse within the Catholic diocese of Ballarat were due to be heard.

Victims present in the courtroom applauded McClellan's decision. McClellan told Myers, 'If the cardinal's health has not sufficiently improved by then to enable him to travel, we will further consider the position, which may include further delaying his evidence to a date when he can safely travel to Australia.'

Pell's office in Rome said he had been suffering an unspecified 'heart condition' for some time.

'His symptoms have recently worsened, with a specialist cardiologist in Rome advising only a few days ago that it is not safe for him to undertake long-haul flights in his current condition,' a statement from the Vatican read.

'Cardinal Pell realises there may be some who will question the decision to remain in Rome; however, it would be unwise for him not to heed medical advice. The Cardinal has consistently expressed his intention to do everything possible to assist the work of the Royal Commission.'

When Pell's solicitors first emailed the commission about Pell's health, they requested that McClellan meet privately with Myers to discuss allowing him to appear by video-link. McClellan rejected the plea for confidentiality. The whole point of the royal commission was to establish public accountability.

'It is not appropriate that the essential requests contained in the letter be confidential, and it was not appropriate for me to meet with Mr Myers on a confidential basis,' McClellan told the hearing.

Survivors and advocates were furious, unsympathetic to Pell's health problems. Many of them were elderly and suffering from their own ill health, but had planned to travel to Melbourne from all over the world to witness Pell's appearance in person. Now they would have to change their plans.

And then, on 5 February 2016, Pell once again applied to give evidence via video-link from Rome. Lawyers for victims told the commission that Pell's medical conditions were 'very common' to anyone of the cardinal's age – he was 74 at the time – and that those conditions should not prevent him from flying.

Lawyer Paul O'Dwyer SC, representing victims, told the commission that Pell's medical condition 'fades into insignificance' considering that 'witness after witness has had to spell out the most intimate details of their life in the witness box, sometimes not anonymously'.

He called for Pell's medical report to be made public. His comments were supported by other lawyers for victims. However, lawyers for the victims told the commission it was also important that the matter be resolved quickly. Many abuse survivors were unwell and elderly, and were anxious as Pell's evidence was repeatedly delayed. Some of them were running out of time.

McClellan revealed that Pell's medical conditions were hypertension and ischaemic heart disease. While it would be preferable for Pell to fly to Australia to give evidence, McClellan said the commissioners were satisfied that doing so would pose a risk to Pell's health and that his condition was unlikely to improve.

'Although people with the conditions that Cardinal Pell has may fly long distances, it is apparent from the medical report that in the case of Cardinal Pell there is a risk to his health if he undertook such travel at the present time,' McClellan told the commission.

'... [W]hen the alternative that he give evidence by video-link is available, the commissioners are satisfied that course should be adopted.'

O'Dwyer asked McClellan, 'What if that view that those conditions [that] preclude the cardinal from safely flying to Australia are wrong?'

McClellan replied, 'I've made the decision, Mr O'Dwyer.'

He said Pell would appear via video-link over a four-day period from Monday 29 February. This prompted a very public campaign led by child sexual abuse survivors and their supporters to raise money to send victims of the Church to Rome to witness Pell give his evidence instead. More than $200,000 was raised.

Writer, musician, and comedian Tim Minchin also penned a song, called 'Come Home (Cardinal Pell)', which he performed on national television in Australia on 16 February 2016. The scathing song included the lyrics:

I know what it's like when you're feeling shitty.
You just want to curl up and have an itty-bitty doona day.
But a lot of people here miss you, Georgie.
They really think you ought to just get on a plane …

I mean, with all due respect, dude,
I think you're scum!
And I reckon you should
Come home, Cardinal Pell …
It's lovely here, you should
Come home, you pompous buffoon.
And I suggest do it soon.

And then, as the Minchin song went viral, a bombshell hit. Eleven days before Pell was due to finally give evidence to the commission via video-link, *Herald Sun* reporter Lucie Morris-Marr revealed on 19 February 2016 that Pell was being investigated for 'multiple offences' while serving in senior positions within the Church in Australia. Morris-Marr's exclusive report said that detectives from Taskforce SANO – Victoria's police unit established to investigate child sexual abuse – had compiled a dossier containing allegations that Pell had committed the offences when he was a priest in Ballarat, and also when he was the Archbishop of Melbourne. According to the report, the investigation by SANO detectives had been underway for a year. The dossier said that Pell had allegedly sexually abused minors 'by both grooming and opportunity'.

In a statement, a spokesman for the Vatican told reporters that the allegations were 'clearly designed to do maximum damage to the Cardinal and the Catholic Church and undermine the work of the Royal Commission'.

Pell vehemently denied the allegations, describing them in a statement as 'outrageous', 'without foundation', 'utterly false', and 'designed to embarrass'. He also called for an investigation into the Victorian police force to identify the source of the claims.

It was in this context that a group of about 20 Ballarat survivors flew to Rome to witness Pell's evidence.

It was because of those allegations against Pell, and the police investigation and court case that followed, that the findings of case study 28 were not released along with the rest of the royal commission's final report tabled in parliament in December 2017. Releasing the Pell findings might have prejudiced a jury and jeopardised his trials. Once again, victims and their advocates would have to wait for answers.

Paul Levey, one of the Ballarat survivors of Ridsdale's abuse who gave evidence to the royal commission, was born in 1968, and is an only child. His mother was a staunch Catholic, and his father converted to Catholicism in order to marry her. Levey was 12 years old in 1980 when he first met Ridsdale, who at the time was studying at the National Pastoral Institute in Elsternwick, an inner suburb of Melbourne. A nun who was friends with Levey's mother introduced Ridsdale to the family.

'The nun suggested my mother and I go on a camping trip to White Cliffs with Ridsdale and some other boys,' Levey's statement to the commission said. 'My mother and I went to White Cliffs, and camped there for about two weeks. This was in early 1980. This is the first time I ever spent any time with Ridsdale. Ridsdale sexually abused me on this trip by masturbating me and forcing me to touch him.'

After that, Ridsdale embedded himself in the family, and visits became much more frequent, as did his abuse of Levey. During 1980, Ridsdale asked Levey's parents if he could pick Levey up on Friday afternoons after he had finished school and take the boy with him to stay at the National Pastoral Institute for the weekend. This happened about six times. Ridsdale had a self-contained unit at the institute, and abused Levey each time. Ridsdale became more involved as Levey's parents went through a divorce that same year. Ridsdale would stay with Levey and his mother in their house overnight, under the guise of attempting to help and support the family.

'Around Easter 1982, when I was 14, Ridsdale and Dad decided to send me to live at the presbytery at Mortlake where Ridsdale was serving as parish priest,' Levey's statement said. 'I had no real say in that. I went to school at the Catholic Regional College at Noorat. I lived with Ridsdale from Easter to about October 1982. I was sexually abused all the time, just about every day. I had my own bedroom at the presbytery but that was a front. I always slept in Ridsdale's room where there were two beds. No one else lived at the presbytery.'

In October 1982, Levey was moved without explanation out of the presbytery, and sent to live with a local family. Levey recalls feeling relief, because he was friends with one of the boys in the family and he would be able to escape Ridsdale. Around the same time, Ridsdale was shifted from the Mortlake parish in Victoria to a parish in another state, New South Wales, where he continued to abuse children.

When Ridsdale was outed by news outlets in 1990 as the worst paedophile in Australia, Levey told his dad about the abuse he had suffered for years. His father took Levey to the Sunbury police station to report the crimes, and after a court case that was traumatising for Levey, Ridsdale was found guilty.

'My dad has now passed away,' Levey's statement said. 'The criminal proceedings brought up a lot of memories and there was no real support. I blocked a lot of it out. In recent years Mum has told me that whilst I was in Mortlake, she rang Bishop Mulkearns several times because she wanted me to come home. She told me that it took her a while to get through to the Bishop, and when she did he virtually said to her, "Bad luck, it's an arrangement between Ridsdale and Paul's dad."'

I met Levey in Ballarat when I was covering the early rounds of hearings into case study 28. He was unwell, suffering from deep-vein thrombosis, and required a walking stick to get around. Levey was outside the courtroom with Leonie Sheedy from the Care Leavers Australasia Network (CLAN), which represents children abused in orphanages and as wards of the state. As I drove up to the court, I could see Sheedy and her 'Clannies', as she calls them, at the roundabout outside the court, holding up signs that read 'Churches need to be made accountable', 'Pope Francis, send Pell back to Ballarat', and 'Suffer the little children'. Around the corner outside the church, a red caravan was parked, emblazoned with the words 'Pope must act: Sack Pell now'. An artist held up a portrait he had painted of Pell with the words, 'Go to hell Pell'.

Levey told me that despite suffering from serious health

conditions, he would be flying to Rome to watch Pell give evidence. Because of his poor health, his doctor said he would need to make a 24-hour stopover along the way. But he wanted answers about what Pell knew about Ridsdale's offending and about any action taken to stop him. He and his partner, Michelle, paid for their flights before they knew about a crowdfunding campaign to get survivors to Rome. Levey was also hopeful of meeting with Pell in person.

Any desire Levey had to meet Pell in Rome was shattered as Pell gave evidence. I covered Pell's evidence before the commission for *Guardian Australia* live for four days straight. I had by then heard countless stories from survivors who had appeared before the commission about the profound impact of abuse on their own lives and the lives of those around them. When Levey got to Rome, he refused to leave the room at the Hotel Quirinale where Pell was giving evidence, despite the pain he was in and despite his deep-vein thrombosis requiring him to frequently stand and walk around. He sat and listened to all of the evidence over four days. Levey would provide comments to me from Rome while I was in Melbourne watching the live-stream and frantically blogging.

Day one of Pell's evidence started softly, with counsel assisting, Gail Furness, clarifying Pell's roles within the diocese of Ballarat and who he worked with.

But on day two, Furness comprehensively questioned Pell about how it was he could not have known that Ridsdale was abusing children. At times, Pell appeared to grow frustrated with the questioning, but Furness was unmoved. She and McClellan systematically pressed Pell about what was known about child abusers within the diocese during the period he served as a parish priest at Ballarat East from 1973 to 1983.

The commission heard that by the time a meeting of consultors was held in 1982, at which Pell was present, Mulkearns and the majority of consultors knew Ridsdale was abusing. At that meeting, they decided to move Ridsdale between parishes for a sixth time.

Pell maintained that, despite the widespread knowledge of Ridsdale's abusing, he was not told about it and did not hear about it. Ridsdale had been abusing from the 1960s onwards, the commission had previously heard. In 1973, Ridsdale and Pell lived together in the parish house of St Alipius in Ballarat East.

> **McClellan:** You, as a responsible consultor, would want to know, you would be very concerned to know, whether or not the reason [for moving Gerald Ridsdale to a new parish] was because Ridsdale's activities had become a matter of public scandal, wouldn't you?
>
> **Pell:** I would have been much more – it would have been important to know whether the public scandal touched on underage sexual activity or the public scandal was of another nature, say drinking or quarrelling or adult sexual activity.
>
> **McClellan:** Whatever it was, public scandal brings real problems for the Church, doesn't it?
>
> **Pell:** Yes, it does.
>
> **Furness:** I think where we're up to, Cardinal, is that you don't have any recollection of what was said at the meeting, although you have a recollection of what was not said, is that fair?
>
> **Pell:** I have studied the minutes of this meeting that took place over 30 years ago and, in the light of those minutes, I am quite happy to accept them.
>
> **Furness:** That was not my question. I will repeat it. You do not have any recollection of what was said at the meeting although you have a recollection of what was not said, is that right?
>
> **Pell:** I wonder whether that is misleading … Independent of the minutes, I do know the basis on which we proceeded. That was … when a priest could be shifted for non-criminal activities and the reasons would not necessarily be given.

The evidence was at times explosive. Pell attracted gasps from those watching the live-stream in Sydney when he told the hearing that the widespread child abuse at the hands of Ridsdale, was 'a sad story and it wasn't of much interest to me'. Pell said he did not think people with no knowledge of abuse should be held accountable for failing to protect children. He was accused by Furness of trying to 'exclude yourself from all responsibility' from abuses that occurred within Ballarat.

Asked if he accepted any responsibility for Ridsdale being moved from parish to parish, rather than being removed from the Church or reported to police, Pell responded, 'No, I don't.' At times, survivors of abuse watching the evidence at the Sydney hearing walked out, angered and distressed by Pell's responses.

Furness put it to Pell that it was implausible he did not know about the abusing by Ridsdale and that he was being moved between parishes for that reason.

Pell replied, 'That is a complete nonsense.'

Levey struggled as he listened to this evidence. To him, Pell seemed arrogant, and still clueless about child sexual abuse and the experience of victims and survivors. Levey told me, 'I did originally want to meet with him, but after the evidence where he said Ridsdale's abusing wasn't of much interest to him, wasn't significant enough for him to look into, that just destroyed any will to meet him. What would be the point?'

But it was important for Levey to at least be in the room while Pell answered the commission's questions.

'I didn't think it was fair that we had to sit in rooms with the Church hierarchy looking at us giving evidence before the royal commission in Australia, while he got to hide in Rome and not be looked in the face by survivors and their families,' Levey told me. 'But it turned out to be a big kick in the teeth. He didn't care. He didn't want to know. The church seemed to think if they ignored children being abused, it would go away. And I think that's how Pell treated it.'

On day three, Pell admitted that he recorded the reason for the resignation of paedophiles from the Church as 'ill health' rather than criminal activity or paedophilia. Furness did not accept Pell's evidence that senior figures who worked alongside him who knew of the abuse deliberately didn't tell him about it.

For the second time in two days, Furness told Pell his evidence was 'implausible', adding that it was 'designed to deflect blame'.

The survivors from Ballarat had by then had enough. They held a press conference, calling for a meeting with the head of the Roman Catholic Church, Pope Francis, saying they had grown frustrated with Pell's evidence. That meeting was never granted to them. Even News Ltd columnist Andrew Bolt, a staunch defender of Pell, conceded that Pell's evidence before the commission was 'disastrous' and that the case against him was 'very damning'. Bolt withdrew those comments one day later, and secured an exclusive interview with Pell, to be held after his evidence was complete.

The fourth and final day of Pell's evidence drew more ire. A lawyer for abuse victims put it to Pell that the death of at least one child-abuse victim could have been prevented had Pell gone to police so an investigation could be launched. The statement was met by applause from survivors watching from the Ballarat town hall.

Pell said that when a young schoolboy came to him to say that Brother Edward Dowlan was abusing children, he 'didn't do anything about it' aside from telling a chaplain, because he believed then that was all he had to do. He was strongly challenged on this point by Justice McClellan.

McClellan: What did that boy say to you?
Pell: Um, he said something like 'Dowlan is misbehaving with boys.'

McClellan: That was a very serious matter to be raised with you, wasn't it?

Pell: Um, yes, that is the case.

McClellan: What did you do about it?

Pell: Um, I didn't do anything about it.

McClellan: Should you have done something about it?

Pell: Well, I eventually did. I eventually inquired with the school chaplain.

McClellan: You didn't go straight to the school and say, 'I've got this allegation, what's going on?'

Pell: No, I didn't.

McClellan: Should you have?

Pell: Um, with the experience of 40 years later, certainly I would agree that I should have done more.

McClellan: Why do you need the experience of 40 years later? Wasn't it a serious matter then?

Pell: Yes, but people had a different attitude then. There were no specifics about the activity, how serious it was, and the boy wasn't asking me to do anything about it but just lamenting and mentioning.

McClellan: You and I have had this discussion on more than one occasion: why was it necessary for people to ask you to do something rather than for you to accept the information and initiate your own response?

Pell: Um, obviously that is not the case and my responsibilities as an auxiliary bishop and director of an educational institute and archbishop, obviously I was more aware of those obligations in those situations than I was as a young cleric. But I ... don't excuse my comparative lack of activity.

The former premier of New South Wales Kristina Keneally, a Catholic who also has a masters in theology, followed Pell's evidence closely. In an analysis written for *Guardian Australia*, Keneally wrote that many found Pell's evidence shocking:

> Let's set aside that perhaps any priest – indeed, any human with a functioning conscience – might have shown some interest once stories and rumours started to swirl in Ballarat. Pell shared a presbytery with Ridsdale, Pell sat on a committee of priests who made decisions to move Ridsdale from parish to parish, Pell was vicar for education when Ridsdale was a school chaplain at St Alipius, and Pell accompanied Ridsdale to court when he was finally charged.
>
> Pell had more reasons than most to turn his mind to what Ridsdale was perpetrating.

Once the commission's questioning was over, Pell addressed the media. He said the process had been 'a hard slog, at least for me. I'm a bit tired.

'But the royal commission process is designed to try to make the situation better for the future, for the survivors, and to prevent the repetition of all this suffering in the future,' he said.

'I hope that my appearance here has contributed a bit to healing, to improving the situation. All the leadership of the Church in Australia is committed to avoiding any repetition of the terrible history of the past and to try to make things better. I was born in Ballarat. I'm very, very proud of my Ballarat connections. I grieve for the suffering of the people whom I regard as my own people. I will be meeting with the Ballarat survivors tomorrow. Please God [I hope] that will take us a little bit forward.'

A reporter then asked him, 'It was put to you that perhaps this might have appeared to be a witch-hunt, and you said it had crossed your mind. Why did you think that?'

With that, Pell promptly ended the press conference, replying,

'I think I will leave you to work that out. Thank you very much, one and all.'

It was over.

Levey returned from Rome traumatised. What few know about the group of Rome survivors was that the experience took a toll not only on them personally, but on their cohesion as a group.

'When we went to Rome there was a lot of support around us,' Levey said. 'There was a lot of commotion … and it just exploded on us with the media and GoFundMe and everything like that. And then when we got home, everyone sort of went their own way. I think that's one of the things that a lot of people don't realise about being in this situation you're in. You have a group of people who are incredibly vulnerable and who are all survivors and … you're all a support group for each other and you grow to love each other. But then [support drops away].'

In Rome, certain Ballarat survivors were approached by media for comment, and they became the spokespeople for the group. Except, Levey said, the spokespeople didn't always share the views of others in the survivor pack. 'The steam train didn't have a driver,' he said.

In the lead-up to going to Rome, too, there was conflict. There were disputes about who should get to go to Rome and how far the money from the crowd-funded sum would stretch. There were also allegations that a member of the group had been responsible for abusing children. People stopped speaking to each other. Levey struggled to cope in the aftermath of the Rome experience. 'Before and during Rome, I think everything was just so much of a rush, and then everything just collapsed. I think I had too much time to sit and think. I ended up in hospital due to an overdose.'

Anthony and Chrissie Foster also found Rome excruciating.

Chrissie describes the survivors and advocates being outnumbered in the hotel room by 'about 100 priests'.

'The night before we left for Rome, we heard on the news that George Pell's private secretary had called for any seminarians or priests to attend the hearing to support Pell, which filled me with dread at being surrounded by clergy at the hearing,' Chrissie told me.

'The room held about 200 seats. Around 40 were for media, plus our 20, left the balance of 140 or so to be clergy and religious in the forms of monks, brothers, and nuns.' The room is officially called the Valdi Room, but unofficially is known as the green room, decorated in pale shades of green.

While some of Pell's evidence drew gasps from those watching the evidence from the commission's end of the proceedings in Sydney, Chrissie Foster said those in Rome dared not make a squeak for fear of being asked to leave the room.

But she recalls a moment when the Sydney survivors expressed the feelings of those in Rome for them. It was when Pell described the young schoolboy coming to report being abused to him, and his decision not report it to the school authorities.

'There were speakers, of course, in the room in Rome, so what was being said by the commissioners in Sydney could be heard,' Foster recalls. 'Our jaws dropped at Pell's comments, and then a gasp of horror came out of the speakers. It was like their gasp was coming out of our mouths for us. And I remember Pell looked around ... he couldn't work out what he'd said wrong.

'It was amazing, and it was traumatic. It really was. We were all invited to meet Pell afterwards, and after that, Anthony and I said, "No way."'

Of the 4,029 survivors whom the commissioners heard from in private sessions about child sexual abuse in religious institutions,

2,053 (52.9 per cent) said their alleged perpetrators were people in religious ministry. Around two-thirds were priests (30 per cent), religious brothers (32 per cent), or religious sisters (5 per cent). Just under one-third (29 per cent) were lay people. Almost one-quarter of survivors told the commissioners their abuse occurred in places of worship or during religious activities. The commission's final report said:

> In private sessions and case studies we heard about children experiencing sexual abuse in places of worship or related locations such as a confessional, a priest's residence or a ritual bathhouse; in seminaries and houses of religious formation; and during religious activities such as altar boy duties, Bible study or Sunday school.
>
> Most of the perpetrators we heard about in places of worship or during religious activities were adult males who were people in religious ministry. We frequently heard about the trust and respect shown by religious communities and families to people in religious ministry, and how this was a factor in perpetrators gaining access to, grooming and abusing children.
>
> Survivors who spoke with us during private sessions took, on average, 23.9 years to tell someone they had been sexually abused. Some survivors may never tell anyone.

The culture of secrecy in the Catholic Church perpetuated child abuse, and internal religious beliefs and practices, including canon law, acted as barriers that prevented anyone outside the Church, including the police, from being informed, or perpetrators from being held to account by broader society. Abuse victims had nowhere safe or trustworthy within the Church to report their abuse, and the fear and reverence instilled in victims for religious figures prevented them from disclosing abuse to family members or police. Often, members of the hierarchy of the Church were abusers themselves, covered for abusers, or were more interested in protecting the Church's reputation than children, the royal commission revealed.

'In several of the religious institutions we examined, the central factor, underpinning and linked to all other factors, was the status of people in religious ministry,' the commission found.

> The power and authority exercised by people in religious ministry gave them access to children and created opportunities for abuse. Children and adults within religious communities frequently saw people in religious ministry as figures who could not be challenged and, equally, as individuals in whom they could place their trust.

> Clericalism is linked to a sense of entitlement, superiority and exclusion, and abuse of power.

> We heard that the culture of clericalism continues in the Catholic Church and is on the rise in some seminaries in Australia and worldwide.

It was clear that being in a high-profile clerical position in the public eye did not make a person less likely to commit abuse. In fact, it meant if that person did choose to abuse, it was more likely they would be believed when they denied it, or protected when they were found out.

CHAPTER THREE

Mistrial: part I

'I'm more and more disgusted with what happened. Before
I wasn't, I had a naive sort of view of things. I'm still incredibly
confused, but now I have the perspective of a parent, who can
see that if that was going on with their child, that it would
be a totally criminal matter.'
– Tracie's story, Royal Commission into Institutional Responses
to Child Sexual Abuse

How do you find 12 unbiased jurors to hear the trial of one of the
world's most powerful Catholics for crimes of child sexual abuse, at
a time when many people around the world are reeling at news of
the Church's profound failure to protect children?

This was the question that the chief judge of Melbourne's
County Court, Peter Barrington Kidd, found himself considering
as he presided over the trial of the financial controller of the Vatican
and confidant to the Pope, Cardinal George Pell.

Kidd is no stranger to complex, high-profile cases. In 2015, at the
age of 49, he became the County Court's youngest chief judge. Born
in Adelaide, South Australia, on 4 October 1965, he studied law
at the University of Adelaide before spending two-and-a-half years
working at the prestigious corporate law firm Mallesons. According
to an interview with Kidd in the summer 2015–16 edition of
Victorian Bar News, he didn't take to corporate law, and almost

considered leaving the profession after his experiences. 'And that's when I saw an advertisement in the paper for the Commonwealth Department of Public Prosecutions,' he told the publication. 'In some respects, it was really me saying to myself, "I'll try this before I make the decision to move on [from law]." I applied and got the job, and I never really looked back after that point. I suddenly realised I could be excited by my work.'

Over the decade that followed, he prosecuted high-profile cases that made headlines in Australia, including the Bega schoolgirl murders, and the murder trials of Victoria Police officers Sergeant Gary Silk and Senior Constable Rodney Miller. After moving with his family to Switzerland in 2004 and studying international humanitarian and criminal law at the University of Geneva, Kidd was appointed as an international prosecutor with the War Crimes chamber of the state court of Bosnia-Herzegovina, in Sarajevo. While there, he prosecuted people for heinous war crimes – including murders, beatings, and tortures – committed in detention camps.

So when Kidd returned to Australia and settled in Victoria in 2008, taking on the role of Crown prosecutor, he was accustomed to cases that presented complex legal questions, and which dealt with historical crimes for which few witnesses remained alive.

After being promoted to senior Crown prosecutor in Victoria and spending a couple of years in that role, Kidd was appointed to the highest-ranking position within the County Court of Victoria – chief judge. Asked by *Victorian Bar News* what his focus as chief would be, Kidd responded that he was interested in the complexities around evidence presented in sex-offence trials. 'As we know, in many sex trials there are multiple complainants, which immediately raises the question of tendency and coincidence evidence,' he said. 'In fact, even with single complainants the issue is raised – that in itself is controversial. I intend to get involved in trials myself, including multi-complainant sex trials. I intend to have a hands-on role in this particular field.'

There could be few cases more challenging or controversial than that of the highest-ranking Catholic ever to be charged with historical child sexual abuse offences, Cardinal George Pell. Prior to trial, a series of directions and pre-trial hearings were heard before the County Court, as is usual practice. In these hearings, which are usually brief, the judge or magistrate sets a timetable for the defence and the prosecution, and deals with any administrative matters to ensure that both sides have everything in order before the trial goes ahead. Directions hearings are also used to get challenges to evidence out of the way in order to avoid delays during the trial – the parties may dispute the calling of a certain witness, for example, propose introducing new witnesses, or want to establish the terms of a cross-examination to ensure inappropriate lines of questioning aren't ventured into before the jury. One of the most significant administrative matters that Kidd needed to address during these directions hearings in Pell's case was what measures the court needed to take to ensure that jurors would not be prejudiced towards or against Pell, given his high profile and the Church's public and international fall from grace. How could he ensure that the Cathedral trial would be run fairly for both Pell and the complainant?

In a directions hearing on 2 August 2018, Kidd decided, with the agreement of both the prosecution and the defence, that a pool of 250 potential jurors would be brought into the basement of the County Court, and a video-link would be established between the basement and a courtroom on level three. Any potential juror with an excuse or a reason for not being able to sit on the case would write their reasons down on a sheet of paper containing their juror number, and those reasons would be brought to Kidd to consider.

Kidd decided to run the jury selection in this way partly because of the sheer number of potential jurors – having them explain their excuses to him one by one would be time-consuming – and also because he was concerned that 'there will be a number of people in the pool who will say things we wouldn't want the other potential jurors to hear'. 'I imagine several comments [will relate to] some antipathy towards the Catholic Church,' he said during a directions hearing. 'Those people will obviously be excused, but I don't want the rest of the court contaminated with those kinds of excuses.'

The empanelment of a jury is an essential part of the court process. Failures to run the empanelment process in accordance with strict statutory requirements may lead to the discharge of the jury, and in some cases may provide grounds for an appeal against a conviction.

It was clear that Pell's status, the background of the child sexual abuse royal commission, and the worldwide reckoning with the Catholic Church would present some challenges to Kidd. There was much talk from the moment it became known that Pell was being investigated for historical sexual abuse crimes that he could never get a fair trial because of his status, and because jurors would be incapable of casting irrelevant facts and emotions relating to the Catholic Church aside. One way that courts may deal with concerns about juries being prejudiced towards defendants or victims – an issue more pronounced in high-profile cases – is to run a judge-only trial. However, Victoria is one of three Australian jurisdictions that does not offer this option for those charged with the most serious offences. Pell's trial revived debate about whether Victoria needed to introduce this option. (For a brief discussion of the debate over jury trials and judge-only trials, see Appendix B.)

On the morning of 15 August 2018, the first official day of Pell's trial, the empanelment process began, and the written excuses were brought up to the third floor from the holding room for Kidd to consider, as a small group of journalists watched on. This process was held in courtroom 3.3 of Melbourne's County Court, the same room in which many of the royal commission's hearings had taken place. Kidd sat at the front of the room at the raised bench, his staff taking their seats at a table below. On the next step down were two long tables, with the prosecution seated at one and the defence at the other. To the side was the jury box, and on either side of the room were screens that could be linked to the basement and to the holding room. Behind the tables for the respective parties were seats for the public. In the front row sat Detective Sergeant Chris Reed, who had led the investigation, and Katrina Lee, an executive advisor for the Catholic Archdiocese of Sydney and a longtime friend of Pell, who was present every day he faced court. Behind them sat the journalists, and the few members of the public who had kept track of proceedings and court dates, and who attended throughout.

Overall, the trial itself was a significantly less frenzied affair than the committal, which struck me as strange. Australia's most senior Catholic was facing his first day on trial, and there was no long line to enter the court or struggle for a seat.

A video-link to the basement, where the mass of potential jurors was held, was established. The screens were not large enough to capture the entirety of the basement at once, so the camera would pan to different sections of the room. Kidd went down to the basement and made some preliminary remarks to the potential jurors, telling them that they were being considered for empanelment in the trial of Cardinal George Pell, and that the trial was expected to run for five weeks. I couldn't help but wonder what was going through the jurors' minds when they learned which trial they might be deciding. It struck me that there must have been at least some in the room unaware of who Cardinal George Pell was, and who only learned of his significance later.

'Good morning, everybody,' Kidd told them once he was with them. 'My name is Peter Kidd. I'm the chief judge, and I will be the judge presiding over this trial. It's the trial of the matter of DPP [Department of Public Prosecutions] v George Pell. Now, I declare this room where you're all sitting an extension of the courtroom where we will be sitting. When I return to the room, the accused will be arraigned; that is, the charges he faces will be read out to him and he will plead not guilty to each of the charges.' Kidd returned to courtroom 3.3, and Pell was formally arraigned and pleaded not guilty.

The jurors were then given more information by Kidd about the trial. 'Many, if not all, of you would have heard of Cardinal George Pell. That may be because of a connection to the Catholic Church or because of media publicity. The fact that you have heard of Cardinal George Pell does not necessarily mean that you should apply to be excused. That is different from knowing the accused man.'

Kidd outlined the basics of the case. Pell was accused of having offended against two children aged 13 inside St Patrick's Cathedral in Melbourne in 1996. The potential jurors were told that one of the victims was now dead, and that the offences were alleged to have occurred while Pell was the Archbishop of Melbourne.

The potential jurors were then invited by Kidd to write down on a piece of paper any reasons they felt they should be excused from jury duty for the trial, along with their jury number. They were also asked to complete a questionnaire, included on which was a list of witnesses and potential witnesses, as well as a list of places to be discussed in the trial. On the questionnaire, jurors were asked if they knew any of the witnesses, lawyers, or court staff involved in the case.

'Now, self-evidently, the accused man, Cardinal George Pell, is a very senior member of the Catholic Church,' Kidd continued. 'He is, in fact, a cardinal of the Catholic Church. Just because you are of Catholic faith or identify with the Catholic faith doesn't automatically disqualify you from sitting on this jury. On the other hand, if, because of your Catholic faith or identity, you feel that you cannot bring a fair and impartial mind to the trial, you must seek to excuse yourself. Similarly, if you have strong feelings against the Catholic Church which you cannot put aside and which would prevent you from bringing a fair and impartial mind to this trial, you must seek to be excused. If you are not able to put aside your personal experiences or any bias or sympathy that may arise from the fact that this case concerns a cardinal of the Catholic Church, then you must seek to excuse yourself.'

Kidd homed in on this point, stating that it was 'critical' that Pell only be judged on the charges against him and the evidence presented at trial. 'This trial must not be used as an opportunity to make Cardinal Pell a scapegoat for conduct not contained in the charges or for the conduct or failures of the Catholic Church generally.' This point was drilled into the potential jurors, and would be repeated to the selected jury frequently throughout the trial.

Kidd also told the potential jurors that if they had read or knew about a book by journalist Louise Milligan entitled *Cardinal*, they must seek to be excused. The same went if they followed any blogs or websites campaigning against child sexual abuse, Kidd told them.

'Finally, can I advise you and remind you that if, for any reason, you do not end up being a juror on this trial, you are not entitled to talk about this process with anyone else, or that it involved a trial for Cardinal Pell. Let me be clear about that. If you aren't selected on the jury, this will be one of the last opportunities I will have to tell you this. If you are not selected on the jury, then you must not talk about the fact that this case involved Cardinal Pell.'

The slips of paper containing juror excuses and questionnaires were brought up to Kidd in courtroom 3.3 to consider. One by one, Kidd read out the juror number, and either excused them from jury duty or found their reason unacceptable and ordered that they remain in the jury pool. In some cases, he would call individual jurors into the courtroom to ask them to further explain their excuses before he decided whether to dismiss them.

The jurors remaining in the pool after this process, known as the jury panel, had their numbers placed in a ballot box. The panel was then brought up to the same level of the court where Kidd and the legal teams were, and those who did not fit in courtroom 3.3 were taken to a holding room down the hall. The empanelment process then began. Journalists left the main courtroom at this point to make room, and sat in the holding room with the overflow of jurors. Fourteen jurors were then drawn from a ballot box and had their numbers and occupations read out by the court tipstaff. As they were called, they made their way to the jury box, walking in front of Pell. Pell was allowed to challenge up to three jurors without giving any reason, but chose to accept all 14 of those drawn, which included eight women and six men.

While only 12 jurors would deliver the verdict, two extra jurors were drawn in case they might be needed, because the length of the trial meant that any number of things could happen to the jurors, including some of them falling ill. If more than 12 out of the 14 remained by the end of the trial, another ballot would be held to decide the final 12. The excess jurors drawn would be excused and sent home, their five weeks of hard work ending before verdict deliberations began.

Following this process, which took all morning and early afternoon, the case was transferred to courtroom 4.3 for the remainder of the trial. This courtroom was much smaller and more contained, and as such the jurors were closer to the legal teams, could get a much clearer view of Pell, and would likely have identified the small group of journalists furiously taking notes. For five weeks, all of us would file in and out of this little courtroom, although the jurors, judges, and court staff would go through a separate entry and exit. This provided plenty of time for me to get a stronger sense of how Kidd operated, and how the legal parties perceived him. It was also plenty of time to come to know the other journalists covering the case, who would prove to be an essential source of support and humour as it developed and intensified. The courtroom was also frequented by a combination of curious lawyers, Pell supporters, and child sexual abuse victims and advocates. Courtroom 4.3 and the four tiny meeting rooms outside in the hallway became my offices.

Once everyone was gathered in the courtroom, and the jury was brought in from their room shortly after 2.00 pm, it was clear there were only 13 jurors. It was revealed that one juror, a woman, had already dropped out, having been excused to care for her child. Kidd addressed the jury and told them what their role would entail over the following weeks. The jurors listened intently, many of them taking notes as Kidd again outlined the charges: two charges of sexual penetration of a child under 16; two charges of an indecent act with a child under the age of 16; and one charge of indecent assault of a child under the age of 16.

'It's for you and you alone to decide if he is not guilty of these charged offences,' Kidd told them. 'You are the only ones in court who can make a decision about the facts. It is also your task to apply the law to the facts you have found and by doing that to decide guilty or not guilty.

'It is my role to ensure the trial is fair. It is not my responsibility to decide this case. The verdict you return has absolutely nothing to do with me. So while you follow directions I give about law, you are not bound by any comments I make about the facts.'

Kidd then ran the jurors through the different types of evidence that would be presented to them during the trial. He reiterated numerous times that they were not to share this evidence with anyone or to speak about the case with anyone aside from each other, and only when the entire jury was present.

They were also told that they were not compelled to accept any comments made by counsel – that is, the legal parties – during their addresses to the jury. 'Of course, if you agree with an argument they present, you can adopt it,' Kidd told them. 'In effect, it becomes your own argument. But if you do not agree with their view, you must put it aside.'

'Dismiss feelings of sympathy or prejudice you may have, whether it is sympathy for or prejudice against the accused or anyone else,' Kidd continued. 'No such emotion has any part to play in your decision. You must dispassionately weigh the evidence logically with an open mind, not according to your passion or feelings. You must use your intellect, not your heart. You must not make your decision based on any information obtained outside of court. Ignore media. That is just so important. You must ignore that. It must play no role at all in your decision-making process. None of that media coverage or what you have heard is relevant to this trial. None of it. Anything you have previously heard or which you might hear on TV or radio is completely irrelevant to what you hear in this case. Cardinal George Pell is entitled to a fair trial. A fair trial can only be had if he is judged on the evidence placed before you in this case, and if you follow my directions.

'Most importantly, you must not make any investigations or inquiries, or conduct independent research concerning any aspect of this case or any person connected with it. That includes research about the law that applies to this case. You must not use the internet to access legal databases, legal dictionaries, legal texts, earlier decisions in this or other courts, or any other materials of any kind relating to the matters in this trial. You must not search for information about this case, Cardinal Pell, or the Catholic Church on Google, or conduct any similar searches.'

Kidd told the jurors that this direction was so important that if any of them heard that another juror had conducted their own research, they had to inform him or his staff immediately.

'You must report your fellow juror. The immediate outcome is that the jury may need to be discharged, the trial will be brought to an end, and the trial may need to start again. This would cause stress and expense to witnesses, prosecutors, and other jurors.'

It was also a criminal offence.

'Jurors have been sent to jail for discussing a case on Facebook,' Kidd cautioned.

'You may ask yourself this question: what is wrong with looking for more information? Seeking out information or discussing a matter with friends may be a natural part of life for you when making an important decision. As conscientious jurors, you may think that conducting you own research will help you reach the right result.'

However, there were significant reasons for not conducting research into or discussing the case, Kidd continued. Media reports could be wrong or inaccurate. Deciding a case on information not known to the parties was unfair to both prosecution and defence. And, finally, a verdict could only be true if it was made according to the evidence presented in the trial alone.

'You would cease being a juror – that is, a judge of the facts – and have instead taken on the role of investigator if you started making these inquiries and acting on outside information.'

Jurors conducting their own research undermined public confidence in the jury system, he said.

'The jury system has been a fundamental feature of our criminal justice system for centuries. And one of the reasons that you must not discuss [the trial] with people not on your jury is that those people have not heard all of the evidence. People not on the jury have not heard my instructions as to law or the arguments of counsel. They can't possibly contribute to your thinking fairly.'

The jurors were told that when assessing the evidence of witnesses, they should consider credibility and reliability. While credibility concerned honesty and whether the witness was telling the truth, reliability might be different.

'A witness may be honest but have a poor memory or be mistaken,' Kidd told them. 'It is for you to judge whether the witnesses are telling the truth and whether they correctly recall the facts about which they are giving evidence.

'This is something you do all the time in your daily lives. There is no special skill involved. You just need to use your common sense. In making your assessment, you should appreciate that giving evidence in a trial is not common and may be a stressful experience. So you should not jump to conclusions based on how a witness gives evidence. Looks can be deceiving. People react and appear differently. Witnesses come from different backgrounds and have different abilities, values, and life experiences. There are just too many variables to make the manner in which a witness gives evidence the only or even the most important factor in your decision.'

Jurors should also keep an open mind about the credibility of witnesses until all of the evidence had been presented, he said.

Kidd emphasised that Pell did not have to prove his innocence. Rather, it was up to the prosecution to prove Pell's guilt. They had to prove this beyond reasonable doubt.

(It should be noted that, unlike in the US, Australian courts do not observe a definition of reasonable doubt. Australia takes the approach that to define the terms is to diminish them. In Victoria, jurors can ask the judge for some guidance as to how to interpret 'beyond reasonable doubt' if they are stuck, but this question was not asked by the jurors in Pell's case. However, the jurors were given very strong directions by Kidd about factors to consider when assessing whether they should hold a reasonable doubt.)

'You've probably heard these words before and they mean exactly what they say, proof beyond reasonable doubt,' Kidd told the jurors. 'This is the highest standard of proof that our law demands. For now, you should know that it is only if you find that the prosecution has proven all of the elements beyond reasonable doubt that you may find the accused guilty of that charge.' Kidd then repeated this for emphasis, and added, 'If you are not satisfied that the prosecution has done this, your verdict in relation to that charge must be not guilty.'

The jurors were told that they would need to appoint a foreperson, who would not be able to be balloted off at the end of the trial. The foreperson would be the person communicating with the judge, including relaying any concerns or questions from the jurors. The jurors went on to appoint a woman in this role.

They were reminded yet again by Kidd, 'This trial is for you 13 people to sit on. So, no research, no discussions.'

It was with these directions ringing in their ears that the jurors left the court for the day. Once they had left, Richter mentioned to Kidd that Pell was on medication that required him to go to the toilet frequently. Kidd assured Richter that if Pell needed a break at any time, it would be accommodated. It was before jurors entered the court for the morning or after they had left that matters such as these and administrative issues would be discussed. Richter also brought up another administrative matter: the cardinal's robes.

Richter told Kidd that he intended to show the robes to the jurors. He intended to prove to the jurors that the robes could not be manoeuvred in a particular way. The prosecution had no objections to the robes been shown.

Kidd said he did not have 'any difficulty' with the robes being shown by Richter, 'so long as it's not overly dramatic, Mr Richter'.

'It won't be, your honour,' Richter responded. 'I don't intend to re-enact the impossible.'

Day one of court was adjourned.

On day two, the jurors heard the opening addresses from the defence and prosecution, including more elaborate details for the first time about what Cardinal George Pell was alleged to have done while Archbishop of Melbourne in 1996.

Pell was not remanded in custody at this stage. He had relinquished his passport, and was not considered a travel risk. He arrived each morning from his accommodation in Melbourne in his private car, accompanied by Katrina Lee. Police would be waiting to swiftly escort him from the car and into the building. He would often be met by members of the defence team outside the court, who would walk inside with him. Due to his pacemaker, Pell was unable to walk through the security screening gates, and instead received a pat-down. He was then whisked up to level four of the court and into one of four small meeting rooms adjacent to the courtroom. Once court commenced, he would be escorted by a police officer into the dock at the back of the courtroom. His outfit, like at the committal hearing, was always the same: a black buttoned-up collared shirt, black pants, and sometimes a beige jacket. He would sit in the dock, sometimes with his head bowed as he took notes, at other times looking intently at the judge or bar table.

By this point, the number of journalists attending the case had dropped down to Australian media and a couple of international organisations, including representatives from *The Wall Street Journal* and Reuters. There were no more than a dozen reporters present.

Senior prosecutor Mark Gibson led the case for the Crown. Compared to the flamboyant Richter, Gibson was calm and measured, never raising his voice or changing his tone. Richter's grey hair and beard was thick and full, at times with a certain unkempt quality to it, while Gibson's beard was always neatly trimmed, his hair always combed and parted. Richter favoured round John Lennon-style spectacles; Gibson, more standard, thin rectangular frames. Richter, a longtime smoker, could be seen sucking on a vape pen during court breaks. Gibson walked directly between court and his office, rarely dallying. Both men would have encountered each other frequently in previous trials and would have been familiar with the other's style of prosecution and defence. There was an air of respect and, at times, camaraderie between the two.

Gibson had only been appointed to the role of senior Crown prosecutor a few months before Pell's trial began, prior to that having been a senior counsel. He had been a barrister for more than 30 years, and is described in legal and police circles as a 'nice guy' who leaves no stone unturned. He has been known to bring senior detectives into meeting rooms of the court before a trial and run them through a mock cross-examination, playing the role of the defence in order to prepare them for any line of questioning. In his spare time, he coaches umpires for Australian Rules football – he has been umpiring matches since 1985. In a profile of his career on the website of Victoria's Office of Public Prosecutions, Gibson is quoted as saying there are similarities between law and umpiring.

'In umpiring you can't be swayed by the crowd or the players, and need to be impartial at all times,' he said. 'Like the courtroom, you also can't let emotions get in the way of your decisions.'

It was in a calm, chronological manner that Gibson outlined the prosecution's case against Pell before the jury for the first time. He could not have been given a more complex or high-profile case to mark the start of his role as a senior prosecutor.

On a Sunday morning sometime in the second half of 1996, Gibson told the jury, Archbishop Pell was saying mass at St Patrick's Cathedral in East Melbourne, having recently been installed as the archbishop of the Melbourne archdiocese. As was customary during Sunday mass at the cathedral, the church choir was singing, consisting of a large number of boys aged between about 10 and 18. These choristers included scholarship students from the prestigious and exclusive St Kevin's College in the blue-ribbon eastern suburb of Toorak. Their scholarships had been awarded as a condition of having successfully auditioned for and committed to rehearsing and performing for the St Patrick's Cathedral choir. The complainant and his friend were among the choristers at the time. They were both 13 years old.

Once mass had ended and the choir had finished singing their hymns at the end of the service, they would proceed out of the building by walking through the front door and then in an anti-clockwise direction around the southern side of the cathedral to an area at the back of the cathedral, where the choirboys would re-enter the building, change out of their robes, and get ready to go home. On the day the first alleged offences occurred, once the choir had proceeded outside the cathedral after mass, the complainant and his friend decided to have some fun, relieved that their singing duties were over.

The boys decided to slip away from the procession once it was outside the cathedral and away from the public gaze.

'You'll hear both boys, having departed from the procession, went back into the cathedral through one of the doors on the south side entry wing, and that's the side you may know faces Fitzroy Gardens,' Gibson said. 'Once inside the cathedral, they went into an unlocked door and walked down a corridor that led down to the sacristies, the private rooms at the rear of the cathedral and off-limits to choirboys. One of those sacristies was for the priests to use and get changed in, and the other one was for the archbishop to get changed in. Upon reaching the priests' sacristy, both boys entered that room. No one was in there, mass having recently ended.'

Inside the room, to the left, was a wooden-panelled bifold door covering a storage cupboard. The boys opened it, finding sacramental wine inside. They each took a few swigs.

'Cardinal Pell happened to walk in the room, and caught them in the act of being in a place of being off-limits and drinking church wine,' Gibson told the jurors. 'You'll hear that the boys were told by Cardinal Pell that they were in a lot of trouble. Cardinal Pell was still wearing his church robes. The boys came out from where they were swigging wine, and Pell approached both boys. Then you'll hear he proceeded to manoeuvre his robes so as to expose his penis to the boys. One of the boys asked, "Please let us go."'

Pell instead stepped forward and grabbed the complainant's friend by the back of head and forced his head onto his penis. This comprised the first charge of sexual penetration of a child under the age of 16. After a short while, Pell moved on to the complainant and grabbed him by the back of his head, and forced his head down onto his penis. This comprised the second charge of sexual penetration of a child under the age of 16. Pell then stopped and told the complainant to remove his pants. The complainant pulled down his pants and underpants, and Pell knelt down and fondled the boy's penis while at the same time masturbating himself. These acts comprised the charges of an indecent act in the presence of a child under the age of 16. After a couple of minutes, Pell finished and stood up. The boys left the room, hung up their robes, and left the cathedral. They did not say anything to anyone, including each other, about what had happened.

At least one month later, another incident allegedly occurred following Sunday mass at the cathedral. The complainant was walking along the corridor leading to the choristers' change room, adjacent to the archbishop's sacristy. Pell pushed the boy against the wall, grabbing his genitals and squeezing them before letting go and walking off. The encounter was brief, and again the complainant didn't tell anyone. At the end of 1997, when they were in year eight, the boys left the choir and St Kevin's College.

Gibson told the jurors that police had conducted an extensive investigation. This included interviewing numerous witnesses. (In a court case, a witness is anyone who gives evidence; it does not mean that they witnessed the offending firsthand.) None of the witnesses except the complainant had firsthand evidence about the offending. The other boy Pell had allegedly offended against had died in 2014 at the age of 34, and had always denied ever having been abused when asked by his parents if anything had ever happened to him.

'The Crown has a duty to call all relevant witnesses, whether helpful or not to the Crown case,' Gibson told the jurors. He also told them that 'it will become apparent there are a number of conflicts between the complainant account and other witnesses called by prosecution'.

As well as evidence from the complainant, the jurors would hear from other choristers and people involved in the Sunday Solemn Mass service at the time. Choirmaster John Mallinson, church organist Geoffrey Cox, master of ceremonies Charles Portelli, and sacristan Max Potter would all give evidence. Some of them would give seemingly contradictory evidence, Gibson said. Some would say that the choir procession was a highly regimented process both inside and outside the cathedral and that, therefore, two choirboys peeling off from the procession would have been noticed. Some would speak about the door to the priests' sacristy being locked; others would say it was unlocked. Some would say the sacramental wine was always locked away and could not have been accessed by the boys. Some witnesses would speak about Pell standing on the steps of the cathedral after mass and greeting people for an extended period of time, and therefore it would be claimed that he could not have made it to the priests' sacristy to assault the boys shortly after mass had ended. Some would speak about the robes that Pell wore as archbishop being layered, heavy, and cumbersome, conflicting with the complainant's account of Pell being able to manoeuvre them to expose his penis.

By flagging with the jurors that there would be numerous witnesses giving contradictory evidence, Gibson presumably hoped that the jurors would not be surprised when these discrepancies in accounts arose.

Prosecutors are obliged in a criminal trial to call all witnesses who can help with the narrative of events and facts in the case, unless there is a good reason not to do so. The defence is not obliged to call any witnesses. If the prosecution fails to do this, the defence can ask the judge to give the jurors a direction telling them that a certain witness had not been called, and from this that they would be entitled to conclude the witness would have been detrimental to the prosecution's case. There are a few situations in which the prosecution is not obliged to call a witness: if, in their view, the witness is unreliable and incapable of being believed, or if they would not add anything significant to the case that hadn't already been covered comprehensively by the other witnesses. For example, in the Cathedral trial, the prosecution did not have to call every choirboy in the choir at the time simply to establish that mass was held on Sundays and that Pell sometimes presided over these masses. Enough witnesses gave corroborating evidence to establish these facts.

The prosecution is allowed to cross-examine its own witnesses in circumstances where the witness is unfavourable to its case. In a directions hearing before the Cathedral trial, the parties discussed before the judge the fact that several of the witnesses being called by the prosecution would present evidence that might prove inconsistent with its own case. Gibson sought permission from the judge to cross-examine the witnesses. But due to the complexity of the case, it became clear that Gibson and his colleague, barrister

Angela Ellis, would have to run this cross-examination carefully.

Gibson told Kidd during the directions hearing: 'The witnesses tend to speak in absolutes. It is going to be a matter for the jury as to whether or not moving the vestment in such a way is impossible. Next is access to wine. [The complainant] says it was there and he took a swig. Other witnesses say it was locked away. The basis for the Crown case is simple. The accused whilst alone came upon the complainant. If that was impossible, then the Crown case fails. If the jury do have reasonable doubt as to whether or not the accused was alone when he walked along that corridor, if they do have reasonable doubt as to whether or not the sacristy was unlocked … whether vestments could be manoeuvred … the duration the accused stayed outside on the steps … and if two boys could detach from the procession without being noticed, then the Crown case could fail.'

What Gibson clearly wanted the jurors to conclude was that several of the witnesses, such as Potter and Portelli, were loyal to Pell, and that this loyalty could have influenced their evidence.

Kidd told Gibson that cross-examining the witnesses to test their memory was one thing. But cross-examining them in an attempt to show they had a motive to protect Pell out of allegiance to him could trigger or feed into the notion of a Church cover-up, and arouse emotions in the jurors prejudicial to Pell.

Gibson assured Kidd that the cross-examination would be performed in a 'narrow, seamless way'. He would simply ask the witnesses questions such as 'How long have you known Cardinal Pell?' and 'Describe how it is that you know him.' Kidd said that so long as the prosecutor was not seeking to put to the witness that they were lying, his proposed line of questioning would be allowed. (There are strict rules about cross-examination, and in a courtroom it is an art. Witnesses must not be invited to give evidence based on hearsay, or on what they think might have happened. Questions must not be confusing or misleading.)

Gibson echoed Kidd's directions by clearly telling the jury towards the end of his opening address: 'Put aside feelings of sympathy or prejudice [towards Pell]. The last thing the prosecution would want is for a determination to be made based on a bias or prejudice towards the accused man, Cardinal Pell, because of his position in the Catholic Church.'

Gibson then handed the jurors a book of photographs that he said would assist them when they were taken on a tour of the cathedral as part of the trial.

Gibson's opening remarks had taken half a day. He had wasted no time in getting to the heart of the case, and did not shy away from Pell's prominence in the Church. Gibson had been considered and reserved, using eloquent, clear language. When Richter began his opening address at around noon, he put the events in relatively crude terms, made pop-culture references, and his booming voice conveyed tones ranging from incredulity to disbelief. He did not attempt in any way to shy away from or downplay the offences that the cardinal had been charged with.

'This is an extraordinary case in the sense that Cardinal Pell is the most senior Catholic cleric ever to have been charged with actually committing sexual offences,' Richter told the jurors. 'Some of you may have seen a movie called *Spotlight* concerning a cardinal in Boston, and his alleged misconduct consisted of covering up a for a priest. But in terms of actual sexual assaults – and let's not mess our words – we are talking about forcible oral rape. And I use the word rape to emphasise the importance of what's alleged to have happened here.

'The cardinal's case is it did not happen. Period. And it couldn't happen for reasons that will become apparent during the trial.'

Richter quickly zoned in on Gibson's reference to the date the abuse occurred – sometime in the second half of 1996. Richter had gone a step further than the prosecutors. He had tracked down church records, and was able to demonstrate that there were only two occasions in 1996 when Pell presided over Sunday Solemn Mass after having been inaugurated in August that year: those dates were 15 December and 22 December. This provided only two opportunities for Pell to have offended.

But Pell could not have offended on these dates, Richter continued, because the choir processions at the cathedral following mass were ritualistic in nature.

'Deviation from ritual is looked upon as a no-no,' he said. The choir procession was organised according to pitch, and therefore those with the highest voices and likely the youngest were in front of the procession, going back to the oldest choristers with the deepest voices. Behind the choirboys in the procession came the clerics, with Archbishop Pell at the very end. If the two boys, who were towards the front of the procession, had taken off, they would have been seen by at least one person behind them, 'if not the whole lot', Richter told the jurors.

'How probable is it that they nick off like that without anyone noticing?' Richter asked the jurors. 'This is a disciplined procession. There is a gentleman called [Peter] Finnigan who was the choir marshal in charge of discipline. These were times when sexual misconduct was a subject of conversation in the community, and older people felt they had a duty of care to look after young children.' A disciplinarian like Finnigan would not tolerate two young boys slipping away from the procession at a time when the community was increasingly vigilant about and aware of child abuse, he said.

Shortly after being inaugurated as archbishop, Pell had introduced the Melbourne Response, the scheme aimed at providing support and compensation to child sexual abuse survivors. It made no sense that Pell, 'the man who's supposed to be raping two young boys in a sacristy', would introduce such a scheme if he were an offender, Richter said.

Sunday masses were the most well-attended masses at St Patrick's Cathedral, aside from those at Christmas and Easter. Tourists, special guests, other clerics, and dignitaries all attended. 'And so, as a new archbishop conducting his first formal Solemn Mass on a Sunday, you'd imagine it would be well attended, there would be a lot of people to shake hands with to say, "How are you?" and "God bless you", and whatever else one says to guests and congregants.'

There was no way that Pell could be on the steps speaking with congregants after mass and also have the time to abuse the boys in the sacristy before anyone noticed, Richter said. There was simply no opportunity for the two boys to run off and not be seen by anyone, especially since there were witnesses who would say that certain doors the boys would have needed to go through on their way to the sacristy would have been locked.

'Whether it's deliberate lies or a fantasy – and we all know children can have fantasies, and sometimes they come to believe them over the years – whether lies or fantasy, malicious or whatever, it does not matter,' Richter said. 'It did not happen.'

There was no evidence, Richter added, that Pell knew either of the boys by name. There had been no grooming. He did not know their families. There was also no evidence that Pell locked the sacristy door while attacking the boys. While the first boy was being sexually assaulted, the complainant did not run away, Richter told the jury. It was impossible that one of the boys would not have yelled or called out during the attack; and if they had, there would have been people in the corridors outside who would have heard them.

But there was an 'even greater improbability' that spoke to why the offending could not have happened – the archbishop's robes. Richter – not any investigating detectives – had obtained the robes, and he brought them into the court and submitted them as evidence. Jurors would later have the robes brought into the jury room to hold and to try on. Richter asked one of his defence team to hold the robes up during his opening address while he pointed out the foundation garment, called an alb. 'It's quite heavy. It's supposed to go right down to the ankles,' he said.

'On me, it will trail on the floor, and on him,' Richter continued, gesturing towards Pell, 'down to the ankles. The one thing you don't see here is any parting. It's a single shift that goes all the way to the ground. So how he could push this aside to show an exposed penis is something you'll consider as a serious issue with the evidence.' Pell would also have been wearing suit pants underneath this, Richter said, making manoeuvrability even more difficult.

All up, there were about 13 points of improbability in the prosecution's case, Richter said. 'It's a bit like TattsLotto,' he told them.

'The fact is, to say something is possible gives you not the slightest idea how likely it is. It is possible, ladies and gentlemen of the jury, that a meteor will come out of space and strike this court while we're sitting here. It's possible physically. But do you plan your life on that basis? I don't think so.'

Richter was not finished with outlining the impossibilities of the case, however. He told the jurors that if the boys had been abused, they would not have continued to attend the choir the following year. He also asked why the two boys did not discuss their abuse among themselves at any stage, 'along the lines of "That bastard, why did he do this to us? What are we going to do about it? Are you going to tell Mum about it? Are you going to tell Dad about it?"

'Just picture this,' he went on. 'Twelve-year-old boys that have been orally raped. On [the complainant's] evidence, they were crying. Did they say, "What about next week's mass, next Sunday, are we going to go? He might come at us again." The evidence of [the complainant] will be he had never discussed this with [the other boy]. Never.'

Finally, Richter turned to the other victim. The jurors were told he had died in 2014 from a heroin overdose when he was in his early thirties. They were told that he never disclosed being abused to anyone before he died, and that he had in fact had denied being abused when his parents directly asked him. The other boy did not turn to heroin because he had been abused, Richter told the jurors, but rather he had told his father he took heroin because he liked it.

He concluded his opening address by saying, 'If it's not probable, it's not likely to be the truth.

'When you take into account all known facts, the simplest explanation is likely to be the truth. In the end, we will be arguing to you that the simplest answer to this is it did not happen.' If there was even a possibility that the jurors believed it could not have happened, they must find Pell not guilty, he concluded.

Following these opening addresses, Kidd gave some further directions to the jury.

A clear issue in the case for the jurors to determine was whether the events happened at all, he said.

'The prosecution case will be that they did happen in the way described by the complainant ... the defence case will be the incidents just did not happen, they are false.

'You, of course, will always bear in mind it's for the prosecution to prove its case ... from beginning to end. And the defence does not need to prove anything.

'You must be careful not to allow convenience to override justice. You would be wrong to say just because Pell is guilty on one charge, he must be guilty or not on another.'

The arguments had been made. Gibson's case was that the events had occurred; Richter's, that they had not. And the judge had made it clear to the jurors that they alone were responsible for determining the truth.

CHAPTER FOUR

Mistrial: part II

'These leaders, these people, are the ones who are the biggest miscarriages of justice. They will do anything to protect themselves, their reputation and their institution, and that's what's so astounding and so offensive to the core. They didn't get up and say anything. I was left alone as the victim, as the advocate, as the troublemaker, as the person that is bringing the community into disrepute.'

– Abuse victim Manny Waks, CEO of Kol v'Oz

According to the City of Melbourne, St Patrick's Cathedral is the largest and oldest church in Australia, built in stages between 1858 and its completion in 1940. An example of Gothic Revival architecture, the grand building is at once beautiful and dark, the bluestone walls and its tall, black spires extending upwards becoming particularly pronounced when Melbourne has bright-blue skies. Grotesque gargoyles supposedly protect those seeking salvation within the church from the evil outside it. The inside is filled with archways and stained glass, but their colours do not distract from the chill. Between 1992 and 1997, parts of the cathedral were closed while restoration work took place, and during 1994 it was closed to the public altogether so that the restoration could be completed in time to celebrate the centenary of the church's consecration.

It is where state funerals for prominent Catholic public figures are held, and where some memorial services take place following public tragedies such as terrorist attacks or plane crashes. And it is where the Archbishop of Melbourne presides over Sunday Solemn Mass. In 1996, the Archbishop of Melbourne was George Pell. He had been inaugurated in August of the same year. And months later, jurors had by now heard, he allegedly sexually abused two 13-year-old choirboys after Sunday Solemn Mass, before assaulting one of them again a few weeks later by grabbing his genitals briefly in a church corridor.

Following the opening addresses from Gibson and the initial directions from Kidd, the 13 jurors were taken on a tour of the cathedral to complete day two of the trial. The court staff changed out of their legal robes and into everyday clothing so as not to attract attention. Journalists were not allowed to attend. Strict conditions for the tour were set by Kidd. Jurors were not to speak to anyone at the church. If they had any questions, these were to be directed to the judge's assistant. The jurors had already been given a photo book containing photographs of key areas of the church. Now they would be able to see the corridors and rooms for themselves, and to walk the same route the complainant said he took to get back inside the cathedral following Sunday Solemn Mass. This took a couple of hours. Parts of the view of the cathedral were filmed so that jurors would be able to refer back to the footage when they retired to deliberate over their verdict in a few weeks' time. They were also given a transcript from the tour. The jurors were told that they were not to return to the cathedral at any point during the trial.

The jurors returned to court briefly following the tour of the church. Before they were brought from the jury room into the courtroom, Richter raised a concern with Kidd.

'There have been a couple of incidents where, just walking past the jury, they smile and, if we're on our own, we look down,' Richter said. 'It would be really nice if your honour told them that it is not because we are rude and we hate them.'

Kidd replied, 'All right.'

With that, the jury was brought back into the court, and Kidd thanked them for being diligent throughout the church tour, referred to throughout the trial as 'the view'.

'You may have noticed that in the course of the view, we all crossed paths quite a bit and no doubt you crossed paths with counsel and solicitors, and I am sure from time to time counsel and the solicitors perhaps looked down or turned away rather than engaging with you as they normally would in ordinary day-to-day life,' Kidd told them.

'Of course, they do that for a reason, and that is because they have a particular role in the case; they are very conscious that they shouldn't be engaging with you in a social kind of way. Just don't hold it against them, though. Don't take it that they are being rude. They are just doing their job.'

The jurors had three questions for Kidd following the view, and all related to the priests' sacristy where the offending allegedly occurred. The jurors wanted to know if there had been any changes to the room over the 22 years since the offending. Kidd assured the jurors that they would be presented with evidence over the coming weeks of the trial that would answer this question. The jurors also wanted to know the exact location in the sacristy where the abuse occurred. Kidd again said that evidence about this would be presented during the trial.

Their third question related to when security locks on the priests' sacristy were installed. 'If any evidence is led about that, you will hear it,' Kidd told them.

The jurors were sent home, again with strict directions not to speak about the case to anyone or to conduct any research.

In the three days following, the jurors heard from the most important person on whom the prosecution's entire case hinged: the complainant. His would be the only first-hand account of the alleged crimes. Cases such as these, where there is only the complainant's and accused's first-hand accounts of events, are known as 'word-against-word' cases. While Pell would never be called to the witness stand to give evidence, he had pleaded not guilty, and his case was that the events that had allegedly unfolded were improbable, if not impossible, and did not happen. The complainant's evidence was not open to the public, including the media. His evidence was given via a video-link, as is customary in cases involving sexual abuse.

In 2017, new provisions were added to the *Jury Directions Act 2015* to improve jurors' understanding of the directions they are given by judges or magistrates. Numerous reforms to jury directions had already been occurring over several years in Victoria in order to address known problems with jury directions, including that they were overly complex, not clearly understood, and at times overwhelming. Some of the changes introduced in 2017 were particularly relevant to Pell's trial.

Although only rarely used in Victoria, a direction known as 'The Markuleski direction' was expressly abolished. This direction, still used in some states, requires the judge to tell jurors that if they have any doubts about the complainant's evidence in relation to one charge, they should therefore doubt the truthfulness and reliability of the complainant's evidence generally, in relation to all charges. In its submission to the child sexual abuse royal commission, the Law Council of Australia had recommended keeping the direction. 'At its core, the purpose of such a direction is to ensure that a jury is not misled by a direction that they should consider each count separately and that different verdicts may be reached on different counts,' the submission, dated October 2016, stated. 'A danger may exist that a juror, having doubts about a complainant's account in respect of one count, will believe that those doubts should be disregarded when considering the complainant's account in respect of another count. A judicial direction may be necessary to ensure that such an erroneous approach is not taken.'

But in its final report, the royal commission said the arguments it had received against the direction were 'considerably more persuasive' than arguments it had received in favour of keeping it. States and territories should consider abolishing it, it said, because it was inappropriate in cases where the jury had enough evidence to convict on one charge but to acquit on others. The direction might mistakenly lead jurors to believe that they would have to apply their view on one charge to every charge being faced by the defendant. It could be a confusing direction, given that jurors are also instructed to consider each charge separately. Victoria's 2017 amendments to the *Jury Directions Act* abolished it altogether.

A direction was also added to address misconceptions that victims of sexual offences should be expected to describe the offending in the same way every time. This was because strong research has found that differences in a victim's account, and in fact in anyone's account of the past, are not uncommon, and do not mean they are not being honest. A direction was added to inform jurors that differences may be seen in both truthful and untruthful accounts. It is now up to jurors to determine if these differences are significant and point to dishonesty. The direction does not stop defence lawyers from highlighting inconsistencies in a complainant's or other witnesses' evidence, or from outlining to jurors why those differences should be viewed as significant and as a blow to the complainant's credibility.

Other changes to directions have been made over the years. In the past, jurors were often directed that a delay in complaining about an alleged sexual assault might cast doubt upon the credibility and reliability of the complainant. Now a trial judge is obliged to direct a jury that there may be good reasons why a complainant has delayed making a complaint. Ultimately, a jury will consider the reasons for delay in the specific case, and will be assisted by the arguments advanced by both the prosecutor and defence counsel. Richter made much of the fact that Pell's alleged victim did not speak out until he was an adult.

But courts have been frustrated by the lack of successful prosecutions against sex offenders and the historical procedural unfairness to victims, so evidence requirements have changed. There is overwhelming evidence that many victims do not speak about their abuse until decades later. The vast majority of sexual assault cases come down, understandably, to the complainant's word. To ensure that trials are still fair, legislation now requires the judge to give jurors specific directions to balance any unfairness against the defence or complainant when it comes to word-against-word cases.

Jurors are commonly told that they must consider that the defendant might be deprived of an alibi (if the complainant cannot specify the time of the alleged offence) and could be at a significant forensic disadvantage due to the passage of time. They are told it is up to prosecutors to prove guilt, not up to the defence to prove innocence. They are told it is not uncommon for child-abuse victims to forget exact dates and peripheral details, or to report their abuse only as an adult. The jurors in the Pell case were given clear directions along these lines.

Dr Vivian Waller, a solicitor and the managing partner of Waller Legal in Victoria, which specialises in representing people who have been physically, sexually, or psychologically abused or neglected as children, represented the complainant in Pell's case. While the complainant's legal case was, of course, managed by the prosecutors and the Crown, Waller managed media inquiries, and offered advice and support to the complainant.

Waller told me she was not surprised by the calls from some for the court to make the transcript of the complainant's evidence public. But there was good reason for courts not to release this evidence, she said.

'It's very important to protect witnesses in criminal trials, especially victims of sexual abuse. What person would ever come forward and report to police if in fact every word of their testimony was going to be broadcast around the world and scrutinised by anyone and everyone?'

Waller was right. It would send a terrible message to sexual assault victims yet to come forward if they were told they had the right to anonymity and to have their evidence given in a closed court, only to see a court turn around in Pell's case and order that the entire transcript of a complainant's evidence be made public. Not only would the complainant in Pell's case have been misled, but potential complainants in future cases would surely lose faith in the justice system.

'I think it's appropriate that complainants give their evidence in a controlled environment where scrutiny can be given to their evidence and where it can be tested,' Waller said. 'But it's not proper for them to be exposed to social media trolls and trials by media commentators. We have trial by jury in this country, where jurors are coached and trained about what they're allowed to take into account or not.

'If no one reported sexual offending, sexual abuse of children would run rampant. It's perfectly appropriate to have in place something that protects the survivor from an onslaught of everyone picking over every detail of their life.'

What the Pell trial revealed was a general lack of understanding of this process, Waller said. 'Most of the rules in place in sexual assault trials serve to protect the accused person and to preserve the notion of innocence until proven guilty. The only thing there to protect the complainant is anonymity and the ability to give their evidence via video-link and not in an open court. All the other rules of evidence, the overwhelming preponderance of them, are about protecting the right of the defendant to be innocent until proven guilty. For example, the fact that the jurors are not told of any other allegations. Or not letting the jury know of previous convictions.'

In Pell's case, the jurors were not told that the complainant had disclosed his alleged abuse to a sibling. They were not told that the other boy's turning to drugs as a teenager had been swift and seemingly unprecedented, and that he withdrew his interest in the choir soon after the alleged offending occurred and was ultimately expelled from it. They were not told that the other boy's father suspected his son had been sexually abused, even despite his son's denials – they were only told of the denials. They were not told that the complainant disclosed having been abused just weeks after attending the funeral of his childhood friend, the other alleged victim. They were not told that the complainant and the other boy, once close, had stopped hanging out together in the months after the abuse occurred. They were not told that the death was after years of heroin and drug abuse by the boy, and a decline in his mental health. This was all done to ensure fairness to Pell.

Those who were there in the room while the complainant gave evidence and was cross-examined described the 34-year-old as honest, eloquent, and compelling. Although the media were not allowed to hear his evidence or to read transcripts of it, parts of his evidence were comprehensively quoted by the prosecution and defence throughout the five-week trial. What we learned was that his scholarship to St Kevin's College was significant to his family. Without it, his parents would not have been able to afford the fees for the exclusive private school.

He gave an insight as to why he never told anyone that Pell had sexually abused him. 'I knew a scholarship could be given or taken away even at that age,' he told the court. 'And I didn't want to lose that. It meant so much to me and my family. And what would I do if I said such a thing about an archbishop? It's something I've carried with me the whole of my life. I refrained from telling anyone.'

In his police statement, the complainant said he remembered Pell as 'being a big force in the place'.

'He emanated an air of being a powerful person. I've been struggling with this a long time ... and my ability to be here. Because I think Pell has terrified me my whole life ... he was [later] in the Vatican. He was an extremely, presidentially powerful guy who had a lot of connections.'

The court learned that after he began singing with the choir, the complainant's parents began divorce proceedings. He told the court that he did not want to cause any further trouble for his family by losing his prestigious scholarship as well. So, he told the court, he had immediately pushed the alleged attack to the 'darkest recesses' of his mind.

What the jurors were not told at any point, and therefore did not consider in their deliberations, was that the complainant had disclosed his abuse to his sister in 2013, two-and-a-half years before he first made a statement to police. Her evidence given at the committal hearing was never mentioned, and she did not give evidence at the trial. The complainant told his sister about the offending 17 years after it occurred. In a directions hearing, Gibson argued that it used to be the case under the *Evidence Act* that whether or not an event was deemed fresh in a complainant's mind depended solely on how much time had elapsed between the abuse and the disclosure. But under changes to the Act, whether an event disclosure could be considered fresh also came down to other factors, such the age and health of the complainant at the time of the offending. For example, some sexually abused children do not remember specific details of their abuse as an adult, or even any aspects of it at all. Their memory might be sparked by returning to the scene of the abuse as an adult, or by children of their own turning the same age as they were when they were first abused. In the absence of leading questions, it is unlikely that a spontaneous recollection of abuse is false, he said. But, ultimately, it was decided that evidence from such witnesses was not allowed in Pell's case.

The 2017 research report of the child sexual abuse royal commission titled 'Empirical Guidance on the Effects of Child Sexual Abuse on Memory and Cognition' found that because testimony from sexual abuse victims was typically not supported by medical and forensic evidence or eyewitness accounts, especially in historical cases, their testimony came under more rigorous scrutiny.

'The evidence of the victim is often met with disbelief and subjected to vigorous challenges by police officers and defence counsel that imply that it is not valid, in part because the alleged abuser is an older, trusted or high-status adult,' the report found. 'In turn, this generates more intensive scrutiny of the investigative interview procedures conducted after the victim reported their abuse to the police. Normal adult autobiographical memory often includes self-contradictions about dates, times and the number of people present at an event. People are particularly poor at reconstructing the time frame of an event.'

The report went on to find that 'it is possible, temporarily, to entirely forget an experience of child sexual abuse or aspects of the abuse. Dissociation and complete forgetting were significant among a sample of victims whose age at the onset of abuse was in early childhood. The abuse may have been so severe that stress interfered with the encoding and recall of these experiences.'

Gibson told Kidd during the directions hearing that the complainant's disclosure to his sister of being abused by Pell was spontaneous and not prompted by leading questions. Kidd responded: 'What am I to make of the fact that he's affected by alcohol?' Gibson replied: 'It's a disinhibitor, and a person up until that age might be extremely reticent to complain but being in a disinhibited state he's more likely to reveal it … it's not something to go against memory … common sense tells one when one is disinhibited they're more likely to admit things.'

The complainant's memory of allegedly having been sexually abused by Pell was as follows:

> We were in the corner of the room near the cupboards when he [Pell] planted himself in the doorway and said something like, 'What are you doing here?'
>
> He started moving underneath his robes. He pulled [the other boy] aside and [Pell] pulled out his penis and I could see his [the other boy's] head being lowered toward his [Pell's] penis. And then [the other boy] sort of started squirming and struggling. I could see [Pell's] hand on the back of his head. [The other boy] was crouched and sort of flailing around a bit.
>
> I was no more than a couple of metres away. [The other boy's] head was being controlled and it was down near Pell's genitals. I couldn't see his [Pell's] penis at that time. It went for a minute or two.

The complainant said he remembered saying to Pell: 'Can you let us go? We didn't do anything.'

> I saw his [the other boy's] head being pushed down … and then it stopped. Then he [Pell] turned to me and then he pushed his

penis in my mouth. It occurred closer to the corner of the room
… I was pushed down, crouching or kneeling. Pell was standing.
He was erect and … I was pushed onto his penis. It was for a
short period of time, two minutes. He instructed me to take off
my pants and I did that and he started masturbating or trying to
do something with my genitalia with his hands. Pell was touching
himself on his penis with his other hand.

The complainant said this lasted for one to two minutes:

Pell was crouched onto me almost, I was standing upright. It was
two to three metres from the doorway. I put my clothes back on.
I corrected myself, my pants had been dropped but not taken off.
We went back into the choral change room area.

We didn't mention it to anyone. We didn't complain. It felt
like an anomaly and I was in shock in the days and weeks and
months following. I was proud to be at that school. My parents
were going through a divorce. I didn't want to do anything to
jeopardise my education. I was young and didn't really know
what had happened to me. I didn't really know what it was, if it
was normal.

Journalists and other members of the public were allowed back
into the court on 22 August, once the complainant's evidence
was complete. When we returned, we learned that another juror
had asked to be excused because she had a seven-month-old
granddaughter who was unwell and distressed by her absence. The
juror was her granddaughter's primary carer. Kidd had the option
to either discharge the juror immediately, or delay the trial for a
couple of days to see if her granddaughter's condition improved.
Kidd decided to send the jurors home for the day, and to get an

update about the juror's granddaughter and her condition when they returned the next day. By 23 August, when the jurors returned, the woman was not among them, disobeying the judge's orders to return and give an update before he made his final decision. A decision was made, with agreement from all of the parties, to discharge her from the jury to avoid further delays. On day seven of the trial, the jury was already down to 12: six men and six women.

The first witness to give evidence in the open court was retired schoolmaster John Whalley Mallinson, who in 1996 was the director of music and an organist for the St Patrick's Cathedral choir. When he gave evidence at Pell's trial, he was 84 years old. He had retired as choir director in 1999. Mallinson was the first of numerous churchgoers to outline in sometimes tedious, agonising detail the layout of the church and who had access to which rooms. Much of this evidence was repetitive and, often, too much time had passed for witnesses to recall with certainty which doors were kept locked and unlocked during mass, who had access to those rooms and when, what certain rooms were used for at different times, and whether Pell was ever left alone during Sunday Solemn Mass, or whether he was always accompanied by someone else. Choirboys and clergy were also asked about these details. A few of the journalists had already sat through weeks of such evidence in the committal hearing, and now we were hearing it again in the trial.

Mallinson drew a diagram of St Patrick's Cathedral that included various rooms, including the priest's and archbishop's sacristy, and this was tendered as evidence. Mallinson told the court that the room he identified on his diagram as the music room in 1996 was used as the room where choirboys robed and disrobed, and it was where their robes were stored. Gibson asked Mallinson whether the doorway into and out of that room was locked or unlocked in 1996.

'I think I have said that I – it was always open,' Mallinson responded. 'But I may be wrong. There may have been times when it was locked. But it was always open, as I recall, on Sunday mornings ...'

Mallinson was asked whether he recalled the frequency with which Pell celebrated Sunday Solemn Mass at the cathedral in the second half of 1996.

Mallinson could not recall this. 'It's a long time ago,' he said.

Mallinson was asked for his recollections about how many boys and men were in the choir, and whether the choir processed outside the building after mass or internally. Mallinson could not remember on what occasions the choir processed internally through the building and back to the choir room to disrobe, and on which occasions the choir processed externally. He said that 'there may well have been' external processions, but he could not remember them specifically.

When Mallinson was cross-examined, Richter asked him whether he was aware of the allegations against Pell.

'Yes,' he replied.

Richter asked Mallinson if he recalled Peter Finnigan being the choir marshal in the second half of 1996, and Mallinson confirmed that he did. Richter wanted to know whether Mallinson considered Finnigan a disciplinarian, a strict authoritarian who did not allow choirboys to step out of line. A key aspect of Pell's defence was that choir processions into and out of the church were a regimented, theatrical production in which the choir was expected to look its best before the public. But Mallinson's responses to this were rather vague. Asked if he had ever heard Finnigan telling a choirboy off if they turned up late to return their robes after mass, Mallinson replied, 'It's probable, yes.'

Asked if Finnigan was a disciplinarian, he simply responded, 'Yes.'

Richter put it to Mallinson that because of public concerns about clergy abuse at the time, there would be senior adult men with the choir at all times.

But Mallinson responded, 'I certainly wasn't aware of it [clerical abuse] then that I can recall.' He said while he knew that Pell had introduced the Melbourne Response, he did not recall exactly when that was. The court heard that on occasions when Mallinson played the organ during mass and as the choir processed after mass, he would play a prelude, and depending on which one was played, that could last between six and 15 minutes, and might continue after the choir had exited the cathedral.

Richter then put it to Mallinson that on occasions when he played the organ, he would have been in a position to see two choirboys slip away from the procession as it exited the building because of the direction the organ faced.

'No, I wouldn't see them,' he replied.

Richter pressed the point, saying that if he had his head down, playing music, he wouldn't have seen them, but he would have looked up from time to time and noticed two boys running off.

Mallinson repeatedly said that the organ console was quite high and would have been difficult to see over, but Richter would not let it drop.

'It might have been difficult, but what I'm saying is, if the choir see the organist making a motion or signalling to them, it follows that the organist can see them?'

Mallinson responded, 'I would say at St Patrick's Cathedral it is very difficult for the organist to look over the top of the console or for small boys to look over the console and see the organist.'

Richter later put it to Mallinson that 'if a couple of choristers decided to nick off from the procession at any stage, someone would have noticed'. Gibson objected to the question, saying it was a question that asked about the state of mind of other people, which Mallinson could not possibly answer. The objection was allowed.

Richter then came to the matter of the corridors outside the priests' and archbishop's sacristies, which were off-limits to the general public. He was asked if he recalled whether the sacristan, Max Potter, would have been in these areas then, taking things from the cathedral and putting them back in the sacristies. But Mallinson responded that Potter would not begin clearing things from the cathedral immediately. He would wait until most of the congregants had left the main chapel. Mallinson agreed that he usually had altar servers and clergy assisting him in clearing up.

When Richter asked Mallinson if Pell was always accompanied in and out of the sacristy, Mallinson replied, 'Possibly? Yes. I don't remember.' He did recall that on several occasions, Pell did not process outside with the choir, but came down the side aisle of the chapel and through to the back corridors that way.

On Friday 24 August, the other cathedral organist in 1996, Geoffrey Arnold Cox, was brought in to give evidence. He had also served as the assistant choirmaster to Mallinson at the time. He told the court that another man, Peter Finnigan, was appointed the choir marshal because Cox 'didn't have eyes in the back of his head and I was often busy playing the organ or doing something else, and it was very useful to have one other adult who had some sort of disciplinary responsibility, I suppose'.

He was questioned by the prosecutor assisting Gibson, Angela Ellis. She asked him where Mallinson would be on the occasions that Cox was playing the organ.

'He may well have processed out with the choir at the rear of the choir, or he may well have ducked through the sacristy corridor in order to open the glass door,' Cox responded. 'I really can't recall.'

He told Ellis that after mass, once the choirboys had exited the building, 'they were on their best behaviour until they got to the west door, then they had to be watched like hawks, because they'd start talking and ambling and getting out of line, you know, the way kids do. But generally, they stayed in two by two, right around to where they entered [the building again] through the glass door.'

Cox's evidence continued into Friday 24 August. Under cross-examination by the defence barrister assisting Richter, Ruth Shann, Cox said that two boys taking off from the choir 'couldn't happen really'. 'There's nowhere to nick off to,' he said.

Cox said that by the time he finished playing the organ and returned to the choir room via the sacristy corridor, sometimes the priests' sacristy and the work sacristy doors were not locked up and there'd be hardly anyone there. He added that the doors to those rooms were 'sometimes left open for quite a while'.

Next, Peter Finnigan, the choir marshal, was called to give evidence. The role of choir marshal involved supervision and pastoral care, the court heard. Finnigan was important in the trial because the defence painted him as a strict disciplinarian who would not have tolerated two choirboys slipping away from the choir, and, more importantly, he would have noticed it.

He confirmed that after processing out of the church after Sunday mass, the boys would gain entry to the building again through a glass door on the side of the building where the sacristies connected to the cathedral. Finnigan said he would open the door for the boys, and 'pin it open with a mat'. Once the boys were inside, he would pull the mat away and the door would shut. The fire door inside the building that then led to the sacristies and choir disrobing room was also pinned open with a mat, he said. But he said that if the door was open for too long, an alarm would sound, so it never remained open for long.

The jurors were excused for their morning break, and before the legal parties also left, Kidd revealed that the jurors had submitted some questions: 'Can we get confirmation how many Sunday masses did Archbishop Pell attend [not necessarily lead]?', 'What dates specifically, if possible?', and 'Did he wear robes on those dates?'

With agreement from the parties, Kidd said he would tell the jurors in response to all questions that they simply had to listen carefully to the way the case was being put forward. It was still early in the trial.

With that, Kidd adjourned the court for the morning break. 'I'll find out who our prime minister is,' he told the parties. The day before, the former immigration minister, Peter Dutton, had secured the numbers for a leadership spill against the prime minister, Malcolm Turnbull, who had then resigned. The treasurer, Scott Morrison, defeated Dutton and Julie Bishop to become prime minister. What few Australians knew while they were being distracted by federal politics was that the trial of Australia's highest-ranking Catholic to be charged with child sexual abuse offences was underway in Melbourne.

When the court adjourned for breaks, Pell, Katrina Lee, and staff for the defence would gather in one of four meeting rooms adjacent to courtroom 4.3. For a time, the journalists would gather in the meeting room ext door to Pell's, until staff realised that the walls were not sound-proof and that the journalists would occasionally catch wind of scandalous details such as Pell's lunch orders [Uber Eats, sausage rolls, milkshakes, and sandwiches].

After this, the room next to Pell's was locked, a security guard would remain nearby, and the journalists would occupy one of two meeting rooms several metres away from Pell's down the hall. In these rooms, we would discuss the evidence, the dreariness of listening to witness after witness struggling to recall details of the church layout, which way the choir processed, and which doors were locked or unlocked. We would charge our laptops and compete for one of the handful of power points found throughout level four. Occasionally, we would stop Gibson or Richter as they headed towards the elevators and ask them questions, and they would be cordial and happy to answer if they could. Sometimes, the journalists would talk about anything but the trial. But all of us helped each other out. A camaraderie developed.

We were all stuck in this thing together, without transcripts, without the evidence of the complainant, without access to court exhibits tendered as evidence. We relied on each other to clarify facts. We also speculated: did he do it? And if he did do it, was there enough evidence beyond a reasonable doubt? All of us agreed that it would be a difficult case for the prosecution to prove, but also that it was extremely difficult to weigh in without having heard the complainant's evidence. It was also becoming clear that quite a lot of the evidence from the committal had been deemed inadmissible at the trial, although that was not entirely unusual.

When court resumed and Finnigan returned to complete his evidence, he was cross-examined by Richter, whose forensic work had uncovered back editions of the archdiocese newspaper, *Kairos*, which listed the dates of Sunday Solemn Masses throughout 1996, including who presided over them. The newspaper listings revealed that there were only two dates when Pell had said Sunday Solemn Mass in 1996: 15 and 22 December. Finnigan said while he could not specifically remember back to those dates and who presided over mass during them, he did not dispute the accuracy of the newspaper listings.

Richter asked Finnigan if he recalled two boys missing from the choir in 1996.

'No, I don't,' Finnigan replied. But he disagreed with Richter that he would have been so disciplinarian as to record whether a choirboy had turned up to choir rehearsals 10 or 15 minutes late following mass. He also disagreed with Richter that even returning a music sheet that was torn or tattered would have led to the boy responsible being reprimanded.

Richter put it to Finnigan, 'If two young choirboys had gone missing [after mass], you would have waited around until they showed up?'

Finnigan responded, 'Had I known they were missing, I certainly would have.'

Finnigan's evidence continued on Monday 27 August 2018, when another key aspect of the defence's case – that Pell was never unaccompanied while at the cathedral presiding over Sunday Solemn Mass as archbishop, and that he was always assisted in robing and disrobing – was put to Finnigan by Richter.

Richter asked him if he ever saw Pell fully robed in his archbishop's regalia going back into the sacristy unaccompanied.

'I can't remember,' Finnigan replied.

Richter pushed: 'It would be something that would stick in your memory, if it happened?'

Finnigan replied, 'Not necessarily.'

One of the key witnesses whom the defence had expected would back up their case that an archbishop would never be left alone at Sunday Solemn Mass, and would therefore never have an opportunity to offend, had just told the court that seeing the archbishop alone was not something so remarkable that it would stick out in his memory.

When Richter asked Finnigan if he knew of the charges against the cardinal, Finnigan responded, 'I've deliberately chosen not to know and have not sought to know.'

Once his evidence was complete, Finnigan walked past Pell in the dock, shaking his hand on the way out.

The next witness was Maxwell Potter, the man who had served as sacristan during the period that Pell was the Archbishop of Melbourne. The sacristan's main role, Potter told the court, was to prepare liturgies for the cathedral. He also opened the cathedral in the morning, prepared for masses, and set up for any special ceremonies. Potter, essentially the caretaker, was another crucial figure in the defence's argument. The defence had argued that Potter would be one of many people around Pell, particularly at times when Pell was using the sacristies after mass, because Potter would have been busy clearing up and returning precious items such as chalices and missals from the chapel to the sacristies. He told the court that after mass he would also return the candles from the altar to the altar server's sacristy, along with the thurible, a metal vessel suspended by chains containing incense. Potter said he had to clean out the thurible after every mass, a process that took up to 10 minutes. He would also disconnect the microphones and clear the lectern.

Potter said he always walked in and out of the sacristy where the archbishop was – the court had heard that in 1996, the archbishop was using the priests' sacristy rather than the archbishop's sacristy because of work being done in the latter. Neither party disputed this, and in any case the complainant's evidence was that the offending had occurred in the priests' sacristy. However, Potter did not recall this, saying Pell did not robe or disrobe in any room aside from the archbishop's sacristy.

Potter was also asked about Pell's custom after Sunday Solemn Mass of speaking to parishioners outside on the cathedral steps before returning to the sacristy to disrobe. He was asked by Gibson if there were any occasions when this practice did not occur. Potter responded that if Pell had another commitment after mass, he might not stand at the steps speaking, and would instead head directly to the sacristy. When he did speak to parishioners on the steps, however, Potter said Pell would be there for anywhere between 10 minutes and half an hour.

Potter said that when Pell returned to the sacristy to disrobe, either he or Charles Portelli would accompany Pell. 'It was our responsibility to open those rooms for him to go into,' Potter said.

When the court resumed after the morning break, and before the jurors were brought back into the court, Kidd raised a matter of concern with the parties. The jury would have seen the previous witness, Finnigan, walk past Pell in the dock and shake his hand, Kidd said.

'What you do with that is a matter for you,' Kidd told the parties. 'I'm just telling you that's what happened, and the jury saw it.'

Richter responded, 'Of course, when Mr Potter is finished, I would prefer that he not do anything of the kind.'

Potter was present in the room, waiting for the jury to be brought in so his evidence could resume.

It was agreed that witnesses from then on would be directed to and from the witness box via a route that took them straight down the side of the room and across the room behind the bar table. In this way, they would avoid walking past Pell.

The jury was brought back in, and the trial continued.

In the next part of his examination, Potter was asked about another matter that the defence said was a key point of contention in the credibility of the complainant: the wine stored in the sacristies. The complainant said that the wine he and the other boy had drunk before being abused by Pell was red. But the court heard that the dean of the cathedral at the time, Monsignor William McCarthy, only drank white wine, and insisted that it be white. (McCarthy could not be called as a witness, because he was elderly, senile, and had been declared mentally unfit.) Potter told the court he recalled the sacramental wine being white. He knew this because he was responsible for ordering the wine and storing it in a vault in the priests' sacristy.

After the lunch break, the parties returned to the courtroom and had a discussion before the jurors were brought in, and Potter was asked to leave the room. Gibson told Kidd that he would seek to have Potter declared an unfavourable witness, because Detective Sergeant Chris Reed's interview with Potter contained the note that it was 'quite possible' wine was left out to be cleaned up after mass, contrary to what Potter had said in the court.

Gibson told Kidd that prosecutors had therefore expected Potter to say something similar when brought into court to give evidence. Instead, Potter said he always returned the wine to the vault. Gibson also added that Potter had given inconsistent evidence about Pell being alone. The notes from Reed reported Potter as saying that he could not categorically state that Pell was never alone. But Potter had told the court that he agreed with Richter's proposition that Pell was never left alone.

Kidd dismissed Gibson's application, saying it was unclear from Reed's notes whether he was directly quoting Potter. Rather, it was a summary of the interview. The jury and Potter were brought back into the court.

He was excused shortly after, and the next witness, a former choirboy called David Dearing, was sworn in. In 1996, Dearing was 13 years old, the same age as the two boys who were allegedly abused. He, too, was in the choir as part of the choir scholarship program to attend St Kevin's College.

He gave evidence that he recalled Pell standing on the front steps of the cathedral after mass, speaking with parishioners. He told the court that there was about 200 metres between the choir processing outside of the building after mass and the door through which they re-entered the cathedral. He said that as the choir processed outside, other people would be coming out through the side doors of the cathedral, 'possibly tourists taking photos'. 'That was quite normal,' he said. He added that his father, Rodney Dearing, was also in the choir at the time, and took the responsibility seriously. His father would sometimes help to ensure that the boys maintained order, he told the court. He said that Finnigan and his father expected the procession to remain in an orderly two-by-two format until everyone was back inside the building, and that if one or two boys had slipped away prior to this, he would have seen them.

Richter's colleague, barrister Ruth Shann, put it to Dearing that he would also have noticed if two boys were missing once he was back in the choir room disrobing.

'I'm going to say no,' Dearing said, 'because I wouldn't have looked at every person in there … It's possible that someone might not have been there, yes.'

Under examination by Gibson, Dearing was asked if he saw Pell standing on the steps himself. 'I can't recall an exact time of that happening. I just know that was what happened,' Dearing said.

> **Gibson:** Okay, so let me understand that answer. Is that not something of your own personal knowledge, but just something that you believed occurred?
>
> **Dearing:** I knew that occurred because I could have gone to the rooms, unrobed, and done what needed to be done and then come back to the front of the cathedral and still he [Pell] would be there.

Gibson asked Dearing if there were occasions when Pell might have departed from this practice of standing at the front steps after mass. But before Dearing could answer, Richter objected, saying the question invited speculation.

The jury was sent to the jury room and Dearing was sent outside so that the parties could debate whether the line of questioning would be allowed. It was bordering on cross-examination, rather than re-examination.

It was decided that the line of questioning indeed came too close to cross-examination, and would not be allowed. Dearing was brought back into the courtroom, along with the jury, and was promptly dismissed.

On Tuesday 28 August, the tenth day of the trial, a Basha hearing was held. A Basha is held in the absence of the jury, usually when prosecutors wish to call a witness who has not appeared at the committal hearing. Without a Basha, the defence would have little idea as to what the witness's evidence might be, and would not have an opportunity to prepare its defence. If, after the Basha, it is decided the witness will be added to the list, he or she is then examined again in much the same way as part of the trial with the jury present. According to the Judicial College of Victoria, 'The judge may control the range of questions that are permitted on a Basha. He or she may require the parties to focus on specific issues that need to be determined in order to allow a fair trial.' A Basha may also be ordered if it appears that a witness will change their evidence between committal and trial, so that the defence can prepare a response according to the new information. Like many administrative discussions in the absence of the jury, these Bashas were held prior to the jury assembling for the day's hearings or after the jury had been excused. Journalists and the public were allowed to witness these hearings. Our days most often started before the jury's, and finished after they had gone.

Martin Welch, a former choirboy who had made a statement to police in June 2017 – after the committal hearing – was called next. In his police statement, Welch said that Pell would drop in on rehearsals sometimes held immediately after mass to say hello to the choirboys. 'Can I suggest this,' Richter said to Welch, 'that if he did that it would have been after singing and he would have popped his head into the choir to say, "Congratulations, you did well," or something like that?' Welch replied, 'Yes.'

Richter continued, 'But he was not robed at that stage – he was unrobed, it was after he unrobed.'

'Yeah, yeah, it was,' Welch replied.

Central to the defence argument was that Pell was never alone while robed around choirboys; this was important, because the complainant said Pell was in his robes during the alleged abuse.

The defence case was that this was virtually impossible.

Richter then asked Welch, 'On processing out of the building after mass, did you ever notice any choirboys nicking off during the procession?'

Welch responded, 'Um, I feel like it might have happened, but I really can't recall.'

This went against Richter's argument that two boys taking off from the procession could not have happened, because they would have been noticed and disciplined.

> **Richter:** When you say you feel like it might have happened, if someone was trying to nick off, they were actually yelled back?
> **Welsh:** Yes.
> **Richter:** People at the back or anyone who noticed it would yell out and say, 'Get back into line'?
> **Welch:** Yes.

Richter's argument was now supported by the witness.

Welch was dismissed from the Basha, and was told he would be recalled to give evidence in front of the jury later that day.

Before the jury was brought in, Kidd asked Gibson whether there was any dispute that Pell only presided over Sunday Solemn Mass in December 1996 on two dates: 15 December and 22 December. Remember, Richter had found diary entries from a former altar server, Jeffrey Connor, and newspaper records that listed mass dates and who presided over them, to arrive at those two dates. Gibson agreed that the two dates were not contested by the prosecution. In other words, it could now be presented to the jury as a fact agreed by both the prosecution and the defence that the two dates in the second half of 1996 when Pell was known to have presided over Sunday Solemn Mass as archbishop at St Patrick's Cathedral were 15 December and 22 December.

Kidd also told Richter, 'I just don't see the point in taking a witness like this gentleman [Welch] to a diary when he's given evidence that he's got no memory [of specific dates that Pell presided over mass], he is vague, and I just can't see how that can ... be productive in the circumstances.'

'I agree,' Richter responded.

The next witness brought in for a Basha was Christopher O'Hanlon, another former choirboy, who joined the choir in 1996. In his police statement, O'Hanlon said, 'Sometimes he [Pell] would call by and congratulate us on our performance. As far as I can recall, he was by himself; he wasn't escorted or anything.'

Richter put it to O'Hanlon that when Pell did this, he had disrobed and was wearing his normal 'priestly garb, pants and whatnot'.

'Um, I can't recall specifics,' O'Hanlon replied.

In his police statement, O'Hanlon also attested, 'On a particular day, sitting in the hall while waiting to be called into the choir room, George Pell walked past and greeted me.'

Pell must not have been in his archbishop robes at this stage, Richter told O'Hanlon. O'Hanlon attempted to answer, 'Um, I would say not that I recall ...' but Richter cut him off. 'Where was he going?' he asked O'Hanlon.

Gibson interjected. He had not allowed O'Hanlon to finish answering the question properly.

O'Hanlon clarified that he could not say for sure whether Pell was in his robes or not when he saw him.

The witness was excused from the Basha. The parties went over some administrative matters, including the order of witnesses for the day. At this point, Gibson clarified with Kidd and Richter that while the prosecution had no issue with the proposition that the 15th and 22nd were the only dates in December 1996 when Pell said mass, they did not yet agree that those were the only dates in the second half of 1996 – the period in which the complainant said the abuse occurred – that Pell might have said mass. Connor, the diarist who was yet to give evidence at the trial, had been overseas in November, so it could be that Pell had presided over mass at some time during that month, Gibson said.

At 10.40 am, the jury was brought in, and the trial resumed. Carl Mueller, another former choirboy, gave evidence via video-link from Perth, Western Australia. He was among the choirboys who recalled Pell speaking with choirboys 'as a group and individually'. Later, a video would be played to the jury of Pell being interviewed by detectives in Rome, in which he would say he had 'nothing to do with choirboys'. A number of the choirboys gave evidence that contradicted this.

Mueller told Richter that he recalled at least one occasion when Pell came and spoke to the choirboys in their choir room dressed 'in the full regalia and the big archbishop hat on and … the ceremonial outfit, so I recall that occasion quite clearly'. On other occasions when Pell popped in, Mueller said he could not remember what Pell was wearing.

'Mr Mueller, could I ask you this?' Richter said. 'Your recollection of those days is quite hazy, because you were young, yes?'

'Yes, that's correct,' Mueller responded.

In his statement, Mueller said he also remembered occasions when Pell was alone, because he was usually accompanied by the master of ceremonies, Charles Portelli. He said he found it amusing when he saw Pell alone, because he usually never saw one without the other. Richter put it to Mueller that on the occasions that Pell was not accompanied by Portelli, he would have been accompanied by another official. It was something of a leading question, but was not disputed by Gibson.

'I do not recall,' Mueller responded.

The witness was excused, and Welch was brought in to give his evidence for a second time, this time in the jury's presence. His evidence was similar to what he had said during the Basha earlier that day, as was O'Hanlon's when he returned to give evidence before the jury.

The evidence from most of the choirboys had been brief. Their memories were vague. Decades had passed since they were children in the choir. They recalled some aspects of the procession, but not others. They could not pin their memories to specific dates.

The Archbishop of Brisbane, Mark Coleridge, gave evidence via video-link next. Between 1995 and 1997, he lived at the St Patrick's Cathedral presbytery, was the celebrant for mass from time to time, and was master of the Theological College and a media spokesman for the Church in Melbourne. He told the court that although he had lived at the presbytery, he had not been attached to the cathedral staff, and had no memory of how frequently he celebrated mass at the cathedral. After Pell became Archbishop of Melbourne in August 1996, he said, Pell presided over mass 'quite frequently, much more frequently than his predecessor', but Coleridge said he personally did not play any role during those masses, because he was ancillary to the staff at the cathedral. 'I never – I don't even recall being at St Patrick's Cathedral when Archbishop Pell celebrated eleven o'clock mass,' he said. 'I had other duties.' Therefore, he could not be an eyewitness in relation to the procession, or to Pell's movements before, during, and after mass. That was why, when Richter asked Coleridge whether Portelli's function was 'to actually shadow and be at the beck and call of the archbishop at all times', Gibson objected to the question.

Kidd sent the jurors out, the archbishop was put on mute on both ends of the video-link so he could not hear what was being said, and Gibson elaborated on his objection that Coleridge was in no position to comment on what Portelli would have been doing, because Coleridge had already told the court he was never there.

Richter responded that all he wanted from Coleridge was to understand the function of the master of ceremonies, Portelli. 'But I won't press it,' he told Kidd. 'Having regard to the witness's answers, it seems to me that almost nothing in his statement will pass muster.'

Kidd agreed that 'because he's not an eyewitness, because he can't comment directly, any answer he gives is so far removed that even if it had probative value at all, it's likely to be misused in the circumstances of a case where we've got all the direct witnesses, including the master of ceremonies himself'.

The jurors were brought back in, and Coleridge was unmuted. The jurors were told that Coleridge's evidence would be cut short for the very important reason that he had told the court he was never present when Pell presided over Sunday Solemn Mass at the cathedral. He was excused.

The next witness was Rodney Dearing, the father of former choirboy David Dearing. He had become a member of the choir at the same time as his son. He was asked by Gibson about the distance the choir would travel out of the building after mass and down the south side of the building before re-entering the cathedral.

'It's a long distance,' Dearing replied. He said once the choir had moved outside and had rounded the corner at the front of the cathedral, the procession was more 'relaxed'. He said sometimes he would assist with bringing music sheets into and out of the cathedral, and sometimes he would walk down the corridor and past the sacristy where Pell was taking off his robes. Dearing said the master of ceremonies would regularly accompany Pell at this time. Gibson then asked Dearing if Portelli was a smoker.

'I don't know,' was Dearing's response. Gibson was trying to imply that Portelli, a heavy smoker at the time, may have slipped away for a cigarette after mass and therefore may at times have left Pell on his own. It was a line of questioning that Gibson would pick up again when Portelli gave evidence on Wednesday 29 August, the 11th day of the trial.

But first, another two Basha hearings were held for former choirboys Damian Nenna and Farris Derrij. After this process, the prosecution decided that Nenna would not be called to give evidence before the jury. The Basha had made it evident he recalled almost nothing from the time he was in the choir in 1996. Derrij was, however, officially sworn in to give evidence before the jury immediately after his Basha hearing. He was 12 years old in 1996, and a soprano in the choir. Derrij said that once the choir had processed outside, it broke up when it was out of sight of the public. He said that while he would have noticed if two choristers had slipped away, he might not have noticed if they had done so as the precession re-entered the building, because that was the point where the procession would start to break up. He said, 'I don't know what people did' at that point.

Next up was Portelli, who served as Pell's master of ceremonies for the entire time he was Archbishop of Melbourne, until the end of 2000. Portelli resided at St Patrick's Cathedral at this time.

He told the court that he would wait for Pell to arrive before mass at the car park near the back door of the cathedral, and that he would usually have a cigarette while he waited.

Gibson asked him, 'How many packs-a-day smoker were you back then?'

'Far too many,' Portelli replied.

He would then accompany Pell to the archbishop's sacristy to prepare for mass, or, if that room was not available, they would go to the priests' sacristy.

Gibson asked why it was that the archbishop's sacristy wasn't always available to Pell.

'The archbishop's sacristy was used for many things,' Portelli replied. Because it was a large room that could be locked, paintings and furniture were stored in there, and it was sometimes used as a day chapel and would be full of chairs. He confirmed that Pell would not have been able to use the archbishop's sacristy after he became archbishop in 1996 because of this kind of work going on. Portelli said he had no knowledge or recollection of Pell speaking to choirboys before mass.

Portelli had drawn a diagram of the floor plan of the cathedral when he was interviewed by police in December 2016, and this diagram was submitted as evidence. He told the court that smaller valuable items used during mass tended to be stored in the priests' sacristy, the larger ones in the archbishop's sacristy, and that Potter would be responsible for this.

He said that the sacristies and the vaults in them would be locked during mass and were always off-limits to choirboys. However, he confirmed that the choirboys could use the hallway that ran past the sacristies. Portelli said the vaults inside the sacristies were not visible from the corridor.

Portelli said Pell nearly always remained on the cathedral steps talking to parishioners after mass, unless he had another engagement to get to. On the occasions he remained on the steps, Portelli said he stayed with him. He said that when they returned to the sacristies, they would be unlocked by either himself or Potter in readiness for Pell to disrobe.

Portelli also confirmed that mass usually went on for between 65 and 70 minutes.

'You said earlier that you were a smoker. Would you have a smoke after mass?' Gibson asked him, as though to imply that an hour or more was a long time for a heavy smoker to wait to have a cigarette.

'Not at all,' Portelli replied.

'Would you have a smoke at some stage after mass?' Gibson asked.

'Not at all,' he responded.

Portelli went on to say that while it was 'possible' there were occasions when Pell disrobed in the sacristies without him there, it was 'most unlikely' because Portelli, too, would have to disrobe, and would also help Pell to remove the heavy garments.

But Portelli then added it was not possible that Pell was ever alone in the latter part of 1996 when disrobing.

Gibson asked him how he could be sure of this.

'As I said, since they were the first times that he was using the cathedral as archbishop, I would've made it my business to make sure that I was with him at – at all times.'

Next, Gibson questioned Portelli about the robes Pell wore as archbishop. 'They could be physically lifted?'

'Well, they had to be, to be put on,' Portelli replied.

Gibson: 'The alb was not a tight-fitting garment?'

Portelli: 'No, the alb was a loose-fitting garment, but the way it was worn – and still to this day we do it – it's stretched fairly tightly across the front to stop your foot from catching it when you're climbing stairs. So, therefore, the cincture, the rope [tied around the waist], holds it in place'.

Worn above the alb is a chasuble. Portelli said disrobing would take between two and three minutes.

Portelli was asked if Pell ever had any interaction with choirboys, including after mass.

'The only times I can remember him speaking to choristers was if he met one or two of them who might have been coming late to church,' Portelli said. 'Then, he might acknowledge them.'

Under cross-examination, Richter asked Portelli to demonstrate how the cincture was tied around the waist.

'So, it's actually knotted five times,' Portelli said as he stood in the witness box and demonstrated.

'Five times?' Richter responded.

'Mmmm.'

The robes and albs worn by Pell at the time were then tendered as evidence. The jurors would be able to examine them, and even put them on if they wanted to, in their jury room.

Portelli said he specifically remembered Pell presiding over mass in December 1996 'precisely because they were the first two [where Pell presided over mass as archbishop] and we were still working out, basically working out the bugs, trying to work out how this was going to work properly and smoothly'. It was also the reason that Portelli said he remembered Pell standing on the cathedral steps following mass. 'People were wanting to meet him because many of them were meeting him for the first time,' Portelli said.

Portelli was re-examined by Gibson, and was asked whether the presbytery was smoke-free. It was, Portelli confirmed.

'If you wanted to smoke, you'd have to go outside?'

'Certainly.'

'And the closest area from outside the priests' sacristy would be along that corridor that goes past the public toilets, through the metal gate, and outside to the courtyard area?'

'Yes, yes, yes, yes, yes,' Portelli replied, in a somewhat impatient tone.

Gibson asked Portelli what Pell would do if he needed to go to the toilet. Would Portelli accompany him then? 'Well, no,' he replied.

Richter then re-examined Portelli on this point further.

'Do you have any recollection of the archbishop, whilst robed, ever going to the toilet by himself or with anyone, whilst robed?'

Portelli responded, 'It's impossible, it's impossible to do so while robed. It's physically impossible wearing all of this to use the toilet in any form.'

Portelli was excused.

Another former choirboy, Robert Bonomy, was then called to give evidence, and his evidence was similar to many of the other former choirboys'. He remembered Pell congratulating the choirboys or popping his head into their room 'on multiple occasions', but he could not remember whether he was in robes when he did so. He said that once the choir processed outside after mass, there was a feeling of relief among the choristers that their official duties were over. He also said he would see Pell walking along the corridors after mass – sometimes robed, sometimes not.

The next former choirboy, Luciano Parissi, also said Pell would sometimes come by the choir room while the boys were disrobing, and would 'generally be on his own' when he did. But Parissi said something different from the other choirboys. He said that once they had processed outside, the choir would wait until Pell had passed them and had re-entered the building. This was done as a mark of respect, Parissi said. He added that this period of waiting for the archbishop happened about '80 per cent of the time'. This was new evidence not previously given at the committal. He said that by this point, the choristers were just looking forward to going home, and that there was a sense of relief. 'Just a general feeling of, *Let's hurry up and go home.*' Parissi confirmed that the sacristies were off-limits to choirboys.

In cross-examination, Shann put it to Parissi that, given he was a member of the choir from 1991 to 2001, he might be confused about waiting outside for the archbishop and refraining from entering the building until the archbishop had done so. That may have been the custom for other archbishops that Parissi sang for, she said, but it was not the custom when Pell was archbishop. Shann told Parissi that no other choirboys who had given evidence mentioned waiting for the archbishop to pass.

Parissi responded, 'Look, there's a very good chance I'm wrong about that. It could have happened in Archbishop Little's time – sorry, Hart's time, as opposed to Pell's time.'

He later told Shann that if any choirboys ran off, 'they would be pulled back into line … they really wouldn't go too far if that happened. It's hard to miss a child running in a robe, really.'

The next former choirboy to give evidence, Stuart Ford, told the court that the procession broke down and was not 'rigidly double-filed' by the time it was out of the cathedral and out of view of the congregation. 'Our job for the day was done,' he said. He added that someone had usually chocked open the first door they had to go through in order to re-enter the building. He said the next door they had to pass through once they were inside, a security door, was also chocked open or held open by an adult, but he could not remember specifically. He said the choir was still being supervised by adults at this stage.

Another former choirboy, Anthony Nathan, who was 13 years old in 1996, was asked similar questions. He described the procession outside the building after mass as 'orderly', and said that they would sometimes get in trouble for laughing, joking, and talking. He also said he recalled an occasion when a boy had run off from the procession to the toilets, because he was unwell. Nathan, too, recalled Pell popping into the choir room after mass while the boys were disrobing, but said he could not remember whether Pell was alone or not when he did so.

In cross-examination, Richter pointed out that it was interesting Nathan could still remember an unwell boy running off, years later, which he said demonstrated both how an unusual and noticeable event a boy running off would be.

But under re-examination by Gibson, Nathan said he never saw the boy run off with his own eyes. He just remembered people asking where the boy was. 'And then he came back into the choir rooms afterwards, and he was quite pale.' The boy was not the complainant or the other boy who was allegedly abused, Nathan confirmed.

Aidan Quinn, yet another former choirboy, gave evidence next, confirming that the choir processed out of the building in two-by-two formation, with the highest-pitched and youngest boys at the front, through to the older boys with deeper voices. Behind them were the clergy, and at the back of the procession, Pell.

Andrew La Greca was the next former choirboy to give evidence. Under questioning by Gibson, La Greca said that when choirboys walked past the priests' and archbishop's sacristies, the doors would be open and therefore 'available' for choirboys to walk into. However, he said, the boys assumed that those rooms were off-limits.

La Greca was 13 years old in 1996, when the two other 13-year-old choirboys were allegedly abused. He said that once the choir processed outside the cathedral after Sunday mass and had passed by the gate and were out of view of the public, they would 'just start going crazy'. They could not wait to get home, he said. They would start talking among themselves and moving out of line. He said there would be about 50 to 60 choirboys in the procession, and that 'it wasn't military, shall we say, in the way we processed out'.

After Gibson finished his questioning, it was close to the end of the day's hearings. La Greca would face the bulk of his cross-examination by Richter the next day. It would prove to be one of the lengthiest cross-examinations of a former choirboy during the entire trial.

The next morning, on Friday 31 August, before the jury was brought in and Richter's questioning of La Greca resumed, there was debate as to whether the prosecution should call a witness named John May, who had supplied the sacramental wine to St Patrick's Cathedral in 1996. The prosecution wanted to call May because Pell's defence had made the colour of the wine an issue. The complainant had said the wine was red. The defence had presented evidence that the only wine kept at the cathedral in 1996 was white. It was up to the jury to decide how significant this issue was – whether it was possible that there were also bottles of red still around, or whether it would be understandable for the child victim of a sexual assault to be mistaken about details such as the colour of the wine. Kidd told Richter and Shann that he understood that, overall, it did not appear that the colour of the wine was a major issue in the trial so far. 'However, it has been cross-examined about [by Richter] and it is going to be referred to in [his] closing address ... as I understand it, and therefore it is an issue. In my submission, it is a relevant issue about which evidence ought to be given.'

During his evidence, the sacristan, Max Potter, had told the court he recalled the bottles of wine being made of white glass, but later said the bottles were clear and see-through. May, in his statement to police, had said that the colour of the bottles was in fact called French green.

Shann objected to May being called as a witness. She said the prosecution wanted to call May to support the complainant's testimony.

'But the problem with that is that he's given three different versions of the colour of the bottle,' she told Kidd. 'In the evidence in chief, he said the bottle was a dark brown. At the committal, he said it was a green-amber bottle and then shortly after that, in cross-examination, he referred to it as a murky bottle.

'Now, if the prosecution wants to say something which affects Mr Potter's reliability on this topic, there's an obligation upon them to ... put that to Mr Potter as a matter of fairness ...

If the relevance [of calling in May as a witness] is to suggest that Mr Potter lacks reliability, that's an issue there and ... if the purpose of eliciting this evidence is to suggest that whilst, as I understand it, the prosecution accept that it was, in fact, white wine that was being used at the cathedral at that time, but they wish to suggest [the complainant] may be mistaken because the colour of the wine was somehow obscured by the appearance of the bottle and so he's made a mistake about the colour, that is an invitation to speculate.' The complainant had never said in his evidence that he may have been mistaken about the colour of the wine itself, Shann added.

Kidd responded that Potter had introduced evidence as to the appearance of the colour of the bottle, not the colour of the wine, and that the prosecution should be able to present evidence around the bottle's appearance.

Gibson told Kidd that the credibility and the reliability of the complainant was the key issue in the trial. 'So the more relevant question, in my submission, is not what did the wine look like to Mr May, but rather, what was the colour of the bottle? So as to explain, or assist in explaining, why a [13-year-old] boy, who'd not tasted wine, or not known what Burgundy wine was at that age, might describe it as red wine.'

Gibson added that the prosecution were not seeking to attack Potter's credibility, but to 'head off an attack on [the complainant] as being an unreliable witness based on something as insignificant as his description of the wine'.

Kidd decided to withhold his decision as to whether May would be able to give evidence, and the jury was brought in to hear La Greca complete his evidence.

Richter asked La Greca if he had ever told police or the committal hearing that he had seen Pell on his own dressed in his archbishop's vestments after Sunday Solemn Mass. La Greca, who had a transcript of his previous evidence from the committal hearing given to him, pointed out a line in the transcript where he had said Pell would pop his head into the presbytery complex, where the choir sometimes rehearsed after mass.

Richter was growing impatient. 'Yes, yes, and what do you say about his robing then?' Richter asked.

'Well,' La Greca replied, 'it was straight after mass. So he would still be in his robes.'

'You're joking, aren't you?' Richter responded. 'You know he would disrobe before going back to the presbytery, don't you?'

'There were occasions where he wasn't unrobed,' La Greca insisted.

'You're just making this up,' Richter retorted. 'He has no reason to go in full archbishop robes back to the presbytery where he is going to have his lunch.'

La Greca accepted that he might be mistaken.

Later, Richter suggested to La Greca there were rules that when the choir was in sight of the public, it needed to conduct itself with proper decorum.

'That was the rule,' La Greca agreed.

'And there were people there to enforce that rule, weren't there?' Richter continued.

'There were people who put themselves in that position ...' La Greca began, but he was cut off by Richter disagreeing, 'No, no, no.'

La Greca continued, 'But they weren't respected.'

Richter repeated, '"Put themselves in that position"? Who put themselves in that position?'

Kidd interrupted the exchange, telling Richter to let La Greca finish answering the question.

La Greca continued, 'But it was ongoing within the choir that we didn't respect the authority that these people held.'

Richter asked him whether he respected Finnigan, to which La Greca replied, 'To a certain degree.'

Richter replied, his voice rising, 'Do I detect in that notion that rebellious youth wouldn't just accept someone putting himself in a position of authority that he may not have had, is that it?' La Greca responded, 'Well, he [Finnigan] was never ...'

Again, he was interrupted by Richter, who was shouting.

'Look, he had an official title, didn't he?'

'Yes,' La Greca responded. 'He was a Christian Brother.'

'No,' Richter shouted. 'He was entitled as choir marshal, was he not? Just answer my question.'

Kidd interjected, 'Mr Richter, we're just going to take a break.' It was just after midday. The jury left the room, and La Greca was also asked to leave.

Kidd turned his attention to Richter.

'Mr Richter, I know you've got a job to do, but I'm not going to tolerate shouting like that. I'm not going to tell you off in front of the jury.'

'I'm grateful for that,' Richter replied.

'I am trying to be as even-handed as I can here,' Kidd continued. 'And I must say, thus far, counsel at the bar table have behaved impeccably during this trial. So let's not see it go off the rails now.'

When the jurors returned, Richter asked La Greca about his relationship with the other of Pell's alleged victims, the former choirboy who had died in 2014. Richter put it to La Greca that they were friends. La Greca confirmed that they were, and that they spent time together inside and outside the choir.

Richter asked him if he ever had any recollection of his friend running off from the procession.

'No,' La Greca responded.

Yet another former choirboy, Aaron Thomas, was sworn in once La Greca was excused. He, too, was 13 years old in December 1996, when the alleged abuse occurred. His evidence was similar to that of many of the former choir members: after mass, the choir would turn left once outside the cathedral and would walk around to the moat and fountain area, before re-entering the cathedral through a door at the south side of the building. Like the others, he said that if it was raining, the choir would proceed back to their choir room through the inside of the building; but aside from those occasions, the choir headed outside.

As soon as the boys came to the moat area, Thomas said, 'most of us broke straight through and ran and tried to disrobe and just get out of there'. The choirmaster, Mallinson, would still be playing the organ at that point, or if Cox was playing the organ, 'we would pretty much just be supervising ourselves ... when we get to that area, everyone just bolts'.

Sometimes he would see Pell after mass: on some occasions he was still robed, and on others he had disrobed, Thomas said. He was sometimes alone, sometimes with another priest, or sometimes with altar boys, he added.

Thomas said that the doors to the building were chocked open ready for the boys to re-enter it after mass. Under cross-examination by Richter, Thomas agreed that Pell would always be accompanied when he went to disrobe after mass. He said he could never recall an occasion when two boys had taken off from the procession.

Thomas was excused, the jurors were again reminded not to talk about the case with anyone, and they were dismissed for the day. Once they left, there was a discussion about how the death of Pell's other alleged victim would be handled during closing addresses. Saying that he had died through an accidental heroin overdose might lead jurors to believe he had turned to drugs because of having been abused. The parties agreed to simply say he had died in 2014 in 'accidental circumstances' when he was 30.

There were some preliminary discussions about what directions the judge might give the jurors after the closing addresses. The trial was nearing its end. Kidd adjourned the court, and week three was complete.

When the court reconvened on Monday 3 September, before the jurors were brought in, Kidd said that he had reached a decision as to whether May's evidence about the wine would be admissible. It was, and May could be called, he ruled.

Richter then said he had another witness he would like the prosecution to call to give evidence – a man named Jeffrey Connor, the former altar server at the cathedral who, the defence had found, kept a meticulous diary about events at the cathedral, including during 1996.

Gibson contested this, saying Connor should not be called. 'If one looks at the diary carefully, there is different ink within the – within a same entry,' he said.

'Different ink, different stylised writing and it seems, well, at least one could ask questions about this, that the reference to the accused man has been written in a different ink and therefore at a different time from the reference to the solemn pontifical mass.' He did not accept the diary's accuracy, he added.

Richter told Kidd that Connor had to be called, because he was an eyewitness.

'I don't know about that,' Kidd responded. 'He's not an eyewitness to the offending.'

Nevertheless, Kidd decided the witness would be called. Both the defence and prosecution had endured a win and a loss when it came to additional witnesses.

The jury was called in, and another former choirboy, Christopher Doyle, who was 15 years old at the time of the alleged offending, was sworn in. His evidence was that while the choir procession after mass was usually orderly and disciplined, there were times when it became 'a little bit haphazard'.

'Guys would walk [out of line] and talk to people they knew,' he said. 'Sometimes, we'd go a little bit astray – they wouldn't be walking two-by-two. But it happened very, very rarely.'

Next was the final former choirboy to be called, David Mayes, which came as a relief to many of the journalists who had heard similar questions asked and similar responses for three weeks. The end of all this was in sight.

Mayes confirmed that the priests' and archbishop's sacristies were off-limits to choirboys. He said that on occasions the choir processed outside after mass, and they would sometimes have to wait for up to five minutes near the pond, getting 'restless' and 'irritable' while they waited for someone to unlock the iron gate. But they would usually remain orderly while they waited, he said.

When Richter cross-examined Mayes and put it to him that Finnigan was a disciplinarian, Mayes responded, 'Not really. I recall him actually being quite approachable,' he said. 'I wouldn't refer to him as an enforcer.' He confirmed to Richter that he had been friends with the dead alleged victim, and that he had never said anything to Mayes about being abused by Pell.

With the evidence from all of the choirboys complete, Detective Sergeant Chris Reed, who had led the police investigation, was sworn in to give evidence.

He told the court that he first took a formal statement from the complainant on 18 June 2015, and then, six weeks later, took a further statement from him on 31 July. During this second meeting, Reed told the complainant it appeared that he had 'made an error in his years counting back on his maths' in his initial statement when he said the offending had occurred in 1997. The complainant agreed that he had counted incorrectly, and corrected his dates, saying it had occurred in 1996.

As part of search warrants executed, police had obtained records from 1996 from the Catholic Archdiocese of Melbourne. But Reed said police had not been able to obtain Pell's personal diary from the period in question. He said while he did not ask Pell for his diary, the search warrant issued to the Church had asked for a number of documents, including diaries. He said he had obtained the dates that mass was held in the cathedral during 1996 from archive copies of the Catholic newspaper *Kairos*; but while the paper listed the dates of mass, it did not list who presided over them.

On 29 March 2016, the complainant did a walk-through of the cathedral with detectives, indicating where the abuse had occurred. This was video-recorded.

In October 2016, detectives travelled to Rome to interview Pell at the Hilton Rome airport hotel in Fiumicino. This interview was video-recorded.

A video screen was unrolled, and the jurors were told that the video of this interview would be played to the court. This was a remarkable moment in the trial, given that Pell himself would not be giving evidence. This was not necessarily out of any unwillingness by Pell to testify, but because it was the prosecution's case to prove, and Pell maintained that he was innocent and that the offending had not happened.

While we can never know what the jurors thought about this, there may have been some who wondered why such a high-profile, articulate, and intelligent person did not take the stand. Presumably, there were several elements to the defence's strategy. It is known, for example, that of the hundreds of successful defence cases Richter has led, he has called the defendant to the stand only a handful of times. As well, Pell's wooden demeanour while talking about child sexual abuse at the royal commission had been widely criticised, and there may have been a view held by Pell's defence team that, due to this demeanour, testifying would do him no favours. The defence would also have known that the video of Pell being interviewed in Rome would be played, which did, to some extent, allow Pell to speak for himself. It has by now been played by media outlets and seen by many members of the public.

But when we were in court, it had never been seen before by journalists or the public. And given that the jurors had not heard anything from Pell, these 45 minutes would become a defining moment in the trial. Pell's stance in the face of the serious claims against him was to be on full display.

The video opened to show Pell looming large on the screen, sitting at a table in the hotel's small conference room. Pell was on the left of the screen; beside him, to the right, was Detective Superintendent Paul Sheridan. A small painting hung on the off-white wall behind them, the image too difficult to make out. On the opposite side of the table, out of view, was Reed, who asked most of the questions as Sheridan watched on. Pell was dressed entirely in black, bar the flash of white on his neck from his priest's collar. His arms were crossed in front of him, and remained that way.

Before Reed could elaborate on the allegations against him, Pell read a prepared statement.

'I have to rely on the law and my conscience, which says that I am innocent, and I have to rely on the integrity of investigators not setting out to make a case but actually searching for the truth,' he told them.

He said he would give police a list of names of people to interview, who he said would speak 'authoritatively' about his conduct in 1996 and 1997, when the alleged offences were said to have occurred.

'I would earnestly hope that this is done before any decision is made whether to lay charges, because immeasurable damage will be done to me and the Church by the mere laying of charges which on proper examination will be later found to be untrue,' Pell said.

Less than nine months later, on 28 June 2017, detectives did charge him.

Once Pell had read his statement, prepared with the assistance of his solicitors, Reed tried to begin his questioning. Reed told Pell a former choirboy had alleged that Pell had exposed his penis to him after mass.

'Oh, stop it,' Pell interjected. 'What a load of absolute and disgraceful rubbish. Completely false. Madness.' He then invited Reed to 'go on ... what happened after the mass?'

Reed replied, 'It's alleged you stepped forward and grabbed [a boy] by his head and forced his head onto your penis.'

Again Pell interrupted, 'Completely false.'

'You don't have to comment at this stage,' Reed replied. 'I can continue on.'

Pell: 'Please do.'

Reed told him it was alleged that sometime in the second half of 1996, while Pell was Archbishop of Melbourne, he had come across two choirboys in the priests' sacristy of St Patrick's Cathedral after Sunday Solemn Mass. It had been alleged Pell orally raped one of the boys, forcing his penis into his mouth, and that he had also performed indecent acts on them.

Pell, sucking on sweets throughout the interview, repeatedly interrupted Reed to confirm: 'This is after mass?' and 'This is in the sacristy at the cathedral after Sunday mass?' When Reed confirmed that this was indeed the allegation, Pell replied, 'That's good for me, because it makes it even more fantastic and impossible.

'The most rudimentary interview of staff and those who were choirboys at the cathedral in that year and later would confirm the allegations are fundamentally improbable and most certainly false.'

At times, Pell scoffed as Reed outlined the allegations. 'What a load of garbage and falsehood, and deranged falsehood,' he said at one stage.

At the end of the interview, Pell was asked if he had anything more to say in answer to possible charges that might be laid.

'That I'm certainly not guilty,' he said. 'I believe on many, many details I've been able to prove that the charges are false, and I believe with more work and information we'll be able to further enhance the strength of those denials.'

Pell said a couple of things that directly contradicted evidence given at trial by some of the former choirboys. He told the detectives that he was 'always out at the front of the cathedral' after mass, and that he 'never came back with the kids'. As we'd heard, choirboys, church staff, and some of the clergy who gave evidence said that there were occasions when Pell would indeed go back with the procession. Pell, however, told detectives that he only walked with the procession if he had to 'race off to another mass or something'.

By the time the interview had finished playing, another day of court was complete. Pell's denials to police had marked the day's end.

CHAPTER FIVE

The evidence ends

'Although the primary responsibility for the sexual abuse
of a child lies with the abuser and the institution of which
they were part, we cannot avoid the conclusion that the
problems faced by many people who have been abused are
the responsibility of our entire society.'
— Justice Peter McClellan AM,
chair of the Royal Commission into Institutional Responses to
Child Sexual Abuse, final-sitting address

As the trial entered its final two weeks, the mood among Pell's
defence team seemed jovial. Richter would speak with Pell before
and after court, and sometimes they would share a joke and a
smile. The journalists, too, were glad that the case was coming
to an end. For weeks, we had moved between the courtroom and
the tiny meeting rooms outside it, often passing Pell on the way
in and out of the courtroom. It became normal to spend each day
with the cardinal, and to do so while few people knew what was
happening inside courtroom 4.3. We were with the same group of
people throughout the trial, the same faces walking in and out of
the courtroom each day, with a few barristers and judges sneaking
in on their breaks to watch the unique trial unfold.

Although there was a collegiality and friendliness among the
reporters, we had also been engrossed in the trial for weeks on end.

It would be a relief to soon be busy with other things, to be working from anywhere else. It had been exhausting paying close attention and taking hours of notes day after day, knowing we could not immediately access transcripts, which added pressure not to miss key information.

Tuesday 4 September began with another Basha, this time for the supplier of wine to the church, John May. Immediately after the Basha was held, May was sworn in to give his evidence once again, this time before the jurors. May, aged 89, had taken over the running of Sevenhill Winery in 1972, which supplied sacramental wine to the Catholic Church, including to St Patrick's Cathedral. May was manager of the winery until 2001.

The sacramental wine bottles supplied to the cathedral in 1996 were 'French green [in colour], screwtop claret-type bottles, 'cause we bottled all our wines, our reds and whites, in the same colour bottle in those years,' May told the court under questioning by Gibson. 'It was a light shade of green.'

The same type of bottle was used for all of the sacramental wines produced – a sweet white, a sweet red, and a dry wine, he said.

He said he never supplied the wines directly to St Patrick's Cathedral, but sent them to distributors, who then delivered the wine to the cathedral.

Under cross-examination by Richter, May was asked if there were any other sacramental wine suppliers in Melbourne at the time who might have packaged their wine in a clear bottle rather than the French green bottles used by Sevenhill Winery.

'That I do not know,' May replied.

He elaborated that the bottle his winery used for sacramental wine in 1996 was 'a white bottle with a tinge of green'. Richter asked whether, by picking up the bottle and looking at it, people would be able to identify whether the wine was red or white. 'Yes,' May replied.

Under re-examination by Gibson, May added that all of the bottles had a black-and-white label on them with a photograph of the Sevenhill church and a description of the type of wine inside.

Once his evidence was complete and the jurors were sent away for lunch, Gibson told Kidd that police had interviewed the former altar server Jeffrey Connor, who Richter had requested be called as a witness because he had kept a diary during his time serving the church. Gibson told Kidd that the prosecution would call the witness that day. At 2.40 pm, the jurors returned to the court, and Connor was sworn in. The 62-year-old said he had been an altar server at the cathedral between 1994 and late 1997, and that he recorded his attendance at, and activities in, the cathedral in a diary.

He recorded the time he started and when he finished work, where he was working, and the social functions he attended, even recording the names of restaurants he visited, who he was with and how much the meal cost. Connor told Gibson, 'I also recorded when I attended mass and what function I had in mass, if any.'

Connor said he recorded who presided over mass only for those masses he personally attended, and that he attended nearly every mass in 1996, except when he was unwell or overseas.

'Normally I'd write up my diary three or four weeks in advance,' Connor told the court. 'So I'd put, "Solemn Mass, St Patrick's Cathedral", and then I would leave it blank and find out on the day who the celebrant was.'

Independently of his diary, Connor said he had no recollection of when Pell presided over Sunday mass in 1996. Gibson asked May why there was whiteout on the entry for 15 December 1996, which named Pell as the mass celebrant. He said it was likely he had originally written 'Solemn Mass', but upon later finding out that Pell would be presiding over it, he would have whited it out and changed it to 'Pontifical Solemn Mass', which is what mass is called when the archbishop presides over it.

He also said there were occasions when Pell attended mass while he was archbishop but did not preside over it. Under cross-examination by Richter, Connor said Pell would have been wearing different regalia on those occasions.

Richter then asked Connor if he knew what the allegations were against Pell. 'Vague, yes, vague,' Connor replied.

Richter continued, 'And vaguely speaking, two young choristers are alleged to have snuck away from the choir procession and made their way into the priests' sacristy and there fossicked around and allegedly found some wine of which they took a swig or two, I don't know how many, and were then confronted by the archbishop in his regal archbishop robes and sexually assaulted.'

Gibson objected, saying that Richter's statement asked Connor for an opinion. Kidd agreed, and Richter apologised. After Connor was excused, Chris Reed, the detective who had led the investigation, was recalled to finish giving his evidence.

Under questioning from Gibson, Reed confirmed that the other choirboy who was allegedly abused by Pell and who died in 2014 had been asked to leave the choir in November 1997 for misbehaving, which saw him lose his scholarship to attend St Kevin's College. Reed confirmed that the victim's parents told police their son had denied having been abused when asked in 2001, and never went on to disclose any sexual abuse to them before he died.

Gibson's questioning of Reed was brief. Richter's cross-examination of him, which began on 5 September, was not.

Richter focused on the timeline of the abuse. He pointed out that in his original police statement, the complainant had specified that the abuse had occurred within the same calendar year, in 1997, while he was in Year 7, after he had been attending St Kevin's College for about six months. But Richter was told by Reed that he recalled having a conversation with the complainant during which the complainant said that he was not certain about the exact timeframe in which the abuse had occurred. However, Reed had made no note of this conversation.

In the committal hearing, Richter said, the complainant had said the first incident (in the priests' sacristy) and the second incident (in the corridor) both occurred in 1996, before Christmas. By the time Pell faced trial, prosecutors said the first incident had occurred in December 1996, and the second incident in about February 1997.

Richter said to Reed, 'What happened at committal ... was that it became clear that it was going to be alleged [by the defence] that the only Sunday masses said by Cardinal Pell in 1996 were on 15 December and 22 December. So, that meant that if they were the only occasions in 1996, someone later had to say, "Goodness, well, we can't fit in the second allegation in 1996, the second incident, so we better expand it to 1997." That follows, doesn't it?'

Gibson objected to the question on the basis that the decision to change the dates on the charge sheet had been made by someone other than Reed, so he could not factually answer the question.

Kidd upheld the objection. Gibson added that Richter was seeking to attack the complainant based on the charges and dates written down by police and prosecutors, and that this was unfair. The jurors were asked to leave the room, and the parties discussed the objection, with Kidd telling Richter that 'what conclusion police officers drew, what was put to Cardinal Pell in the interview, and the timeframe elected by the draftsman down at the Department of Public Prosecutions are irrelevant to that issue [of the complainant's credibility]. It is one thing for police officers and prosecutors to draw conclusions and to make judgements. You cannot infer from that the complainant has made a prior inconsistent statement. The only way you can establish a prior inconsistent statement is to point to it.'

He added, 'You're not entitled to cross-examine the informant to somehow undermine either the credit of [the complainant] beyond establishing the prior inconsistent statement or the credit of the prosecutorial authorities. And I'm concerned some of the questions tend to be flirting with that.'

Richter accepted the argument, but said he intended to cross-examine Reed about the integrity of the police investigation. He wanted to bring before the jury the fact that additional choirboys had given statements to police, but they had not been called upon to give evidence at trial because their evidence was unfavourable to the prosecution case.

Gibson pointed out that the defence had all of the statements from all of the former choirboys interviewed by police, and that at no point did the defence ask that every single one of them be called as witnesses.

Kidd agreed, telling Richter, 'The fact is, I think it is unfair – if you want to make the point the police have got this material, so-called exculpatory statements from a whole lot of choristers who they have chosen not to pursue, then the jury need to know police have never hidden that information, they've made full disclosure to the defence, and the defence had an opportunity, if they wanted to, to request statements to be obtained and that wasn't made.

'I just can't believe it. If there was a so-called exculpatory statement made by a chorister, to the effect that Cardinal Pell could not have committed this offending, I can't believe for a minute that you wouldn't have asked for that statement.'

Gibson added, '[I]t is disingenuous to cross-examine along the lines of a deficient investigation when the witness [Detective Sergeant Reed] has provided all of the notes, both his and all police officers to whom choristers or other potential witnesses who exculpate the accused had spoken; readily supplied all the notes so the defence have had them.'

Richter hit back. 'Speaking of disingenuity,' he told Kidd, 'I thought it was the prosecution's task to gather all of the evidence.'

Kidd raised an important point at this moment about the comprehension of the jurors. 'The problem with you going down this path,' he told Richter, 'is that you're moving the inquiry away from an assessment ultimately of the credit and reliability of the complainant's account. You're shifting it on to the police and the prosecution, and the jury, they don't know how the system works. You are right, it's for the prosecution to introduce all material and evidence, but we know the way the system works also, that where there are notes handed over there needs to be full disclosure ... if there are witnesses the defence believes ought to be called, they can make a request for them to be called, as has, in fact, happened in this case. I think it's problematic for you to open that up without the jury being in the full picture.'

Kidd's concern was that this was not only an unfair attack based on the evidence, but that Richter would be effectively opening up an attack on police investigators that argued they had somehow been dishonest, as well as incompetent. The jury was not aware of the way the system worked; they could not be expected to know that, in fact, Pell's legal team, led by Richter, could at any time request that certain witnesses be called.

'You need to know that my thinking is that if there is a suggestion of some kind of concealment or disingenuous, dishonest behaviour on the part of the authorities ... then I'm not going to allow that impression to be left with the jury without them being given the full picture as to the way things work,' Kidd said.

With that argument in the absence of jurors over, Kidd said he was going to give Richter 15 minutes to think, and that he himself was going to get a cup of tea.

When they returned, Richter had moved on to something else. He told Kidd that when the jury came back he intended to ask Reed whether he had ever asked the complainant for his psychological records.

'I know the answer is going to be no, Richter said, 'but it's important that he, as the principal investigator, ought to have at least found out whether there might have been some psychological problems.'

He pointed out that the complainant had said during the committal hearing that he had sought counselling. '[Y]ou don't have counselling and see psychologists for some time unless you have some issues,' Richter said. He said it would be unfair to Pell if jurors used his lack of psychological issues as evidence of his reliability.

But Kidd did not agree the question was relevant. There were laws under the *Evidence Act* that meant psychological information and other confidential information could only be subpoenaed if it was considered relevant to the evidence. It was relevant, Richter responded, because the complainant might have given the impression to jurors that he was someone who had never had any psychological issues. Richter added that he did not want to present jurors with confidential documents from the psychology sessions, but just with the fact that he had sought counselling.

Gibson objected, saying that asking Reed, a third-hand witness, about counselling, would be unfair to the complainant and might cause the jurors to unfairly speculate as to why counselling had been sought. He accused Richter of placing undue significance on the counselling the complainant had sought. The complainant had said in the committal hearing that he had previously seen a counsellor, and that he had previously been on medication.

'He had a few counselling sessions in his mid-twenties, and he was given some medication for depression,' Gibson said.

He also reminded Kidd that on his own ruling on a request to subpoena the complainant's counsellor, he had found there was nothing in the protected documents about the complainant that suggested he was suffering from any mental-health issue at the time of the alleged offending that affected his ability to observe or recall the offending.

Richter tried a different approach. He said that what he wanted to highlight was that the complainant had never disclosed his having been abused to his counsellor. He was arguing that if the complainant had been abused as a teenager, surely he would have admitted to being abused during one of these counselling sessions in his twenties.

Kidd stood his ground. The line of questioning would not be allowed.

The jury and Reed were recalled, and Richter's cross-examination continued. Under Richter's questioning, Reed confirmed that his investigations had uncovered no evidence of sexual grooming. There was no evidence of a prior relationship or familiarity between the boys and Pell, and no evidence of a motive.

Richter went on to ask Reed about his interview with a potential witness, the dean of the cathedral, Monsignor William McCarthy. The jurors heard that Reed was ultimately unable to take a statement from McCarthy due to his age and cognitive state. He would have been an unreliable witness for either side.

But Richter let the jury know that McCarthy had told Reed that any offending by Pell would have been impossible. Gibson objected, and again the jurors were sent away.

What was the relevance of anything McCarthy might have said if he was incompetent and senile, Kidd asked Richter.

'I mean, if we've got a man here who has some competence problems, who asserts it's impossible – without any foundational facts being led – how can that be relevant aside from speculative opinion?' Kidd said.

Another critical point Kidd made was this: even the witnesses who had given evidence and claimed that Pell was always accompanied – the sacristan, Max Potter, and the master of ceremonies, Charles Portelli – had at no point said the offending was impossible.

How could McCarthy, who, unlike Portelli and Potter, had not had any role shadowing Pell around the cathedral, reliably know that any offending was impossible, especially given that he had been declared senile? Kidd told Richter he had no problem with Richter making the point to jurors that Pell was at a significant forensic disadvantage due to the lapse of time and the age of witnesses. But it was unreliable hearsay to suggest that McCarthy had given evidence that the alleged offending was impossible. Richter was not permitted to pursue that line of questioning further.

When Reed completed his evidence just before 1.00 pm, it marked the end of all the evidence in the case, and meant that closing addresses from the prosecution and defence could begin. The end loomed. The jurors were sent away for lunch, but the legal parties remained in courtroom 4.3, and important matters of charges and timing were discussed ahead of the closing arguments and directions from Kidd.

Originally, Pell had been facing two charges of sexual penetration of a child under the age of 16, and three counts of an indecent act upon a child under 16. However, during the trial, it emerged that the complainant had not witnessed the other choirboy being orally raped. From where the complainant stood, he saw Pell expose his penis before pushing the other boy's head down to it. But he did not see Pell's penis enter the boy's mouth. So, after a discussion between the parties, one of the charges of sexual penetration was downgraded to an indecent act.

Gibson told Kidd he would like the following day, Thursday 6 September 2018, to complete the writing of his closing address. He would prefer to come back on Friday 7 September to read his address before the jury.

Richter objected. Taking an entire day off to write a closing address seemed 'excessive', he said. He added that he did not want jurors to go into the weekend with the prosecution's argument at the front of their minds for two days without the defence's closing address to balance it.

Kidd ruled that Gibson would have to begin his closing arguments on Thursday afternoon. He would have to work all night to finish. Once the jury returned, they were told they would begin to hear closing addresses the following day, before being sent home for the day.

'Obviously you have now heard all of the evidence in this case,' Kidd told them. 'I'm obviously not talking about you individually, you're a body and, as I've always said to you as a jury, you're entitled to speak about the case among yourselves as, no doubt, you have been. But as you go away today, just be more vigilant than ever that you are the only ones, you are the only people that have sat here judging this case on the facts and have heard all of the evidence and directions that I have given you. No one else outside of this courtroom has been hearing the evidence in the way in which you have been with the directions that I have been giving you. So don't talk about it with anyone, and don't do any research.'

Again, once the jurors left, the parties remained behind to discuss what directions Kidd should give to the jurors when considering their evidence. These lengthy discussions between the parties about key legal issues and directions are something that journalists have no space to go into with their limited word-counts or time on air. Indeed, many readers would find the details of these discussions tedious. But in a case such as Pell's, which has been so scrutinised and indeed criticised by those who were not there, and particularly by those who did not hear the minute and detailed discussions about procedure and protocol, it is essential that at least some of these discussions are recorded, and that the public is informed about how carefully Kidd ran this trial.

One of the issues that the parties discussed was how to direct the jurors on inconsistent evidence. For example, when he gave evidence at the committal hearing, Geoffrey Cox, the organist and assistant choirmaster, said Pell would remain on the steps of the cathedral after mass for 20 to 30 minutes. At trial, Cox said this timeframe was five to 10 minutes.

One of the directions discussed was the Azzopardi direction, in which the judge tells the jury that they must not draw an adverse inference against the accused if the accused fails to give evidence during trial. Kidd expressed surprise that Richter had not asked that this direction be given, but said that, given the quality of Pell's legal team, he would not question the decision.

But it made sense that Richter would not want that direction given to jurors. It might only have served to highlight the fact that Pell did not take the stand, and pointing this out might have led the jurors to think there was something significant about it.

Jury directions are essential to help jurors not become bogged down by irrelevant or peripheral information, and are especially useful in simplifying and clarifying important information heard during lengthy or difficult trials. According to the *Jury Directions Act 2015*, when summing up the case for the jury, the trial judge must, among other things, 'explain only so much of the law as is necessary for the jury to determine the issues in the trial'.

As the law around jury directions has become increasingly complex over the years, it has become essential that the prosecution and the defence work with the trial judge to help determine which directions should be given. Judges must make these directions as simple, as concise, and as free from legal jargon as possible.

To assist the jurors, Kidd wrote what he described as a 'road map' for them. This was a folder that identified each of the party's main arguments, as well as the key legal issues that jurors should keep at the forefront of their minds. Both parties approved this document before it was handed to the jurors. This indexed document included references to witnesses who had given evidence that was relevant to each issue. The road map did three key things: it highlighted who had given evidence on what issue; it directed the jurors to where in the transcripts they could find that evidence; and it included exhibits such as photographs and diagrams submitted by the parties throughout the trial.

As the day came to an end, on the eve of the commencement of the closing addresses, Richter made a remark to the chief judge, Kidd.

'All I can say is that my wife tried to persuade me to accept a judicial appointment, and I said no, because they were just as hard, if not harder [than being a defence barrister].' The case of George Pell, Richter said, 'just proves it'.

'Well,' Kidd responded, 'it is what it is, Mr Richter.'

CHAPTER SIX

Hung

'I felt dirty, and responsible for what happened to me as a child.
I have isolated myself ... hidden my true feelings. The loneliness
I have experienced is overwhelming.'
– Survivor testimony to the Royal Commission
into Institutional Responses to Child Sexual Abuse

When the jurors returned to the courtroom on 9 September 2018, Kidd began by directing them that there was insufficient evidence to convict Pell on the first charge of sexual penetration of a child under 16, that being the rape of the now-deceased choirboy. The jurors, of course, did not know the discussions that had occurred in their absence the day prior that led to this direction being agreed to by the parties.

Kidd told them, 'The complainant's evidence was that he did not actually see the penetration. He was situated, on his account, behind Cardinal Pell at the time. He said before you that he had simply assumed there had been oral penetration. And, at law, I have decided that is just simply not enough.'

Kidd said the jurors had therefore been discharged from deciding Pell's guilt on that charge, and formally directed them to enter a 'not guilty' verdict on the record in respect of that charge.

'However, the prosecution will substitute that charge, effectively, with an alternative charge of committing an indecent act with a child under the age of 16.'

And, with that done, Gibson's closing address began.

He began by urging jurors not to focus on Pell or the parade of witnesses they had heard from over the previous month, but on one man – the complainant who gave evidence and said that, when he was 13 years old, Cardinal George Pell had raped him. That Gibson chose to focus their attention in this way highlighted just how compelling a witness he must have been, but also just how reliant the prosecution case was on his evidence to succeed.

'I want you to step back for a moment and simply think about what overall impression you were left with [about the complainant],' Gibson said. 'While overall impressions are, of course, by no means conclusive, they do provide a good starting point in your assessment of the strength of the Crown case.'

Gibson asked them to recall what the complainant said about his family, his education, and what that education had meant to him and his family.

Throughout the trial and after it, I spoke to numerous defence barristers, prosecutors, lawyers, and senior detectives with direct experience of encountering Gibson. One senior detective described him to me as 'everything you'd want from a Crown prosecutor'.

'He's got all the precision of the great barristers,' the detective, who had sat through dozens of cases led by Gibson, told me. 'He's got the ability to keep a jury interested, but without the flare and flourish of a defence counsel.

'It shouldn't be dismissed how hard that is. Defence have the full armoury of weapons available. They get all the theatrics, and can get away with sailing pretty close to the breeze. However, the Crown are required to show some restraint.'

It's hard enough to compete on a level playing field when opposed by a barrister of the calibre of Robert Richter. I often found myself imagining what it must be like to have to compete in a trial like Pell's. Of course, all the legal parties were professional, and gave an air of treating each day in court like any other. But they must, at times, have allowed their minds to turn to how they would be scrutinised and spoken about once the trial was finally made public.

In the trial of Pell, by all accounts and my own observations, Richter pulled out all the stops, but he was known for doing so for all of his clients. Gibson remained collected and restrained.

'The consummate prosecutor,' another source with direct court-room experience of Gibson told me. 'Sensible, ethical, strategic, methodical … a rare talent.'

'He's not into telling war stories or grandstanding,' one senior detective told me. 'He's like an accountant. He's just there to crunch the numbers and get the job done. But he really commits himself to the task. Some prosecutors don't care about their cases. They commit themselves to the cause, but they deliberately remain removed. I always feel like Gibson cares about the case, and although he doesn't show it, I reckon a loss hurts him.'

And so, although he may not have been granted the time he desired to prepare his closing statement, when Gibson stood at the bar table before the jury, he appeared prepared. He laboured his main point with the jurors. Did they really think the complainant was a liar? If they did, they would have no choice but to acquit. But if they believed him to be honest, what then?

'Most importantly, you got to spend some time observing him – indeed, it was an extended period of time, you will recall – under pressure, being cross-examined and probed extensively by Mr Richter,' Gibson told them. 'You will have your own views as to how he performed under that enormous pressure.'

Gibson put a series of questions about the complainant's integrity to the jurors to consider. Did the complainant strike them as frank? Did he seem to be recounting actual events and experiences? Were any mental blanks that he did have troubling to the jury, or were the facts that the complainant struggled to recall simply the sort of unimportant, peripheral details anyone would struggle to remember after nearly two decades, and after being sexually assaulted?

Interestingly, Gibson also asked the jurors to consider whether the complainant might have been making things up. Rather than only focusing on the complainant's honesty and integrity, he directly invited the jurors to seriously ponder if the complainant was dishonest.

Did he exaggerate and embellish at every opportunity, putting a positive spin on things to his advantage, he asked them. Did he recount minor details with an accuracy that one wouldn't normally be expected to be able to recall?

'We submit that when you step back, the impression you ought to be left with was a person simply doing the best he could to describe, as well as he could, what had happened to him all those years ago as a 13-year-old.'

The complainant was a person genuinely recounting his experiences as a boy though the eyes of a 32-year-old man, he said. He was not indulging in fantasy. He did not have a rampant imagination, or an inventive mind. Gibson put it to the jurors that what they had seen was simply someone telling the truth.

He also reminded them that the standard of proof, beyond reasonable doubt, was an exceptionally high one.

'There is no standard higher known to the law,' he told them. He added that at no stage was it up to Cardinal Pell to prove his innocence. Rather, the burden was on the Crown to prove his guilt.

So why was it that he, as a prosecutor, was standing there urging the jurors to convict Pell?

'The answer, we submit, lies not only in the powerful and persuasive account of [the complainant], but also in [the complainant's] evidence indeed fitting with the overall evidence of the witnesses.'

What Gibson did, very methodically, was tell the jurors, using evidence from the case and referring to witness testimony while he did it, that the accounts of various clergy staff did not disprove the complainant's account, but in fact supported it.

Richter had suggested to the jurors that the abuse could not have happened. It was a fantasy. Impossible.

Step by step, Gibson walked the jurors through the long, tedious evidence heard over some five weeks, laying it out chronologically, directly quoting witnesses along the way, and giving the jurors transcript references so that they could easily check for themselves. He made a complex and high-profile case seem rather black-and-white.

According to the diary of altar server Connor, there were two occasions in the second half of 1996 where Pell presided over Sunday Solemn Mass as Archbishop of Melbourne. This point was also accepted by Portelli: there would have been at least two occasions, perhaps more, where Pell presided over mass in the second half of 1996, when the complainant said the abuse occurred.

The evidence given throughout the trial was that the choir processed after these masses sometimes internally, sometime externally. The complainant said that his abuse occurred on one of the occasions the choir proceeded externally. At some point during the external procession past the south transept, around the corridor with the iron gate and before re-entering the building through the glass door, the complainant and the other boy slipped away from the procession.

In his own words, the complainant had told the court: 'We sort of broke away from the main choir group. It was sort of scattered and a bit chaotic, as a bunch of kids are after mass. We managed to separate ourselves from that group. I don't recall specifically when we broke away.' He added that by the time the choir reached the iron gate, 'people were all over the place'.

If the complainant had really wanted to lie, or if this was a fantasy, wouldn't he have just lied to the jurors about at what point in the procession he and the other boy had slipped away? Wouldn't he just say that no one thought much of it, that no one saw, that if they did it, it was not a big deal?

Gibson put it to the jurors that this slipping away was one of those peripheral details that might not be front-of-mind or embedded in memory in the context of a traumatic event. He asked the jurors to reflect on their own experiences in recalling matters from many years before. Was it even reasonable to ask someone the exact point at which they and another child took off, especially when it preceded something much more traumatic such as sexual abuse? The exact point at which he and the other boy left the procession was not something the complainant had even been asked to turn his mind to until he faced cross-examination by Richter some two decades later in a committal hearing.

Gibson put it to the jurors that it was not problematic that none of the choirboys or clergy could remember two boys ever taking off from a procession. This was because it would only have been a big deal, something memorable, if they *had* noticed it. Why would they remember an event that either no one noticed or wasn't out of the ordinary? In fact, several former choirboys had given evidence that the procession did sometimes break down and become a bit chaotic and disordered when it got to a certain point outside. People would talk to each other and move out of line. Would two boys breaking away and entering the building a bit earlier than the rest of the group really be so memorable?

Even Cox told the court that the boys were only on their best behaviour until they got to the west door. In his evidence, former choirboy David Dearing had told the court that it was 'possible people could go missing and I would have been looking the other way, but I don't recall it happening'.

Further, as the choir exited, the men who assisted with watching the boys at various points, Mallinson and Cox, would have been at the organ – one playing, and the other turning the pages. They would not have been able to see two boys take off.

Once the boys were through the glass doors and back inside the building, they made their way down the sacristy corridor and headed towards the priests' sacristy. Gibson told the jurors that, around this time, Pell would have been leaving the front steps of the church, having paused to shake parishioners' hands, ready to make his way back inside the cathedral.

'Now, in considering the question of the duration of the meet-and-greet at the front steps, remember it is at an early stage of the cardinal's tenure as archbishop and at a very early stage, according to Mr Connor's diary, as to Archbishop Pell saying Sunday Solemn Mass.' Pell's practice of hanging around the steps for lengthier periods of time speaking to parishioners might have been customary eventually, but protocols take time to develop, Gibson said. Pell himself said during the recorded police interview that if he had another engagement to get to after mass, the meet-and-greet would be cut short. Perhaps, Gibson said, this was one of those occasions. He referred to evidence from Portelli and Mallinson that supported this idea.

Portelli had also told the court that Pell was using the priests' – not the archbishop's – sacristy at the time to robe and disrobe in. Portelli said that Potter would have unlocked the sacristy door ready for the archbishop to go into to disrobe, and Mallinson told the court that after unlocking the door, Potter would leave a 'suitable interval that decorum would require' before returning to the sacristy to put items from the service away.

'So,' Gibson continued, 'you have the door being opened, Cardinal Pell at the steps, the boys making their way down the corridors, Potter having to wait for a suitable time to let parishioners finish praying, and the door being open and available in readiness for the return of Archbishop Pell to disrobe.'

At this time, the boys entered the unlocked priests' sacristy to poke around.

The complainant had told the court, 'We were being naughty kids, having a look around. We entered the room and noticed to the left of us, as we entered, there was a wooden-panelled area resembling a storage kitchenette kind of thing. We were poking around this cupboard, and we found some wine.'

The wooden-panelled surface with storage cupboards was 'a little bit concealed, but not too concealed. We found some wine in that panelled area in the cupboards. The wine was in a, like, a dark-brown stained bottle. We were excited, feeling mischievous. We found the bottle and we opened it, and we started having a couple of swigs of it.'

If the abuse had never occurred, how could the complainant have been able to so accurately describe a room so off-limits to choirboys and that was ordinarily locked, Gibson asked the jury. While there had been a few changes to the room over the years, the complainant had accurately described the room as it was in the latter part of 1996.

Potter gave evidence that supported the complainant's description of the room, the location of the bench and the sink, known as a sacrarium, and confirmed the storage location of the wine.

'How does [the complainant] know it's a kitchenette kind of thing without having actually been there, as he says he was?' Gibson asked the jury. 'We know from Potter that there were wood panels back in 1996. How does [the complainant] know where the wine was kept?'

If the complainant was having a fantasy, it was a very accurate one.

In his cross-examination of the complainant, Richter had put it to him that he would have been given a tour of the priests' sacristy as part of his induction to the choir. The complainant could recall no such part of the tour. But, Gibson said, '[W]hether he had or hadn't had a tour of that room doesn't mean that he would remember the intricacies of the room as to where things were, including whether it's got an alcove where the wine was stored.'

At one point during the cross-examination, Richter had said to the complainant, 'Prior to the incident that you alleged happened, the assaults, you had seen inside the sacristy.' Richter did not ask it as a question, but stated it as though it were a fact.

The complainant had replied, 'I can't recall.'

Richter: You were taken, were you not, on a tour of the cathedral when you joined the choir?
The complainant: I would have [been], yes.
Richter: And you were shown the sacristies?
The complainant: I have no recollection of that, no.
Richter: Do you dispute it?
The complainant: No.

When Pell entered the sacristy, the complainant said, '[W]e're in the corner of the room where the cupboards were and we heard a bit of noise approaching, and we were trying to quiet down a little bit, and then he entered the room. He was alone. He was in some robes. He planted himself in the doorway and said something like "What are you doing in here?" or, "You're in trouble." There was this moment where we all sort of froze, and then he undid his trousers or his belt, like he started moving underneath his robes.

'He pulled [the other boy] aside and then he pulled out his penis and then grabbed [the other boy's] head. I could see his head being lowered toward his genitalia.

'And then [the other boy] sort of started squirming and struggling. Archbishop Pell was doing something with one of his hands. I could see the back of [the other boy's] head and his other hand was around the back of [the other boy's] head and shoulders. I could see his hand on the back of his head. [The other boy] was sort of crouched and sort of flailing around a bit. Pell was standing and he had [the other boy] crouched in front of him.

'This was towards the centre of the room. I was no more than a couple of metres away. [The other boy's] head was being controlled and it was down near Pell's genitals. I couldn't see his penis at the time. It went on for a minute or two. I saw his head being pushed down, with his back to me. And then it stopped.'

This incident was the basis of charge one: an indecent act with a child under the age of 16.

'Then he turned to me and he pushed his penis into my mouth. I was pushed down and crouching or kneeling. Pell was standing. He was erect, and he pushed it into my mouth, he pushed it into my mouth. I was pushed onto his penis. It was for a short period of time. Two minutes.'

Charge two: sexual penetration of a child under the age of 16.

The complainant continued, '[H]e instructed me to undo my pants and take off my pants and I did that. Then he started touching my genitalia, masturbating or trying to do something with my genitalia. With his hands.'

This constituted charge three: an indecent act with a child under the age of 16.

'Pell was touching himself on his penis with his other hand.

Pell crouched on – was crouched on – the knee almost. I was standing upright.'

Charge four: an indecent act with a child under the age of 16. This lasted, the complainant said, one or two minutes.

'It was two or three metres from the doorway,' the complainant said. 'I put my clothes back on. I corrected myself. My pants had been dropped. They weren't taken off. He didn't yell. I made some objections. We got up and left the room and went back into the choral change room area. We walked out of the south entrance, and around.'

Gibson had asked the complainant during his evidence why the boys did not just go straight from the sacristy to the choral changing room.

'We were trying to join back up with the choir and not go through a door in an area we weren't supposed to be in at that time, but going through a door where no one else was going through at the time. Going directly to the choir room may not have been the most discreet way to rejoin the choir. The choir was outside. We were trying to get there again to rejoin the choir again.'

Gibson reminded the jurors that the complainant had gone on to describe being picked up by one of their parents and not mentioning on the way home what had happened. He didn't complain to anyone, and nor did the other boy.

'It felt like an anomaly, so foreign and I was in shock,' the complainant said. 'I just didn't tell them. I was proud to be at that school. My parents were going through a divorce at the time. I didn't want to jeopardise anything to do with my education. It meant so much to me and my family. I refrained from telling anyone.'

From the complaint's point of view as a 13-year-old boy, he was the one who should have been in trouble. He'd broken away from the choir. He'd snuck away and into the priests' sacristy, which he knew was off-limits to choirboys. He had drunk wine. He had been caught in the act.

At this point, Gibson had run out of time. His address would need to continue into Friday.

When the court resumed the next day, however, Richter was absent. The court had received a note that, due to family circumstances, he would not be present, but that he would like the closing address by Gibson to continue. There was a discussion about what Kidd should tell the jury. Richter's colleague, Ruth Shann, said they should be told that Richter had a family situation and would be back on Monday, and that the court would proceed as normal in his absence.

'In that case, we will go ahead. Ms Shann, if you could just send Mr Richter my best wishes,' Kidd told her.

With that, the jury was brought in.

Gibson told them that the significance of the scholarship to the complainant and his family, and his fears of it being stripped away, was a sufficient, understandable, and reasonable explanation as to why he did not disclose the abuse as a child.

Next, Gibson addressed the issue of the archbishop's robes. In his first police statement, the complainant had said that Pell was 'wearing robes and he moved them to the side to expose his penis. I can't remember exactly what he had on underneath his robes.' In the trial, he had said that Pell moved the robes aside, pulling them apart and revealing his penis.

Gibson told the jurors that both of his accounts were effectively saying that Pell manoeuvred his robes in such a way as to expose his genitals. The jurors were given the exact robes that Pell would have been wearing that day. They were allowed to take the robes into their jury room, just as all the other exhibits such as maps and photographs were in that room. The jurors could touch the robes themselves, manoeuvre them, lift them, and even try them on if they wished. Gibson asked them, given that they had seen and touched the robes themselves, whether the robes struck them as too heavy or cumbersome to allow manoeuvring in the way the complainant had described.

'They can easily be lifted or moved to the side to expose a penis,' Gibson put to them.

The alb was loose-fitting. The garment was more of a poncho, and certainly not a straitjacket.

Addressing the issue of access back into the cathedral after mass, Gibson pointed to the direct evidence from numerous witnesses about the various and easy ways in which people regained access to the building. Sometimes the door would be unlocked; sometimes it would be chocked open; sometimes a doorbell would be rung and the glass doors would be opened by whoever was nearby; sometimes it would be unlocked in anticipation of people coming and going. Given the hive of activity some witnesses described around the cathedral during and after Sunday mass, why would anyone notice two boys if they went back inside the church, Gibson asked them.

The complainant had said that the next incident involving Pell occurred at least a month after the first. All along, the complainant had said he could not definitively say when the second incident occurred. Richter had homed in on this during the trial. If the records showed that Pell as archbishop only presided over Sunday mass twice in 1996, and those dates were in December, how could a second incident have occurred some weeks after the first and in the same year? But Gibson highlighted the point that the complainant's own evidence was not inconsistent with the possibility that the second offence might have occurred in early 1997. The complainant admitted he did not know the exact date, and Pell was still presiding over or attending Sunday Solemn Mass a few weeks after the first incident occurred.

Once again, after Sunday Solemn Mass, the complainant said, '[W]e were walking down the hallway that goes past the sacristy, [when] the incident happened.

'And I saw him, and he pushed himself up against me on a wall, and Archbishop Pell squeezed my genitalia, my testicles, my penis. Nothing was said, it was all within a matter of seconds. One, two, three seconds.'

Charge five: an indecent act with a child under the age of 16.

'It was a Sunday mass, and the whole choir at some point had moved through that route that day, and I was one of them that was moving in that direction. Past the door, going towards the rear of the cathedral, Archbishop Pell was in robes and I was in robes. He squeezed and kept walking. I didn't tell anyone at the time because I didn't want to jeopardise anything. I didn't want to rock the boat with my family, my schooling, my life.'

He did not mention the second assault to the other choirboy who had been with him when they were first assaulted, he said, because 'I had no intention back then of telling anyone ever.' The incident occurred on an occasion when the choir processed internally, and specifically between the priests' sacristy door and the archbishop's sacristy door.

Gibson pointed out that despite telling police he had never had anything to do with choirboys, Pell had also at another point said the choirmaster would be in the choral change room making sure everyone was changed out of their robes after mass. How would Pell know that, Gibson asked, if he never had anything to do with choirboys and always remained on the steps?

'He seemed to be speaking from personal observation [of the choir room],' Gibson told the jurors.

Having walked the jurors step by step through the charges, the complainant's testimony, and all of the evidence from a parade of witnesses, including former choirboys and clergy, that supported his account, Gibson concluded his address.

'We say that you can and should accept that [the complainant] was a witness of truth and reliability. If you do accept him beyond reasonable doubt then you will find the charges proven and the accused man guilty. The opportunity existed for these two incidents to have occurred.

'We urge you to accept the complainant's account of what happened and to find the accused man, Cardinal Pell, guilty.'

With Richter absent, the defence team could not immediately begin their closing address. The jurors were sent away for the weekend.

On Monday 10 September, the jury would witness Richter in his element. Before they were brought in, Richter walked up to the lectern in the middle of the bar table, facing Kidd. The jurors sat to the right of this table, along the wall. Richter grabbed the lectern, lifted it, and moved it to the far end of the bar table, positioning it so that, rather than facing Kidd, he would be facing the jurors head-on.

'I hope your honour doesn't mind my moving the lectern,' Richter said.

Kidd replied, 'I'm fine with that, Mr Richter … let's bring the jury in.'

And so when the jurors returned and took their seats, they looked straight ahead to see Richter staring at them. He began with an emotional statement: 'After 40-odd years, it still never gets easier addressing a jury in a case that involves the fate of a man, whatever his station in life, and what I want to say to you will take a bit of time.'

Richter would go on to take – it would turn out – almost two days,compared to Gibson's four hours. His address would also be full of analogies, pop-culture references, and even references to the Holocaust, jumping from event to event, in stark contrast to Gibson's steady, chronological, and comparatively succinct and easy-to-follow closing address. If journalists had begun to grow exhausted from the trial, tired of hearing the same facts stated or disputed again and again, it was Richter who made things interesting again.

Gibson had begun by focusing on the story of a 13-year-old boy, now 34. Richter asked jurors to consider 13-year-olds and their behaviours in general.

'None of you,' Richter told the jurors, 'come here from a desert island or some outer-space settlement. Some of you have children who will have been 13. You all have experiences of 13-year-olds who have sleepovers with good friends and the kinds of things they discuss in the privacy of a shared room late at night when they're trying to go to sleep. This particular case is peculiar, in a sense. It is peculiar because we have the names of two 13-year-olds who, according to [the complainant], were supposedly subjected to a terrible event. The question is, what would they have discussed?'

I thought that Richter was ready to make the point here that two 13-year-old boys would have shared and spoken about what had happened to them, if not with friends then certainly with each other. However, he diverged to speaking about American trial movies. And he did so to labour a point from early on in his address: once the jurors had made their decision, there would be no going back. If they convicted an innocent man, they would not be able to change their minds. It was an extraordinary amount of pressure to put on the jurors, and one that saw a few raised eyebrows in the room. Kidd looked calm as this unfolded, but we would later learn, once the jurors left the room, that he was anything but.

In the meantime, Richter continued. 'You would have seen how juries are selected in America … when you see an American television movie or series about trials, you see that the accused person sits next to his counsel at the bar table, at the defence bar table.

'We [in Australia] maintain the tradition that the accused person sits at the back of the court in what's called the dock. That in itself seems to have the possibility of engendering the kind of thinking that says, *Well, he's [back] there, there must be something [wrong with him]*. That's why I prefer the American system, because it doesn't start off with an accused person being isolated at the back of a dock.

'But we don't have that.

'Instead what we do have is a system where we trust the collective conscience of you 12 men and women in terms of the kind of introspection you might be expected to show about your own beliefs and your own belief systems and your own biases and prejudices – because we all have them. The important thing is to bring them to the fore of the mind in order to decide whether or not we are genuinely judging on evidence or genuinely judging on predisposition.

'But that is not to say that you don't use your common sense as you've acquired it in life in order to make judgements, and I mean serious judgements, judgements that affect the course of your life as well as judgements that may affect the course of the life of the man in the dock. We know nothing about you except you have a number of occupations … those of you who've watched prominent trials yourselves or might have been in juries know that there's a kind of frenzy surrounding juries where jurors might be interviewed after a trial or the jurors might be asked, "What do you think?" or "How did you come to that conclusion?"

'We do not have that. And we trust in your capacity to reason logically about it, because the task of a jury is an intellectual task. Any mistakes you make in reasoning the way that you do is going to be left to no one after you have delivered your verdict, other than yourselves and your individual consciences. As to your thought processes, your thought processes are final in this when you make a verdict. I mean, yes, you have heard things about judgements being appealed – they are usually because of errors that were made in the course of a trial – but no one appeals a verdict on the basis that you, as an individual juror, had some thought process which was not permissible.

'None of you will be responsible for the consequences of your verdict to anyone other than the accused person, Cardinal Pell. Whatever impact your verdict may or may not have on [the complainant] … he may or may not feel let down. That is not the point. Your verdict has no impact on him. There is only one person on which your verdict will have impact. What can be known is that Cardinal Pell's future, the future of a fellow human being, is in your hands.'

The jurors looked at Richter intently. Many took notes. If the jurors were not aware of it at the start, by the trial's end it must have been clear to them how high Pell's profile was, even in the absence of media coverage and a large media presence. The core group of reporters who were there every day for even the most tedious and unhelpful witnesses, the constant reminders from Kidd not to talk about or to research the case, and comments made by Richter could have left them in no doubt that, even if they were not overly familiar with Pell and his background, or even the Catholic Church, they had been selected for the trial of a lifetime. Now Richter was asking them whether they could live with themselves if they got their verdict in one of the most high-profile cases in recent memory wrong. It was an extraordinary weight for them to bear. The jurors looked earnest, but focused.

One of the principal issues the jurors had to consider, Richter urged them, was whether it was possible for Pell to ever have been on his own long enough for the offending to have occurred. In fact, Richter said, it was unlikely Pell was ever on his own at all.

'Is it possible, in relation to the second episode, an archbishop of St Patrick's Cathedral, in his robes, violently pushes a child of 13 against the wall and decides to grab their genitalia and squeeze it hard?' Richter asked the jurors.

'All things are possible.' But, he said, imagine it was the complainant on trial, not Pell, for perverting the course of justice. 'And if [the complainant] is on trial for telling lies about this or for not telling the truth about this, counsel would be addressing you in his defence by saying, "Well, it's reasonably possible." And in my respectful submission, it wouldn't be. Not in these circumstances.'

Richter was not looking at his thick binder of notes. He barely referred to them at all. It was difficult to tell if the jurors were impressed by this, or whether, like me at times, they found Richter's dancing between pop-culture references and explanations of possibilities and impossibilities needlessly drawn out and, at times, hard to follow.

Richter said Gibson's final address urging them to find Pell guilty seemed to be entirely based on the proposition that the offences could have happened, not that they had.

'Of course it's possible,' Richter said. 'It's theoretically possible [but] … It's a matter for you whether its reasonably possible. When I opened this case, weeks ago now, I said that it was possible, it was theoretically possible, that a meteorite might strike this court. But you do not lead your life on the basis that may happen. Just as it is possible that when you go home, those of you who drive might have a car crash, but that is not going to stop you from driving your car home.

'So the notion of possibilities is not one with which you're concerned here, although my learned friend was at pains to point out that certain things are possible. Oh, it's possible that boy X in the choir was looking away at the time when [the boys] left the procession. But then you ask yourself, is it possible that something was happening in the celestial atmosphere that caused forty pairs of eyes to look up and not notice something which would otherwise have been noticeable?

'And when you come to think of it that way, the final address by my learned friend, the prosecutor, about what is possible misses the point. And the point is, we have evidence which is clear – evidence of the way things are done.'

This included evidence of procedure, ceremony, and standards. The choir procession was regimented. The boys were expected to behave to a standard that being a part of a choir attached to St Patrick's Cathedral, attended by dignitaries and senior clerics, required. Richter described Charles Portelli as 'the most important witness whose evidence you heard in this case'.

Richter told the jurors that when Portelli had told them, 'He would have done this,' or 'He would have done that,' what he was actually saying was that Pell *did* do it. He remembered the first two occasions when Pell presided over Sunday Solemn Mass because Pell being appointed was memorable and significant. The first two Sundays on which Pell presided over Solemn Mass as archbishop were in December 1996, when the offending was alleged to have occurred. Portelli was there. And he was always by Pell's side, according to his evidence.

'He said that he was there to assist Archbishop Pell to disrobe after the service, after Solemn Mass,' Richter told them. 'And when you consider what that means, you might realise just how significant it is. Whatever else he could have done or might have done pales into insignificance when you consider what it is that he says he did.

'This is a new archbishop, who comes into what you might describe as his kingdom in order to say Solemn Mass, which is the epitome of liturgical process in the Catholic Church.' Portelli's key job was to greet Pell, take his car keys from him when he arrived for safekeeping, assist him in and out of his robes, and generally assist him, Richter told them.

Portelli had a key ceremonial function. It was unlikely he would stray from this, especially during the first occasions of Pell presiding over mass as archbishop, Richter said.

'You might think to yourself, when the Queen goes on some ceremonial occasion, does she waltz around saying hello to corgis and saying hello to somebody and then go into some room and put on her robes of state, etcetera,' he continued.

His voice boomed. 'No, she doesn't. There are people whose functions are defined and given to do certain things. She's not left alone, and the archbishop in his kingdom is not left alone.'

When Gibson questioned Portelli, he had asked him about his smoking habits at the time. Richter addressed this, too. Upfront, he told the jurors that Gibson was trying to imply that, being a heavy smoker, Portelli might have 'sneaked out for a quick fag at some stage and left the archbishop alone'. But that would be akin, Richter said, to himself ducking out of the courtroom for a quick smoke.

'I have a function here; my learned friend has a function here. I used to be a heavy smoker, but I don't believe that I ever snuck out from the courtroom to have a quick cigarette whilst the process was in place.'

He pushed the point: 'The overwhelming evidence is that the archbishop was never alone in the sacristy, just like the Queen is never alone, what with footmen and everything else, during ceremonial occasions. It does not happen, and it did not happen on these two occasions.'

The jurors also needed to consider that Pell had not groomed the boys, Richter said, yet supposedly suddenly decided to abuse them.

'This case is about the elephant in the room, and it's best to deal with elephants by recognising them, because we know, over the years, Archbishop Pell, first of Melbourne, then of Sydney, then a cardinal, has become what I might describe as the face of the Catholic Church in Australia.'

By the time he became archbishop, child sexual abuse tragedies and crimes within the Church had been exposed, along with failures by clergy to address or stop the abuse. As a result, 'Archbishop Pell has almost become the Darth Vader of the Catholic Church. Some people consider that he is responsible for everything that has happened there. The charge against him – and he is the highest Catholic official that I know of to be charged with actually performing acts of sexual abuse – are unique. And that's what you're concerned with. Not whether he is the leader of the dark force, not with the fact that we know that sexual abuse has gone on for decades, not only in the Catholic Church but in other institutions.'

But the jurors were not to judge Pell according to the failures of the Catholic Church. They were not to judge him based on whether he might have known other children were being abused, and might have failed to have acted appropriately. They were to judge Pell only on the charges and the evidence in front of them. And, according to Richter, the evidence should show that the offending outlined by the complainant could not have happened and did not happen.

Richter even brought up the song by comedian Tim Minchin, 'Come Home (Cardinal Pell)'. Richter told the jurors that if they had heard the song, it was irrelevant. What was relevant was that when the allegations relating to him abusing children were made, Pell allowed himself to be interrogated by Victoria Police.

When he was interviewed by police, Richter said, Pell answered every question and did not prevaricate. Richter encouraged the jurors to refer back to the transcript of the police interview.

Next, Richter turned his attention to the dates of the alleged offending. Pell was told during the police interview that both incidents were said to have happened in the second half of 1996, and within the same choral year.

'All five charges are supposed to have happened between 1 July 1996 and 31 December 1996, so we span a six-month period without specificity as to when or what. We know why that's so – it's because police had no idea at that stage of when it was that he actually said Solemn Sunday Mass at St Patrick's Cathedral. They had no idea. So by the time police come to Cardinal Pell, he is supposed to remember what happened in the six months leading up to 31 December of 1996.'

In the first police statement, Richter reminded the jury, the complainant had said it all happened in 1997, before changing it to 1996 in his second statement. Regardless, he still said it had all happened within one choral year. But because of entries in the religious publication *Kairos*, which recorded the dates of Sunday Solemn Mass and who presided, along with diary entries kept by Connor and uncovered by Pell's defence team, it had become clear that Pell only said Sunday Solemn Mass on two occasions in 1996, in December, and that only a couple of weeks had elapsed between those two occasions, Richter said. The complainant originally said the second offence took place a few weeks after the first, and that did not add up with the facts of when Pell is recorded as having said mass, Richter told the jurors.

'A month or so after [the complainant] makes his first allegations, he remembers – or is reminded, we don't know – that this couldn't be so, because he is supposed to be in Year 7, and all of these events took place in Year 7. So, everything is changed from 1997 to 1996 in his second statement to the police, but it is still in the same choral year. And that is crucial.' Richter reminded jurors that it was Pell's team that first constructed a timeline, found Connor, and examined archival copies of *Kairos*, and that prosecutors did not examine those archival copies until just before the trial, after Richter had revealed the information during the committal hearing.

Richter then referred to Gibson and the prosecutors, saying that the evidence the defence had uncovered had left the Crown in 'something of a quandary about how to present this case the best they can, and my learned friend Mr Gibson, an experienced Crown prosecutor, an honourable man ... may feel like there are ashes in the mouth because [he] has to deal with things not on the basis of

"We have now proved beyond reasonable doubt what Cardinal Pell did to [the complainant]", but rather a defence of [the complainant] saying, "X is possible" and "Y is possible."

'If you think in terms of probabilities, what we now have is a case which builds one improbable interpretation upon another.'

At 11.40 am on 10 September, Kidd sent the jurors off for morning tea, with Richter's closing address still in its early stages. And with the jurors out of the room, Kidd told the court that the grandfather of one of the jurors had passed away. The funeral would be held the next day, on Tuesday 11 September. Kidd said he intended to grant the juror leave to attend the funeral.

'It would be unfair and unkind if I didn't give that leave,' Kidd said.

The parties agreed that Tuesday would therefore need to be a day off for all involved, and that court would resume on the Wednesday. At 12.05 am, the jurors were brought back in after morning tea to hear the rest of Richter's closing address for the rest of the day.

After the break, Richter told the jurors the law had changed when it came to child sexual abuse cases. The law no longer required – 'quite appropriately,' Richter conceded – that a complainant's story needed to be consistent from beginning to end. The law had over the years changed to accept that memory is fallible. But Richter told the jurors that they should not take this to mean they were required to accept the complainant's account beyond reasonable doubt; nor did it require them 'to destroy this man's life', he added, motioning towards Pell in the dock.

Pell, as always, watched on, sometimes staring intently ahead; at other times, taking notes.

On day five of the trial, the jurors had, through their foreperson, sent a question to Kidd. The question was this: 'Can we have a doctor or a psychologist to explain the behaviour [of the boys] after the incident, is it normal after sexual assault?' The jurors' question added they wanted to assess whether the two boys would have spoken to each other about the assault they had endured together if it had happened, as Richter had said throughout the trial.

In response to their question, Kidd told the jurors, 'Experience shows that people react differently to sexual offences, and there is no typical or normal response to a sexual offence. Some people may complain immediately to the first person they see, while others may not complain for some time, and others may never make a complaint.'

Richter reminded the jurors of their question during his closing address, as well as of the fact that the other boy, who had died in 2014 of an accidental death, never complained of having been abused before he died. Further, he reminded the jurors, he denied having been abused when his parents asked if he had ever been assaulted. 'Children don't always lie,' Richter told the jurors. 'Sometimes they don't lie at all.' What Richter seemed to be saying was that they should take the dead victim, but not the complainant, at his word.

Richter added that they should consider the case of two boys being assaulted together differently from, for example, a young girl being raped on her own and not feeling strong enough to come forward for twenty years. The boys had apparently been raped together. The rationale of not discussing it out of fear or shame should not apply when two boys had been assaulted together by the same person at the same time, Richter argued, because they had a shared experience, and it would be expected that they would go on to discuss that shared experience at least with each other.

'It's not believable' that they would not have discussed it with each other, Richter told the jurors. (It should be noted that there is no research that shows children abused together necessarily discuss this abuse with each other.)

Even if the complainant could not bring himself to talk about it, Richter asked the jurors to ask themselves whether the other victim would feel the same way. How likely was it that neither boy would discuss it, with each other or with others?

'You see, it takes two not to discuss a subject,' Richter said.

'Now remember, the evidence is they remained friends [after the incident],' Richter told the jurors. 'They had sleepovers even after they left the choir. "What do we do if he attacks us again?" Do you think one of them may have said that, if it had happened? Common sense says, of course, they would have.' Thirteen- and 14-year-olds who have sleepovers share secrets and discuss intimate thoughts, Richter said. He took a long time on this point, going over and over it. The second time the complainant had been abused, in the corridor, when Pell pushed him against the wall and squeezed his genitals, he would have said to the other boy, 'Be careful, because that bastard Pell had another go at me,' Richter said.

He went on to tell the jurors that he had had the experience of talking to concentration-camp survivors. When he mentioned this, a few of the reporters looked at each other in surprise. What point could Richter be possibly be about to make here?

Concentration-camp survivors, Richter continued, 'when they're sitting together, and I happened to be at the door listening, they do talk about what happened to them at the concentration camp because it's in-house'.

He asked jurors to think about what they shared with friends who had been through similar catastrophes in life. Was it conceivable that people with a shared traumatic experience would never speak with each other about it?

At this point, Kidd interjected, asking Richter if it was a convenient time to adjourn for lunch.

Richter: 'Except for one sentence.'

Kidd: 'All right.'

Richter: 'It is conceivable, if it never happened.'

With that, Kidd sent the jurors for their lunch break a few

minutes early, at 12.56 pm. Once they had left, he turned his attention to Richter. He asked Richter to move away from the end of the bar table and to return to the middle of it. Richter obliged. Kidd, usually measured, was noticeably irritated.

'Twice today,' Kidd told Richter, 'you've told the jurors that they've got to be satisfied of [the complainant's] account, effectively, before they destroy this man's life.'

'Yes,' Richter replied.

'And I don't think it's proper for this jury to be told that,' Kidd said. 'They're not being asked to destroy a person's life. They're being asked to apply the law to the facts to decide whether he is guilty. The consequences which flow are legal consequences, and they [the jurors] don't bear any moral or legal burden for destroying somebody's life.'

It spoke to Kidd's professionalism that he had waited to reprimand Richter after having asked the jurors to leave at a point that would have seemed perfectly normal to them – lunchtime – some time after Richter had made his comments. If the jurors had suspected they were being sent away because Richter had done something Kidd took issue with, they might have wondered what was going on once they left the room. Kidd chose to address Richter during the lunch break, but he did so sternly, making it clear that pushing the point further would not be tolerated. Richter had got away with telling the jurors they could not change their minds if they wrongfully convicted Pell once, and he had then laboured the point again after the morning break. Kidd would not let this stand. Richter, being a seasoned defence barrister, must have known he was crossing a line in putting that kind of pressure on jurors – the possible responsibility for destroying Pell's life. He must have known he stood a good chance of being reprimanded for it. And he must have decided that the risk of being reprimanded was worth it if it allowed him to at least plant the idea of such a burden in the jurors' minds. It was inconceivable that someone of the ilk of Richter did not know what he was doing.

Rather than defend the point he had made, he immediately told Kidd, 'I accept that, Your Honour. I may have got carried away with the fact that this man's professional life is destroyed, whatever happens.'

Kidd was not finished. He told Richter, 'Well, I think that's the case with everybody … that sits in that chair [the dock] and faces significant consequences both professional and incarceration, but the jury has got enough pressure on them not to bear the burden, a moral burden, of that kind.'

Kidd told Richter that rather than correct him in front of the jurors when they returned from lunch, he would give Richter the opportunity to correct himself during the rest of his closing address.

Richter said he would 'certainly' appreciate that opportunity.

There was more. Next, Kidd admonished Richter for having suggested that the jurors' verdict would have little consequence or impact on the life of the complainant compared to the impact it would have on Pell. This had been a 'complete distraction', Kidd said. 'It may well be the case that the impact [on the complainant] will be very significant, as it would be in most cases of victims who come before the courts and allege sexual abuse. We shouldn't be making assumptions one way or the other, and it's irrelevant, so that's another concern to me.'

Richter responded, 'I will correct that.' Again, it was better for Richter that he correct the record before the jurors than the judge.

There was more.

'Thirdly, your experience with concentration-camp survivors is completely irrelevant to the job that this jury has.' Kidd repeated for emphasis, 'It is [irrelevant], Mr Richter. I know the point you're making.' Richter was perfectly entitled to make his argument that the boys would have spoken about the abuse if it had occurred, Kidd said, but bringing concentration-camp survivors into it was a step too far.

'Perhaps it was a bad example,' Richter conceded.

Kidd said he usually wouldn't raise such issues in the middle of a closing address, but given that the jurors would not be returning to court on Tuesday, owing to the funeral that one of them needed to attend, he did not want them leaving the court that day with the weight of destroying a man's life, and of concentration-camp analogies, on their minds.

Kidd then turned to Gibson, asking if he had anything to add.

'No, Your Honour,' he replied.

With that, court was dismissed until 2.15 pm.

When the jurors returned after lunch, Richter went straight to an apology.

'Reflecting on what I was saying before lunchtime, I think I kind of got carried away by the enormity of what this trial involves into saying things I should not, and are not your concern and that you must not have regard to.' Richter told them that destroying Pell's life was none of their concern. He added that whether their verdict had an impact on the complainant was not part of the evidence in the case, was not of their concern, and that he 'got slightly carried away by the enormity of what is involved in this trial into saying things that were emotional, in some sense'.

He added that he should not have used concentration-camp survivors to illustrate his point about survivors of abuse. He offered them a different analogy instead.

'You've got two 13-year-old boys who decide to pinch a bicycle, and they ride along, and there's a bit of an accident, and they're bosom buddies, and they discuss among each other ... what to tell their parents. Are they going to tell anyone anything? The one thing you can be sure of is there would be some discussion between them.'

Finally, Richter moved on, going into the issue of timing, referring to witnesses who had said that Pell would have been at the end of the procession and that, when it moved outside, he would remain on the cathedral steps for some time, speaking with congregants and dignitaries.

'You have the evidence of Mr Potter. You have the evidence of Mr Mallinson. Of Mr Cox, Mr Finnigan, of Rodney Dearing, Mr Mayes, Mr Nathan, Mr Quinn, Mr Thomas, Mr Welch, Mr Connor – Jeff Connor, an extraordinary witness, because he was a lately discovered witness and his diary was a late finding which, when considered, was considered important enough for the prosecution to have it [the diary] so they could examine it. He was a witness of impeccable credit both for reliability and honesty, and no one suggests he was doing anything other than recounting what happened … that the archbishop would stay on the steps for 10 minutes or so, maybe even more, maybe 15.'

The other improbability that Richter then urged the jurors to consider was that the offending was alleged to have occurred during Pell's first or second time presiding over Sunday Solemn Mass as Archbishop of Melbourne at St Patrick's Cathedral. He asked jurors whether it made any sense that he would offend during these early masses, given he had only been inaugurated as archbishop a few months earlier, in August.

Richter referred to evidence from the other star defence witness, Portelli, who had given evidence that he would accompany Pell to the sacristy and help him remove his vestments, and that Potter would also often be there, putting vestments and other special items away in the sacristies. Portelli had told the court, 'I was always there when Pell disrobed.' Portelli had also told the court that there was no need for privacy during the robing and disrobing process, because

Pell and other officials wore trousers underneath their robes. There was no need for decorum, for them to be left alone.

'There is no evidence to say the archbishop ever robed or disrobed by himself,' Richter said.

'So the Crown case is that during this interval of unlocking of the priests' doors by Max Potter and the ferrying of the vessels, that's when it could have happened. So, assume there is a period of two to five minutes before Potter starts moving between the sanctuary and the sacristies. That would be more or less the exact time [the complainant] is putting himself and [the other boy] and Pell in the room. And so, is that possible? There is no open possibility there for this particular episode to have happened in that kind of bustling atmosphere.'

Richter focused extensively on the archbishop's robes. In his statement to police, the complainant had said, 'I watched him take his penis out. He was wearing robes and he moved them to the side and exposed his penis. I can't remember exactly what he had on underneath his robes.'

Richter told the jurors that pulling the robes aside was not possible with the particular robes Pell had been wearing, and which had been made available to the jurors to examine. There was no slit down them that allowed for them to be pulled aside. The complainant had been challenged on this point during the committal hearing.

'So what happens when he gives his evidence in chief [at trial]?' Richter asked the jurors. 'He invents things he had never said before, not to police, and not at committal.' During his evidence at the trial, the complainant had said that Pell had undone his trousers under the robes and pulled his penis out.

'So all of a sudden, he's inventing the undoing of trousers or a belt,' Richter said. Pell's archbishop regalia was 'cumbersome', he continued. 'It's not impossible altogether to expose your penis, not impossible, but it takes a fair bit of doing and you need a sort of third hand to do some of those things. And the archbishop didn't have a third hand. And that might indicate to you that what he [the complainant] is recreating is fantasy.'

When the jurors left for the day, the parties remained behind, as usual, to discuss legal issues. Gibson told Kidd he had been considering the Azzopardi direction, which the defence had told Kidd they did not want given to the jurors. This is the direction to jurors that they are not to view the defendant negatively for not taking to the witness stand to give evidence. Gibson told Kidd he wanted him to reconsider his decision not to give that direction.

Kidd responded that Richter was a highly experienced and knowledgeable defence barrister, and if he had decided he did not want the direction given, he was inclined to follow that. Kidd told Gibson that there needed to be a substantial and compelling reason to give the direction, and he had not been presented with one.

'Your Honour,' Gibson said, 'the accused is a cardinal of the Catholic Church, and therefore the concern the Crown has is that there's a high risk of an adverse inference being drawn against the accused, given he's not given sworn evidence. Now, to prevent that risk, Your Honour could give an Azzopardi direction.'

To that, Kidd responded that giving the direction might simply highlight the very fact that Pell had not given sworn evidence. Pointing it out might make it seem significant.

Kidd turned to Richter. 'And you're concerned that if I give the Azzopardi direction, I undermine the approach you're taking?'

'Yes, Your Honour,' Richter replied.

A judge must give directions asked for by the legal parties, unless there are good reasons for not doing so. If there is disagreement between the parties, the judge must look at previous cases and directions given, make a decision, and give reasons for it. Ultimately,

Kidd told the parties that when the court returned on Wednesday 12 September, he would not be giving the direction.

When court returned a couple of days later, Richter continued his closing address by making another reference to a television show, this time *Rumpole of the Bailey*, a British show from the 1970s created by barrister John Mortimer. The fictional show follows the cases of Horace Rumpole, an elderly London defence barrister who often defends underdogs.

'He [Rumpole] used to talk about the golden thread of the law, the golden thread which is the presumption of innocence,' Richter told the jurors. 'Well, that thread is only as golden as juries attend to it, and juries adhere by it.' He then gave the jurors a long-winded definition of the philosophical principle of Occam's razor, which Richter had mentioned early in his closing address, but which he said he realised jurors might not know the meaning of, given Kidd's direction that they were not to research the case. After reciting some Latin and talking about the definition given by Wikipedia, Richter told the jurors that Occam's razor essentially meant that 'the simplest solution tends to be the right one'.

The simplest, most plausible, explanation in the case of Cardinal George Pell was that the offending did not happen, he told them.

He addressed the second incident, in the church corridor, when the complainant's genitals were grabbed by Pell.

'What sort of insanity would you require for an archbishop who is dressed like that, who is six foot four, to violently shove a kid against a wall and then grab his testicles and squeeze them hard, not expecting a child to say "Ow" or not expecting someone to see a physical assault by an archbishop because it was a physical assault pushing against a wall,' he told the jurors. Those who had been abused within the Church were always referred to by the media as 'victims', Richter told the jurors. 'The real question is, do you find beyond reasonable doubt that he is a victim of this man? That this man did things to him that made him into a victim?'

Shortly before 11.30 am on 12 September, Richter completed his closing address.

He reminded the jurors, in a slightly more gentle way than he had at the beginning of his closing address, that they needed to rely on and live with their own consciences.

'You are sitting in judgement of a fellow human being,' he said.

He told them that if they decided to find Pell guilty and woke up the next day with doubt, it would be 'too late'.

'We do not have a situation where the jury can write to the court and say, "I made a mistake,"' he told them.

'I thank you for your attention, and I know that you will take your task as seriously as the law expects you to, and return a verdict of not guilty. Thank you.'

Kidd reminded the jurors of a few points before they left.

'It is not my responsibility to decide this case,' he began. 'That is your role. The verdict you return has absolutely nothing to do with me. You are not bound by any comments I make about the facts.

'You may believe all, none, or some of the witnesses' evidence,' he said. 'Don't look for hints from me. I'm not going to give you any. I absolutely assure you of that. My role is not to express a view one way or another about the guilt or not of the accused man.'

He began giving the jury some directions.

'You will recall that Cardinal Pell participated voluntarily in a recorded interview,' Kidd told them. 'He made strong denials of the allegations, and when I say to you constantly you must take into account all of the evidence – it includes evidence that he said that from what he'd been told, [the allegations] involved "vile and disgusting conduct" contrary to everything he holds dear.

He said the allegations are the product of fantasy. He said he did not know any choirboys in 1996. He said the interviewing of staff at the church would show the allegations were fundamentally impossible.

'Now, in this case there is a clear conflict between the evidence of [the complainant] and the evidence of the accused. You must acquit the accused if evidence on the recorded interview gives rise to reasonable doubt. It is not sufficient for you to merely find the prosecution case preferable to the defence case. So even if you do not think the accused is telling the truth but are unsure where the truth lies, you must find the accused not guilty. Even if you are convinced his statements in the recorded interview are not true ... you simply put it to one side and ask yourself if the prosecution has proven the accused's guilt beyond reasonable doubt.

'Now, in this case the defence argues the account of [the complainant] is a fantasy. It's for the prosecution to prove beyond reasonable doubt that the account of [the complainant] is true. That it is not a fantasy.' He reiterated that Pell did not have to prove he was innocent. 'It does not work like that,' Kidd told them.

Kidd turned his attention to the parties' arguments about the opportunity for Pell to offend, in his robes and on his own, unnoticed. The complainant's account required numerous opportunities to offend for the assaults to have occurred.

'If any of the opportunity evidence, whether alone or collectively or in combination, raises a reasonable doubt as to whether [the complainant's] account is true, you must acquit.'

He said the fact that aspects of the complainant's evidence had changed between the committal hearing and trial might mean he was less likely to be truthful; on the other hand, Kidd told them, 'truthful witnesses may make mistakes about details'.

'When you are assessing this evidence, I direct that you also bear the following in mind. Experience shows people may not remember all the details of a sexual offence or may not describe the details of a sexual offence the same way each time. Trauma can affect how you recall events. It is common for there to be differences in accounts. Both truthful and untruthful accounts of a sexual offence may contain differences. It is up to you to decide whether differences in [the complainant's] account are important and whether you believe all, none, or some of his evidence. Ultimately, you need to decide whether the prosecution has proved beyond reasonable doubt that Cardinal Pell committed the offences.'

When Kidd concluded his directions on 13 September, he reminded jurors that it was a common occurrence for there to be a delay in making a complaint about a sexual offence.

A significant consequence of this delay and the fact that the police investigation did not take place until 2015 – almost 20 years after the alleged offending – was that it had impacted on Cardinal Pell's ability to defend himself against the charges.

'You must have regard to the following significant considerations,' Kidd told them. 'Because of the delay that I've referred to, Cardinal Pell lost the opportunity to make inquiries at or close to the time of the alleged incidents. Cardinal Pell lost the ability to explore the alleged circumstances soon after the alleged offences were said to have occurred. Most of the church or cathedral witnesses could only give evidence on practice or protocol or routine rather than what they recalled occurring on specific dates. If this trial was being held proximate to 1996 or 1997, then one might expect more witnesses to give specific recollection of the dates in question.

'More specifically, there is also a lost opportunity to explore an alibi or an absence of opportunity. For example, had the investigation and trial occurred close to 1996, the defence could have explored with parish or Church officials whether they specifically recalled spending time with Cardinal Pell on the front steps of the cathedral at the time the alleged offending is said to have occurred.

'It's obvious that some of the witnesses have had their memories affected by the passage of time. That is a matter that would not have arisen to the same degree had these charges been laid proximate to 1996. While it is common ground that Cardinal Pell delivered mass, the defence has not formally conceded that Cardinal Pell did not deliver mass on other occasions in 1996. The diarist was away for several weeks in November.

'Dean McCarthy, who lived at St Patrick's, was present most of the time at Sunday masses. Dean McCarthy would have been a material witness on a number of topics ... you've heard evidence that he's mentally infirm and effectively unable to give reliable evidence. There is thus the lost opportunity of Dean McCarthy giving evidence before you.'

Kidd finished by telling the jurors that, whatever their verdict, they all had to agree on it. And on 13 September, just before 2.00 pm, they retired to their jury room to deliberate.

If the parties expected a quick verdict, they were to be proven wrong. It was clear that Richter, at least, believed the case was cut and dried, that a 'not guilty' verdict could be likely within hours. But after the first day of the jury's deliberations, with no verdict returned, Richter declared that he needed 'a sleep and a double whisky'. On Friday afternoon, as the court closed and the jury still had not delivered a verdict, and with an anxious weekend of waiting ahead of him, Richter offered Pell some reassuring words and a pat on the shoulder. Kidd ordered the jurors as they went into the weekend not to discuss the case, saying, 'This is a key stage, and there has never been a more important time for you not to discuss this case with anyone or conduct your own research.'

By Tuesday 18 September, Richter implored Kidd to ask the jury how their deliberations were going. 'Progressing,' was the terse answer that came from the foreperson.

Four days into their deliberations, it appeared from the outside that some of the jurors must have agreed with Gibson that the sole complainant's testimony was compelling and believable. As improbable as Richter had said the case was, the complainant's evidence had given the jury reason to ponder.

By this point, the toll was showing on both Gibson's and Richter's faces. Because the verdict could come at any time, journalists had no choice but to wander the hallway outside the courtroom each day, waiting for movement, for the lawyers to return to the courtroom, or for the security staff to unlock the doors – some sign that something was happening, that a verdict had been reached. The entire time the jury deliberated, Pell was locked away in the tiny meeting room just outside the courtroom. Journalists took over meeting rooms nearby.

On Wednesday 19 September, a note was delivered from the jurors to Kidd. 'We have reached an impasse,' it read. 'Please can you advise further instructions?'

When it became clear that the jurors would not reach a unanimous verdict, Kidd told them at about 2.30 pm that he would accept a majority 11–1 verdict. Still, by the end of the day, they could not agree. The jurors looked utterly distressed by the prospect of having to return to deliberate once again. They did not seem thankful at only having to reach an 11–1 verdict.

At 4.00 pm on Thursday 20 September, almost a week into their deliberations, Kidd recalled the jurors to the courtroom again to ask for their progress. The foreperson said that nothing had changed. Kidd asked her whether one more night to sleep on it before resuming to deliberate in the morning would help. The jurors returned to their jury room to discuss this while we waited in the courtroom. A short time later, they returned to the court, and the answer was clear. No, it would not help, the foreperson told Kidd, before she began to cry.

With that, Kidd looked at the legal parties, and said gently and somewhat apologetically, 'Well, it seems the time has come, hasn't it?'

He declared a mistrial.

Journalists knew instantaneously that the trial notes they had gathered so meticulously for weeks were now almost useless should a retrial occur. A mistrial is meaningless and irrelevant during a retrial, both legally and also in terms of covering the story. People would be most interested in the final outcome of the retrial, not in what had happened months before, during a trial in which the jurors had not been able to reach a verdict. As journalists wondered what to do with their notes, and faced with the prospect of sitting through the evidence again, Kidd offered reassurances to the exhausted jurors.

'In some cases, the burden is much greater than others,' he told them, as they listened while in visible distress. By this point, five of the jurors were in tears. The burden had clearly been enormous, their deliberations and disagreements surely intense.

'From the moment you were empanelled over a month ago, the burden was going to be greater than most,' Kidd continued. 'It's obvious to all of us how much work you've done. I don't think you should be hard on yourself. I think you should be very proud of the effort you've put in. You go with our thanks and our best wishes.' He excused them from performing jury duty for another 10 years, given the enormity and stress of what they had just been through together.

He again told them not to speak to anyone about the case because, he warned them, 'You cannot win. You will place yourself in an impossible position.' As kind and as empathetic as Kidd had been, he also left them with a warning: 'Whatever took place in that jury room must stay there.'

And it did, until some three months later, when an extraordinary and unexpected verdict was delivered by a new jury in the retrial.

CHAPTER SEVEN

The missing witness

A pivotal but absent person in the Pell case was the other boy allegedly abused by Pell, alongside the complainant, when he was 13, and who died in April 2014, about three months shy of his 31st birthday. Outside court one day, I asked his father, whom I will only identify as 'R', what his son was like.

He smiled as he told me that his son was 'a typical boy' when he was a child.

'He liked helping his grandparents,' he said. 'He'd always disappear, and I'd ring up my mum and she'd say, "Oh yeah, he's been here for the last two hours helping me cook."' He remembered going to AFL games with his son, always sitting in the members' area, and the way his son would go and buy bottles of water for the elderly Carlton supporters that sat behind them. 'Every week they'd come along with containers of lollies and cakes and things, and there would always be a cake there for my son,' he said.

On 14 June 2019, I drove from Melbourne to Ballarat, and arrived at the house that R had just moved into with his partner, whom I will identify as 'K'. There were boxes yet to be unpacked, and the internet was yet to be connected. The move had been difficult for R – it happened amid Pell's case, and he had over the years suffered multiple strokes and heart attacks. He had five stents in his heart. He also had diabetes, and suffered from chronic ill-health. But he was happy to speak with me, despite all of this, greeting me at the front door and inviting me inside, slowly guiding me down the hallway and into the living room. Due to his health problems, walking was difficult for him. He sat in an armchair opposite me, and spoke in a soft, considered voice.

'The reason they did not call me for evidence at the trial was because it would have been indirect evidence. In other words, I am not the actual victim – I am the victim's parent,' he told me. His evidence would have been hearsay. His son had never disclosed being abused to him. Had the jurors heard from R, it would have been unfair to Pell.

His son and the complainant had been good friends as children, R told me. They were attending the same primary school when someone from the St Patrick's Cathedral came to their school and held auditions for the boys to join the cathedral choir.

There were three boys selected from the school, R's son and the complainant among them. They received a scholarship to the all-boys Cathedral College in East Melbourne as part of the deal to sing with the choir. However, in 1994, the director of Christian Brothers' Education advised the principal that Cathedral College was to close. St Kevin's College, an exclusive private school in the prestigious suburb of Toorak, in Melbourne's east, agreed to take the choirboys instead. But in the first months of being a part of the St Patrick's choir, the boys went to Cathedral College.

'They were both going to the school, and they had to start at eight o'clock in the morning for choir rehearsals, so my ex-wife and I said to [the complainant's] parents he could stay at our house, we can take him to school. His mother was living on her own with several kids in the house, so it was less pressure for her. He lived at our house for about four months.' R's now ex-wife would usually be the one to drive the boys to the college, leaving Brunswick West, where they then lived, at about seven-thirty in the morning to get the boys to rehearsal on time. The boys would make their own way home from school together in the afternoon, using public transport.

R said that his son, initially at least, enjoyed being in the choir.

'But I don't think he enjoyed getting up extra early,' R told me. 'On a weekly basis, it was every morning at eight o'clock, so you'd have an hour of choir before school. Sometimes, especially with Easter or Christmas, there would be an hour or so after school, too. They would come home, and we would drive them back for an hour and a half of rehearsal.'

R said he enjoyed having the other boy living with his family during the time.

'He was a little bit of a nerdy kid, you know, very insular, and he was lovely. Absolutely no trouble. He helped out where he could, and he always asked my ex-wife could he help around the house, if could he do something. We'd always say, "No, you've got homework to do, go do your homework." I found him to be a very honest kid – I could leave money out and it wouldn't be touched. He was a part of the family. He knew he could help himself to the fridge, we used to say, "There's soft drinks there and biscuits there. Help yourself."' The boys, R said, were good, close friends.

When the boys transitioned to St Kevin's College later in 1996, getting to rehearsal was easier – the train stop was at the school's doorstep. R's son turned 13 in July 1996. Up until around that age, he said, his son was full of energy, with several hobbies. He particularly loved playing lacrosse, and represented Victoria at a couple of national championships.

'He loved to be competitive,' R remembered. 'He enjoyed skating, riding his bike. He used to spend a lot of time at my mum and dad's, and they lived about 800 metres away from us, in the Brunswick area. He would walk about 15 minutes to their house, and he used to go there a lot. My father was a toolmaker by trade, and he had a workshop set up at home, a four-car garage with machines and tools. You couldn't even walk in there. So he used to enjoy that.'

But more than that, he enjoyed cooking with his grandmother. She taught him to bake biscuits, cakes, and scones. He learned how to do different types of roasts, and to cook meat on a skewer. He mastered different pastas, learning from his grandmother how to make sauce from scratch.

'He announced to us when he was about 12 that he was going to be a chef,' R said with a smile. He managed to get work experience at an exclusive club for women in the city, frequented by the well-to-do wives of judges, lawyers, and doctors. He baked the women scones using his own recipe.

'The women used to crave these scones,' R said, laughing as he remembered. 'One day, the ladies said to the boss, the owner, "Who the hell have you got making the scones? They're fabulous." They brought my son out and introduced him, and the women adored him. He did so well that at Christmas we got a phone call from the owner. He wanted my son to come work during the school holidays in the kitchen, and they were so impressed, they said when he does leave school, they'd be happy to put him on as an apprentice.

'They said, "He's absolutely a joy." He was a joy to have working there. We were proud.'

When he was 12, in the summer of early 1996, R's son decided he wanted a bike. R recalled how his son would wake up around five every morning to do a paper route before school, and before having to do his early-morning rehearsal with the choir each day.

'He wanted to buy himself a BMX. A silver flash or some fancy, expensive bike,' he told me. 'He would be home from the paper round in time to have a shower, get dressed, and go to choir. And he worked for almost a year to get that bike.' On weekends, R would take his son and daughter, who was a few years older, to watch AFL games. They would go out for dinner as a family to bistros.

But this normal family life began to change when his son was almost 14 years old, R told me. The change in his son was totally out of character, and seemed sudden.

'He was somebody who cared, who was mindful, who basically looked after other people, and he went to being somebody who didn't care,' R told me, his voice low. 'I always wondered why.'

R began to notice bits of aluminium foil screwed up in the bathroom, and his mother, who his son was still visiting, noticed the same at her home, too.

'One day, she undid the foil, and it had been burnt on one side,' R said. 'Something had been burned in it. And that's what I found, in his bedroom, in the toilet. Bits of foil. So he was obviously smoking it.'

What was he smoking, I asked.

'Heroin,' R told me bluntly. 'You put a bit in there,' he said, motioning folding up foil, 'put a cigarette lighter underneath it, and you inhale the smoke. You're getting basically heroin through the nose.' R found out there was a boy at St Kevin's College who lived in Richmond, then a delinquent area known for its drug culture, and a scene still associated with the neighbourhood by some today. 'He lived in Housing Commission flats. Not a really nice area. And I found out, he told me in fact, that his father used to sell drugs. And that's where my son got them.' R asked me to imagine what it was like for boys like his son, and the boy living in a government flat in Richmond, to be taken from their public school lives and thrown into the prestigious world of St Kevin's College, which the most affluent children in the state attended – sons of dignitaries, lawyers, doctors, and businessmen.

'Kids were driving into the school in limos, and cars with chauffeurs,' R told me. 'There was a parade of them. It was amazing, amazing, amazing. When you consider 1,200 kids at the school, with 30–40 limos, that's a lot. A lot of wealth.'

By 1997, his son was no longer interested in the choir, telling R he was thinking of leaving, but never giving a reason why.

'We weren't seeing his friend [the complainant] anymore at all, which was interesting,' R said. 'They were quite inseparable before.' Around this time, R realised that the BMX his son had worked so hard for an entire year to buy was gone. 'I said to him one day, "What happened to your bike?" He ummed and ahhed, and said, "Somebody stole it."'

R told me matter-of-factly, 'He sold it for drugs.'

Around this time, R and his then wife received a phone call from the choirmaster, whose name he could not recall. 'He was an older gentleman who had been there quite a while, and he rang and said he wanted to talk to us about our son. So we went along to the cathedral, and he said he couldn't have our son in the choir anymore because he was very disruptive, he kept coughing – he had asthma – but he kept coughing. I'd say that the smoking caused that problem. But he basically said he couldn't have our son in the choir anymore.'

Being in the choir was a condition of the scholarship for St Kevin's College. Having lost his scholarship, his son began attending a public school in North Melbourne – R and his wife could not afford the fees to keep their son at St Kevin's. But within about a year, when he was in Year 8 or early Year 9, his son was expelled from that school.

'By then he was living wherever,' R told me sadly. 'He sometimes used to come home and then disappear, and we wouldn't see him for three or four weeks, and then he'd come home, sleep with us for one or two nights, then disappear again. My parents were quite sad, he stopped going to see them as well, and that didn't help.'

Of course, R confronted his son at different points. When he was about 14 or 15, R said he asked him if something had happened to him. 'He was in the choir, around older men, and I thought maybe someone had yelled at him or he was in trouble, or something worse. And I asked him, "Did anybody interfere with you?" I first asked him that when he was late 14 or 15. He … his reaction … if nothing really happened to you, you'd say, "Oh no, nothing happened." But he would get really upset. He would be affronted. I look back and I think, *Why was he so over the top?* I've been wondering about that for a while now. Why was he so affronted? To sort of blow up over what I've asked him?' R said his son never denied being abused. He would just become angry, and refuse to engage with the question.

R and his ex-wife tried to help their son many times, enrolling him in rehabilitation programs.

One day, when his son was a bit older, about 18, R suspected he was using drugs again after having completed a month-long rehabilitation program. R worked for 11 years as an honorary probation officer for young people, and he knew the signs of drug-taking.

'And he got so upset that I asked, he didn't talk to me for two years,' R said. 'I think he'd been to every rehab place in Melbourne.'

Unfortunately, life did not become easier for R or his family. By the time his son was in his twenties, he was in jail for drug use. He did a couple of sentences of three months each for possession, and later he served a six-month sentence. In between stints in jail and rehab, his son would sometimes come and stay with R or his ex-wife. Sometimes, he would stop by at Christmas. At his worst, R told me, his son was using one gram a day.

'That is huge. Huge,' he told me. 'Most addicts would be a quarter of a gram.'

When his son was about 28 or 29 years old, he was living for a time in a cheap motel next door to some friends who were also addicts. A police sting led to them all being arrested. One of them got five years. R's son was sentenced to 18 months for possession.

'He came out of jail on a Sunday,' R told me. 'His mother had his bedroom all set up ready for him. He stayed there Sunday, Monday night. Tuesday, he went out, smashed the car, came back, stayed the night, and Wednesday he went out and died of an overdose.

'Because he was in jail, he probably got clean, and if he tried to use when he got out, his system probably wasn't used to it.'

It is a heartbreaking story, one familiar to many who have loved an addict.

'I was expecting it,' R told me calmly, although sadly. 'Drug addicts don't live long. It's a simple fact of life.'

His son died on 8 April 2014, at the age of 30, the month after Cardinal George Pell had given evidence to the child sexual abuse royal commission in Sydney.

The next time R saw his son's childhood friend, the complainant, was at his son's funeral. R was shocked to see at least 100 people at the service, including former choirboys and one of his son's drug counsellors. Many people had to stand at the back of the church, as the pews were all full. At the funeral, R played a recording of the cathedral choir, which had been recorded back when his son was just a boy, when he had sung with them many years before.

At the end of the funeral, the complainant approached R. It was the first time they had seen each other since about 1997. He was with his partner, R recalled.

'He came up to me and talked to me, and he said, "It's so sad." He was very sombre.' He asked R about the recording of the choir played during the service.

'He asked me, "Was that the choir, the cathedral choir?" I said, "Yes." He said, "I'm on that. I'd love a copy." I said, "Yeah, I'll get you a copy." But I didn't get his phone number.'

R said he has since been told that just a few weeks later, the complainant disclosed his alleged abuse by Pell to a family member for the first time. In July 2015, he made a formal statement to police.

But at the funeral that day, R knew nothing of what had occurred to either of the boys.

'I found out the year after the funeral, in July, when the police rang me from SANO.' R was referring here to Taskforce SANO, established in 2012 to investigate sexual abuse during the Victorian parliamentary Inquiry into the Handling of Child Abuse by Religious and other Non-government Organisations.

'They rang me and said they had a matter they wanted to talk to me about, about my son.' R was told by the detective that he could not discuss the matter over the phone, that it needed to be done in person. 'It will only take an hour,' the detective told R. It took closer to five.

'I thought it was about my son's drugs, or his past, that he might have done something stupid,' R told me. 'So he's come, and I let him in and we sat at the table, and he started telling me the story about … you know [the complainant and my son]. That my son had been sexually abused or assaulted by Pell.

'I thought, *Huh? Hang on. He's now the cardinal. But he was the archbishop then. They don't do that.* And he's telling me all these things. And, really, it was a bit of a shock to the system.' R's partner, K, said that R went into shock after the interview with the detective. His health took a turn for the worse. The reality began to sink in for R over the course of a couple of weeks, K told me.

'When the detective came, it was very hard, extremely hard for him to be a parent and have that come at him, and the fact that he didn't know. He felt like he'd failed, and because he passed away there's no way of fixing it – to say, "I'm sorry." It's done so much damage to our relationship, this whole thing. It's a good job I love him, because he's a different person. He's had all kinds of health issues now. All of that stems back to what happened and not being able to fix it. He has me, but I only knew his son while he was a drug addict. But I didn't know his son the way he was before.'

R has been supported by good friends and survivor advocates since learning about the alleged abuse and having to wait as the court cases unfolded. He said that detectives kept him updated throughout the process. He said detectives also told him about the way the complainant had stood up to cross-examination in the trial.

'The police gave me information. They said they've [the defence] had him up there for days cross-examining him to the point that they just couldn't get the answer they were looking for, because he stuck to the facts and kept telling them what happened, and it got to the stage where they bullied him. And that didn't go down well with the jury. He just kept saying the same thing. For days. He stuck to his guns.'

Having lived in Ballarat for several years, R had come to know many of the community members who have lived in the town their whole lives, over the period when abuse by clergy in the town was overlooked, ignored, and covered up. Many of the victims of those crimes and their families remain in Ballarat, and some have reached out to R. They have told him stories about Pell, who also grew up and started his clerical career in the town.

A friend told R that her family had been good friends with Pell's while they were growing up. 'They would go on holidays together and do Christmases together,' R told me. 'She was saying that he has always been a spoiled brat. They were very arrogant as children, both he and his brother.'

Locals also told R about Ballarat's history being steeped in abuse by clergy. Police in the area were historically involved in concealing such crimes. 'A friend of mine who used to be a station sergeant here in Ballarat in the eighties and nineties, he said he got a notice from command in about 1991 that said, "If anyone comes to complain about our priests, you show them the door." That was an order from head command. From Ballarat police. The clergy were above the law.

'It's all a boys' club. There are still a lot of people who are well-to-do in Ballarat who say, "Oh no, Pell couldn't do that. He's our George."'

R said he was willing to speak to me about his feelings about the case to give the alleged victims a voice. The complainant's lawyer, Viv Waller, has said the complainant is intensely private and just wants to move on with his life. R said he spent many mornings at St Patrick's Cathedral watching his son sing in the choir, and he said there were many Sundays when the cathedral was not busy and was not the 'hive of activity' some witnesses in the case described. He said he believed the complainant, and would be forever grateful to him for coming forward.

'One of the messages I keep repeating is that if you are a victim, come out. Tell us. Talk to a friend. Report it. You'll feel much better for it.'

CHAPTER EIGHT

Retrial: part I

'At the time all of these things took place, I wasn't in a position
to tell anyone as I feared I wouldn't be believed. Priests had so
much respect from parents and the like, Catholic families at
that time almost idolised the local priest.'
— Survivor testimony to the Royal Commission into Institutional
Responses to Child Sexual Abuse

The prospect that we would be facing the same witnesses, questions,
and evidence all over again was clearly tough for everyone, including
Pell, the journalists, and the two legal teams. It must have also
distressed the complainant, although he was not at the court. The
journalists had spent five weeks on a case they could not write about,
returning to their newsrooms with notes unable to be transformed
into stories that could be run. The legal teams had spent months
preparing their cases, dealing with an agonising wait as the jurors
deliberated, and they would now have to go through the entire
process again.

While journalists knew that the suppression order would
eventually be lifted, it offered little comfort to them or their editors
in the immediate aftermath of the mistrial. It did not change their
feeling that weeks of work had been for nothing. If the prosecutors
decided that it would be too expensive to run the trial again and
dropped the case altogether, we would still be unable to report on

the Cathedral mistrial until after the Swimmers' trial had occurred, because of the suppression order in place. Reporting on the mistrial risked prejudicing the jury chosen for the Swimmers' trial.

If the legal teams decided to delay the Swimmers' trial – due to commence in November 2018 – in order to run the Cathedral trial a second time, the public would be much more interested in the result of the second Cathedral trial once the Swimmers' trial was over, and only a few details of the mistrial would be reported. Jurors in a retrial are not told that a previous jury could not reach a verdict. A retrial is considered to be an entirely new trial, run independently and without prejudice from previous cases. So the big news from a retrial, once we could report it, would be whether Pell had won or lost the Swimmers' trial and the second Cathedral trial; not the fact that, months earlier, a mistrial had been held, resulting in a hung jury. While, of course, we would still report the fact of the mistrial, no news program, publication, or website would have the space or airtime to run the full details of all three trials once the suppression order was lifted.

There is no doubt that almost everyone in the media who was present from day one, and who stayed the course of the mistrial, believed this was Richter's case to lose because of the sheer passage of time that had elapsed since the alleged offences and the prosecution's reliance on just one witness, the complainant. We were much less informed than the jurors when it came to considering the case, because we had not seen the complainant testify or be cross-examined. We had heard whispers in court corridors that he was brilliant and compelling. We hadn't seen this for ourselves, though. We had relied on his evidence being quoted by the legal teams throughout the case to get an inkling of what he had said. We had no direct experience as to what his demeanour and manner had been over the four days he was examined and cross-examined.

We had all been determined not to let our own uncertainty cloud our coverage. All of us, at varying times during the trial, had admitted how tough this case was to adjudicate. And it wasn't our job to do so, anyway. It was the job of the jury. We reported the facts and cross-checked those facts with each other. We helped each other. We were careful. We all respected the legal parties, and took care not to embellish the facts or speculate about them in our draft stories. Of course, we had intense private conversations about the case in meeting rooms over shared packets of lollies and chips, in hallways, and in private over drinks. But, speaking for myself, I did not walk into the courtroom on day one convinced of either Pell's guilt or innocence. I, along with the jurors, was about to learn a lot. I kept an open mind.

By the time the Cathedral mistrial ended, I was less sure that this was Richter's case to lose. While I cannot speak for others as to how they perceived his arguments, to me it seemed that his closing address had been confused, needlessly lengthy, and, at times, condescending when I am sure he was trying to be relatable. But it must be tough for one of the most well-known and highly paid defence barristers in Victoria, used to defending gangland criminals and winning, to truly come across as relatable to about a dozen citizens pulled together to consider a case of historical child sexual abuse. I wondered constantly what jurors made of him during the trial. He could switch from being likeable, razor-sharp, and amusing to being condescending and loud. Perhaps this method worked before a jury considering gangland criminal offences, but may have been less endearing before jurors considering horrific details of child sexual abuse.

It quickly became clear that the prosecutors had no intention of dropping the Cathedral trial and focusing on the Swimmers' trial instead. They would run the Cathedral trial again, before turning their attention to the Swimmers' trial. They would not give up.

There was now a question of whether newsrooms would commit to once again sending journalists to a trial spanning five weeks that they could not immediately report on and that might even, for a second time, result in a hung jury. While anyone could come and go from the courtroom, you still had to know that the trial was on and where it was being held. To know which witnesses were coming up or had been dropped, you had to be there. Matters could move quickly: people could fall ill, the court could be dismissed for a day, directions hearings could happen at any time. Few alerts were being sent out to the media, so we were not being regularly updated to each day's events. There was no public listing for the case on the court website. It was public, but only kind of; possible to keep up with, but only if you attended every day or knew someone else who did. Ultimately, a handful of news organisations – including the ABC, *Guardian Australia*, Reuters, the *Herald Sun*, AAP, *The Washington Post*, and *The New Daily* – committed to sending reporters every day for the retrial. In most cases, they were the same reporters who had been present at the first trial. By this stage, we knew each other professionally quite well, sharing notes, asking each other legal questions, relying on seasoned court reporters such as the ABC's Emma Younger, *The Age*'s Adam Cooper, AAP's Karen Sweeney, and the *Herald Sun*'s Shannon Deery to explain some of the procedures.

We also approached Richter and Gibson in the hallways, and they helped us to understand the road ahead. Even for the full-time court reporters, some of what was unfolding was unprecedented. This was a once-in-a-lifetime trial for us all. How often do reporters dedicate months of their lives to the trial of a man as high-profile as this, under highly suppressed circumstances, in regards to a complex and emotionally charged issue, with the prospect of multiple trials unfolding? It was in everyone's interest in such a thorny case that all involved in reporting it got their facts right. Often, however, I wished that a dedicated, informal, and off-the-record question-and-answer session with Kidd and the legal counsel could be arranged for us to ask purely about legal procedures and processes – much like the child sexual abuse royal commissioner had offered journalists before the Melbourne hearings began.

In the absence of such guidance, all we could do was call lawyers not involved in the case for assistance with making sense of events that occurred, but often I found that even mentioning the name Pell led to them hanging up the phone, so fearful were they of being quoted or misquoted. There were about a dozen seasoned legal and police professionals I relied upon to call spontaneously when I was confused about a legal principle or occurrence, and while I cannot name them in order to protect their professional reputations and identities, I am very grateful to all of those who trusted me enough to answer my off-the-record questions about how certain legal processes worked. Of course, this was not the same as being able to talk at length to people involved in the case itself. But it was often all I had.

It was decided that the retrial would be held in November 2018, in place of the Swimmers' trial, which would be moved to early 2019. Before court ended for a final time at the mistrial, and once the jurors left the room, Kidd said there would be a mention held on 12 October 2018 to discuss the next steps in the case. Time to do it all again.

It appeared, at first, that this would be a more streamlined trial. For a start, it was agreed that much of the evidence from the first trial, which had been video-recorded, would be played to the court during the second trial, rather than calling witnesses back. Since the complainant had given evidence via video-link the first time around, this would be played in the retrial, including the questioning and cross-examination. This would spare him from having to go through the ordeal once again. Other key witnesses, however, would return to give evidence in person. Charles Portelli, for example, was to return to the courtroom. All of this was done according to the wishes and agreement of the legal parties, and was not unusual. Some of the witnesses' video evidence was to be partially edited – for example, to remove questioning that both the parties deemed irrelevant to their cases. Changes had to be made to avoid another hung jury. But the evidence to be heard would largely be the same, except for a couple of significant changes, including hearing from a new key witness, and slight but important alterations to the opening and closing addresses. Of course, things had to change. A mistrial represents a failure, essentially, of the opposing legal counsels to convince the jurors of their case. Without making some changes, the case risked failing again.

A new jury needed to be selected for the retrial, and that process began on 7 November 2018. As with the first trial, journalists watched via video-link from a courtroom on the third floor as 250 would-be jurors crowded into a room on the lower level of the County Court.

As they took their seats, Kidd told them that they faced selection for the 'Director of Public Prosecutions versus Pell' trial.

There was an audible gasp in the room as he clarified: 'That is, Cardinal George Pell.' A potential juror in the room who was, in the end, dismissed from jury duty due to an upcoming overseas trip, told me he did not recall specifically being told that it was unusual for there to be 250 jurors called, but he remembers the person in charge of the jury pool telling them that, normally, if their number was not called, they would be excused from jury duty and not have to come back. But the staffer told him, 'This is not a normal day.' Some of those not chosen for the Pell trial were instead chosen for the trial of

James Gargasoulas, who would later be jailed for life for committing mass murder when he used a stolen car to mow down and kill six people in the busy Bourke Street mall on 20 January 2017.

'It was also explained to us that, due to the large number of potential jurors to be part of the process, the room was going to be temporarily declared a courtroom so that they could use it to do the jury selection via a video feed,' the potential juror told me. 'It took a while to get everything going, to herd us all into the room and have us sitting in number order. There was a slight sense of fluster among the staff – you could tell that things weren't business as usual.

'There certainly was a sense of being witness to something momentous when Pell entered his plea.' That plea, of course, was not guilty.

'One hundred and fifty-six: church pastor. One hundred and thirteen: mathematician. Eighty-five: tram driver. One hundred and seventy-eight: dietician. Five: head chef.'

One by one, the jurors' numbers were called by the tipstaff. They made their way from where they were seated to the jury box, and Pell challenged none of those selected.

All of the jurors were sworn in for duty on the Bible, but more out of confusion than any religious affiliation – the process of taking either an oath or affirmation was explained quickly and somewhat haphazardly, it seemed, and the jurors looked confused.

Either way, the retrial had begun, and Kidd addressed them in the way he had addressed the jurors in the first trial. They were to use their heads, not their hearts. They were not to make Pell a scapegoat for the failings of the Catholic Church. Talking about the case outside of the jury room was a serious criminal offence, and they were not to do so under any circumstances.

The next morning, on Thursday 8 November, after Kidd completed his opening directions to the jurors, Gibson began his opening address. Again, he laid out the case calmly, and step by

step. For the first time, the new jury heard details about exactly
what it was that Pell was accused of.

After outlining the alleged offences and where and how they
occurred, Gibson explained to the jurors that the evidence of the
complainant had already been given at an earlier point in time.
He did not say, nor would it have been right to say, that the
complainant's evidence had been recorded during a previous trial.
Rather, Gibson told the jury that video and audio of his testimony
had been recorded, and that recording, including of the cross-
examination by Richter, would be played to them later in the week.

'The law provides for that pre-recording procedure to take place
as already indicated by His Honour to you. It does not mean, as
you have been told, it is to be treated any differently because it's
pre-recorded. It does not mean you give it greater or lesser weight.
It is simply an alternative means by which a person in his position
may give evidence. What that means is that the parties, my learned
friends and us, already know it is evidence in this trial. So, in
giving you a summary of the Crown case, I'm able to refer to [the
complainant's] evidence that will be before you rather than trying
to anticipate what his evidence is likely to be.'

He repeated what had allegedly happened once the boys reached
the priests' sacristy. Again, the abuse was described to the jury as it
had been to the first jury; but this time, the abuse of the other boy
was described from the outset as an indecent act with a child under
the age of 16, rather than sexual penetration of a child under the
age of 16 – given the changes to that charge that had been made at
the previous trial.

Once again, Gibson described how Pell forced his penis into
the complainant's mouth; but this time, with the benefit of already
knowing the evidence from the witnesses, he was able to describe it
in more detail. 'Pell was standing and he pushed [the complainant]
down to a position where [the complainant] was crouching or

kneeling. [The complainant] was then pushed onto Cardinal Pell's erect penis so that Cardinal Pell's penis was in [the complainant's] mouth. This act of fellatio or oral sex lasted for a short period ... a couple of minutes. You will hear that Cardinal Pell then stopped and told [the complainant] to remove his pants.'

Gibson told the jurors how the complainant didn't say anything at the time because he did not want to jeopardise his prestigious scholarship in any way. 'He was also cognisant of the position held by the accused man and the possible ramifications that might flow from saying something about what had happened,' Gibson told them.

After describing the second, brief incident that occurred a few weeks later, when Pell shoved the complainant against a wall and grabbed his genitals, Gibson told the jurors that at the end of the 1997, when the boys had finished Year 8, both boys left St Kevin's College and the choir.

Gibson knew more clearly, this time, the evidence that was to come, so he was able to outline early and in detail conflicts between the prosecution and defence cases, and prepare jurors for any challenges to the Crown's case. He said that a number of witnesses – including some choristers; the choirmaster, John Mallinson; the organist, Geoffrey Cox; the master of ceremonies, Charles Portelli; the sacristan, Max Potter; and the choir marshal, Peter Finnigan – would speak of the procession being a regimented procedure, both inside and outside the cathedral. Therefore, the defence would argue that any choirboys separating or peeling off or detaching from the procession as it was leading down the side of the cathedral outside would have been noticed.

Gibson told the jurors that those witnesses would be asked about the notion of two boys leaving the procession and ducking back into the cathedral, and some of them would say the door to the priests' sacristy was usually locked when the sacristy was unattended.

'That obviously conflicts with the account given by the complainant that he entered the unlocked sacristy,' Gibson said. 'It's just sensible, I think, at this stage for you, at the outset, to know what some of the issues are going to be in this case, because ultimately the Crown will be asking you to accept, beyond reasonable doubt, the account of [the complainant].'

Gibson went through other matters, such as the fact that some witnesses would say the wine would have been locked away. Some witnesses would speak about Cardinal Pell standing at the steps of the cathedral after mass on some occasions and greeting people for an extended period of time that was inconsistent with the offending having occurred within a short period of time after mass, as described by the complainant. Gibson highlighted the problems that Richter would have with the Crown's case early and often, so that there would be no surprises for the jury.

'Some of the persons whom I referred to a short minute ago will speak about Cardinal Pell and how he was always accompanied whilst robed by his master of ceremonies, Monsignor Portelli, or by the sacristan, Mr Potter,' Gibson said. 'So, this is inconsistent with the offending having occurred when Cardinal Pell was alone ... Again, an issue you will have to consider.'

Portelli would describe the robes as being multi-layered, heavy, and cumbersome; as such, that conflicted with Pell's ability to move them to expose his penis, Gibson continued. This time, Gibson's opening address was focused more on what the witnesses who opposed the complainant would say and all of the inconsistencies that arose from that, rather than on the complainant's account alone. It was an interesting revised strategy.

'Now, you've already been told by His Honour that the Crown has the burden of proof,' Gibson continued. 'There is no burden on the defence to prove anything. You have been told that yesterday and again today.

'The burden rests with the prosecution from start to finish, and it must prove these charges beyond reasonable doubt based on the evidence. It is imperative in this case that you make your determination based on the evidence as His Honour has told you, putting aside any feelings or prejudice or sympathy. The last thing that the prosecution would want in this case is for a determination to be made by you based on some bias or prejudice against Cardinal Pell because of his position within the Catholic Church. That is not what we want.'

And with that, Gibson concluded the Crown's opening of the case.

It was Richter's turn, and this time he did not wait until the end of the case to move to the head of the bar table and address the jurors head-on. While Gibson's sentences had been short and concise, Richter laboured each point, once again rarely using notes, and was sometimes distracted by new thoughts halfway through current ones. It is impossible, of course, to know how the jurors perceived him, but in terms of addresses, Richter's were, to me at least, compelling because he was entertaining and a bit baffling, but he was also sometimes hard to follow to a conclusion.

'Some of you might well have heard a song by a fellow called Tim Minchin which went viral and made the news and made lots of things, entitled "Come Home (Cardinal Pell)",' Richter began. 'Well, he came back, and he came back of his own accord to clear his name. Although he had diplomatic status at the Vatican, and as we know there is no extradition treaty with the Vatican and Australia, he came here voluntarily. So the notion that he had to be brought here to face justice has to be clear. Because that song [was] a toxic song at the time and an offensive song, but it made a lot of media.'

What Richter did not tell the jurors was that the song was about

Pell's failure to fly to Australia to face questioning before the child sexual abuse royal commission. It had nothing to do with flying back for the trial. Richter then jumped to when Pell was interviewed by detectives in Rome about the charges he faced.

'Cardinal Pell was not obliged to be interviewed by police interrogators,' Richter told the jurors.

'There was no way that they could interview him when he was at the Vatican unless he wanted it and allowed it. And the fact was that the interview, which you will see a video of … was set up in a hotel room by the police officers, including Detective Sergeant Reed, who was what is called the informant in this case. He laid the charges, and that was done at the invitation of Cardinal Pell. And it wasn't a situation where he just said, "No comment," as a lot of people would say in those situations. It was a situation in which, given very limited facts about what it was that he was to be questioned about in terms of detail, he had prepared a statement which he handed over, and he then opened himself to any questions that the interrogators might want to ask, and he answered them, and he answered them as fully and as honestly as he could.'

Richter described once again all of the improbabilities in the case, and the problems with the dates on which the complainant had first alleged the abuse occurred.

This time, it was made clear to the jury from the outset that the only dates upon which Pell would have said Solemn Sunday Mass in the second half of 1996 were the 15th and the 22nd of December.

Richter asked the jurors to focus on what the case was not about, saying again that the jurors were not to blame Pell for the failings of the Catholic Church to respond to child sexual abuse or to protect children. Pell was not on trial for that, the jurors were reminded.

Richter went on to say that whether or not Pell knew about paedophiles in the Catholic Church, and whether or not he did enough to stop them, was irrelevant.

'That, of course, was the focus of the royal commission,' he said. 'That was its focus: the institutional response to allegations of child sexual abuse. And that having been the case, a lot of people, when they heard that Cardinal Pell had been charged, had assumed that it had something to do with not dobbing in or dealing with errant clerics.

'That is not the trial here. The trial here is of the most senior Catholic cleric charged with – actually, let's call a spade a spade – actually orally raping a child of 13 and doing some other disgusting things with two children. That's what this trial is about. It's not about what he knew about whether some other priests, 20 years even before then, had been doing things to little boys and failed to report.'

Richter removed references to meteorites from his opening address this time around, but told the jurors they would have 'had to have lived on the Moon' not to be aware of the coverage of Pell in the media.

For the retrial, Richter presented a definitive list of 12 issues in the case that, he argued, meant the abuse could not have happened. He told the jurors he would outline these 12 issues throughout the trial. They would primarily show it was not practically possible that Pell was in robes and alone immediately after Sunday Solemn Mass. Again, the Queen was referenced.

'He was just not alone when he was robed; he was always accompanied,' Richter told the jurors. 'It's a little bit like the Queen, I suppose, although he wouldn't like that comparison at all. But the Queen, when she is in state, when she is robed, is never unattended, never unattended. She is not expected to dress and get undressed on her own; there are always attendants.' Pell would have been in a similar situation as the archbishop presiding over mass at the cathedral, Richter said.

'Since the 16th century or whatnot, bishops and archbishops were not to be left alone,' he continued. 'The mass isn't finished until you've de-vested yourself and certain prayers have been said in relation to articles of clothing, so we say that was the case.'

Richter tried to appeal to the mathematician among the jurors. He said estimates of how long Pell had remained on the cathedral steps after mass, or how long corridors would have been empty, or when doors would have been unlocked were in contention. 'We say that the arithmetic will be a significant issue in whether or not what happened was practically possible.'

Finally, Richter asked the jurors, where was the motive? There was none, he said, answering for them.

'When you listen to the evidence, and it will be your intellect that's called for, not your passions or your feelings of compassion or prejudice or bias or pity for a man who's 76, sitting in the dock. Forget that. That's not what it's about. It's about intellect and analysis. That's what judges do, and you are the judges of the fact. Was there an opportunity on the evidence, a credible opportunity [to offend]? Secondly, the means. Well, we can assume that the archbishop has a penis. You can assume that. But the means of manoeuvring it when in robes … did he have the means to do it in that way? In the way that [the complainant] describes?

'But if you eliminate the opportunity, and you eliminate the means, the only way he [Pell] could have taken the kind of risks involved in what [the complainant] described is if he was mad. And he's not.'

The jurors in the retrial took fewer notes. They listened intently, letting each piece of evidence sink in. They had access to all the transcripts and exhibits in their jury room. They could check the evidence at any time. While the previous jury seemed at times more intense and unsettled, their emotion evident on their faces, writing furiously, this jury seemed calmer and more difficult to read. It may have helped that Richter did not tell them this time around that the life of a man was in their hands.

From Friday 9 November 2018 until partway through Wednesday 14 November, the court was closed to the public, including the media, while the complainant's evidence and cross-examination was played to the jurors. On 14 November, the jurors were taken on a tour of the cathedral in the same way that the previous jury had been.

The video evidence from Carl Mueller, the former choirboy who had given evidence via video-link from Perth in the previous trial, was played to the court. He had told the court that he recalled Pell always being accompanied by someone shorter than him who was bearded and a bit 'rotund'. The laughter this comment had provoked from those in the courtroom was caught on the tape and could be heard. Did the jurors at the retrial wonder where the laughter was coming from?

Next, the video evidence from Aidan Quinn, another former choirboy, was played. It became apparent that the Crown and the defence had agreed to drop several of the former choirboys as witnesses altogether, choosing not to play videos of their evidence, because their testimony had added nothing to the case. However, this did not result in a shorter trial, with a new witness later added – criminal barrister Daniel McGlone – and changes made to the closing addresses.

Along the way, Kidd directed the jurors as to how they were to treat different kinds of evidence.

'Evidence can come in many forms,' they were told. 'It can be evidence about what someone saw or heard. It can be an exhibit admitted to evidence … Some evidence can prove a fact directly. For example, if a witness said that he or she saw or heard it was raining outside, that would be direct evidence of the fact it is raining. However, other evidence can prove a fact indirectly; you infer it.

For example, if a witness said that he or she saw someone enter the courthouse wearing a raincoat and carrying an umbrella, both dripping wet, that would be indirect or circumstantial evidence of the fact that it's raining outside. You can conclude from the witness's evidence that it was raining, even though he or she did not actually see or hear it rain … That's called drawing an inference. A reasonable inference. As far as the law is concerned, it makes no difference whether evidence is direct or indirect, and by indirect I am talking about "indirect" being another word for circumstantial evidence …

'People often believe that indirect or circumstantial evidence is weaker than direct evidence, [but] that is actually not true,' Kidd said. 'It can be just as strong, or even stronger. What matters is how strong or weak the particular evidence is, not whether it is indirect or direct evidence.'

Kidd warned the jury that they were not to make guesses.

On Thursday 15 November, the seventh day of the hearing, a statement of agreed facts was read to the jurors by Angela Ellis, the prosecutor working alongside Gibson. These were facts that both parties – the defence and the prosecution – had agreed to and that were not in contention. In other words, the jurors did not need to decide if they were true or false. (Outlining the agreed facts to jurors allows them to focus on other evidence, and saves time.)

It was not in dispute that there were extensive restoration works occurring at the cathedral, including to the sanctuary and to the main body of the cathedral, during 1996, Ellis said. Nor were the dates that Pell presided over mass in December 1996 in dispute. The full statement of agreed facts was tendered as evidence to the jury as a document, or exhibit, so they could it have with them in the jury room.

John Mallinson was sworn in next. He must have been perceived as a key witness by the parties, as his video evidence from the first trial was not replayed. The 84-year-old told the jurors that his role had been to recruit choirboys and to choose music for mass, as he was choirmaster and organist at the cathedral.

Part of the choirboys' expenses were paid in return for singing in the choir, he confirmed. When asked by Gibson whether he recalled Archbishop Pell celebrating mass in 1996, he responded, 'I'm sure he did. He must have been there. I'll have to say yes, but I can't remember a particular occasion.' He said that the choir included about 50 boys, along with some adults. If Sunday mass occurred on an occasion when he was playing the organ, Mallinson told the court, he 'would not be aware of anything else going on in the cathedral', including whether Pell had joined the procession or had remained on the stairs. He described Portelli as 'very conservative' and as a 'stickler' for church protocol.

'The console is quite high, the music desk is quite high,' he explained. 'You've got a lot to think about when you're playing the organ. You're not aware of anything, unless somebody distracts you.'

To many questions, including about the pathway the choristers took to get inside the cathedral after processing outside, how they would gain access through doors, and whether those doors were locked and unlocked, Mallinson responded, as others did, that he could not recall exactly. It was a long time ago.

He said that he had seen Pell returning to his sacristy following mass, usually accompanied by Portelli or Dean William McCarthy. Mallinson drew a diagram of various areas of the cathedral as it was in 1996, and this drawing was tendered as evidence for the jurors. His evidence continued through the morning and into the late afternoon – a lengthy time for an elderly man to endure, especially given that he had undergone a similar experience just weeks before in the mistrial.

He said the sacristan, Max Potter, would leave a suitable interval that 'decorum' required after mass before collecting sacred vessels from the main altar and moving them back into the sacristy. He did not want to be moving vessels around while congregants were still praying after mass.

He also said he could not recall Pell exiting the cathedral with the procession accompanied by Portelli, or standing by the western door at the steps speaking to guests after mass.

Richter asked him whether it was ever reported to him that two choirboys had 'nicked off' from the procession.

'I can't recall,' he replied.

Richter: 'But it was an extraordinary thing to have happened, if it had happened, and you would have recalled it, would you not?'

Mallinson: 'I'm pretty sure I would, yes.'

On re-examination, Gibson put it to Mallinson that any choirboys nicking off would have to have been caught in order for it to be reported to him.

'Yes,' Mallinson replied. 'How else would I have known?'

Gibson: 'If they hadn't been caught, you wouldn't have expected it to be reported to you?'

Mallinson: 'I wouldn't have known otherwise, unless I've got eyes in the back of my head or something.'

On Friday 16 November, the other church organist, Geoffrey Cox, was sworn in. He told the court, under questioning from Ellis, as he had before, that the choir was highly disciplined and regimented. He said he had no specific memory of who presided over Sunday Solemn Mass on exact dates at the cathedral in late 1996 and early 1997. 'After several years,' he said, 'one Solemn Mass blurs into another.'

Like Mallinson, he was sometimes part of the procession, depending on whether he was playing the organ or not. Unlike Mallinson, he did not refer to a period of decorum before items were removed from the cathedral and returned to the sacristy. He told the court that people started moving items as soon as the procession had left. He said 'it never happened' that choirboys would run ahead of the procession to get ahead of it in an attempt to re-enter the cathedral earlier.

He said that by the time he or Mallinson finished playing the organ after mass, the 'hive of activity' at the cathedral 'had sort of simmered down'.

Richter asked Cox if there were times, while playing the organ, that he had observed altar servers entering the priests' sacristy after Sunday Solemn Mass.

'Look, I had my back to them,' Cox replied. 'They would pass behind me. I don't remember any detail about what they were doing.' He said he was not sure about exactly what went on in terms of clearing the cathedral and returning items to the priests' sacristy.

'The sacristies were, in my experience, sometimes left open when I walked back after playing the postlude. And that would sometimes be after everyone had gone, and perhaps Mr Potter had gone down for a cup of tea – he might have been returning later.'

Richter asked him whether, if children were in the priests' sacristy, he would have heard their voices if the door was open, especially if their voices were elevated as they protested Pell's alleged abuse of them.

'Certainly,' Cox replied.

The evidence of wine supplier John May was then played to the court as a video recording before the court adjourned for the weekend.

On Monday 19 November, before the jurors entered the court, Kidd told Richter there was a matter he wanted to discuss with him.

He said that Richter's line of questioning to Cox about whether he would have heard children's voices in the priests' sacristy was impermissible. This was because he was asking Cox to guess, to offer an opinion, rather than to recall something directly from his memory. Richter did not disagree with Kidd.

'It's not observational evidence,' Kidd told Richter. He added that 'elevated voice' was a vague term. What was meant by it? Yelling? Speaking loudly? Screaming?

'The sacristies ... the jury have seen them, they are rooms, there's no magic to them, they are just rooms, and there's a corridor, and we have all seen that, and the jury will make whatever judgement they are able to on the basis of your common-sense arguments,' Kidd told Richter.

Their exchange continued:

Kidd: It's another thing to get a witness to give evidence, expert lay evidence, to the effect that the complainant's voice would have been heard.

Richter: Yes. One of the problems is that we didn't carry out any experiment because the acoustics there, and I tested them on number of occasions, the acoustics there are pretty good in terms of what's heard in the hallway and what's heard in the workers' sacristy. We weren't in any position to carry out such experiments, but someone like [Cox] would be in a position to talk about how there is essentially an atmosphere of silence and the acoustics coming out of the sacristy are pretty clear.

Kidd: But is there an atmosphere of silence? I mean, there's plenty of evidence, in fact you've mentioned it in cross-examination, that there was a hive of activity taking place around the corridor, which would include people walking, talking, and the like. And all sorts of noise is taking place, so that just shows you how artificial the questioning is.

Richter: Except for this: if that proposition is accepted, then the Crown case is dead.

Kidd: If what proposition is accepted?

Richter: There's continuous traffic there.

Kidd: That's an argument you can put to the jury.

Richter: Yes.

Kidd: I'm focusing on how it is that questioning about the capacity to hear an elevated voice ... how that doesn't invite speculation in this case.

Richter: Your Honour, what I will do, I suppose, is address the jury on [the complainant's] dealing with the notion of elevated voice.
Kidd: Like you did last time. And you made your good points, and they're there to be made. But last time you didn't go down this path. You didn't.
Richter: I didn't last time. That's true. I suppose it's a retrial. One tries to improve.

Peter Finnigan, who was the choir marshal at the time the offending was alleged to have occurred, was sworn in, being another of the witnesses required to return to the court to give evidence. He told the court his role had been similar to that of a schoolteacher, to supervise the boys and to discipline them if necessary. His role also involved compliance around safety and first aid.

He said once the choir had finished proceeding after mass, and had returned to the choir rehearsal room, 'The boys would take off their robes and hang them up, they'd be just piled onto a coat hanger. That was one of my jobs. To make sure everything was hung up neatly. And then the boys would sit down in their chairs. Everyone had an allocated place to sit in the rehearsal room and wait to be dismissed by the director of music, who was playing the postlude, the final piece on the organ.' He said there was no one ticking boys' names off as they returned to the room or as they left it to go home. He said while the boys were allowed to use the church corridors, they were not allowed into the sacristies. He said the mood of the choristers after mass was 'often excited'.

'You know, they were boys,' he said. 'They had been there since nine o'clock, they were hungry, they were ready for lunch and ready to be home and, you know, having the afternoon off.'

When he was cross-examined by Richter, he was asked, 'If two young choristers had decided to nick off and run into the southern transept, it's unlikely you would have missed that?'

Finnigan agreed. 'It would be pretty unlikely I'd miss that. Unless I was distracted. But most likely I would have seen it.'

Richter put it to Finnigan that he was a strict disciplinarian.

'I certainly was,' Finnigan agreed. He said that after mass he would wait until all of the boys had been collected by their parents.

Richter: What if one was missing?

Finnigan: I might not know if they were missing.

Richter: If two young choristers were missing for any length of time from the procession or later after the procession from rehearsal, you would know about it?

Finnigan: Not necessarily.

Richter: How do you mean?

Finnigan: Well, because if I'd noticed them missing I would know about it, but if, as you said earlier, they managed to slip away without my noticing, I wouldn't know because … we did not take a roll.

Finnigan said he recalled that after mass Pell would stand on the steps of the cathedral speaking with parishioners.

'That would be what, 10 minutes or something?' Richter put to him.

'Something like that,' he replied.

Richter told Finnigan that he had been reading Wikipedia about the role of the master of ceremonies, which at the time was Portelli, and put it to Finnigan that it was a traditional role that went back to the Middle Ages. 'I didn't know that,' Finnigan replied.

Richter: His principal job was to look after the archbishop.

Finnigan: I think he had to look after the liturgy as well.

Richter: He was like the impresario of a liturgical sort of drama unfolding?

Finnigan: Yes.

Richter: And that liturgical drama would take place, and while it was taking place the principal function [of Portelli] was to make sure that the archbishop was looked after?

Finnigan: No. His principal function was to make sure the liturgy – the whole liturgy – went well. Not just the archbishop. But the whole thing.

It is pure speculation what the jurors may or may not have found significant in this exchange. But it struck me as a blow to the defence that while Richter emphasised throughout the trial that Pell was never alone, and that he would have been accompanied by Portelli for a large portion of the time, the choirmaster told the court that, actually, Portelli would have had responsibility for more people that just Pell. The inference that jurors could have drawn from this was that Portelli could not be with everyone at once, and therefore could not have been with Pell all of the time if he also had responsibilities elsewhere in the cathedral.

Richter put it to Finnigan that Portelli would always process with Pell outside the cathedral to the stairs.

'I don't recall,' Finnigan replied. But he did agree with Richter that he did not recall ever seeing the archbishop on his own while he was in robes.

Max Potter, the sacristan, was the next witness to be recalled to give evidence. Gibson asked Potter if it was correct that he had first met Pell in the early 1980s. Potter confirmed that this was the case, and the line of questioning was then objected to by Richter.

'I wonder what the relevance of that is, Your Honour,' Richter said. 'I object.'

Gibson replied, 'Simply the history between the two men. That is that they have known each other for a long period of time.'

Of course, what Gibson was trying to do was demonstrate that Potter might have an allegiance to Pell, given how long they had known each other. That perhaps there was bias.

Kidd told Gibson to keep the line of questioning limited to that, but Gibson had made his point and chose to move on, asking Potter about his duties after mass. I found it interesting that rather than cite his duties as sacristan as being to keep vessels and valuable items safe, and to move them between the sacristies and the cathedral, to return the altar wine, and to keep rooms secure, like he had in the first trial, Potter responded this time that his role was to follow the archbishop to the main door.

'The archbishop would stay and greet people … on the steps of the cathedral, sometimes for 20 minutes or half an hour,' Potter said. 'Father Portelli and myself would stay with the archbishop. If Father Portelli was there, I would go back into the cathedral and clear the sanctuary, things from the sanctuary, and take them back to the sacristy.'

Gibson asked Potter whether after mass there would be an interval, for reasons of decorum and to allow people to finish praying and leave the cathedral, before he started clearing away items.

'Occasionally, yes,' Potter said. 'Occasionally I would …'

Richter interjected with an objection. 'These are very leading questions,' he told Kidd.

The jury and the witness were sent away for an afternoon break; once they left, a discussion between the parties ensued.

Once the jurors and Potter had left the room, Kidd told Richter that Gibson's line of questioning seemed relevant to him, because 'it goes to the very opportunity for the complainant to have access to the sacristy corridor without Mr Potter being there'.

Richter responded that if this were the case, Gibson could 'put it to him rather than having a whole lot of cross-examination to confuse him'.

Once the jurors returned from their break, Gibson asked Potter how long after mass it was before he would start returning candles, chalices, cruet sets, and other items to the sanctuary.

'Could be five minutes,' Potter said. 'I make sure that the procession's cleared from the cathedral first. And people will be walking up to the sanctuary area kneeling, so we didn't disturb them for five or six minutes, we gave them their private time, and then we would move in after that.'

Gibson asked Potter what the choir would have been doing when he unlocked the priests' sacristy in preparation for the archbishop to return to disrobe after mass.

'They'd be outside the cathedral,' he replied. He clarified that he would not accompany Pell to the front steps of the cathedral until 'later on' into his term as archbishop, once Pell had got used to the building. During this early period, Potter said he would leave Pell with Portelli on the steps of the cathedral, and then go back to the cathedral and start clearing the sanctuary.

Gibson asked Potter whether he could categorically state that Pell was never alone when he went back to his sacristy to disrobe after mass. Potter confirmed, 'There was always an assisting priest, or one of us in the sacristy with the archbishop.'

> **Gibson:** Mr Potter, I want to put something to you now, given the last two answers that you've given. Is it the case that you had a conversation with Sergeant Christopher Reed, who's leading this investigation? On 5 December 2016?
> **Potter:** Yes.
> **Gibson:** And the topic of Archbishop Pell being alone or unaccompanied when he returned to the sacristy came up in the discussion that you had with Mr Reed, didn't it?
> **Potter:** Yes, but he asked me quite a few questions that day and I wasn't too sure – it wasn't just that, those questions.

Gibson: Mr Potter, in speaking with Sergeant Reed, did you indicate, firstly, that it was possible that Archbishop Pell was in the sacristy without you present after mass?

Potter: If ... if I was doing something special and he was there, but he would have an assistant if I wasn't present with him.

Gibson: Well, the second thing I want to put to you is did you indicate to Sergeant Reed that you cannot categorically state that Archbishop Pell was never alone when he returned to the sacristy?

Potter: Well, because sometimes I was in another area and when I'd come back in, one of the priests or Father Portelli would be there, but I'm not necessarily saying I saw him every time.

On Tuesday 20 November 2018, Potter's evidence continued. Gibson asked him about the robes worn by the archbishop.

Gibson: The chasuble doesn't prevent access to the groin area, does it?

Potter: The design of the chasuble Archbishop Pell was wearing ... they were long and heavy, and he would sometimes wear another vestment underneath it called the dalmatic. Therefore he would have sufficiently heavy robes that he could not move his hands anywhere except hands joining or holding the crossier. The weight of those vestments are not light, and they are fairly heavy vestments.

Gibson: The chasuble is a free-flowing garment, is it not?

Potter: Yes, but the design of Archbishop Pell's robes were very long, and the side ... they went right down both ways. They went full length over his arms and right down past his knees.

Gibson: The chasuble does not prevent one putting one's hand to one's groin if one wanted to, do you agree with that?

Potter: No, I'm sorry, I disagree with that because, knowing the type of vestments used by Archbishop Pell, it was [not] possible to do it.

He told Gibson that Pell would only robe and disrobe in the archbishop's sacristy.

On 20 November, Potter was cross-examined by Richter. Potter said he had specific memories of 15 December, when Pell first presided over Sunday Solemn Mass. Potter said he specifically remembered it because it was his responsibility to ensure that 'everything was ready for him'.

'I was there to make sure the robes fitted correctly on him and to help him put the chasuble over his head,' he said.

While the jurors were on their morning break, there was a discussion between the parties, during which Gibson called Potter's reliability into question. The day before, Gibson had asked Potter in a non-leading way about the procession after mass, and Potter volunteered that on such occasions he would accompany the procession to the front of the cathedral. In the afternoon, when Gibson returned to this topic, Potter added that he would not attend the front steps but would go to the sanctuary, where he would wait while people finished kneeling and praying after mass.

'Today, he seems to be saying that he did move down to the front steps and was in a position to observe Cardinal Pell [the first times he presided over mass as archbishop] staying at the front steps and speaking to parishioners,' Gibson said.

'Secondly, he was most adamant that the archbishop sacristy was the sacristy in which the archbishop would robe and disrobe, and yet today he's added that "he used the archbishop sacristy for most the time", in other words inferring not all of the time. That is a second example of his evidence being at odds from yesterday's.' Gibson said Potter had gone from only having general memories of Pell presiding over mass when he was questioned by him, to having specific recollections of 15 and 22 December when Pell presided over mass under questioning by Richter.

'He said today that he agreed with the proposition put by my learned friend that he would go to the front steps that the archbishop processed to, and the altar servers who were carrying the mitre and the crozier relieved the archbishop of those things at the front steps. I understood his [previous] evidence to be that he would stay in the sacristy in the area that he pointed out to me in one of the photographs, behind the wooden structure, and wait a period of time before he started to clear out the sanctuary. Now, I didn't understand any of his evidence yesterday to be that he would go back with the altar servers who were carrying the mitre and the crozier back to the sacristy door to unlock it.'

'Yes, I think that's right,' Kidd said. 'Let's assume for the moment that he has shifted, and I can absolutely say I'm absolutely confident in a couple of matters that he shifted noticeably on the archbishop's sacristy, the priests' sacristy point, and I also think he shifted on the altar servers' point as well. You make your points to the jury that ultimately he's unreliable. Why do you need to put it to him that he's unreliable?'

Gibson said he was concerned after reading about a case where the Court of Appeal had overturned convictions as unreasonable and unsupported by evidence after the Crown prosecutors failed to put theories to witnesses that they later went on to put to jurors in their closing addresses. Gibson did not want a situation where, in his closing address, he suggested Potter was an unreliable witness, only for a conviction to ensue, Pell to appeal, and the appeal to be upheld because prosecutors had never allowed the witness himself to answer as to whether or not he was unreliable.

The witness needed an opportunity to respond, Gibson said. 'I don't want to come in for any criticism at the end of this trial,' he told Kidd. He said he wanted to put it to Potter that he was not just agreeing with Richter, but was doing so to enhance Pell's chances of acquittal.

I had no idea, then, how significant Gibson's point would prove to be more than one year later when it came to the High Court.

Richter objected to this being put to Potter by Gibson. He reminded Kidd that he had previously told the parties he would not allow any cross-examination raising the suggestion that Portelli or Potter had a conscious or unconscious allegiance to Pell.

Richter added that if Gibson wanted to put it to the jurors during his closing address that Potter was unreliable, Richter would not later appeal any guilty verdict on the basis that this point had not been put to Potter himself.

'It's a legitimate observation,' Richter said. After all, Gibson was not suggesting Potter was lying; simply that he was unreliable.

Given Richter's assurance, Gibson said he would be content to use his closing address to assert that Potter was unreliable. But he was not allowed to go so far as to say he was a liar.

With that, Potter and the jury were brought back into courtroom 4.3. Potter's evidence concluded a short time later, and the next witness, Charles Portelli, Pell's master of ceremonies while he was archbishop, was sworn in. His evidence continued through to 21 November 2018.

Was there any occasion, Richter asked him, that he could recall the archbishop processing back to the sacristy, pushing anyone aside or pushing anyone? It was a clear reference to the second incident of abuse, when the complainant alleged he had been pushed up against a wall by Pell and had his genitals grabbed.

'No,' Portelli said.

The archbishop's robes were presented to Portelli. He was asked to demonstrate once again to the jurors how to tie the cincture – the rope that wrapped around the waist of the vestments.

Without prompting, and as he stood and demonstrated the way the cincture was tied, Portelli said, 'One needs to be like Houdini to get in and out of this.' This comment struck me as odd. Why did Portelli believe that was an important point to make?

Richter responded, 'By the time we've seen the knots, we might agree.'

Portelli demonstrated how to tie the cincture into various knots around the waist to hold the garments in place.

Richter asked Portelli how tight the knot would have to be.

'It has to be tight enough to stop the alb moving,' Portelli replied.

Portelli told the court that the robes Pell wore as archbishop needed to be specially commissioned.

'He was six foot four, and a bit stooped, and so the style police used to say to me, "He always looks badly dressed," because albs tended to ride up at the back, so I had them made in such a way that they're longer at the back than they are at the front,' he said.

Portelli demonstrated how the stole would be held in by the first loop of the cincture. After he tied three knots in it, it was still too long and trailing on the ground, so Portelli tied a further two knots. 'That's five,' he told the court.

Portelli confirmed that he would help Pell out of the robes, untying the knots, and once the robes were off he would hang up and store them.

Richter asked him about Pell's first Solemn Sunday Mass as archbishop on 15 December 1996. Portelli said he remembered the occasion. He said Pell was 'always' with him as the choir processed out of the church. Richter asked Portelli whether, on the first two occasions when he said Sunday mass in 1996, Pell would stand outside greeting parishioners after mass.

'Yes,' Portelli said. 'He would be there at least 10 minutes.'

Gibson re-examined Portelli, putting it to him that he seemed to have strong and specific memories of the two occasions in 1996 when Pell presided over Sunday mass. He asked Portelli what he did after mass on 15 December; whether it was one of the occasions when he or Pell had an afternoon engagement and needed to rush off afterwards. Portelli had given evidence that he would drive Pell to these engagements.

'I'm not sure we had an afternoon appointment that day, did we?' Portelli replied.

'Well, I'm asking you,' Gibson said. 'This is the occasion that you say you remembered, it being the first mass that you say Archbishop Pell said in the newly renovated cathedral. Do you know where he went immediately after?'

'I'm sorry, I don't have the list in front of me,' Portelli said – presumably referring to a list of engagements.

What about 22 December, Gibson asked. Did he and Pell leave for any engagements after mass on that occasion?

'It would be unlikely, but I don't think there was anything in the afternoon that day.' This line of questioning was important, because Gibson wanted to show jurors that Portelli in fact had no specific recall of the dates in question.

Gibson asked Portelli whether he knew of any occasion when Pell was alone in the sacristy.

Portelli: No, I've never ... I am not aware of any time he was alone.
Gibson: *I never saw him alone in there.* Is that what you were about to say?
Portelli: No, I didn't say that. I said that I am not aware that he was ever alone in there.

He also clarified with Portelli that the long cincture that went with the robes, the one that Portelli demonstrated as being extra long and therefore requiring five knots to keep it from dragging along the ground, might not have been the exact cincture that Pell wore when he presided over mass in December 1996. Portelli said the cincture was one of several in a drawer for the archbishop.

Portelli completed his evidence just before noon. It was impossible to say what the jurors thought of a key witness who, though called by the prosecution, seemed to be a key to the defence. From my perspective, Portelli seemed to be someone whom jurors might reasonably and justifiably have perceived as being a willing and eager participant in Richter's lines of questioning, and close to Pell.

In the afternoon, another former choirboy, Farris Derrij, was sworn in. He had been in Year 7, and a soprano in the choir in 1996. He was asked how the choir would process externally out of the cathedral after mass, as many of the other witnesses before had been asked. 'The sopranos were first,' he responded. 'They were at the front, and as each row went back they sort of snaked out in two rows. It was generally pretty orderly until we got outside, and then less orderly as we got closer to where we were out of sight.' There were fewer people on the outside of the church, Derrij said, so some boys would start talking and would move out of the orderly procession.

Under cross-examination by Richter, he accepted that his memory of those years was hazy, and said he had never seen boys take off from the procession.

Following Derrij, another former choirboy, David Dearing, was sworn in, who had just turned 14 at the time the offending was alleged to have occurred, and who sung alto. He said that by the time the choir returned to the rehearsal room and returned their robes after mass, they, 'could be a bit boisterous'. 'We were all just wanting to go home,' he said. When asked by Richter's colleague, barrister Ruth Shann, if two choristers taking off from the procession line would have been a serious disciplinary offence, he responded, 'I would have thought so.'

Once Dearing's testimony was completed, the recorded evidence of choirboy Anthony Nathan from the first trial was played to the court.

On Thursday 22 November, former choirboy Luciano Parissi was sworn in. In the mistrial, he was the witness who had said that Pell would sometimes come by the choir room while the boys were disrobing and that when he did, he would 'generally be on his own'. He had also said in the mistrial that once the choir had processed outside, the choir would often wait until Pell had passed them and re-entered the building, as a mark of respect. Parissi was 16 years old in 1996, when the offending was alleged to have occurred, a little older than some of the other former choirboys who gave evidence. Again, he said that after Sunday Solemn Mass, when the choir processed outside, Pell would initially be at the end of the procession, but once outside, 'he would walk by us and just sort of acknowledge us, and then walk back in [the building] and then we would follow after'.

Parissi said there was a mood of relief among the choirboys by the time they were back in the rehearsal room, and they were glad the morning was over. He said once the boys were back inside the building, there was a rush to get back to the choir room to disrobe and go home. There would sometimes be a bottleneck of boys in the corridor trying to get back into that room.

He said that 'on the odd occasion', Pell would come by the choir room after mass 'and say thank you and congratulations on a well-sung mass'. He said that sometimes Pell was accompanied, but not always. He confirmed that sacristies were off-limits to choristers and that he had never been inside one. Gibson asked him whether it was possible that two choirboys could have taken off from the procession.

'It would be very hard to [take off], but it could be possible,' he said. 'Being at the opposite end of the procession [from the adults], absolutely.'

Rodney Dearing, the father of David Dearing, was sworn in after the morning break. He had been one of the adult members of the choir in 1996. When he was asked by Richter about the orderliness of the choir as it processed outside, he responded, 'The choir is on show.'

'So even though some of them were young boys, order and discipline were required, because they were sort of the face of the cathedral in some respects, so that mucking up wasn't tolerated.'

He said that once the boys processed outside the cathedral and took a left-hand turn around a corner, he could no longer see them and so he could not say whether orderliness was maintained beyond that point. This was because, having a deeper voice than most of the choirboys, he was situated towards the back of the procession. However, he said, he did not think it was possible for two boys to detach themselves from the procession and take off unnoticed. Their robes were distinctive, he said, and they would have been seen.

Robert Bonomy, another former choirboy, was next. In 1996, at the time of the alleged offending, he was 15 years old. After mass, he said, the choirboys 'wanted to get out of there'. He said he saw Pell walking around the cathedral corridors over the years, both robed and unrobed, sometimes accompanied and sometimes not. He said he had never heard of two boys running off from the procession and slipping back into the cathedral.

The following witness, Stuart Ford, who gave evidence on Friday 23 November, also said the choirboys were more orderly when on public display inside the church, and while they were perhaps less orderly once they were outside the building, it was 'nothing too extreme'.

Former choirboy Christopher Doyle, who was 14, turning 15, in 1996, agreed: 'When we were inside the cathedral it was very ordered because obviously the mass was still going on technically, and the whole pageantry and formality, I guess, [was maintained]. And then we'd walk out, down the main steps of the cathedral, and then we'd start walking anticlockwise and we were still rather orderly. There was another gate we'd walk through on our path, and sometimes you'd get little less orderly because we're out of the public view for the main part, but, yeah, we still kept some reasonable sort of order until we got through those main doors and then went back through the southern transept. Again, we'd still be in some form of order, but again it would be a little less organised from there as well.' He said that once the choristers passed through the outside gate, 'It'd become a little bit more relaxed. You could sort of see guys sort of switch off a little, but I guess in terms of having to worry about their tasks and, yeah, just went back to like normal kids were, we'd walk off and, yeah, the demeanour would be relaxed – relaxed is probably the best way to describe it.'

The video evidence of former choirboy Aaron Thomas, from the mistrial, was then played to the jurors before they adjourned for the weekend after receiving a warning from Kidd.

'You have now heard several weeks of evidence and you know that we're heading towards the end of the evidence, so in some respects it might be more tempting than ever to talk about the case and the evidence. I've got no doubt that in the confidentiality of your jury room you've already had discussions about issues, and that's to be encouraged, because that's what you're there to do. But just remember that they are absolutely strictly confidential. Only you 14 have heard the evidence thus far, no one else, so your family members haven't heard the evidence, your friends haven't heard it, they haven't seen the cross-examination. They don't know what the issues are; only you do.

'So don't talk about it.'

CHAPTER NINE

Retrial: part II

'I feel that the mental health and healing of survivors are not
the core issues driving the Church's approach to the issue,
but the protection of the institution via suppression and
silence is utmost.'

– Survivor testimony to the Royal Commission into Institutional
Responses to Child Sexual Abuse

On Monday 26 November, the fourteenth day of the trial, a new
witness was called, whose evidence, from the accounts of many who
were present, would inadvertently prove to be a turning point in the
case. Whether the jury saw it the same way, we can never know.
But months afterwards, senior detectives and members of the legal
community told me that they, at least, believed his evidence must
have been crucial in solidifying the impression of Pell's guilt in the
minds of jurors.

The witness was Daniel McGlone, a 48-year-old lawyer and
barrister who was 18 in 1996 when the two boys were allegedly
abused. He had been an altar server at the cathedral between 1987
and the start of 1997.

McGlone was sworn in, and told the court his work included
administrative law, policy law, and some human-rights and refugee
work. McGlone was among the witnesses the defence asked the
prosecution to call, clearly because they believed he would add

something important to their argument that the offending was improbable, if not impossible. However, the defence team was careful never to refer to the evidence of McGlone or that of its other key witness, Portelli, as providing an alibi for Pell because the evidence was not strong enough to go that far. It would later be revealed that McGlone had approached Pell's defence team after the mistrial, and had offered himself as a witness in the case.

McGlone told the court that he had attended most Sunday masses held during the decade in which he had been an altar server, but said he could only recall one occasion when he had served at a Sunday Solemn Mass celebrated by Cardinal Pell, although he could not remember the exact date. He recalled that before the service the altar servers assembled in the priests' sacristy, and that it was the first time Cardinal Pell had said Sunday mass in the cathedral. McGlone said he was the thurifer – carrying the thurible, a metal censer containing incense and suspended from chains – on that occasion.

Under questioning by Gibson, he confirmed that he knew altar server Jeffrey Connor, a witness in the trial, but had only learned his surname in recent months, and that Connor was a 'friend of friends'.

'Did you not know him back in 1996 as an altar server?' Gibson asked him. McGlone confirmed that he did.

McGlone told the court that the priests' sacristy, whenever he saw it, was unlocked. The only sacristy that was ever locked was the archbishop's, he said. He told the court that he could specifically remember the occasion he had served as altar server for Pell, even though he could not remember the exact date, because his mother had made a rare visit to attend the Sunday mass that day, most likely to have lunch with him afterwards.

'I was aware my mother was in the congregation,' he said, adding that he quickly excused himself after mass after returning the thurible to the priests' sacristy to meet with her. He said on this occasion, he and his mother arrived at a step on the outside of the cathedral, and 'we stopped there ... and I start talking to her, and George Pell is to the left-hand side, and he's doing the meet and greet, and I'm talking to Mum'.

The previous archbishop, Frank Little, did not do this meet-and-greet, McGlone confirmed. Given that fact, the date his mother attended must have been on one of the early occasions that Pell said mass, since McGlone had stopped being an altar server by 1997 and Pell was only inaugurated in August 1996. Gibson asked McGlone why he described what Pell was doing as 'a meet-and-greet'. The term 'meet-and-greet' was one used by Richter throughout the trial. Why, Gibson asked McGlone, did he not just say that Pell was 'meeting and greeting people'?

'Well,' McGlone replied, 'it's something you see in Anglican churches a lot ... it's not an unusual phenomenon.

'So, George Pell was doing that,' he continued. 'I was talking to my mum. In an effort to distract her, I asked her whether she would like to meet the archbishop, and before she really responded to that, I just took over and said, "Your Grace, this is my mum," and he said in his usual manner, the usual way he spoke, "You must be very proud of your son."

'And Mum responds by saying, "I don't know about that," which is very embarrassing, of course.'

McGlone said there was 'another cleric' present with Pell at the time of this conversation. Gibson put it to him that given he had served at Solemn Masses for a decade by then, he would know the name of that cleric by Pell's side.

'Not really,' McGlone said.

Of course, these details were important, because if Pell was at the steps, he could not have been in the sacristy abusing children.

McGlone said he then excused himself from the steps and went back to tidy up the cathedral. He walked down the main nave, and back to the priests' sacristy.

'At that stage it looked like everything had been packed away,' he told the court. 'I am conscious that Max [Potter] is about.'

Gibson asked him why, in the 10 years of serving at masses every Sunday, McGlone remembered specifically what had been put away or not on this occasion when Pell said mass.

'Well,' McGlone said, 'I remember coming in and seeing, well, not seeing, you know, the chalice and ciborium, you know, those kinds of items which are sort of valuable.'

Might they have still been in the sanctuary, Gibson asked.

'No,' McGlone said, 'because I checked the sanctuary before I came in.'

Gibson asked McGlone if he had made a statement to the informant in the case, Detective Sergeant Reed, the previous week, on 21 November 2018. He confirmed that he had. Gibson asked him whether he had spoken to Jeffrey Connor before making that statement. He confirmed that he had spoken to Connor and Connor's partner. Gibson asked him how long before making the police statement he spoke to Connor, and McGlone replied that he could not remember the exact date, only that it had been some time earlier that year.

'We are 11 months into the year. Just do your best [to recall],' Gibson said. 'Give us a quarter, a quarter of the year.'

'I'm still not confident, I'm sorry,' McGlone said.

Gibson: How many times have you spoken to Connor prior to making your statement, the police statement?
McGlone: Well, I became aware of the allegations at the cathedral sometime after the committal, which I felt was a dissonance to the memory that I had with my mum. I had a pretty clear memory about what had taken place with my mum, and when

I checked my academic records it all seemed correct, but I was still not 100 per cent, because I had a clear … as a lawyer you can have a clear memory about something, but memories may be wrong. I don't doubt my memory, but I wanted some sort of external verification, and I know that Jeff [Connor] works down at St Francis because I've popped in and said hello to him previously, very, very rarely, but on occasion I'd done that before, and I asked him about the time, '96, and he then talked about that, it was just in general terms, I can't remember exactly what I asked him or spoke to him about, but just about us being servers at the time, and he said there was a photo that Ray [his partner] had, and on that I then decided to contact Ray to see if I could get a copy of, well, an image of it. I believe it was during this conversation he mentioned that Jeff kept a diary about specific dates. Now, I wanted to contact somebody in regards to all of this specific information because I thought it was relevant.

He said he had done a masters with a member of the defence team, Paul Galbally, and so, after trying but failing to make contact with Ruth Shann, he contacted him.

Kidd interjected, pointing out to Gibson, 'We are getting a long way from your actual question.'

Gibson asked McGlone why, if he was so sure of his own memory, he had sought out Connor.

'It's just, as a lawyer, you know that someone provides an account, and it's an account, it's one thing. It's always worth considering whether there's any other material relevant to that account.' When pressed about why he was so sure that he and his mother met with Pell on the first occasion Pell gave mass, McGlone replied it was because Pell had a 'celebrity status' and it was therefore memorable.

According to Connor's diary, Gibson said, Connor was the thurifer on 15 December, the first Sunday Solemn Mass that Pell was likely to have presided over as Archbishop of Melbourne. But McGlone had earlier told the court that he was the thurifer that day. Might it be that he was confusing the first and second occasions Pell said mass, Gibson asked him.

'I can't exclude that,' McGlone said, 'but I don't believe so.'

During cross-examination by Richter, the photograph that had been provided to McGlone by Connor's partner was produced and tendered as evidence. It was a photograph of all of the altar servers at the time. During questioning by Richter, McGlone said the first time that Pell said mass at the cathedral was of deep liturgical significance to him. Unlike all the other witnesses, he also told Richter that the priests' sacristy was 'a very public space, to my mind'.

In his re-examination of McGlone, Gibson asked him why, if Pell being archbishop was of such liturgical significance to him, he had not attended the Feast of Christ the King mass on the evening of 23 November 1996.

Richter objected to the question, but Kidd allowed it, saying it went to McGlone's explanation of why he was able to remember specifically the first time Pell had presided over Sunday mass.

'I never attended vigil masses,' McGlone responded. 'I don't agree with vigil masses.'

Gibson then produced another photograph, a copy of which the jurors also had. It was a photo taken of the procession into the mass during the Feast of Christ the King on Saturday 23 November 1996. He asked McGlone to look at the photograph.

'Sorry, I'm struggling to see,' McGlone said.

Gibson continued, 'Do you see yourself depicted in that photo?'

'Well,' McGlone responded, 'it does appear to be me.'

McGlone confirmed he was second from the right in the photograph, from the photographer's point of view. 'Yes, I accept that is me,' he said.

'And so, when I asked you during evidence-in-chief about the first time that you served for Archbishop Pell, this would be the first, or was there one before this occasion?' Gibson asked.

McGlone replied, 'I don't remember this one at all.'

Gibson then picked McGlone up on his comment to Richter about the priests' sacristy being a very public space.

Gibson asked McGlone if the sacristy was, in fact, off-limits to choirboys.

'I suppose that's the more honest answer,' McGlone said. He added, 'though I don't believe that I ever heard of anyone saying places are off-limits.'

Gibson: 'All right. Let me put it to you this way. Do you have any specific memory of ever seeing a chorister within the priests' sacristy?'

McGlone: 'No, I can't say that.'

With this re-examination, it seemed to me, and possibly to the jurors as well, that Gibson had expertly, methodically, and convincingly destroyed the credibility of McGlone. It created a lot of talk among the journalists. He seemed to many of us to have been revealed as an unreliable witness. Richter had asked that he be called by the prosecution, thinking his evidence would aid the defence's case. Instead, McGlone had come across as biased towards Pell and those close to him.

McGlone was interesting as well, because until now it felt like we had heard so much of the case so many times before. McGlone was new, and so was his evidence.

People who were connected enough to know the trial was taking place filed in and out of the courtroom throughout: the Jesuit priest Frank Brennan; the former deputy prime minister and ambassador to the Vatican Tim Fischer; and barristers and judges from surrounding courts who stopped by, still in their robes and wigs, to observe one of the most notable cases in memory unfold.

Chrissie Foster, who fought the Catholic Church for justice for two of her daughters who were raped by a priest, also attended regularly.

Other church supporters and priests came in and out, too, sometimes approaching the dock to shake Pell's hand and wish him well. A priest was ejected by security for being disruptive, making noises in agreement with Pell's defence team, and frequently forgetting to turn off his phone.

Some other abuse survivors and their advocates would plant themselves among the journalists, seeing them as allies, with at least one whispering their thoughts to us while witnesses were being cross-examined. I felt it put journalists in an awkward position – we were there not to take sides, but to record an important trial. I felt uncomfortable when these advocates whispered to me throughout the case, or seated themselves next to journalists. I did not want any of the parties to think I was aligned to any member of the public.

Following McGlone's testimony, Jeffrey Connor was sworn in. He had begun as an altar server at the cathedral in 1994, when he was 37 years old. He held that position until November 1997, and throughout that time kept a meticulous diary of Pell's movements. Connor's evidence was therefore crucial, and rather than video being played of his previous appearance at the mistrial, he was called to give evidence in person. Connor recorded in his diary the role he played as an altar server, such as whether he was the thurifer or cross-bearer, and he would also record the name of the person who celebrated the mass. His diary revealed that Pell was the celebrant of Sunday Solemn Mass on 15 and 22 December 1996. On 23 February 1997, the mass was celebrated by Father Brendan Egan, the diary showed, but was presided over by Pell.

'Presiding means it's the archbishop sitting in the throne, which is his chair being in the cathedral, and he would be in choir dress, not full pontifical vestments,' Connor explained to the court.

Connor said that when mass started, the doors to the sacristies were locked, and that once mass had ended, Max Potter would be the altar server designated to open them so that the other altar servers could begin clearing items away. Potter 'would be usually there waiting for us', he told the court. Connor said he did not have Pell in his sight at all times after mass.

On 27 November, David Mayes, the second-last former choirboy to give evidence, was sworn in. He said that being in the choir was a very serious affair, and he knew that violating the terms of his membership risked jeopardising his scholarship to St Kevin's – something he was constantly aware of. He told the court that Pell would sometimes come into the choir room after mass, 'in the first five minutes while everybody was still there'. He said it was rare to see Pell unrobed. He confirmed that Pell would often be on the steps after mass greeting parishioners.

Gibson asked Mayes for what period of time he would have Pell under observation after mass.

'It varied,' he replied. 'There were some times when we would exit, descend the stairs, and I might observe Pell, and we would go through and complete disrobing, and I'd go home. Sometimes I'd disrobe, then meet my parents close to the staircase, and on some of those occasions Pell was on the stairs of the cathedral talking to people.'

He said that on occasions, as the choir processed outside, it would pause before reaching the moat. 'In that case we would stand as a group,' he said. 'We were told not to fidget around or misbehave. At some point we'd be given the signal and continue on back to the change rooms.

'The longer the wait continued, the more we'd fidget and try to talk to our friends. Some of the choristers would move around a bit more. I was aware some guys would turn around and talk to their mates and make a bit of a fuss. The further away we got [from the moat], the rowdier it got … the boys would start to talk more. Some kids were probably starting to undo buttons from their robes. It was definitely less orderly than earlier in the procession. It was Sunday, and we were keen to get home.'

Gibson asked him if Pell ever popped into the choristers' disrobing room.

> Mayes: I have a memory of him coming into the room at one point, but I can't recall when.
> Gibson: Was he robed or unrobed?
> Mayes: It was very rare to see him unrobed. He would have been robed.
> Gibson: Accompanied or unaccompanied?
> Mayes: I can't say.

Richter asked Mayes whether the priests' sacristy would be open or closed when the choir lined up to process into the main part of the cathedral before mass.

> Mayes: I have memories of it being open and sometimes seeing priests or staff inside.
> Richter: You'd certainly hear them?
> Mayes: I wouldn't say I'd hear them.
> Richter: You could see probably halfway into the room, couldn't you?
> Mayes: No … you couldn't really see into the rooms by the way the doors were left open … the rooms were a mystery.

The police informant in the case, Detective Sergeant Christopher Reed, was the last witness to give evidence, and concluded his testimony on 28 November 2018. His evidence was interrupted by the swearing in and questioning of former choirboy Andrew

La Greca, whose evidence was much the same as he gave in the mistrial. La Greca told the court that as the choir processed outside the cathedral, its orderliness disintegrated somewhat. He also told the court that Pell would 'sometimes … just wait and speak to the congregation … other times he might have just kept on walking with us. I can't recall exactly.'

Toward the beginning of Reed's evidence, the 45-minute video of his interview with Cardinal George Pell in Rome was played to the jury; the lights were turned off, the big screen was rolled down on the wall opposite the jurors, and the recording was played in the same way it had been to jurors in the mistrial.

Eight months after the interview, Reed confirmed to the court, Pell was charged.

While questioning Reed, Gibson read from the complainant's police statement, including a passage that said: 'My mate … and I were poking around after church. There was this little room where I presume the archbishop got changed within his quarters in the cathedral. The room was towards the back of the cathedral, towards the area where the choir sat. This was along the route we took to go to the changing room and there were a couple of older chamber-style rooms along there. The room we were poking about in on that day was one of those rooms.'

As he had done in the mistrial, Reed confirmed that the other victim had died in accidental circumstances. Reed again said that he interviewed the boy's mother, and that she confirmed that, before he died, her son denied having been abused.

When Gibson stood to give his closing address before the new jury on Monday 3 November, he made it clear to them that he was not inviting speculation. He told the jurors that Richter wanted them to think the offending was impossible, improbable, and fantastical.

Even more meticulously than he had done in the mistrial, he walked the jurors through the allegations step by step, laboriously citing transcript page numbers and references as he went, so that all his statements that counteracted Richter's could be supported.

Gibson told the jurors that the trial came down to three critical issues.

'One, whether Cardinal Pell remained at the steps for an extended period of time, which would have effectively nullified, or removed, any opportunity for him to have been back at his sacristy when the offence is said to have occurred,' he said.

'Two, whether there was opportunity after mass for [the] two choristers to separate from the procession, or whether the procession was like a hermetically sealed pack of people from which there could be no escape until inside their building.

'And three, whether Cardinal Pell entered his divesting room alone as opposed to being in the presence of someone, and remained in that room uninterrupted by anyone. A lot of the focus in this trial has been directed to what witnesses recall about those three topics. The evidence from witnesses has varied to varying degrees on all of these topics, and more.

'But can I say this. On these three topics, the Crown case is that, firstly, it's entirely possible that on the occasion of that first incident described by [the complainant], as opposed to the other Sunday masses said by Cardinal Pell during his five-year tenure as archbishop at St Patrick's Cathedral, it's entirely possible that Archbishop Pell did not remain on the steps for an extended period of time.'

He argued that while many practices, such as standing on the steps and greeting parishioners after mass evolved over time, these procedures had not yet been established on the first occasions Pell said mass as archbishop, when the offending was said to have occurred.

'The Crown case is that, secondly, it's entirely possible that on the occasion of the first incident, there was ample opportunity when the procession group got to the toilet corridor, for two choristers to detach themselves from the rest of the group without being noticed ... with regard to the confined nature of that toilet corridor being descended upon by 33 young sopranos. That's 16 rows of young sopranos, and 28 other choristers; tenors, altos, basses, and a further 14 pairs. So that's a total of 61 choristers, or some 30 rows if it's two by two, all of whom have had a long morning, and the flow-on effect that that would have had on the procession as a whole. And more importantly, on the ability of those within the procession, like Finnigan and Rodney Dearing, to keep track of every chorister at that point.

'The Crown case is that, thirdly, it's entirely possible that at the moment that Cardinal Pell set foot in that sacristy, not when he was walking back, but when he entered the sacristy room on the occasion of the first incident, that he was on his own and remained uninterrupted ...

'You'll recall that at the outset, during my learned friend's opening address, he put forward a number of improbabilities and impossibilities. What the Crown says is that upon proper scrutiny of the evidence, [the complainant's] account stands. The day of the first incident, whether it be the 15th of December or the 22nd of December 1996, or whatever day in the second half of 1996 it occurred, the evidence suggests that [the boys] did detach from the procession group. The evidence suggests that Archbishop Pell had left the front steps, that he had returned to his sacristy in a period shortly after [the boys] had entered it, and he had entered the sacristy alone and unaccompanied, and remained so for a period of time. And those things can be satisfied beyond reasonable doubt.'

Early into his closing address, Gibson spoke about the reliability of memory, asking jurors to consider using their own experiences about which types of elements from past events they might remember and which sorts of details they might forget.

'The good thing about having juries decide these sorts of criminal cases is that collectively you bring together a breadth of experience and common sense, and knowledge and understanding of just how things work in the world, much more than any one person can bring to a task,' Gibson told them.

'And we all know how memory works because we all have the ability to remember, and we all have the ability not to remember.

'Considering the evidence of [the complainant], I'd invite you to view his recorded evidence again. It's been three or so weeks since you've last seen it. When you're considering the evidence of all the other witnesses, I'd ask you to consider these things. Firstly, whether the topic spoken about was a matter of routine, something that took place frequently; whether it was a protocol, for example; whether it was a topic that you would expect someone would recall with clarity; [and] whether it was a topic that stood out in the person's mind which would cause that person to remember.'

Gibson pointed out that when the complainant was asked how far he was from the other boy when Pell was assaulting the boy, 'he closed his eyes as though to think back to that time'. He did this again when Richter asked him which hand Pell used to push him against the wall during the second incident.

'And again, he closed his eyes, thinking back, in my submission to you, trying to recount the actual circumstance about which he was being asked,' Gibson told the jurors. 'And in that case he said, "I'm not certain what hand."

'Those things are cues, if you like, in terms of determining his honesty and reliability as a witness,' Gibson told them. If he had been lying, he would have just made up the distance he was from the other boy; would have just guessed the hand Pell used to grope him. Instead, he tried genuinely to think back and answer the question, and when he couldn't, was honest that he could not.

'Did he have the sort of memory blanks you would expect to have about unimportant details or peripheral matters, the sorts of things you'd expect a person not to recall with clarity given the passage of time, and given their lack of significance to the actual event itself? Alternatively, ask yourselves, did he come across as a dishonest witness, a person who is gilding the lily, a person who is embellishing things at every opportunity that he had, making things up, exaggerating things, plugging holes when he could, putting a positive spin on things and recounting peripheral matters when you wouldn't expect a person to be able to do that?'

The Crown believed Pell was guilty beyond reasonable doubt of the five charges, Gibson told the jurors, because of the 'powerful and persuasive evidence' of the complainant, and because his evidence fitted with the overall evidence of the other witnesses.

Addressing the issue of the date on which the offending occurred, Gibson explained that 'you wouldn't expect' him to be able to cite a date without a record or diary.

'In his first police statement, in June of 2015, you will recall that he said he thought it was the spring after Archbishop Pell had been installed as archbishop. And, interestingly, you will recall that Mr McGlone, in recalling the same time period, stated he had served Archbishop Pell, he said, in the months October through to December. So not dissimilar to what [the complainant] is saying. He said spring, and we know that two masses were said in December 1996 by Pell, and one was presided over in February 1997, more than a month after the December masses. So charges one to four reflect that evidence.'

Gibson pointed out that according to the prepared statement that Pell read to police in Rome, he thought he celebrated mass regularly after becoming archbishop, even though records shown to the court revealed that he in fact travelled a lot during the early months, and did not always celebrate Sunday mass.

'We submit to you, [this is] a good example of how people focus on the overall impression of something, or the overall routine that you're doing, rather than a specific occurrence of something happening,' Gibson said. 'Similar, we submit, to the way in which a lot of witnesses gave their evidence in this trial, focusing on the overall effect rather than a specific incident. So the upshot is that in terms of this first incident, said by [the complainant] to have occurred in the second half of 1996, there is evidence before you that there were two Sunday masses celebrated by Cardinal Pell in the second half of 1996, if you accept Mr McGlone, and Mr Connor, and Monsignor Portelli, as to when the first incident could have taken place.

'The 3rd, 10th, and 17th of November are unaccounted for in Connor's diary, but seem to be accounted for by Monsignor Portelli, who seemed to have an excellent memory in cross-examination as to where Cardinal Pell said mass on those dates; but not as good a memory in re-examination when, you'll recall, I asked him to recount where Cardinal Pell had said mass on the 10th and 17th of November, without being told or without him having the list in front of him. And you'll remember that. He said, "Well, I cannot say without you telling me, or without the list in front of me."

'If Mr Connor and Mr McGlone are correct, then this case is somewhat unusual, you might think, in that 22 years later it can actually be pinpointed. This case can actually be pinpointed to a particular fortnight. I'll call it either the 15th or 22nd of December is when this first incident occurred.'

After establishing dates when the abuse could have occurred, Gibson walked the jurors through how it occurred. On one of these two dates in December, the choir exited the cathedral via the main entrance, or the western entrance, walked down the front steps and turned left, walking two-by-two through a solid metal gate, Gibson told them. They then passed the south transept entrance, and made their way around to a corridor where there was an iron gate and the public toilets, and, finally, passed through glass doors back into the building.

'It was at some point during the processional journey, before going back through the glass door in that toilet corridor, that [the two boys] are said to have broken away from the procession,' Gibson said.

Gibson reminded the jurors that, in his evidence, the complainant had told the court, 'We sort of broke away from the main choir group. It was sort of scattered and a bit chaotic, as a bunch of kids are after a mass. And we managed to separate ourselves away from that group. I don't recall specifically when we broke away, away from the choir group.'

Gibson reminded the jurors that they broke away from the procession before the abuse occurred. Surely it was reasonable, he said, that the abuse that came after, and not the processing out of the building, was what stuck more clearly in the complainant's mind.

'Use your own experience about matters in your own life, or lives, from years ago, and ask is that the sort of thing you may well not recall, exactly at what point you broke away from a group when seeking to be mischievous, which is what he said they were doing at that point. Why would you remember it specifically? This is minutes before the abuse is commenced ... he hasn't turned his mind to it [the point at which he broke away from the procession] until being cross-examined about it at the preliminary, or committal, hearing in March of this year. And there's good reason not to turn your mind to it, given it's insignificant compared to the actual traumatic event itself.'

The complainant had simply told the court in his evidence, Gibson reminded them, that he broke away at some point, and that point was when all the restraints of the choir were starting to break down.

'Moreover, do you really think that young choristers, like the ones that we heard from in this trial, given their age, would remember two choristers breaking away from a group at that point, given that they weren't caught?' Gibson asked. 'There was no kerfuffle that went on from Mr Finnigan, or Rodney Dearing, or any of the adult servers. You might think that if there was a kerfuffle about it, that they'd have been caught and reprimanded or chastised, that there would be a reason for choristers or anyone else for that matter to remember it. But not when you've successfully snuck off.

'We know that the congregation was leaving and therefore adding distraction to the dynamics of the situation, consciously or unconsciously. Secondly, we know that tourists, according to some witnesses, would be in that south transept area taking photos. We know that parents would be waiting by the moat and by the metal gate near the public toilets, and that tourists would be milling around the south transept area immediately after mass. We also heard that most of the people were around the water features. So you have people, parents around the gate area, the toilet gate area around the water feature, you have tourists, you have the congregation leaving, adding to all the distractions which might explain, in answer to that very question that was asked by my learned friend in cross-examination, might explain why those two choristers were not noticed detaching from the group.'

Rather than being impossible, there was in fact ample opportunity for two choristers to go back into the building, being unnoticed in the scheme of the wider crowd. It was not improbable at all, Gibson said. Witnesses gave evidence that the south transept doors the boys went through to re-enter the building were often open to allow the congregation to leave the cathedral. At this time, it was likely Cox or Mallinson was still playing the organ.

Having detached from the procession and gone through the double doors, a couple of the boys decided to have some fun. 'You might think that the idea of having some fun at that point in time is perfectly understandable for two 13-year-old boys after having rehearsed since 9.30 in the morning, then singing for an hour, maybe a little bit longer, until just after midday,' Gibson said. 'That's over two-and-half hours of required discipline, and then perhaps the prospect of having to attend another rehearsal for Christmas carols or for the recording of a CD or a tape; this heavy schedule that confronted the boys may have provided the very incentive to nick off and have some fun, just as [the complainant] said they were doing.'

McGlone had told the court that the only sacristy that was ever locked was the archbishop's, though he would not have known it was accepted evidence that Pell was not using the archbishop's sacristy at the time due to renovations it was undergoing. Other witnesses said that the priests' sacristy that Pell was using at the time would be locked during mass, but that Potter would unlock the door and open it as mass ended in preparation for the archbishop and the returning of items to the sacristy. Potter and Portelli both gave evidence to this effect.

'At this point in time, the Crown would say, the accused man, Cardinal Pell, is leaving the front steps of the cathedral, having paused for a short time to speak with parishioners as they are exiting,' Gibson said. 'So let me say something about the front steps of the cathedral, where it is said that Cardinal Pell would meet and greet.

'Much has been made as to the duration of the meet-and-greet at the front of the cathedral, but remember that this is at an early stage of his tenure as archbishop. We know that practices and protocols did develop over the years, 1996 to 2001, the five-year period that he was archbishop at St Patrick's – of course they did – but these masses when this first incident occurred in 1996 are at a time, to use the expression of Portelli, when there were a number of bugs in the system that needed ironing out.

'So when you are considering the issue of him standing around the steps or even considering the issue of him being accompanied into that sacristy, consider whether practices had developed at this early stage. As you know, a practice is by definition something that develops over time. And little time had passed.

'The second point I make is that the meet-and-greet could be as little as a couple of minutes.' Pell, in his recorded interview with police, said himself that the length of time he would spend on the steps would vary.

The complainant had said the abuse occurred in the priests' sacristy, not the archbishop's sacristy, and evidence had comprehensively shown that the archbishop's sacristy was not in use at the time the offending was said to have occurred. How would the complainant have known this if he was making the abuse up, Gibson asked the jurors, especially given that both sacristies were off-limits to choirboys? Not only that, but the complainant had accurately described the room, not as it was at the time of the trial, but as it was back in 1996, as supported by photographs and evidence from people such as Potter and Portelli.

Gibson said that after unlocking the sacristy prior to the archbishop's return, Potter wouldn't immediately go in to start cleaning up after mass. Gibson told the jurors, 'There would be a suitable interval that decorum would require in the order of half [a minute] to two minutes before Potter would attend the sanctuary and start cleaning up.'

'[T]his interval in ritualistic procedure, between the unlocking of the priests' sacristy door and the bowing to the crucifix which we heard about, and the commencement of the ferrying of the sacred vessels, is when the incident took place, as [the two boys] enter the room and shortly thereafter Archbishop Pell enters the room.

'So I am simply making the submission that, contrary to it being impossible or highly improbable, the evidence seems to support the notion that there is this hiatus, this gap, during which the offending occurred.'

The boys entered the room and began looking around, noticing to their left a wooden-panelled area resembling a storage kitchenette. In the cupboard of this kitchenette, they found a bottle of wine and began to drink from it.

Even if the jurors were to accept Richter's proposal that the complainant may have gone on a tour and been shown the inside of the sacristy when he started with the choir, it did not explain how he was able to remember the intricacies of such a room, such as where the alcove was, and where the wine was kept.

Gibson mentioned the fact that Portelli was a 20-cigarette-per-day smoker. He referred to witnesses who said Pell was not always accompanied. Perhaps Portelli had left Pell before returning into the cathedral to have a cigarette after sitting through the hour-or-more-long mass, Gibson suggested to the jurors. There were also witnesses, he said, who suggested they could not say for certain that Pell was never on his own.

Kidd, during a break, asked Gibson to correct this statement about Portelli smoking, because there was no evidence that he had smoked during or after mass, or on the cathedral grounds.

After admitting his error to the jurors, Gibson quoted from the complainant's evidence, reading out his description of Pell entering the room and abusing the boys.

Gibson told the jurors that the complainant was clearly confused about what had happened, and believed he would be in significant trouble if anyone found out. With his parents divorcing, the last thing he would be expected to do, Gibson told the jurors, was to confess he had broken away from the choir, snuck into a sacristy, drunk wine, and been caught by Pell. He was aware, acutely, that being in any sort of trouble could jeopardise the prestigious scholarship that he and his parents, who lived in the working-class suburbs of Melbourne, so valued.

'And so he doesn't complain,' Gibson told the jurors.

The complainant had told the court that 'coming forward took courage much later on for me to even think about coming forward'.

Gibson asked the jurors to consider how things work in the 'real world'. 'Do you really think a 13-year-old boy would be discussing this sort of thing with [the other boy] or warning him about such a thing after it happened to [him] a second time?'

The jurors should also not take the denials of the other boy, when asked by his parents whether he had been abused, as evidence that it did not happen, Gibson said. Reasons such as embarrassment, shame, or a desire to protect his parents and not wanting to burden them might all have contributed to his unwillingness to confide in them, Gibson told the jurors. 'Perhaps he did not want to perceive himself a victim, or be considered less than manly,' he said.

Gibson said the second assault, when the complainant had his genitals squeezed by Pell briefly as he passed him in the church corridor, again after Sunday mass, was 'brief'. Gibson said the jurors should ignore Pell's 'emphatic denials' that this occurred. Pell had also said he never had anything to do with choirboys, Gibson reminded them, and yet several witnesses said Pell would often stop by the choir room to speak to the boys after mass.

Gibson told the jurors that they should exclude beyond reasonable doubt the denials given by Pell in his formal interview with police.

'The archbishop was using the priests' sacristy and had reason to be in there at that time. I ask you to return a verdict of guilty in each of the five charges.'

It was a thorough, powerful, and easy-to-follow closing address.

On 4 December 2018, Richter once again moved the lectern to the head of the bar table so that he could face the jurors. He began,

'Two of you will be balloted out before you go to the jury room to consider your verdict, and I don't know which of you will be chosen, unfortunately, because you've sat here patiently and listened to everything, and have taken part in the discussions in the jury room and the like, and the two of you who are balloted out will no doubt feel let down in some way. But I don't want to talk to you individually. I want to talk to you as a group.'

Once again, Richter had little use for notes.

He described the allegations to the jurors by saying, 'There are episodes of dropping pants or opening pants, or whatever, and some mutual masturbation taking place. There is a time when the three of them, according to [the complainant], are fixing themselves up, and then they leave, or at least, [the boys] leave. I calculate that the best estimate I can make is at least six minutes it would take for all that. For those six minutes, I want you to ask yourselves: where is Portelli, Potter, the altar servers, the other clergy, including the dean of the cathedral?

'And those six minutes take place in a time span that has encompassed the procession that's going out, and Archbishop Pell is standing on the stairs, or just down the bottom of the stairs greeting congregants. Where are they? That is issue number one. I tell you why it is an issue. Because the learned prosecutor has made it an issue. He has given you what you might have perceived as a measured address. He has been calm, he has told you what the Crown case is, but he's made mistakes. He has made some mistakes that are pretty grievous, in my humble opinion. He had the grace to own up to one yesterday, and that was that he was trying to plant in your mind the notion that Monsignor Portelli had somehow created the opportunity by having a smoke outside.

'You will recall the evidence of Monsignor Portelli [that he] did not smoke during mass and the aftermath of mass. It would be like having His Honour go out in the street, robed as he is, and lighting up a cigarette. It's unthinkable. The learned prosecutor had the grace to say that he was wrong, but there were other things that were wrong, completely wrong in what he said.'

But before getting to those errors, Richter asked the jurors to consider the mental state of Pell back when he was an archbishop.

'Who in their right mind – and no one has questioned the mind of Cardinal Pell – who in their right mind would take the risk of doing what [the complainant] says happened? Who in their right mind would do it? Did the archbishop have some kind of mental breakdown? Who would take the risk, knowing what the archbishop knows about the protocols of the Catholic Church?

'And because of an archbishop knowing the liturgical significance, knowing the evangelical significance of his position, knowing what it entails in terms of how positions are formulated, how protocols are carried out, [why would he] assume that for six minutes or so, no one would come into a room, which is an open room?'

Richter described Gibson's explanation that protocols were still being developed as a 'half-hearted' explanation. Mass was a liturgical drama, a performance, Richter told the jury.

'This is a grand, religious, theological opera, orchestrated ... Who in his right mind would take the risk?'

Mass did not finish when the archbishop stood on the steps greeting parishioners, Richter said. It continued until all of the sacred vessels had been returned, until all of the parishioners had left. That Pell would take such a risk while on show was beyond belief.

'The possibility has to be a real possibility, not a theoretical possibility,' Richter said. 'Like the possibility someone might blow up this courtroom. We do not conduct our lives on theoretical possibilities, and we don't decide the fate of a fellow human being on the basis of something being a possibility.'

It was fanciful that Pell would stumble upon two boys he didn't really know and assault them, Richter continued.

'The other furphy is this,' he told the jury. 'There has been evidence along the lines of *We got to the corridor and we're just terribly relieved. And we just want to get rid of our robes and go home.* But they can't be thinking that. Why? Because there's a choir rehearsal to take place immediately after mass on both the 15th and 22nd, so they can't be thinking, *Oh, great, we're all finished, we throw off our robes and get out as soon as we can.'*

He described the complainant's allegations as 'fanciful', and reminded the jurors that it was not up to the defence to prove Pell's innocence or to prove that the complainant had a psychological condition that would lead to him making things up.

'The fact is, we don't know,' Richter said. 'What we know is that the archbishop says it's a fantasy, and it [the complainant's story] may well have evolved over a number of years and have been embellished to a point where, for example, he might start believing it.'

Pell had answered all of the questions put to him by detectives, he reminded the jurors. In considering all of this evidence, the jury had been 'given a very untasty dish to digest', he told them. 'But you have to because that is your sworn duty.'

Next, Richter did something that was new compared to the mistrial. He used the large screen, the same one that the video evidence of witnesses had been played on, and began a PowerPoint presentation.

A slide flashed onto the screen. In large text, it read: 'ONLY A MADMAN WOULD ATTEMPT TO RAPE TWO BOYS IN THE PRIESTS' SACRISTY IMMEDIATELY AFTER SUNDAY SOLEMN MASS.' Richter left the slide on the screen for jurors to stare at, as he continued.

'There's nothing that would preclude the boys from running out and wailing and screaming,' he said. 'The next aspect of the madman theory is there is nothing to prevent one boy from running and screaming from the room while the other is under attack. How would Pell know that was not going to happen? How would he know the other boy wouldn't be running out of the room raising the alarm or running away in tears?' He said it was ridiculous to think that Pell would somehow have been overcome with sexual urges so strong that he would take the risk of assaulting two boys in the sacristy. 'I don't know that the saying of mass is a particularly sexually stimulating subject,' Richter said.

As he had done in the mistrial, Richter made the point about Pell being similar to the Queen, who was never left alone during public ceremonies. Like the Queen, there were people charged with looking after Pell, he said.

Richter took the entire day, and still had not finished his closing address. When court resumed on Tuesday 5 December, but before the jurors were brought into the room, Richter told the legal parties and Kidd that he intended to show the jurors a 19-minute video animation. This animation would show the movements of various people, including Pell, the procession, the boys, and various members of the clergy in the cathedral. What followed was a lengthy discussion between the parties as to whether the animation should be allowed or not.

Ultimately, Kidd ruled that it could not be shown. It is impermissible for new material to be introduced during the closing-address stage of a trial. At that point, the parties sum up their cases, based only on the evidence they and the jurors have had the opportunity to see. In this instance, Kidd ruled, there would be a real risk that the jury might perceive the video as evidence. He told the parties that the video was not CCTV footage, was not necessarily an accurate account of the movements of people, and that there was a risk that the jurors might not realise this. 'Whilst everyone has given their pictorial account of things, they're necessarily imperfect and incomplete, and I just don't think you can do this cartoon-like slicing of every minute or thirty seconds, because the evidence just doesn't support that.'

With his animation having been kiboshed, Richter asked the jurors, when they returned, to consider 'where, at every minute', the choir and members of the clergy were after the mass, as the procession left the church.

'When you go out to the jury room, we would ask you to do this,' Richter continued. 'Take a slice of time from the end of mass and going to, let's say, 15 minutes past the end of mass. Ask yourself where at every moment the principal participants in this drama are. Where, at every minute, Archbishop Pell is. Where, at every minute, Monsignor Portelli is.

'It can't have happened. There was no opportunity for it to happen. And if you were to come down to one witness in respect of that, you would say Monsignor Portelli proves that it can't have happened. It just could not have happened; unless we have some reason to doubt his credibility, his accuracy, his veracity, his honesty. His evidence alone would cause you to return a verdict of not guilty.'

'I want to ask you something, and you need not answer, because you're not allowed to talk to me. When you came to take your seats in the jury box, and you looked at the accused, you looked at George Pell, who, in some sense, is the third-most important person in the Vatican. He was minister for the economy, he was secretary to the economy of the Vatican. That's like the treasurer. Did you say to yourself, *This man is innocent*? I bet you didn't.

'You would have had to have been living on the moon not to have realised who Cardinal Pell is when you came in. But the real question is, did you come in and say, *Okay, this man is innocent. Now, let's wait and see the proof that he's guilty*'?

'You didn't get such proof. All you had was a sequence of possibilities.'

Richter alerted the jurors to the fact that Pell had been allowed to challenge the jurors as they were selected, when their ballot numbers and occupations were read out.

'You noticed you were picked without any challenges at all. You were the first 14 people that were chosen; no one was challenged. And the reason no one is challenged is that we repose enormous faith and trust in your own integrity, in your own consciences. What you do will be between you and your conscience. No one can ask you how you arrived at a certain conclusion. But our system would be a complete failure if someone on the jury had decided not to disclose that they had some preconceived notion.

'And what that means is, as I said right at the beginning, this is not a trial of the Catholic Church or what happens in the Catholic Church. You will simply be asked whether, on the totality of the evidence, you are persuaded beyond reasonable doubt that the cardinal is guilty. Whatever verdict you come to will be answerable to no one. No one can ever ask you anything about it. Unlike American jurors who go on TV and give interviews, we're prohibited from doing anything of the kind. Our system depends on jurors like you acting fairly. So, I ask for a verdict of not guilty. Thank you.'

Richter finished at about 3.00 pm, having taken almost two full days to deliver his closing address.

As he had done in the mistrial, Judge Kidd then began reading out his comprehensive list of directions to the jurors, taking until late into the afternoon of Wednesday 6 December to finish his orders, telling the jurors not to look to him for hints as to how to decide the case. 'Only you must decide this case,' he said. 'It has absolutely nothing to do with me.' He told the jurors that, while they had to follow his directions about legal matters, they were not bound by any comments he made about the case. It was entirely up to them as to whether they wanted to believe all, none, or some of a witness's evidence.

'In order to convict, you must be satisfied beyond reasonable doubt the account of [the complainant] is true,' he told them. 'That is, the offences, as described by him, actually happened. It follows that it is clearly not enough that you think that this account is merely possible or even probable. These are criminal charges, so you are required to accept his account beyond reasonable doubt before you can convict.

'You must not be influenced by any emotions which you may feel by the fact that the accused man, George Pell, is a cardinal of the Catholic Church, evidently a very senior member of the Catholic Church, and you must not, in any way, be influenced by any knowledge of child sexual abuse allegations within the Catholic Church. Nor should you be influenced by any knowledge of suggestions of cover-ups within the Catholic Church. It has got nothing to do with this trial. Such emotions just play no part in your decision.

'You must not scapegoat Cardinal Pell.'

Before the jury retired to consider its verdict, two jurors were balloted off. Four women and eight men remained, including the church pastor and the secondary school teacher. And then, once again, we had to wait, roaming the corridors outside the courtroom as the jury deliberated. An unlikely collective of people – journalists, Pell supporters, and abuse-survivor advocates – paced the corridor and filled the meeting rooms outside the courtroom as they had once before, in the mistrial. Pell and members of his legal team shut themselves away once again in the tiny room. Richter and Shann, Gibson and Ellis, and Kidd returned to their chambers.

After three-and-a-half days, on Tuesday 11 December 2018, word came that the jurors were done. A verdict had been reached. This was stunning news. There would not be another hung jury. This time, they had all agreed without needing to return to the courtroom to tell the judge they were struggling.

On the surface, Pell's legal team looked relaxed as they took their seats at the bar table. Minutes later, it was hard for Richter to conceal his shock. His client had been found guilty of one count of sexually penetrating a 13-year-old boy and four counts of sexually assaulting two 13-year-old boys.

Pell did not react to the verdict, staring straight ahead from the dock. The room was silent as the foreperson told the court that the jury had found Pell guilty on all charges, repeating the word 'Guilty' five times. The jurors looked calm. This was in stark contrast to the behaviour of the previous jury, many of whom had looked strained.

Richter's confident demeanour evaporated. His voice barely rose above a whisper as he discussed bail requirements and a sentencing date with the judge. He looked as though he felt sick.

Many in the room joined in the defence counsel's disbelief. Doubts of a conviction being recorded had been partly driven by the outcome of the first trial. And only the jurors and legal teams had seen the victim's evidence, which was critical to the prosecution's case.

This meant that the only evidence journalists had heard was from a number of former choirboys and from former church staff who had not witnessed the alleged offences occur, and who often struggled to recall details about the church, Sunday Solemn Masses, and the movements of Pell and the choirboys more than two decades after the fact.

So, when the verdict came, the room was still. No one made a sound.

There was nothing journalists could do but alert their editors. We could not publish a word about it, or share the verdict as breaking news on social media. In many ways, it was also anti-climactic. While editors were aware that journalists were in the court covering the story, there was no urgency or constant pressing for information, because a suppression order remained in place until the Swimmers' trial was held. Kidd allowed Pell to remain out of jail until sentencing in February 2020, because he was booked in for knee surgery later in the month. Pell had relinquished his passport and was not deemed a flight risk, and prosecutors had no objection to Pell remaining out of prison until the court reconvened for sentencing.

Kidd addressed the jurors for a final time. One journalist I spoke to said that Kidd looked shocked, but I felt that the judge's demeanour was impossible to read.

'Thank you very much, members of the jury, for the work that you have done on this case,' he told them. 'I make no comment whatsoever about your verdict. It wouldn't be appropriate for me to do so. That's your decision, and your decision alone.

'The work you have done over the last several weeks has been noticed by us all, and in particular over the last few days you have obviously all worked diligently towards your verdicts in accordance with your oath. So I am really thanking you for all the hard work you have done in listening to the evidence, in assessing the evidence, and then deliberating.'

As he had done for the jurors in the mistrial, he excused them from performing jury service for a decade.

'My advice to you, and really my direction to you, is that your deliberations in the jury room remain confidential. At the end of the day, it is only you 12 who were in that jury room and who reached this decision, and talking about the way in which you reached that decision will get you nowhere, and in fact I have little doubt [that] if you start talking about it in a social environment you just won't win, you will never be able to win, because they just weren't in that room.'

I often found myself considering those words from the judge in the weeks that followed.

I asked Richter, once court was adjourned and he rose from his seat to leave the room, whether he would appeal the verdict. He responded, 'Absolutely,' and hurried towards his client to offer some words of consolation.

Seconds later, before I had even left the courtroom myself, my mobile phone vibrated with a message from a child sexual abuse lawyer, a contact of mine, who had not been at the trial.

'Is it true?' it read.

The suppression order remained in place. But the word was already out.

CHAPTER TEN

Martyr

'I was angry inside. I felt like my son's life was wasted. Why was
it wasted for some guy's two minutes of pleasure? It's not easy to
describe, it's not even easy to even stand here and talk. It's stuff
that destroys families, it destroys people.'

— The father of the deceased choirboy

Two days after the verdict was delivered, a hastily organised hearing
was held in the County Court. The chief judge's calm, considered
demeanour was gone: Kidd was seething.

Some media companies had been unable to resist hinting at the
news of the verdict they had learned from their reporters and other
sources that had emerged from the court. The cardinal had been
found guilty on every charge. He would be sentenced. He would be
going to jail. News organisations, including those that had not sent
a single reporter to cover the trial for even a day, were desperate to
grab hold of the story, even though the only detail they had was the
fact of a guilty verdict.

They tried to skirt around the suppression order that had first
been issued by Kidd on 25 June 2018, which had been applied for
by the prosecution to prevent 'a real and substantial risk of prejudice
to the proper administration of justice'. In their application to the
court, prosecutors had said they wanted a prohibition on publication
of any part of the trial, and that it should apply within all states

and territories of Australia, and on any website or other electronic or broadcast format accessible within Australia. The suppression order issued by Kidd meant that the only detail about the case that the media were allowed to report was the fact that Pell was facing historical child sexual abuse offences. We could not report the number of charges, the nature of them, and the fact that there were two trials involved, the Cathedral and Swimmers' trials.

Every journalist who had attended the court to cover the trials, and most of their editors, including my own, understood the importance of the suppression order, and adhered strictly to it. But before long, other reporters began weighing in with messages on Twitter about suppression orders, spoke on radio programs about a high-profile man 'they could not name' having been convicted, and attempted to be part of, and to get the first story out on, a complex case they knew little about. The journalists who had spent months of their lives in the trial, working long days and taking hundreds of pages of notes, could not respond and did not respond. We knew that doing so risked being found in contempt of court – a serious charge – and because we had been present at the trials, we understood the repercussions to everyone more acutely. The warnings that Kidd had issued to jurors almost daily rung in our ears, too.

Importantly, we respected the parties – including the judge, the prosecution, the defence, and the complainant. This story was not about us. We were there to report on the facts, but only when doing so would no longer jeopardise the administration of justice. Other reporters, in their fight to be first, did not care about this. They did not care that victims awaiting their hearing in court for the Swimmers' trial risked having their trial jeopardised. They did not care that Pell's chances of receiving a fair hearing during the Swimmers' trial was being jeopardised because of their cryptic and, at times, incorrect and foolish commentary. The roughly eight or so journalists who had attended the entirety of the trials watched this circus from the sidelines. We consoled each other, in utter disbelief that we were the only reporters who were truly informed and yet could not correct the record.

As more media outlets apparently broke the suppression order, trying to convince themselves they were not crossing the line, the pressure began to build from our own newsrooms and editors. They were justifiably concerned that if the suppression order were to be suddenly lifted, we would be ill-prepared. When they phoned us to ask whether and when the order might be lifted, we would reply that there was no way Kidd would lift the order while Pell was facing another trial. But this did little to ease their concerns as more reporters tweeted and the online stories grew. There was concern from some newsrooms that once a suppression order was widely broken, it could no longer be deemed effective, and therefore it would no longer be reasonable to adhere to it, or illegal to break it. What if Kidd held a midnight hearing and suddenly lifted the order, knowing that the battle to control the media had been lost, our editors asked us. What if others ran the story overseas? But the few reporters representing overseas news organisations in the trial would not break the suppression order. Other overseas organisations might have found out about the verdict, but they would have no feasible way of getting any detail from the court. You had to be there.

Because we understood the legal context, and had spent months seeing how the judge, the defence, and the prosecution worked, we trial reporters tried to reassure our editors that Kidd would not suddenly lift the suppression order, and that even if he did, he would give us warning. Exacerbating matters was the fact that we could not pretend to know when, even roughly, the order might be lifted. We knew it would not be anytime soon – certainly not in hours or even days. But, of course, some senior (and usually male) journalists who had tapped into the rumour mill began calling our editors.

And when journalists with much more influence and higher profiles than the mostly mid- or early-career journalists covering the trial told the heads of newsrooms that the suppression order might break at any second, a persistent pressure emerged, tinged with panic and urgency.

The pressure put on the journalists covering the case became enormous, coming from all angles. We were asked to immediately prepare features, news stories, and analysis, ready to run the moment the suppression order broke. Of course, we already had enough material to write stories, and had already begun doing so while in court – getting stories ready and prepared for all situations was our job. But we knew it would be months before we could publish them, because the Swimmers' trial was still to come. Even if that trial were to be cancelled, as had been rumoured, it would take weeks for the legal parties to put their reasoning together, to apply for a court date, and for the matter to be heard.

I remember having to leave important commitments long outside of work hours many times during the weeks that followed because of rumours that the suppression order would be lifted imminently. I cut my commitments short, and made frantic phone calls to quash rumours I knew weren't true. It is the way that journalism goes, but I was growing increasingly fatigued, burned out, and frustrated. If anyone were to hear of an impending lift of the suppression order, it would be the journalists who had been covering the case. The court's media officers had worked very carefully with the attending reporters. While Kidd never acknowledged us, he knew we were there. He saw us typing each day in the courtroom. There was a huge part of me that wanted to believe he respected our diligence as much as we respected his, and that he would not screw us over by lifting the suppression order in the middle of the night without notice.

But it seemed that all of our efforts in the court had come

undone. In less than two days after the verdict was handed down, News Corp's *The Australian* and the *Herald Sun*, *The Age*, Macquarie Media, Nine News in Melbourne, an ABC radio program outside Melbourne, and Private Media's *Crikey* reported on the verdict in various ways. The *Herald Sun* published a black front page with the word CENSORED in large white letters emblazoned over it. 'The world is reading a very important story that is relevant to Victorians,' the paper said. 'The *Herald Sun* is prevented from publishing details of this very significant news. But trust us, it's a story you deserve to read.' *The Age* reported that 'a very high-profile figure was convicted on Tuesday of a serious crime, but we are unable to report their identity due to a suppression order'. (Although reporters from the *Herald Sun* and *The Age* were both at the trial, those reporters did not author these stories.) International news sites published the verdict, but some did not geo-block their stories from being read in Australia.

There was always a risk that international media outlets, untouchable by Australian laws, would run the story and the verdict. But their stories were, of course, lacking in detail. To argue that the suppression order had failed because international news websites could and did report on the case – as many journalists and commentators on Twitter rushed to do – was to fundamentally misunderstand the purpose of the suppression order, and the case itself.

Even today, with suppression-order reforms passed by the Victorian government in the wake of the Pell case, it is difficult to see that Judge Kidd would have done anything differently if the case were to run again. The reforms, which passed parliament in May 2019, meant that suppression orders and closed-court orders could only be issued when necessary, such as when publishing information would entail a substantial risk to the administration of justice, or would cause undue distress to victims of a sexual or family-violence offence, or would risk the safety of any person. There had long been legitimate concerns in Victoria that suppression orders were being overused to oppress the media, and that this was against the public interest. But the reforms that have since passed would have done nothing to allow us to report Pell's case. Victims of sexual and family violence are still entitled to protection, and alleged perpetrators of those offences are still entitled to a fair trial. The protection of victims was a key recommendation of the comprehensive child sexual abuse royal commission.

One of the most extraordinary aspects of the suppression order being broken by some Australian media outlets in Melbourne was that none of them had formally opposed the order being issued in Victoria in the first place. Media companies are entitled to send lawyers to court during directions hearings to challenge judges on the issuing of suppression orders, and to argue for certain details of cases to be published.

So, on 13 December 2018, the legal parties gathered back in the court before Kidd for a mention, because a handful of media outlets had broken the suppression order. Some of those outlets then made an application to have the order lifted. The transcript of the mention on 13 December reveals that Kidd was furious. No media were present – we were not told about it until after it occurred.

Kidd said the articles that had been published in the previous hours had 'quite dishonestly' refrained 'from informing their readers that there was no opposition to the [suppression] order being made in Victoria'.

'It is just breathtaking,' he continued.

'And, indeed, it is positively misleading because it tells the community – I think one of the articles tells the community that it [the suppression order] was challenged. Well, my order was never appealed.

'You are supposed to leave the bench when you are angry, but I'll stay for a bit longer to finish this hearing off.'

Kidd's suppression order had stipulated that no information about the case was to be published, and that included news of the conviction. This did not mean that no information about the case and the trials would ever be published. The order would very likely be lifted upon the completion of all Pell's legal proceedings, once there could no longer be a risk to the administration of justice.

Richter told Kidd that even though the media had not named Pell, this was not enough for them to have avoided breaching the suppression order, because many readers would be able to make the connection. He said that the *Herald Sun*'s reference to a very prominent Australian figure, for example, meant that 'the connection cannot fail to be made'. The online public encyclopaedia Wikipedia had also updated its page on Pell to include the guilty verdict, Richter told the court.

'The way I see it at the moment,' Kidd said, 'is that some of this publicity was designed to put improper pressure upon me [to lift the suppression order].'

Richter responded, 'Yes, I suppressed my anger for this morning and hope it will not return other than in a lucid form tomorrow.'

Kidd said that the media coverage 'raises a serious question as to whether my suppression order has been breached in the most egregious way possible. My thinking at the minute, but I will be assisted by what everybody says, is this, that given how potentially egregious and flagrant these breaches are, a number of very important people in the media are facing, if found guilty, the prospect of imprisonment and indeed substantial imprisonment, and it may well be that many significant members of the media community are in that potential position. That being the case, that should inform us as to how the matter ought to be dealt with.' It was clear that numerous reporters and media companies would be facing contempt-of-court charges.

Kidd did not lift the suppression order the following day when he heard the application from some media to lift it. In his mind, many members of the media and commentators had acted appallingly. He was hardly going to reward them. More importantly, he still had to ensure that justice had as much chance as possible of being administered fairly. Lifting the suppression order at that point, before the matters involving the Swimmers' trial had been settled, would be unthinkable.

This also sparked a debate once again about judge-only trials and whether Victoria should move to implement them.

The suppression order was in place only to protect the Swimmers' trial. But would it go ahead? In February 2019, a directions hearing was held to discuss the trial. The first complainant in that case alleged he had been assaulted sometime between 1977 and 1979, when he was aged either 11 or 12, while he was swimming with Pell at the Eureka swimming pool in Ballarat. The complainant alleged Pell had grabbed his left arm, and placed his other hand over his right buttock, touching his testicles with his finger. Pell then lifted him into the air and threw him into the water. The complainant said he felt so uncomfortable he did not get back into the water. He said he could not be sure, however, if the touching was deliberate.

The second complainant alleged that between 1978 and 1979, when he was aged between nine and 10, Pell was playing a throwing game with boys in the pool. When it was his turn to play the game, which involved Pell throwing the boys into the air, the complainant placed both of his feet into Pell's hands, which were cupped in a stirrup formation. Pell allegedly released one hand from his clasp and placed his free hand between the complainant's legs over his swimming shorts, cupping his penis, testicles, and anus area.

The complainant alleged that after molesting him, Pell propelled him into the air, and he landed in the water. The cupping of his groin area allegedly occurred on a number of different days when he attended the pool, and a number of times on those days. Sometimes, Pell would allegedly place his hand under the boy's swimming shorts and rock him back and forth, and, in doing so, Pell's fingers allegedly directly touched the boy's penis and testicles.

There had been more charges relating to Pell indecently assaulting boys in swimming pools that were to be heard in the Swimmers' trial, but one of the complainants died before the case could make it to trial, and allegations made by two other men were dropped due to illness and other reasons not revealed.

With only two charges left to prosecute, the prosecution also wanted jurors to hear from a third witness who could provide detail about an incident that Pell was never charged over. Prosecutors wanted this to be heard by the jurors as what is known as 'tendency and coincidence evidence', to demonstrate that Pell had a pattern of behaviour when it came to the other boys whose allegations had resulted in charges being laid. This third witness said that, in 1975 or 1976, when he was around 10, he and his brother were playing in the water of Lake Boga, Victoria, when Pell was present. They played a game with Pell where they would jump from Pell's shoulders into the water. Pell would hold his hands behind his head to assist the boys to climb up.

The witness said that, during this game, Pell would hold him by his upper thighs, sliding his hands up until his fingers were digging into the boy's groin area. The final time the boy attempted to jump, he allegedly slipped off Pell's shoulders and fell down his front, feeling Pell's erect penis, which hit him in the chin. Pell allegedly smiled at the boy and said, 'Don't worry, it's only natural.'

The primary question for the prosecution was whether they could prove that the alleged touching had been deliberate, or whether the touching had occurred at all. One of the complainants said he was unsure if the touching had been deliberate. The key condition for the admission of tendency and coincidence evidence is the court's assessment that it, taken by itself or with other evidence, has significant probative value (that is, the capacity to prove or demonstrate a claim).

Kidd ruled that it did not. He found:

> In my view the risk of unfair prejudice to the accused in submitting this evidence substantially outweighs the probative value. The case carries with it the real risk that a jury may too readily use the [evidence of the second complainant] to supply what is effectively the missing intentional element with respect to the [first] complainant. This risk could be characterised as substitution reasoning; namely, that because the accused touched [the second complainant] deliberately and indecently then so, too, the touching of [the first complainant] had been deliberate and indecent.

There was a risk that a jury might overestimate the weight of the evidence from the tendency witness, he added.

Kidd's ruling left the prosecution's case substantially, and fatally, weakened. The prosecutors decided on 26 February 2019 to drop the Swimmers' trial, and Kidd subsequently ordered that the suppression order over the Cathedral trial be lifted, given there was no longer a risk of prejudicing a jury. Roughly one year later, in February 2020, ABC journalist Sarah Ferguson would air a documentary series called *Revelation*, in which one of the swimmers who baulked at the idea of giving evidence at the trial and withdrew his complaint went into harrowing detail about what he allegedly experienced at the hands of Pell.

As Pell left the court following the lifting of the suppression order, members of the public who had gathered outside yelled 'Scum' and 'Monster' at him. His loyal friend, Katrina Lee, tried to protect him from being pushed and shoved as he was escorted by police to a car and taken to the Melbourne Remand Centre, where he would spend his days in solitary confinement, allowed out for only one hour a day.

The fact that some international news outlets and local media had already reported the conviction did not dampen the response when the suppression order was lifted. The phones of the handful of journalists who had attended the entirety of the case had been ringing nonstop since the suppression order had been lifted, with requests from media organisations all over the world to give interviews. I felt a sense of obligation to agree to this, given that misinformation about the case was quickly spreading. One of the most egregious rumours that media commentators and Catholic media were reporting was that the jurors in the mistrial had been split 10–2 in favour of acquitting Pell. This was an unverified rumour with no credible source. There were plenty of other rumours about the split in the mistrial that I heard about, including a claim that the split had been more even. One source even told me that the split had been 10–2 in favour of convicting Pell. It would have been completely irresponsible to report these rumours as fact at the time. They remain unverified.

The weight of a split in a jury's determination makes no difference in the eyes of the law. The law requires a unanimous or 11–1 verdict, and anything else results in a mistrial. In the Pell case, even the judge was not told of the split, and he made it clear he did not want to know. Any juror who reveals a split breaks the law. The details of a mistrial split are also irrelevant in a retrial. In the retrial, both parties may learn from their mistakes, change their approach, and refine their arguments. It would be unfair to then judge the verdict in a retrial against the verdict in the mistrial. In Pell's retrial, witnesses were dropped by mutual agreement, and Richter added a PowerPoint presentation to his defence. One new witness was added. The arguments by counsel were similar, but not the same. Focusing on an unverified jury split from the mistrial as though it was relevant to Pell's later conviction was ill-informed, irresponsible, and misleading.

As I spoke about the case to media outlets around the world, I found that even saying that Kidd had been meticulous in the way he had handled the case resulted in me being harassed and accused of bias. This was despite both legal parties having praised him, and my having watched him in action for months. I was bombarded on social media and via email by people insisting that Pell was innocent and attempting to shame me for not reporting this 'fact'. This was despite conservative media commentators receiving plenty of exposure as they insisted that the trial had been unfair and that Pell was innocent, even though they had not attended much of or even any of the trial, and before an appeal had even been heard. This favourable coverage of Pell wasn't enough for some people. For some reason, many supporters of Pell wanted the journalists covering the trial to say it was unreasonable that the jurors had found the cardinal guilty. There was an appeals process available to decide this question, and Pell did appeal. I also began hearing from old friends and acquaintances I had not heard from in weeks, months, or even years, wanting details about the case. I began to feel depressed and very alone as the spotlight became more intense.

On 13 March 2019, Pell was brought back to the court for sentencing, looking noticeably dishevelled and weak as police officers escorted him, using a walking cane, into the dock at the back of the courtroom to hear his fate. Kidd had allowed him to undergo knee surgery before his sentencing.

'Facing jail at your age in these circumstances must be an awful state of affairs for you,' Kidd told Pell sincerely.

Pell sat dressed in a black shirt and beige jacket, and stared straight at Kidd, expressionless. Two police officers sat either side of him, and one directly behind.

Each of the five charges – one of sexual penetration of a minor under the age of 16, and four of an indecent act with a child under the age of 16 – carried a maximum penalty of 10 years' imprisonment. Pell would be a registered sex offender for life, Kidd said, and would be required to allow police to collect forensic samples from him.

He stood as Kidd told him of his fate: a sentence of six years in jail and a non-parole period of three years and eight months.

'Your decision to offend was a reasoned, albeit perverted, one,' Kidd said. 'Certainly you were confident your victims would not complain … the offending which the jury has found you have engaged in was, on any view, breathtakingly arrogant.

'As archbishop, you did have a relationship of approval in relation to the choirboys. In part, the choirboys were performing to please you as archbishop. The choirboys were the least powerful and the most subordinate individuals at the cathedral. The power imbalance between the victims and all the senior church leaders or officials, yourself included, was stark.'

Kidd reinforced the point several times during the sentencing, saying, 'I conclude that your decision to offend was a reasoned, albeit perverted, one, and I reach that conclusion to the criminal standard.'

Kidd said Pell's sentence came 'without fear or favour'.

'There has been extraordinary and widespread publicity and public comment which has surrounded you for a number of years,' Kidd said. 'Some of this publicity has involved strong, trenchant, and sometimes emotional criticism of you. Indeed, it is fair to say that in some sections of the community you are a publicly vilified figure. We have witnessed, outside of this court and within our community, examples of a witch-hunt or a lynch-mob mentality in relation to you, Cardinal Pell. I utterly condemn such behaviour.'

Kidd made it clear that Pell was being sentenced based only on his offending, which he described as 'significantly more serious because of the surrounding or contextual circumstances – namely the breach of trust and abuse of power'.

'This elevates the gravity of each of the offences. In my view, your conduct was permeated by staggering arrogance. There is an added layer of degradation and humiliation that each of your victims must have felt in knowing that their abuse had been witnessed by the other.'

Richter argued that Pell's sentence should be on the 'lower end' because there were 'no aggravating circumstances' to one of the offences. It was 'no more than a plain vanilla sexual-penetration case where the child is not actively participating', he said. Richter later apologised for that description, following a backlash from the public, including from child sexual abuse survivor advocates and victims. It was an extraordinary, tone-deaf term for him to have used, and contradicted his previous characterisation in court of the offence as 'forcible oral rape'. Many people were also confused by Richter's comments on legal grounds, believing that they seemed an admission of guilt. But Richter was required to argue for a sentence based on the jury verdict, not based on Pell's 'not guilty' plea and his maintenance of innocence. The case had been decided, so arguing that Pell was innocent would prove useless in convincing Kidd that Pell should get the lowest sentence possible.

The complainant released a statement in the hours following the sentence, saying it was hard to take comfort in it:

I appreciate that the court has acknowledged what was inflicted upon me as a child, however there is no rest for me.

Everything is overshadowed by the forthcoming appeal.

I am aware of a lot of public comment by people who are critical of my evidence. But only the judge, the jury, Pell and the legal teams have heard my evidence. Regardless of the outcome of the appeal, a few facts will always remain.

I gave evidence for several days. I was cross-examined by Pell's defence counsel. A jury has unanimously accepted the evidence. Pell chose not to give evidence. The jury did not hear from him. He did not allow himself to be cross-examined.

I have played my part as best I can. I took the difficult step of reporting to police about a high-profile person and I stood up to give my evidence. I'm waiting for the outcome of the appeal like everybody else.

Being a witness in a criminal case has not been easy. I'm doing my best to hold myself and my family together. I would like to thank the media for respecting my wish to keep my identity private and keep my loved ones out of the spotlight.

Professor Greg Craven, a lawyer and the vice-chancellor at the Australian Catholic University, did not attend Pell's mistrial and retrial. Nevertheless, he wrote in *The Catholic Weekly* that we 'have witnessed a combined effort by much of the media, including Australia's public broadcaster, and elements of Victoria's law enforcement agency, to systematically blacken the name of someone before he went to trial'. He did not mention the many media commentators who defended and supported Pell, insisting that his trial could never be fair. He did not mention that, come sentencing, Pell had support and character references from himself, and from nine others, including two former prime ministers – Tony Abbott and John Howard. He failed to mention the high-level continuing supportive coverage of Pell, or reveal his own biases that led to him supporting Pell. He did not mention the directions given to the jurors by Kidd. He could not have known them, because he had not been there to hear them. (At this point, only journalists had been into the court to view transcripts from the trial.) He accused the media of spreading misinformation, although he himself did not have the full story.

In an email to all staff, Craven also wrote, 'The university respects the judicial process and will not be making any comment until all legal avenues including any appeal have been concluded'. The same email alerted university staff that Craven had provided a character reference for Pell at sentencing, in which he described the disgraced prelate as a 'deeply sensitive person: thoughtful, considerate; and notably charitable'.

His commentary led to Australian Catholic University staff calling for Craven to be disciplined. The Australian Catholic University branch president of the National Tertiary Education Union, Dr Leah Kaufmann, said she had been inundated with calls and emails from staff at all campuses, including those in Brisbane, Sydney, Canberra, Melbourne, and Ballarat.

'The staff were very consistent in expressing concerns that by having him [Craven] comment publicly people would think he was representing the views of staff,' Kaufmann told me at the time. 'Many said his comments lacked consideration for abuse survivors, who they are committed to supporting, and felt the comments did nothing to rebuild trust in the Church.'

News Corp columnist Andrew Bolt added to the voices stating that Pell had been wrongfully convicted.

'Declaration: I have met Pell perhaps five times in my life and like him,' Bolt wrote in a piece published once the suppression order was lifted. (Bolt would revise this number of meetings to 10 one year later.)

I am not a Catholic or even a Christian. He is a scapegoat, not a child abuser. In my opinion. In my opinion, this is our own OJ Simpson case, but in reverse. A man was found guilty not on the facts but on prejudice. Cardinal George Pell has been falsely convicted of sexually abusing two boys in their early teens. That's my opinion, based on the overwhelming evidence.

The problem was that Bolt had not been present to hear any of the evidence. He had not heard the evidence of the complainant. He had not observed the directions hearings, and had not heard Kidd's orders. He had not heard and therefore did not describe in detail the prosecution case. Yet he claimed to have overwhelming evidence of Pell's innocence. However, just as there is no evidence that judges are more capable of assessing guilt or innocence than a jury of 12, there is no evidence that Andrew Bolt is more capable than a jury of determining the guilt or innocence of a person charged with serious criminal offences. In my opinion.

Conservative Catholic commentator Miranda Devine echoed Bolt's views in a piece for *The Daily Telegraph*. 'It's devastating because I don't believe that Pell, who I know slightly and admire greatly, could be guilty of sexually assaulting two choirboys in a busy cathedral after Sunday mass when he was archbishop of Melbourne in 1996,' she wrote. Again, she had not attended a single day of the trial. She admitted that Pell was someone she knew and liked, without acknowledging that children are abused by likeable people every day. I found it infuriating that members of the public might believe the emotive opinions of an uninformed commentator over considered, factual reports by journalists who had diligently attended the committal, mistrial, and retrial, including endless directions hearings and mentions. We had reported both sides of the story, managing to do so without weighing into these divisive debates.

Pell's defenders continued to be published prominently, regurgitating the defence arguments, rarely citing any facts or evidence about child sexual abuse, and apparently feeling no need to wait for the outcome of an appeal. This included overseas Catholic websites. Where could they have learned all those details about the defence case, since their 'reporters' had not been in court? Jesuit priest and human-rights lawyer Frank Brennan, who attended a few days of the retrial, described the complainant's evidence as 'confused', even though he had not seen or heard the complainant testify. By contrast, in the conversations that occurred between journalists and lawyers in the corridors of the courthouse, I never heard anyone who'd been present during the complainant's testimony say that he had performed badly. Instead, the complainant was described as 'compelling' and 'honest'.

Brennan seemed to lift key phrases and arguments from the defence case, and published them without telling readers that it is entirely open to jurors to disregard all or some of the defence's comments and assertions. Brennan himself may have considered the defence case plausible, but this did not mean that 12 jurors must or should have as well. I found it incredible that commentary such as this was being published and broadcast long before transcripts could have been accessed at the court. (It would take days, at least, to thoroughly review transcripts for a case that ran for five weeks.) Importantly, even when the commentators were not getting it wrong, they were adding nothing new that jurors had not heard or considered. They were, however, omitting crucial information about the way the case had been run by Kidd, and the directions that were given. Despite the number of lawyers weighing in on the case in their defence of Pell, little context was given to the public about how the legal system works and why certain decisions are made.

My colleague, *Guardian Australia* correspondent David Marr, has been reporting on Pell and the Catholic Church for some two decades. His bestselling *Quarterly Essay* and subsequent book *The Prince* investigated Pell's career and how he rose through the ranks of the Church, as well as how he handled the child sexual abuse scandal. In November 2016, Andrew Bolt wrote in News Corp publication the *Herald Sun*, 'No journalist has tried harder than David Marr to smear Cardinal George Pell as a liar who covered up for paedophile priests and even enabled their crimes.' In the same piece, published as police were already investigating Pell, Bolt wrote, 'The evidence against Pell is actually melting away.'

Conservative political commentator Gerard Henderson has attacked Marr's reporting on Pell on numerous occasions as well.

Marr and I recorded a podcast called *The Reckoning* about the royal commission's work and about the Pell case, with producer Miles Martignoni trying to pull us into line as we debated and discussed the trial. Marr told me that the staunch defence of Pell that occurred before, during, and after the trial was driven by what Pell represented – the fundamental culture-war notion that contemporary values are superficial, and that the good of society depends on returning to traditional values. 'Which, when you boil traditional values down, are usually authoritarian notions of how society should be run,' he said. 'But it's dressed up as "fundamental wisdom". There's the general culture-war notion that Pell represents a healthy contrast to progressive values, which might undermine conservative governments.

'Another thing that can't be underestimated with figures like Andrew Bolt is they get off on being wingmen for powerful people.'

Bolt did, on one occasion, briefly, criticise Pell. It came after Pell's evidence at the child sexual abuse royal commission in March 2016, when he said he had 'no reason to turn my mind to the extent of the evils' that paedophile priest Gerald Ridsdale had perpetrated.

Bolt, on Sky News, described Pell's comments as a 'disaster, absolute disaster'. In a column for the *Herald Sun*, Bolt wrote, 'Is the Vatican's third-most powerful leader a liar when he says he never knew what Ridsdale, his colleague, was doing in Ballarat? Or was he just dangerously indifferent to his responsibilities and to the warning signs that children were being raped?' Within hours, Bolt apologised on air for his commentary, saying he felt 'embarrassed' for having criticised Pell. It was an extraordinary walk-back from Bolt, who had secured an exclusive one-on-one interview with the cardinal following the completion of his evidence to the commission.

For conservatives, having a relationship with Pell opened doors, Marr said, giving them intimate access to an inner circle that included people such as prime ministers. Support for Pell was not about Catholicism and maintaining the integrity of the Church. It was about power.

Marr told me that the adoration of Pell by conservative politicians and commentators dated back to the lead-up to the 1998 federal election in Australia, when the conservative Liberal leader, John Howard, unveiled a proposal to introduce a goods and services tax (GST) if elected. The proposition was wildly unpopular with Australians, with 60 per cent believing they would be worse off with such a tax. The 1993 election had been lost by the Liberals despite being described as 'unloseable', largely on the basis of their key policy of introducing such a tax.

In 1998, Pell was the Archbishop of Melbourne as Howard took the GST to the election. The GST was publicly opposed by nearly every Catholic social agency in Australia as a regressive and unfair tax on poorer Australians.

'There was almost a united wall of opposition to it,' Marr recalled. 'All the polls very strongly favoured [Labor] leader Kim Beazley. And then, about 10 days before polling day, George Pell put out a statement saying, "There is no one Catholic position on the GST." Howard used that statement continuously, every day and until polling day as he came to the end of his campaign.'

So it was no mystery, Marr said, why, 20 years later, people like Howard gave Pell a character reference after Pell was convicted of raping a child.

'He is deeply, deeply indebted to Pell. Those conservative columnists, they share that notion of Pell as a key figure in the survival and success of the Howard government and the Liberal Party. It's not about religion. It's not about Pell's stance on gays or divorcees and IVF. It is that, in 1998, Pell made a venture into domestic politics.'

Most Australians, Marr said, didn't care about the culture wars – the battle between groups in society to have their values and beliefs prevail. Support for conservative politics and values existed in Australia long before terms such as 'progressive' and 'correctness' had been seized by the right and reframed into pejoratives as part of those culture wars.

'Hardly anyone outside the loyal readership of the Murdoch press give a flying fuck – and that's a technical term – about the culture wars, which are simply self-important squabble,' Marr said. 'I think, though, we have to steady ourselves to the possibility that if Pell is acquitted on appeal, he will become a culture-war hero. He will become more than that. A martyr of conservative Australians.'

The continuing curiosity about the case from the public, combined with relentless international and local media interviews and misinformation, led me to hold an online 'Ask Me Anything' session on the website Reddit, answering questions about the case from around the world for a couple of hours. But the questions, interest, and harassment did not stop (and has not stopped). It was around the time of the suppression order being lifted and the subsequent frenzy of misinformed stories that I decided I needed to write a book about the Pell case, but I was badly burned out. I participated in the Reddit question-and-answer session from an airport lounge on my way to what was supposed to be a holiday in New Zealand. I had felt able to cope with the intensity of the aftermath of the trials because I knew I had the trip to look forward to, and that I could go on hikes and bike rides through Dunedin, momentarily placing the stress of the previous year or so behind me.

However, a couple of days into my trip, on 15 March 2019, two consecutive terrorist shooting attacks occurred at mosques in Christchurch during Friday prayers. I drove from Dunedin to Christchurch overnight to cover the tragedy – flights had been cancelled and airports shut down, due to security concerns and the fact that, initially, it was unclear how many perpetrators might be involved and trying to flee. My holiday was cut short barely a couple of days in. After having worked nonstop to cover the aftermath of the Pell trial, I now found myself working nonstop covering the New Zealand anti-Muslim terrorist attacks, interviewing relatives of the deceased outside the hospital, and trying to verify information as it came in. I was so sleep-deprived and fatigued that I nearly ran off the road on the drive across New Zealand.

I returned to Melbourne exhausted, and broken. I had a mental breakdown. I felt ashamed. I learned it is not the stories you cover that will break you, but the lack of support that will. The criticism of the reporters covering the trial still did not stop.

CHAPTER ELEVEN

Appeal

'These are insidious, evil acts to which no child should be subject. The individuals concerned deserve the most thorough of investigations into the wrongs that have been committed against them. They deserve to have their voices heard and their claims investigated.'

– Former prime minister Julia Gillard,
announcing the Royal Commission into Institutional Responses
to Child Sexual Abuse

Cardinal George Pell cut a dishevelled figure as he stepped into Melbourne's Supreme Court and took his seat in the dock, flanked by two police officers, on 21 August 2019. His hair had grown long, a large bald patch showing through, and he wore all-black, a pop of white showing from his clerical collar. Prison had taken its toll.

He had hoped to walk free from the building that morning. However, three Victorian appellate judges swiftly shattered that hope when their decision was delivered as to whether 12 jurors were unreasonable in having convicted him for sexually abusing two 13-year-old choirboys in 1996 when he was the Archbishop of Melbourne.

Pell knew his immediate fate within seconds of Chief Justice, Anne Ferguson, the president of the Court of Appeal, Justice Chris

Maxwell, and Justice Mark Weinberg taking their seats at 9.30 am,

'By majority of two to one, the Court of Appeal has dismissed Cardinal George Pell's appeal against his conviction for the commission of sexual offences,' Ferguson said. 'He will continue to serve his sentence of six years' imprisonment.'

Pell momentarily bowed his head, but his face gave little away. The only sound in the court was of journalists typing as Ferguson read a summary of the court's reasons. Filling the court were supporters of Pell, as well as survivors of child sexual abuse and their advocates. Survivors gripped each other's hands as Ferguson continued, saying that she and Maxwell 'accepted the prosecution's submission that the complainant was a very compelling witness, was clearly not a liar, was not a fantasist and was a witness of the truth'.

Two-and-a-half months earlier, on 5 and 6 June, the court had heard Pell's appeal. Usually, a single judge considers an appeal application. If there are grounds for appeal, the matter immediately proceeds to a hearing, usually beginning on the same day, which is overseen by three judges, who review the key evidence. The appellate court does not need to make a unanimous verdict – only a majority of judges need to agree on the outcome. Importantly, an appeal is not a right. A judge needs to decide that there are grounds for appeal based on the papers filed by the applicant, and to grant leave – in other words, permission – for it to be heard.

Pell hired one of Australia's most renowned and expensive barristers, Sydney silk Bret Walker SC, to manage his appeal. According to media reports, Walker charges in the realm of $25,000 per day, and he is frequently cited by university professors and legal professionals as one of Australia's top barristers. He is sharp and eloquent, and speaks in long, verbose sentences. More than once in the court, I needed the assistance of Google Dictionary to make sense of what he said. He has been hired by the executives of big businesses and former Australian prime ministers. He most famously represented the tobacco industry in their ultimately unsuccessful fight against Australia's plain-packaging legislation.

It is not unusual for the defence and prosecution cases to be led by different people at appeal. It allows a fresh mind to examine the case and perhaps approach it from a new perspective. However, Richter and his colleague, barrister Ruth Shann, advised Walker throughout the appeal. Meanwhile, Chris Boyce SC, represented the prosecution at appeal, having joined Victoria's Office of Public Prosecutions in 2016 following a two-decade career as a defence barrister. One senior sergeant told me, 'He's magnificent. By far the best lawyer at the Office of Public Prosecutions … the only competitor would be the director herself [Kerri Judd QC].'

Family members and supporters of Pell and the complainant sat in the front row of Victoria's Supreme Court, which was at capacity. An overflow room was opened with a video-link to the courtroom to accommodate those who could not get a seat. Supporters of the complainant and the former choirboy who had died in 2014 were also in the court.

It is critical that justice is not only done, but is seen by the public to have been done. That is why we have an appeals process. It is why Kidd's sentencing remarks were streamed on television and the internet with only about 30 seconds' delay; and that is why, as arduous as it might be to get them, depending on the court, transcripts are nonetheless available to members of the public. Suppression orders, closed courts, access to transcripts, directions from the judge, the presumption of innocence, a jury trial – all of these things work together to strike a balance between protecting the defendant and the complainant, and ensuring that justice has been carried out fairly and appropriately in the eyes of the public. It may not be possible to strike a perfect balance in all cases.

The chances are that what some members of the public were hoping for in the Pell case – a smoking gun, a definitive narrative of how the abuse had occurred from the moment the boys slipped away from the choir to the moment the complainant decided to report to police – will never eventuate. The questions that many members of the public want answered may remain unanswered forever. This is an uncomfortable reality. What people really want, I feel, is to interrogate the witness themselves, free of any legal constraints, directions hearings, or understanding of the system.

But it is not at all unique that this case largely came down to the word of the victim against that of the defendant, with no direct witnesses. It is also the intrinsic nature of nearly all sexual assault cases. The crimes are usually committed when others are either not present or are not looking, so there can be no other witnesses. It is especially common in historical sexual abuse cases for there to be a lack of other evidence, such as forensic evidence, and this is problematic to all involved. This issue is invariably highlighted to the jurors in the directions given by the judge. As Pell's jurors were told at various points, Pell was at a significant forensic disadvantage, and this was something they were to keep in mind when deliberating. And now an appeals court would examine if those deliberations had been reasonable.

Pell attended his appeal, brought from the Melbourne Assessment Prison in West Melbourne, where he had been held since being sentenced a few months earlier. He dressed in all black and wore his clerical collar, limping slightly as he walked into the court, having undergone knee surgery between the jury verdict and the sentencing. He occasionally took notes on a yellow notepad, and watched Walker and the judges intently. Police officers sat behind him.

Chief Justice Ferguson opened by saying that the bench had undertaken considerable preparation ahead of the two-day hearing, having reviewed 'a considerable amount of the evidence', including recordings, transcripts, photographs, robes, and documents, and undertaking a tour of the cathedral in the presence of both parties' lawyers. She said the bench had also reviewed parts of the parties' closing submissions, and the judge's rulings and charge to the jury. 'As a consequence of the work that we have already undertaken we are quite familiar with the evidence and the arguments that have been made by each party,' Ferguson said.

Some lawyers and prosecutors I spoke with were critical of this approach of reviewing all of the evidence in detail, going so far as to take a tour of the cathedral, as the jurors had done. One lawyer told me, 'They're reliving the trial – and they're going to come up with their own verdict – and that's not their role. They're doing exactly what they're forbidden from doing ... which is substituting their opinion of guilt for the jury's. It's a narrow difference, but an important one ... their role is to establish whether any jury must have had doubt. Not whether they might have.'

In other words, the lawyer was saying that the appellate judges were not there to decide on the credibility of witnesses, which was firmly the role of jurors. They were not there to decide guilt in place of the jury. Rather, their role was to examine whether, in coming to their verdict, the jury had applied the principles of law explained by the trial judge incorrectly, or had decided on something as fact when there was nothing in the evidence to support that fact.

The appellate judges do not consider new evidence, including hearing from new witnesses (except in rare circumstances). They review the key details of the case presented at trial, including transcripts and recordings. They hear arguments from both legal parties based on the existing evidence. The complainant's evidence, including his cross-examination, was video-recorded, so this was among the evidence the judges reviewed. It was open to them to view the transcript of his and other witness evidence, rather than watch the videos.

Pell's Supreme Court appeal was based on a key ground: that the jury was unreasonable in reaching its verdict. Walker also argued on two grounds that concerned the conduct of the trial: Walker said that the defence should have been allowed to play the video animation in the closing address; and that, although a defendant must be arraigned in the presence of the jury panel, Pell was arraigned through a video-link. The last two grounds were flimsy, experts agreed prior to the trial. These days, a video-link is considered an extension of the courtroom. As for the video animation, Kidd gave strong reasons during the trial for not allowing it to be played – it might have been considered by jurors to be new evidence, which is not allowed to be presented during a closing address. Victoria isn't clear on the use of visual aids during closing addresses, and ultimately it's a matter of discretion for the judge. Pell's legal team needed to convince the appeal judges that those two matters regarding the conduct of the trial were so significant that they might have changed the jury's verdict.

It was evident that Pell's greatest chance of success lay in arguing that the jurors should have had a reasonable doubt as to Pell's guilt, and that their verdict was therefore unsafe and unreasonable. Leave to appeal was granted, and Ferguson, Weinberg, and Maxwell heard arguments from the legal parties over two days.

Walker began, highlighting the fact that the Crown had stopped short of calling 'anybody a liar at the trial'. If people such as Portelli, Potter, and Connor were not said to be lying, the jurors should not have dismissed their testimony that Pell was always accompanied and never left alone, he argued. It is open to jurors to convict based on the evidence of one person's testimony. But, Walker said, without any evidence to show that witnesses in support of Pell were lying, this meant there was 'a web, a network of evidence' that people were in and around the cathedral at the critical time when Pell was alleged to be offending in the sacristy. Portelli was among the witnesses who said it was Pell's custom to stand at the cathedral door after mass, speaking with parishioners.

'If he was at the western door at the time, when, on the complainant's account, the offending must have been occurring ... then the law of physics tells us this is literally, logically impossible for the offending to have occurred, according to the complainant's account. And there is no other account. It is in the nature of alibi evidence, unless it is serious and apparently so, or perhaps demonstrated to be so, to raise a reasonable doubt, to put it mildly. It's not just raising the reasonable doubt; it simply renders impossible the offending.' Like Richter, Walker argued that the offending was impossible.

The jurors had heard that the first offences, which involved Pell sexually assaulting two boys after Sunday Solemn Mass at St Patrick's Cathedral, most likely occurred on either 15 or 22 December 1996.

The jurors heard that Pell had offended again about one month later when he grabbed the complainant's genitals, once again after Sunday mass. But the Crown's written case to the appellate judges stated that 3 November 1996 may have also been a possible date when the first offences occurred, as it had not been established during the trial that Pell was not present at mass on that date.

The introduction of 3 November as another possible date was 'in itself disturbing ... and should disturb this court', Walker told the appellate judges. It revealed the Crown's own 'doubts involving the theory that this supposed first event or incident indeed took place on the 15th or 22nd of December', Walker said. 'And if it didn't take place on one of those two dates then the Crown case fails.' This was because the complainant said the second incident – Pell grabbing his genitals – occurred about one month later.

'There's more than a month ... well and truly ... between the 3rd of November and either the 15th or 22nd of December,' Walker said. It was in reviewing this timing that the judges should find a 'lack of realistic probability of this offending taking place'.

Walker also argued that there was a 'formidable list' of factors and events that needed to line up for the offending to be possible, and the jury would have to have believed every one of those factors had occurred. This included believing that Pell was alone for about six minutes with the boys in the priests' sacristy completely undisturbed, and possibly with the door open, after mass.

Justice Maxwell put it to Walker that someone who was in New Zealand at the time they were alleged to have offended in Australia would be an example of an impossibility that they had offended. He questioned whether it was accurate for the defence to argue that Pell's offending was impossible, given there was varying testimony from witnesses in the case in regards to the choirboys' access to the sacristy, Pell's routine after mass, and whether two boys could have slipped away unnoticed.

'The argument for impossibility ... logically loses its force as uncertainty grows,' Maxwell said. 'Your point is ... and you've confirmed it several times ... the evidence established such high improbability verging on impossibility there must have been a doubt. I'm just raising the notion ... the greater [the] uncertainty, the less forceful the argument for impossibility becomes. That must be true, mustn't it?'

Walker responded, 'No. It's very straightforward logic, but with respect, applies just as readily when one is talking about a location at the great west door of the cathedral ... a considerable, physical difference of location, and it suffices entirely for alibi purposes as would being across the Tasman.'

Maxwell then put it to Walker that 'you wouldn't expect perfect recall' about dates of offending and the timing from a child sexual abuse victim. He also told Walker, 'We have to be satisfied, don't we, that the jury must have had a doubt, not might have?'

Maxwell said that, on his reading of the trial evidence, a significant component of the defence's case was that the complainant was a liar. The jurors would have considered the plausibility of this argument in making their verdict.

'It's very common in appeals against conviction in cases of this kind that there will be points properly made about aspects of the circumstances in which it's alleged, or the time at which it's alleged, offending took place, which the complainant doesn't remember.'

Walker responded that the issues with the complainant's evidence, including lapses in memory or difficulty in recalling dates, were not 'trivial'.

Before Walker finished his address, he was asked by the judges to consider the issue of the robes. In the trial and in the appeal, Richter argued that it was physically impossible for Pell to manoeuvre his robes to the side in order to expose his penis as the complainant had said.

Ferguson put it to Walker that the chasuble, which is the outer layer, was like a cape and could be moved to the side. Walker said that would still leave the alb underneath, which could not be manoeuvred to the side.

On Thursday 6 June 2019, the second and final day of Pell's appeal hearing, Crown prosecutor Chris Boyce delivered his response to Walker, saying, 'The complainant was a very compelling witness. He is clearly not a liar; he was not a fantasist.'

Maxwell asked Boyce to guide the judges towards evidence from the trial that supported the assessment he was not fantasising or lying.

In his evidence, the complainant had described the priests' sacristy with accuracy, including a kitchenette area and wooden panels, even though the room was off-limits to choirboys. Boyce said the complainant would not have been able to do this unless he had been in the room and was telling the truth. Boyce also pointed out that the cathedral was undergoing renovations at the time, and the archbishop's sacristy was not in use. This fitted with the complainant's evidence that the abuse had occurred in the priests' sacristy, because Pell had to use that room while work on his usual sacristy was underway.

However, Maxwell pointed out, during his cross-examination at trial, when the complainant was asked if it was possible he had been in the sacristy before, he did not dispute that it was possible. At trial, Richter suggested that the choirboys may have been given a tour of the cathedral when they first joined. The complainant said while he had no memory of such a tour, he also could not state for certain that it did not happen.

But Boyce said there was no evidence presented at trial that such a tour happened or that the complainant had been on such a tour.

Boyce also emphasised the sanctity of jury verdicts. In their written submission to the court, the prosecutors stated, 'When looking at the whole of the evidence, the integrity of the jury's verdicts is unimpeachable. The jury were entitled to accept the complainant as a reliable and credible witness. He was skilfully cross-examined for two days by a very experienced member of senior counsel. The complainant's allegations were not improbable when all of the evidence is carefully considered.'

There was no doubt, however, that to journalists, and those survivors, advocates, and Pell's supporters who attended, Boyce seemed to be struggling. Large chunks of his arguments are difficult to quote directly, as his wording was often garbled and difficult to follow. I later found out that Boyce suffers from a stutter, which those in Victorian legal circles are used to accommodating. But even allowing for this impediment, Boyce seemed to struggle to answer the most basic questions from the judges. In the court breaks, people watching from the courtroom and the overflow room down the hall where the hearing was being streamed onto a screen spoke to each other in disbelief about his performance. Gibson had been so unflappable at trial; Boyce seemed easily flustered.

The hearing was streamed over the internet so that people could watch from their homes or their offices. There was a slight delay on the feed, however, so that any errors, such as the accidental citing of suppressed information, could be censored. It was an eventuality that court technical staff were prepared for. It would be a tough ask for the parties not to utter the names of the choirboys over the course of the two days. But when Boyce accidentally spoke the name of the complainant in the courtroom, he was visibly shaken by the error. Despite being reassured about the delay on the live feed, he found it difficult to regain his composure.

Boyce continued to stammer and stumble in answer to straightforward questions. He was asked by the judges about the argument from Pell's lawyers that it was odd that the victim never spoke to the choirboy who he was abused with the first time about his second assault. Pell's lawyers had argued the victim would have warned the other boy that Pell had abused him again, and to stay away from him.

'Boys talk, don't they?' Maxwell said, to which Boyce responded that boys just want to get on with their lives and 'play footy or whatever they want to do'. In the trial, however, the complainant had told the court he had pushed the abuse to the 'darkest corners and recesses' of his mind. He had feared that talking about it to anyone would jeopardise his prestigious scholarship to St Kevin's College, because being in the choir was a condition of that scholarship. Boyce eventually said that the victim might not have spoken to the other boy about the abuse because he didn't want his parents to find out, and because he was embarrassed.

Weinberg responded, 'Your best answer is surely that this is a matter well within the competence of the jury to assess.' Boyce quickly agreed.

Maxwell, who dominated the questioning, put it to Boyce that it was 'wildly improbable' that someone of Pell's height and stature would not have been seen approaching two choirboys. He was asked why Pell would then abuse those boys in a place with many potential witnesses.

Boyce responded, 'We've said somewhat ad nauseam if you are going to make it up … why make it up?' Many of the issues put by the judges to Boyce had been confidently navigated by Gibson during the five-week trial. Maxwell asked what advantage the jurors might have had over the appellate judges in terms of assessing the evidence, given that the judges had reviewed video footage of the trial, and also had the transcripts. It could not be argued that only the jurors had the benefit of seeing body language and hearing the tone of evidence, he said.

'It's difficult to answer,' Boyce responded. 'Your Honours are not in the same position of the jury. You're just not. I apologise if I'm not being helpful as I might. Generally, a trial has a certain kind of … atmosphere to it.'

Weinberg offered, 'If it helps Mr Boyce … juries almost always get it right. Almost.'

Walker was given 45 minutes to respond to Boyce's arguments, and he was confident as he reiterated his arguments from the day before: the verdict was unsafe; the weight of the evidence showed the offending could not have happened, or at least should have cast reasonable doubt in the jurors' minds.

The hearing finished just after 4.00 pm. Unlike during the retrial, Pell appeared engaged with the appeal, taking notes throughout, and intently watching the prosecutor and judges. He had been in prison for about four months by then. The judges reserved their decision, and did not state when they would return to the court to deliver it. But Boyce's lacklustre performance, combined with Walker's confidence, left many commentators, legal experts, and journalists thinking that Pell's team would succeed. He would likely be acquitted, they said, his conviction quashed, or, in a less likely scenario, a retrial might be ordered. I, however, was not so sure. Some senior police officers and lawyers told me they thought that Boyce had not performed so badly. While it might have appeared that way to someone unfamiliar with courts and appeals, they told me that nothing he said or did was fatal. In any case, predicting the outcome of an appellate court is extremely difficult. The questions asked by the judges at appeals in response to the arguments that are put to them are difficult to read. The questions do not mean they are focused on a particular issue, or have formed an opinion about it. Their job is to test the arguments. It's what they do.

Nonetheless, it was a surprise to many when, on 21 August, the court delivered its decision that, by majority of two to one, it had dismissed the cardinal's appeal. People had lined up before 7.00 am, despite the cold and the drizzle, to ensure they would secure a seat in the courtroom for the decision. An overflow room was needed to accommodate all of them. Pell supporters and victim advocates clashed on the court stairs, exchanging heated words. Advocates held up placards. One man had drawn a large portrait of Pell wearing prison stripes, and held it up for those in line to see.

Throughout his evidence, the complainant had come across as someone who was telling the truth, Ferguson said. 'He did not seek to embellish his evidence or tailor it in a manner favourable to the prosecution. As might have been expected, there were some things he could remember and many things which he could not. And his explanations of why that was so had a ring of truth.'

Ferguson read a summary of her reasons, before the full reasons – spanning 300 pages – were released to journalists. But after reviewing some 30 hours of testimony from the trial, reviewing

2,000 pages of transcript, and examining the robes that Pell wore while he was Archbishop of Melbourne, Maxwell and Ferguson found it was fair that the jurors had believed the complainant. Ferguson and Maxwell had dismissed all of the obstacles to Pell committing the crime that Walker put forward. One of the arguments was that Pell's archbishop's robes were too heavy to be manoeuvred for Pell to expose his penis. Not so, said Ferguson. The three appellate judges had held the robes and picked them up. Ferguson said, 'The robes were not so heavy or immovable as [witnesses] suggested.'

In his dissenting judgment, Weinberg concluded that the complainant's evidence contained discrepancies. But in an appeal, only two of the three judges need to agree.

'Hallelujah – proof there is a God,' a victim advocate yelled outside of the court once Pell had been escorted from the building. After the decision was delivered, people spilled out of the court shortly after 10.00 am, and Pell's supporters dissipated. Only survivors and their supporters were left, taking in what had occurred. Survivors of abuse expressed shock that the victim had received justice, because they had seen so many cases before where victims had not been believed, or their cases had never made it to court. That a cardinal had been held to account – once one of the most powerful men in the Vatican – was profound.

Chrissie Foster, whose daughters Emma and Katie were raped by the Melbourne priest Kevin O'Donnell while they were at a Catholic primary school in the late 1980s and early 1990s, said the dismissal of Pell's appeal showed society's understanding of child sexual abuse had reached a point where being powerful did not offer the protection it once did.

'What a result – it is almost unbelievable,' she told reporters afterwards. 'I was not expecting this. I went to all of the second trial, and I could see it [that the abuse had happened], and I just hoped the jury could see it. And they did. It was forensically argued and debated. Now again. I'm amazed. So often in these cases, hardly any victims come forward. This is a crime fraught with not getting a guilty verdict.'

Shortly after 11.00 am, the complainant who had brought Pell to justice released a statement read out by his lawyer, Viv Waller:

> You wouldn't know my name. I am not a champion for the cause of sexual abuse survivors, although I am glad those advocates are out there. But that is not my path.
>
> After attending the funeral of my childhood friend, the other choirboy, I felt a responsibility to come forward. I knew he had been in a dark place. I was in a dark place. I gave a statement to the police because I was thinking of him and his family.
>
> I would like to acknowledge my friend who passed away, the other choirboy, and pay my deep respect to him and to his family. I would like to acknowledge the courage of those people who reported to the police. For one reason or another, your cases were not advanced. My heart goes out to you.

The reaction from survivors was swift, but the Vatican did not respond. Pell, the one-time financial manager of the Vatican and confidant to the Pope, who many believed would be in the running for the position of supreme pontiff one day, maintained his title of cardinal. The Vatican said all along that it would await the outcome of a further appeal before weighing in. And there was no doubt that Pell would appeal to the High Court, in the final hope of having his conviction quashed. He maintained his innocence. His hope in the High Court's approach would have been bolstered by Weinberg's dissenting judgment in the appellate division of the Supreme Court.

Weinberg had not agreed with the other two justices. In his judgment, he stated that the complainant was 'inclined to embellish aspects of his account. There were inconsistencies, and discrepancies, and a number of his answers simply made no sense.' He concluded that the complainant's evidence 'lacked probative value' and, as a result, he had a doubt as to Pell's guilt. Weinberg said he could not be assured beyond reasonable doubt that the complainant's account was not concocted, particularly in relation to the second incident, where Pell was alleged to have pushed him against the wall after mass in a corridor, squeezing his genitals. The judgment summary stated: 'In Justice Weinberg's view there was a significant body of cogent and, in some cases, impressive evidence suggesting that the complainant's account was, in a realistic sense, "impossible" to accept. To his mind, there is a significant possibility that the Cardinal may not have committed the offences. In those circumstances, Justice Weinberg stated that in his view the convictions could not stand.'

The three judges did unanimously agree that the other two grounds of appeal – that the video animation should have been played, and that it was wrong for Pell to be arraigned via video-link – were to be dismissed.

Richter was livid.

In February 2020, I took the elevator to the fourth floor of a building in the heart of Melbourne's courts district to interview Richter. He led me into his chambers, a room brimming with artwork, papers, books, and vintage furniture. By the door was a 255-year-old leather chair made for Dr Samuel Johnson, who wrote the famous eponymous English dictionary. The relic has sentimental meaning for Richter, who taught himself English after moving with his family to Australia as a 13-year-old boy via Israel and the Soviet Union, where he was born.

I put in interview requests with the prosecution, including Mark Gibson, the County Court's chief justice, Peter Kidd, and Bret Walker SC, but Richter was the only one to eventually agree to be interviewed on the record about the case. While I was writing this book, many people I spoke to – including police officers, child-abuse researchers, lawyers, and senior figures in Melbourne law – spoke of their respect and admiration for Richter. Some described him as kind; most described him as brilliant. However, none would go on the record, so poor are the optics of speaking favourably of someone representing an accused child-sex offender as high-profile as Pell.

I sat on a couch opposite Richter's desk. Richter, contrary to the barrister's black gown I'd become accustomed to seeing him in, was wearing a brown leather jacket. He leaned back into his leather office chair, sucked on his vape, and told me that the reason Pell was convicted was 'three years of royal commission shit'.

'Shit about how he moved people around, and about how he turned up to court as a character witness when [the paedophile Gerald] Ridsdale was pleading guilty, when in reality, Pell just accompanied him to court.' Pell's appearance before the royal commission had damaged his reputation and influenced people's perceptions of him, Richter said. While the royal commission's findings regarding Pell had not been made public at the time of our interview, the media coverage of Pell's evidence, in which he 'came across as wooden and doctrinaire', had turned the public against him, Richter said.

'There was three years of press that painted him as a monster.'

I asked Richter about the years of positive press that Pell received, including in the aftermath of the verdict. High-profile defenders of Pell wrote column after column defending him, despite never having spent a day in the court or having had time to access transcripts. Conservative news programs did the same. Wasn't it disingenuous to suggest that the press influenced people against Pell, when reporters were merely reporting what he said at the royal commission, and when so many powerful media personalities defended him?

The difference, Richter said, was that those defending Pell got it right. He said that while he personally abhorred the politics of some of Pell's defenders, they were correct in their assessment that the offending was impossible.

Pell, just a few years senior to Richter, was 'quite delightful,' Richter said. The two had become friends, despite their stark differences in worldviews. It may seem that Richter, an atheist opposed to drug-prohibition laws and an advocate for civil liberties and human rights, would have little in common with Pell, an orthodox Catholic opposed to the rights of LGBTIQ couples to marry, an anti-abortionist, and a defender of traditional values. In fact, Richter said that one of the reasons he pursued criminal defence after a short stint working in prosecutions was because he knew he could never feel comfortable prosecuting offences such as drug crimes and petty matters. 'I would never prosecute drug cases. There are cases I wouldn't prosecute on a matter of principle, and if someone insisted I had to, my heart wouldn't be in it. I had no objection to prosecuting things, except in cases when the law was a piece of shit.'

Early in his career, he represented Dr Bertram Wainer before the Beach Inquiry, an inquiry into police corruption in Victoria. Wainer had long been lobbying for the inquiry, which exposed police badgering of witnesses and framing of suspects.

Though Pell's and Richter's views differed, it was a meeting of two minds, Richter said, and he enjoyed their conversations and Pell's sense of humour.

'I always thought he was very well read. I mean, he's got a PhD [in church history], for God's sake. I believe Pell's a good man. He's very ambitious, and I think his ambition consumed him in the sense he saw things he wanted to do and had to do theologically, and pursued them rigorously.'

Richter said he never believed at any point that Pell was guilty of the allegations. So, when he was convicted, Richter felt 'shattered', especially because he had believed the case would never make it past the committal hearing.

'I lost my cool after the conviction. I thought it was a perverse verdict.'

Richter fell into a depression. He began to withdraw.

'It was horrible. It was different in this instance, as we had the first trial, which I thought we won hands down. The jury disagreed. So I thought, the second time around, the worst-case scenario would be another hung jury.

'So the conviction came to me as a complete shock. I felt neutered.'

Did he think the outcome might have been different if he had put Pell on the witness stand to face examination and cross-examination?

'I doubt it. Look, the assessment that we made – and we made it collectively with Pell – was there was no point in calling him to give evidence. He'd given an explanation on tape, a voluntary one. He gave his account to the detectives. And how does he prove a negative? Other than by saying, "I didn't do it. It wasn't me"? What else could he say if he was giving evidence? There was no point. To call someone against whom the evidence was as it was, to call them is almost to invite a jury to ask, "Who do you believe? The man who says I didn't do it, or the man who says the opposite?"' That was the wrong question for the jurors to be focused on, he said.

'We didn't need to prove it was impossible for the offending to occur. We just needed to prove there was a reasonable doubt as to whether it happened, and that's what we needed the jury to focus on.'

Richter, who shows little sign of stopping at the age of 74, despite his family imploring him to slow down, said that after the verdict, 'I was going to give it all away.' One of his colleagues and oldest friends calls Richter 'snakeskin,' because when he is under stress, the skin begins to peel off his face.

He also fell into a deep depression. His stress and anxiety once again reared up. These are conditions that Richter does not shy away from disclosing when asked. 'I seriously thought, *I don't think I can take this,*' he recalls. After Pell's sentencing, Richter tried to take a step back from work, contemplating whether it was all worth it after almost five decades.

'I thought about it for weeks. I tried not to work. And then, as time went on, I thought, *No, I'm not giving up. I have certain abilities and skills I don't think should go to waste. I'm not ready to retire.* There are certain cases that come up, and I thought if I could do anything to help, I should. When I run out of energy I want to reduce the workload and start advising more, on tactics and things of that nature. But, at the moment, I'm in full fighting mode. At my age, I can no longer work 48 hours nonstop, but I can still work until two or three in the morning.'

While Walker led the appeal, Richter focused on recovering, and then on offering his services pro bono to other cases. He also took on some smaller sexual assault trials, securing acquittals for his clients in each one. It restored his confidence.

'And that made me think, *I just don't know what to think about the jury in the Pell case,*' he said. 'As a barrister, I have to accept that juries get things right, by and large. But there's a moral panic when it comes to sexual abuse that requires people to assume that because someone claims to be a victim you treat them as a victim, as though that's all that's required as proof to begin with.'

When the Court of Appeal upheld the verdict, it was another blow to Richter, but when I interviewed him he felt resigned about letting the process play out, and he seemed hopeful.

'I also have to accept, as does the High Court, that every now and again the jury will get something wrong, and they'll get it wrong in a way that results in a court quashing a conviction. I've committed too much time and effort to this one to allow myself to think at this stage we will lose.'

Asked if he would run the trial differently if he could do it all again, Richter said vehemently, 'No.

'How could we run the case in any different way? Pell says it didn't happen. How do you prove a negative? Well, you try to bolster that denial with anything you can find. We had to dig it all out. They police never looked at proper Church archives, they didn't go through the Church newspapers, they didn't obtain archival material like diaries about who said when or what. We did all of that. This case cried out for a proper investigation. But the police just didn't do it.'

He does not accept that McGlone or Portelli were unreliable witnesses who might have hampered Pell's case. Even if the jury saw them as biased, there had been no evidence they were lying, Richter said.

Richter told me that Kidd was 'a wonderful judge' who ran the trial well. 'He was completely even-handed.'

He held no regrets about representing Pell, or any of the other alleged criminals he has represented throughout his career. Everyone has the right to a defence, and while the role may not make him popular, he has represented criminals accused on flimsy or false evidence, and has advocated for greater scrutiny of police powers and the protection of vulnerable alleged perpetrators. He has taken on cases to improve access to health care for women. While the public does not always appreciate a defence barrister's role, Richter said, he didn't let these judgements and misconceptions about his work deter him.

'The law says you take instructions from the client,' he said. 'You're obliged to. The only thing you're not allowed to do is tell lies. If a client wants you to tell a lie, you refuse. You test the case. You train yourself not to judge. You'll talk to some clients and demonstrate to them what they're saying doesn't make sense, and to plead guilty. That's your function, too. Not to come to a judgement about guilt, but explain the risks. Most of the work of criminal lawyers is not fighting trials. It's pleading guilty and trying to get a decent outcome.'

His assessment, when it came to the case of Pell, was that the alleged offending did not happen and could not have happened. He never came close to believing Pell was guilty, or that the evidence suggested he might be.

Would he begin to doubt that if the High Court, like the Supreme Court, upheld the conviction?

'No,' he said. 'I do not believe that it happened.'

CHAPTER TWELVE

Acquittal

'This case does not define me. I am a man who came forward
for my friend who, sadly, is no longer with us.'
— The complainant

I flew from Melbourne to Canberra, where the High Court bench
was sitting to hear Pell's case, early on 11 March 2020. Among those
joining me on the red-eye flight were journalists and members of the
prosecution's team, including Detective Sergeant Chris Reed. There
was something surreal about being on a flight with the same people
with whom I had spent weeks in a small Melbourne courtroom.
Almost two years after being committed to stand trial, Pell was
making a last-ditch attempt to appeal his case, taking it to the High
Court, the highest court in the Australian judicial system. Win
or lose, his case was about to come to an end. If the High Court
decided the conviction should stand, Pell would have nowhere left
to go. He would serve the rest of his non-parole period behind bars,
unless he died first.

Across two days in March 2020, the full bench of seven High
Court justices heard Pell's barrister, Bret Walker SC, argue that
Victoria's appellate judges – who had dismissed Pell's first appeal
by a majority of two to one – had been unduly influenced by the
complainant's testimony, and had failed to consider other evidence
rigorously because of that. This had been exacerbated by the justices

watching the video of the complainant's evidence rather than just reading the transcript, Walker argued. It meant the judges may have gone too far, taking on the role of the jury, rather than taking a more holistic approach to establish whether all of the evidence should have led to a conviction to the criminal standard of beyond reasonable doubt.

As with the Supreme Court appeal, there were all kinds of murmurs and predictions as to what would happen. Those who seemed most confident were those who had only taken a real interest in the case once Pell was convicted and began his process of appeals. But if the appellate judges of the Supreme Court had been difficult to predict, the High Court bench was even harder to read. Many media commentators and legal experts were once again saying that Pell would be acquitted, some of them even saying he would walk free from jail that day; that the bench would immediately grant leave for Pell to appeal and, having already decided the verdict was unsafe, would order Pell to be released so that, as an acquitted man, he did not languish in jail.

A couple of sources told me that whatever the outcome, it would likely be a unified one. That, by and large, the chief justice, Susan Kiefel, had unified the court; she was a firm believer that a strong-majority or unanimous decision instilled greater public confidence in the judicial process.

But I largely kept any radical tip-offs or predictions to myself. There can be a vanity in journalism in getting it first and being right, but I knew that were I to predict the outcome publicly and turn out to be correct, it would be through luck rather than any insider knowledge. I had, by now, spent years of my life covering child sexual abuse and the case of Cardinal George Pell, and I had long ago realised that trying to pre-empt court findings was a fool's game. Arguments given weight by the public can also differ greatly from arguments considered by justices behind closed doors.

I was most concerned, however, about my ability to report quickly and accurately. This was hampered by the set-up of the court. Laptops are not allowed in the courtroom, which presents difficulties for journalists needing to send rapid updates to editors and to transcribe arguments. A separate courtroom was therefore set up for the media. In this courtroom, power points were scarce. Eventually, we convinced court staff to find extension cords and adapters for us; they understood that we were there to fulfil a public duty, and should not be unnecessarily hampered in doing our work. Even so, we were not permitted to use the bar tables in the court room, or the power points surrounding them. These precious, historic tables, we were told, were for legal personnel and court staff only.

As a result, a couple of dozen reporters had to try to position themselves in the public seating of the court room so they could see the tiny television screen in the front corner of the room – in the section reserved for legal and court staff – that had a live-stream connected to the courtroom. It was difficult to see the faces of the justices or to discern at first who was speaking, until we became used to their individual voices. We sat crammed in the narrow rows with laptops on our laps and chargers by our sides, electrical cords strewn on the floor, as we fought for a plug on the adapters. We were not allowed to bring our drink bottles into the room. It was a disgraceful set-up for covering a High Court ruling on one of the most high-profile child sexual abuse cases in Australia's history.

Outside the court, Pell supporters who arrived together on a bus gathered holding crosses and a sign that read 'We are praying for you Papa'. A victim advocate held up a sign that read 'Go to hell Pell'.

Walker's central argument was that Pell did not have the time or opportunity to offend. While he accepted that jurors found the complainant believable and compelling, he argued before Kiefel and the other justices that this was beside the point. 'The true question is not, "Do I believe the complainant" but whether, "having believed the complainant, is there any reasonable doubt as to [Pell's] guilt?",' Walker said. The jury's perception of the complainant's credibility should not have alone persuaded them of Pell's guilt beyond reasonable doubt when his evidence, even if it was impressive and believable, did not address questions of doubt raised by the defence, such as a lack of opportunity for the offending to have occurred.

'It is an extreme fallacy for anyone to assume the credibility of the complainant will supply an answer to reasonable doubt raised via evidence to which the complainant says nothing,' Walker said. In his submission to the court, Walker wrote, 'Any conflation of the concepts of "belief" and "elimination of doubt" is an attempt to fundamentally depart from the defining safeguards of the accusatorial system of criminal justice. These safeguards protect people from the risk of being wrongfully convicted of crimes they did not commit.'

He reiterated the evidence given by Pell's master of ceremonies, Charles Portelli, that Pell would usually remain on the front steps of the cathedral after mass, greeting parishioners for anywhere up to 20 minutes. If this were the case, Walker told the bench, there would be no opportunity for Pell to offend in the sacristy. Prosecutors argued at trial that while standing on the steps became Pell's custom, it was not yet customary when he first became archbishop in 1996, and other witnesses gave evidence that there were occasions when this meet-and-greet might be skipped or cut short.

But Walker told the High Court that the prosecution had not discredited Portelli's evidence. His evidence was 'material on the basis of which you cannot eliminate the possibility that the archbishop was on the front steps'. That 'forensically' put a 'full-stop' on any chance to offend, Walker said. 'That's another point that says it was not open to find guilt, on the balance, beyond reasonable doubt.' Even if Portelli could not remember exact dates, his evidence 'shows at least the possibility that he was with the archbishop meeting and greeting at the opposite end of the cathedral where he had to be at the time of the alleged offending'.

Walker brought up Portelli's description of the robes Pell wore when he was archbishop, including Portelli's demonstration of how the cincture around the waist was tied. Pell's defence team argued during trial that it would have been impossible for Pell to manoeuvre the robes in such a way to expose his penis and assault the boys. The jury had before them uncontested evidence that the robes could not be manoeuvred in a certain way, Walker said, to which Justice Virginia Bell replied, 'But the jury did have the robes as an exhibit in the jury room.'

Walker responded, 'Unfortunately, none of us knows what experiments that led to.'

The following day, the director of the Office of Public Prosecutions, Kerri Judd, QC, responded to Walker's arguments. Journalists in the room were quick to admonish her performance, describing her as stilted and scoffing when she paused before responding, or stumbled for words. I had learned my lesson from the Supreme Court appeal, when people had similarly admonished senior prosecutor Chris Boyce. A poor performance by a prosecutor alone would not be enough to sway an experienced bench of seven justices. Pell was the applicant in the appeal; it was no surprise that prosecutors, being the ones responding, were being peppered with questions by the bench. I had asked my legal contacts about Judd, and no one had anything bad to say about her. She was described as a professional, formidable, and whip-smart.

The bench questioned the decision of Victoria's appellate court to watch video evidence from the complainant in Pell's trial, asking Judd what her response was to Walker's argument that it might have caused the majority of judges to give too much weight to the complainant's compelling and believable demeanour rather than to the trial evidence as a whole.

Judd responded by saying that given Pell's legal team made so much of the complainant's lack of credibility and believability, Victoria's appellate court was entitled to watch the video. It did not mean they had elevated it above other evidence, or that they had not given due weight to other evidence from the trial.

Kiefel responded that the difficulty with the appellate judges having viewed the complainant's video was that 'the assessment of a witness by demeanour is so subjective'.

'It's very difficult to say how it [the video of the complainant] affected an intermediate appellate court judge in terms of how they read the transcript. That's why you really shouldn't do it [watch the video] ... unless there is a forensic reason to do it. To what extent is this court to determine the extent to which the Court of Appeal was influenced by the video?'

It remains uncommon for an appellate court to view video evidence, though it is becoming more common as technology is more frequently used. Appellate courts are often cautioned about usurping the jury's role, and by viewing a transcript alone may be more capable of leaving questions of the demeanour of witnesses to the jury, and of taking a more objective and dispassionate view of the evidence. Demeanour is not always a good indicator of truth.

But Judd responded that Portelli did not have convincing specific recollections of what Pell did on the dates in 1996 when the alleged offending occurred. Portelli could not even remember if the choir processed out of the buildings on those occasions internally or externally, she said. Portelli's evidence should not be viewed in isolation, she added. 'Quite a number of choirboys and others do say there were occasions where he [Pell] did not stand on the steps and processed, and the choirboys recall having to wait for him. There's also some evidence from choirboys saying they saw him in the choir room pretty soon after mass. So if he's standing on those steps for a long period of time he's not going to be able to see those choirboys.'

Bell put it to Judd, 'The appeal had to be allowed if it was reasonably established that the archbishop was present on the western steps at the time the complainant was offended against.'

Judd responded the bench needed to consider the evidence on a whole, not just based on Portelli. She added that Portelli's memory was not necessarily reliable.

In his response to Judd on Thursday afternoon, Walker said all the Crown had done was raise the possibility that certain events might have happened that allowed the offending to occur. That was not good enough to prove beyond reasonable doubt that the offending had occurred. There were many examples, Walker said, of the Crown engaging in 'an inappropriate and over-engineered attempt of improvisation to make fit matters which won't fit'.

Judd told the bench that the complainant's accurate description of the priests' sacristy, which was off-limits to choirboys and where the abuse occurred, added to his truthfulness. But Walker responded, 'There is nothing about the knowledge of the room that means the archbishop must have been in it.' He told the bench that if they found any error had been made by the jurors or in the way the case was run, then 'we wish the matter to be over'. 'The best way for it to be over is this court entering an acquittal.'

At the end of the day, Kiefel announced that the bench would reserve its decision until a later date. The court was adjourned. Pell would not be walking free that day.

And then the ABC investigative documentary *Revelation*, led by journalist Sarah Ferguson, went to air, days before the High Court was to deliver its decision. In the documentary, two accusers said that Pell had abused them in the 1970s in Ballarat, including in the YMCA swimming pool. One of the men, identified only as 'Bernie' by Ferguson, was initially going to give evidence in the Swimmers' trial. But, he told Ferguson, the psychological pressure was too great for him to go through with it, and he was among the witnesses to withdraw from the case.

Bernie said that he had been abandoned by his mother at birth, became a ward of the state, and was placed in a Catholic orphanage in Ballarat. Pell would visit boys at the home, Bernie said, and Pell became a father figure to him. He recalls Pell being in the home when the boys would shower.

He told Ferguson: 'Before I know it, he's soaping my genitals … soaping me all over … rubbing his hand up my butt crack. He pulled my foreskin over the head of my penis, and that really, really hurt … he said, "It's normal, it won't hurt as much as time goes on."'

During the committal proceedings, Richter had slammed the notion of Pell having been a frequent visitor at the home, saying Pell had only ever visited the orphanage once, when it was about to close down.

Bernie said he also recalled Pell swimming with boys from local schools and orphanages at the Ballarat YMCA swimming pool. Bernie said Pell would play a game with him, hiding 20 cents down his swimming trunks and encouraging Bernie to find it. He also recalled Pell showering with children in the change rooms. His allegations were supported by another alleged victim whom Ferguson spoke to, named Peter Clarke. Clarke said the boys at the pool would warn each other about Pell's behaviour. 'We'd say, "Watch your nuts, watch your nuts."' Police from Taskforce SANO approached Clarke as part of their investigation, but Clarke said he wanted no part of it.

The world changed drastically in the three weeks between the hearing and the bench delivering their decision on 7 April. Covid-19, the virus spreading throughout the world, had been declared a pandemic as the Pell High Court hearings ended. Countries around the world were gradually shutting down, Australia included, as governments fought to stop the virus spread. The Australian state of Tasmania closed its borders first, and other states followed. By the time the High Court reconvened to deliver its judgment, physical distancing was in place, limiting the number of people who could be in a venue or even in a room at the same time. Domestic and international travel had been effectively stopped, except in exceptional circumstances. Even if reporters were to fly to Brisbane, where the decision was being delivered (the bench travels to Commonwealth law venues around the country for cases, although Canberra is the court's 'home'), there was no guarantee the courtroom would be able to accommodate them, due to the strict physical-distancing measures in place.

The case was about to come to an end, and those of us who had been there for the entirety – by now down to about two or three reporters – would not be there to witness it.

However, the High Court said that the decision would be over in a matter of minutes, if not seconds. Kiefel would read the decision, but not the reasons for it. A summary of the judgment and the full judgment would then be published online within minutes. Thankfully, my colleague from *Guardian Australia* Ben Smee is based in Brisbane as the Queensland correspondent, and was able to head to the court and vie for a seat. From my apartment in Melbourne, I waited for the full judgment to appear on the High Court's website so I could go through it and report the findings. Due to Covid-19, I, along with many other Australians, was working from home. There were not even any colleagues in the room to share and discuss the decision with. I was also concerned that the website might crash with so many people refreshing it while waiting to read the full judgment. The case that had begun with a media frenzy and vocal members of the public demonstrating outside Melbourne's magistrate court was about to end in Brisbane with hardly anyone there to see it.

As Smee and about a dozen reporters gathered at the court, and as reporters in newsrooms throughout the world logged on to the High Court's website, another pack of journalists was gathering outside Barwon Prison, a maximum-security prison for men located about 60 kilometres from Melbourne. They were ready to capture Pell's release if the court decided he was to be acquitted. At the court, Smee described how physical-distancing rules meant that only three journalists and two lawyers were ultimately allowed to sit inside. Another small group, including Smee, stood near the open door to listen in.

At about 10.02 am, Smee shared the outcome. Kiefel dispassionately ordered that 'the appellant's convictions be quashed and judgments of acquittal be entered in their place'.

'And that was that,' Smee wrote in a piece for *Guardian Australia* about being at the court for the historic decision. 'No emotional outbursts, gasps or screams. Just a handful of observers, looking at one another and trying to comprehend how unremarkable and utterly remarkable that moment had been. National history, delivered like an announcement to a doctor's waiting room.' Meanwhile, I was frantically trying to access the court's reasons. As I had feared, the website had crashed. I emailed the court media officer and urged him to email it through. It arrived in my inbox at 10.08 am.

'The High Court found that the jury, acting rationally on the whole of the evidence, ought to have entertained a doubt as to the applicant's guilt with respect to each of the offences for which he was convicted, and ordered that the convictions be quashed and that verdicts of acquittal be entered in their place,' the one-page summary of the judgment said. The decision was unanimous.

The full 36-page judgment stated there was 'a significant possibility that an innocent person has been convicted because the evidence did not establish guilt to the requisite standard of proof'. The judgment gave brief outlines of the prosecution's case, the complainant's evidence, the defence case, and the layout of the cathedral, as well as a general overview of evidence given about how the choir procession exited the building, and the structure of this procession.

Part of the judgment dealt with whether the Supreme Court justices had gone too far by watching video of the trial, including testimony by the complainant and other witnesses. The bench said that while an appellate court watching such video from a trial might be appropriate in cases where there was something particular in the video-recording that would affect their assessment of the evidence, because it could only be discerned visually or by sound, Pell's trial was not one of those cases. In the absence of a forensic reason for viewing video evidence, the appellate court should have refrained from doing so.

'Just as the performance by a court of criminal appeal of its functions does not involve the substitution of trial by an appeal court for trial by a jury, so, generally speaking, the appeal court should not seek to duplicate the function of the jury in its assessment of the credibility of the witnesses where that assessment is dependent upon the evaluation of the witnesses in the witness box,' the judgment said. It also said that the demarcation between the province of the jury and the province of the appellate court had not been superseded by improvements in technology that made video-recording of witnesses possible.

The Court of Appeal majority had also referred to Richter's argument during trial that the offending was 'impossible'. As Weinberg noted in his dissenting judgment at the first appeal, by describing the offending as 'impossible', Richter may have 'set an unnecessary forensic hurdle'. It may have focused the jury's attention on simply whether the offending may have been even minutely possible, rather than whether there was reasonable doubt it could have happened even if it was possible. The High Court said that the appellate judges had done the same as the jury:

> Their Honours reasoned, with respect to largely unchallenged evidence that was inconsistent with those allegations, that notwithstanding each obstacle it remained possible that [the complainant's] account was correct. The analysis failed to engage with whether, against this body of evidence, it was reasonably possible that [the complainant's] account was not correct, such that there was a reasonable doubt as to the applicant's guilt.

This reversed the onus of proof, they said, and may have led the jury to expect Pell's team to prove that the offending was impossible, rather than expect the prosecution to prove beyond reasonable doubt that it happened.

The majority of justices in the Court of Appeal had found there were aspects of the complainant's testimony that would have been difficult to fabricate. For example, they referred to his knowledge of the interior layout of the priests' sacristy. The fact that the archbishop's sacristy was not in use at the time the offending was alleged to have occurred due to renovations taking place added to the complainant's credibility, they found. But the High Court bench were not so impressed by this.

In their judgment, they said that just because the complainant had been inside the priests' sacristy and had described it correctly did not mean that the jurors or the justices in the first appeal should have taken that to mean he was also sexually assaulted by Pell in that room. In other words, while it may have been evidence that the complainant had once been inside the room, it was a stretch to find it was also evidence that he was sexually abused in it.

The High Court found that in order to accept the complainant's evidence, the trial jury and the justices in the Court of Appeal would have needed to also find that, contrary to Pell's practice, he did not stand on the steps of the cathedral greeting congregants for 10 minutes or longer; that, contrary to longstanding church practice, Pell returned unaccompanied to the priests' sacristy in his ceremonial vestments; that no other person entered the priests' sacristy during the offending; and that no one noticed the boys leaving the procession and going back into the cathedral.

But witnesses, including Portelli, Finnigan, Potter, McGlone, and Connor, and numerous former choirboys, all said they could recall Pell greeting parishioners on the church steps for varying periods of time after mass. Portelli, Potter, and McGlone were also among the witnesses who said Pell was always accompanied and never alone during or immediately after mass. All of this, the High Court found, meant that jurors should have had a reasonable doubt as to whether the abuse occurred. The judgment said:

> The suggestion that witnesses' memories may have been affected by the ritual that developed thereafter has echoes of the prosecutor's closing submission, which was that the applicant's [Pell's] practice of greeting congregants may not have developed before 1997. It is a contention that finds no support in the evidence and was not pursued by the respondent on appeal to this Court.

Portelli's evidence was unchallenged, the court found. And yet the majority of the appellate judges had been satisfied of Pell's guilt by 'discounting a body of evidence that raised lively doubts as to the commission of the offences because they considered the likelihood that the memories of honest witnesses might have been affected by delay'. The appellate court was wrong in doing so, the judgment said. 'Making full allowance for the advantages enjoyed by the jury, there is a significant possibility in relation to charges one to four that an innocent person has been convicted.'

And so Pell was acquitted. He was released from prison almost immediately. The large prison gates to the prison car park swung open a couple of hours after the judgment, and a black car emerged with Pell seated in the back. Media captured the moment on video, a large press pack having gathered to capture this moment. Pell was free.

According to Pell, in an exclusive interview with his friend Andrew Bolt one week later, on 14 April 2020, a chorus of cheers emerged from the cells of Barwon Prison when the decision was announced on the news. Inmates had been watching coverage of the decision on televisions in their cells.

Asked by Bolt why he thought the complainant had made the allegations, Pell said, 'I don't know.'

'I wonder whether he was used,' Pell continued. 'I don't know what this poor fellow was up to.' He did not elaborate on who the complainant may have been used by. But he spoke of corruption in the Vatican, and also made allegations of corruption in Victoria. Pell said he was unpopular among some Vatican officials for his efforts to get the institution's finances in order. Asked by Bolt 'how high up the corruption goes', Pell responded, 'Who knows?

'It's a little bit like Victoria,' Pell said. 'You're not quite sure where the vein runs, how thick and broad it is, and how high it goes.' Asked if police had persecuted him, Pell said, 'Well, I think the onus is on them, in the face of that evidence, to show why that's not true.'

Pell said now that he was free, he planned to live in Sydney, with a little bit of travel to Rome.

'I'm 14 years past retirement age in Australia,' he said. 'I'll go quietly. I'll probably do a little bit of writing, keep reading, I'll certainly stay in Sydney. I might go to Rome for a while. I might grow a few cabbages, and a few roses and things.'

The complainant released a statement through his lawyer, Viv Waller, the evening that the High Court decision was announced. He said he accepted the decision:

> I understand their view that there was not enough evidence to satisfy the court beyond all reasonable doubt that the offending occurred.
>
> I understand that the High Court is saying that the prosecution did not make out the case to the required standards of proof. There are a lot of checks and balances in the criminal justice system and the appeal process is one of them. I respect that.
>
> It is difficult in child sexual abuse matters to satisfy a criminal court that the offending has occurred beyond the shadow of a doubt. It is a very high standard to meet – a heavy burden. I understand why criminal cases must be proven beyond all reasonable doubt. No one wants to live in a society where people can be imprisoned without due and proper process.
>
> This is a basic civil liberty. But the price we pay for weighting the system in favour of the accused is that many sexual offences against children go unpunished.
>
> That's why it remains important that everyone who can report to the police does so. I would hate to think that one outcome of this case is that people are discouraged from reporting to the police. I would like to reassure child sexual abuse survivors that most people recognise the truth when they hear it.
>
> They know the truth when they look it in the face. I am content with that.
>
> I would like to thank the police and the Office of Public Prosecutions for their work. I have felt well supported through

this journey. My journey has been long and I am relieved it is over. I have my ups and downs. The darkness is never far away.

Despite the stress of the legal process and public controversy I have tried hard to keep myself together. I am OK. I hope that everyone who has followed this case is OK. This case does not define me. I am a man who came forward for my friend who, sadly, is no longer with us.

I am a man doing my best to be a loving dad, partner, son, brother and friend. I am doing my best to find and hold joy in my life and to provide a safe and loving home for my family.

The spokespeople for the Vatican and the Pope had been silent throughout the case. The Pope had always made it clear that no comprehensive comment would come until the entire legal process was over. Now, with the case ended, the Pope chose the social-media platform Twitter to issue his first reaction. And it was an extraordinary one, which apparently implied that Pell's suffering had been similar to that of Jesus. While the tweet did not mention Pell by name, it came hours after the judgment. It said:

In these days of #Lent we've been witnessing the persecution that Jesus underwent and how He was judged ferociously, even though He was innocent. Let us #PrayTogether today for all those persons who suffer due to an unjust sentence because of someone [who] had it in for them.

An official statement issued by the Holy See said the court decision was a welcome one. 'Entrusting his case to the court's justice, Cardinal Pell has always maintained his innocence, and has waited for the truth to be ascertained,' it read. 'At the same time, the Holy See reaffirms its commitment to preventing and pursuing all cases of abuse against minors.'

Former prime minister Julia Gillard, who had ordered the royal commission into institutional responses to child sexual abuse years earlier, issued a video statement. She didn't comment on the judgment, but spoke about its impact on the community:

> I'm deeply concerned that many, particularly survivors of child sexual abuse and their loved ones, are experiencing waves of despair. Did we learn as a nation from the royal commission into child sexual abuse? Is it worth survivors coming forward to seek justice? My answer to those questions and all the others around them is as follows; today is exactly the right day for every Australian, for every organisation that deals with children, for every church, for every law enforcement agency to commit anew to creating a future where every child is safe from sexual abuse and in which every survivor finds healing and justice, and in which we continue to implement every recommendation of the royal commission.

I had my own questions. What are victims to make of the fact that jurors are told throughout a trial that it is up to them who they believe and whether they accept all, some, or none of the evidence from witnesses? That it was open to them, in other words, to believe the complainant but not in the reliability of other witnesses called?

Ben Mathews, a professor at the Queensland University of Technology's Faculty of Law, told me this was 'a fantastic question that's really difficult to answer'.

'It gets grey and murky, and one thing that helps create this uncertainty is the tension in different court conclusions about the indeterminate notion of reasonable doubt,' he said. 'So you have different courts and individuals making judgements about whether reasonable doubt should have been present when that concept isn't even defined. The reason for that lack of definition in Australia is we put the trust in juries to make the decision.'

Dr Tyrone Kirchengast, a barrister and solicitor of the High Court, said the jury process was sacred, but that also meant it was difficult for studies to be done on how jurors came to their decisions or how much weight they gave different aspects of the evidence.

'Even after the trial is complete, researchers can't interview them about their decision-making processes,' he said. 'The best we have is mock jurors put together to try to study what happens. We should remember that it is only in rare cases where this overturning of a jury verdict occurs, and this is a case of significant notoriety. I think we have to also understand that justice isn't perfect, and it can't always be perfect. It's the case that sometimes innocent people are convicted and guilty people aren't, and what we strive for in Australia is a system that eliminates errors as far as possible. But it's impossible to think of criminal trials as a process of a perfect case being put to a perfect jury.'

He added that trial procedures were being continuously reformed to assist jurors to do their jobs and to lessen chances of error.

Victims of child sexual abuse should not be dissuaded from coming forward and reporting perpetrators as a result, a barrister and professor of law at La Trobe University in Melbourne, Professor Gideon Boas, said. 'It would be unfortunate and legally wrong if the message in the community was that the High Court's ruling has weakened the strength of, or point in, bringing such cases to court or making properly founded allegations. The risk to this kind of messaging is that victims will give up or not bother coming forward. The bottom line is that the ruling will have little or no effect on civil cases and limited effect on future criminal cases.'

He said the Pell case had a set of unique and complex circumstances that would not necessarily be a factor in other jury trials. 'However, any case with an allegation of abuse that is historical and decades ago will have evidentiary issues, especially in cases with only one surviving complainant. It doesn't mean cases with one complainant are not capable of succeeding going forward.' Boas added that the jurors who convicted Pell should not feel as though they had failed, and that the public should not read the High Court decision as a challenge to the sanctity of the jury.

'Victoria's Court of Appeal upheld the jury decision by a majority, and the High Court went the other way,' Boas said. 'I've heard it said a lot in this case, "How could the jury get it so wrong when the High Court decided unanimously it was an unreasonable verdict?" My response is: what's to say the High Court had it right? You had a jury process that functioned, you had a Court of Appeal that by majority agreed with them, and gave it serious consideration, and a High Court who saw it differently. There is no system that is flawless. Some juries will give verdicts that are perverse or unreasonable and, sometimes, so will judges. But victims should know that overturning a jury decision happens rarely.'

Lawyer Peter O'Brien, a barrister who represented victims at the child sexual abuse royal commission and who also represents defendants, told me it was important to remember that not all of those convicted have the opportunity or, more importantly, the money, to have their case considered by the highest court in Australia. In a comment piece written for *Guardian Australia*, O'Brien wrote:

> The only reason they are languishing there [in jail], and Pell is no longer, is because they do not have the funds nor fame to appeal to the High Court in the manner Pell did. And in those rare cases where they are able to attempt it, they are extremely unlikely to be granted special leave to appeal. It is entirely appropriate that an accused can be convicted on the uncorroborated evidence of a complainant. After all, most sexual offences are committed in circumstances where it is only the complainant and the accused

present. Where there is other potentially credible evidence to challenge that account, the jury must apply the high standard of proof to reach their verdict.

He feared this was creating a two-tiered justice system, where those with money and contacts could fight criminal charges and, at most, be held to account in the civil system and ordered to pay compensation, while everyone else would face criminal repercussions, including jail. O'Brien believed there must be better alternatives to this process, which often leaves victims exhausted and questioning if it was worth it.

With Pell's case over, there was, of course, a looming question that had gone unanswered since the royal commission delivered its final report in December 2017. What did Pell know about child sexual abuse in the Catholic Church? On 7 May 2020, one month after Pell's acquittal, Australia's attorney-general, Christian Porter, tabled in parliament the findings from the royal commission relating to Pell. What it found came as no surprise to those who had been present at many of the commission's hearings. Pell knew children were being abused and that priests were being moved from parish to parish in an attempt to deal with them, rather than being reported to police. It meant that these abusers spread like an epidemic through parishes, abusing children in new churches, schools, camps, and communities.

The commission found that Pell was aware of children being sexually abused within the Archdiocese of Ballarat by notorious paedophile priest Gerald Ridsdale, and said it was 'implausible' that other senior church figures did not tell Pell abuse was occurring.

In 2015, at the Ballarat town hall, the commission heard evidence that suggested Pell was involved in the decision to move Ridsdale between parishes once his abusing came to light, including to parishes in Mildura, Swan Hill, Warrnambool, Apollo Bay, Ballarat, and Mortlake. Pell had always denied this or having had any knowledge of children being abused in Ballarat, including by Ridsdale.

But the royal commission found:

> We are satisfied that in 1973 Father Pell turned his mind to the prudence of Ridsdale taking boys on overnight camps.
>
> The most likely reason for this, as Cardinal Pell acknowledged, was the possibility that if priests were one-on-one with a child then they could sexually abuse a child or at least provoke gossip about such a prospect. By this time, child sexual abuse was on his radar, in relation to not only Monsignor [John] Day but also Ridsdale. We are also satisfied that by 1973 Cardinal Pell was not only conscious of child sexual abuse by clergy but that he also had considered measures of avoiding situations which might provoke gossip about it.

As recently as April 2020, Ridsdale pleaded guilty to new child sexual-abuse charges.

Pell said senior figures around him deceived him about the extent of abuse within the Catholic Church. But the commission found:

> We are satisfied that Cardinal Pell's evidence as to the reasons that the Catholic Education Office deceived him was implausible. We do not accept that Bishop Pell was deceived, intentionally or otherwise. It is implausible given the matters set out above that Bishop [Ronald] Mulkearns did not inform those at the meeting of at least complaints of sexual abuse of children having been made.

Pell had also told the commission that it was not his responsibility to investigate paedophile priest Peter Searson, because he believed that the Catholic Education Office and Mulkearns were handling the allegations. Pell gave evidence that he was handed a list of incidents and grievances about Searson in 1989, which included reports that Searson had abused animals in front of children and was using children's toilets. But Pell said this was not enough information for him to act on.

Searson died in 2009 without facing charges. The commission had previously heard that he abused children in parishes and schools across three districts over more than a decade. The commission found that 'these matters, in combination with the prior allegation of sexual misconduct, ought to have indicated to Bishop Pell that Father Searson needed to be stood down'.

> It was incumbent on Bishop Pell, as an auxiliary bishop with responsibilities for the welfare of the children in the Catholic community of his region, to take such action as he could to advocate that Father Searson be removed or suspended or, at least, that a thorough investigation be undertaken of the allegations. It was the same responsibility that attached to other auxiliary bishops and the vicar general when they received complaints. On the basis of what was known to Bishop Pell in 1989, we found that it ought to have been obvious to him at the time. We found that he should have advised the archbishop to remove Father Searson and he did not do so.

During the commission's hearings, Pell had conceded that, in retrospect, he might have been 'a bit more pushy' with all of the parties involved.

'We do not accept any qualification that this conclusion is only appreciable in retrospect,' the commission found.

Victoria Police told me they would receive a copy of the report and would assess the findings. 'At this time it would not be appropriate to comment further about any possible action,' a police spokeswoman told me. While some states and territories, including Victoria, have a concealment offence specifically related to child abuse, no one has been successfully convicted for such an offence. The only conviction for such an offence, against Archbishop Philip Wilson in New South Wales, was overturned by the district court. Victoria did not make reporting of child abuse by clergy mandatory until 2014, and the laws cannot be applied retrospectively. The same difficulties that exist in prosecuting historical child sexual-abuse crime – such as the accused being at a forensic disadvantage, a lack of evidence, and uncertainty around exact dates and times – also exist when it comes to proving crimes of concealment.

There were other findings from the commission about Pell. It was 'satisfied that in the early 1970s Cardinal Pell was told by one or two students, and one or two priests, about [Brother Edward 'Ted'] Dowlan's infractions of a sexual nature with minors'. The commission heard evidence that Pell told the chaplain at St Patrick's College about the rumours, but did not tell the bishop, Mulkearns, or the headmaster of the school, Brother Paul Nangle, about what he had heard.

> Cardinal Pell told us that, with hindsight, he should have done more. In particular, he told us he should have consulted Brother Nangle and ensured that the matter was properly treated. Cardinal Pell said he regretted not doing more at the time. We agree that he should have consulted Brother Nangle and ensured that the matter was properly treated.

A witness identified only as BWF told the royal commission that Dowlan had beaten and molested another boy. But Pell told the commission that BWF was not a credible witness, given he had been convicted of child sexual offences. 'We do not consider that his [BWF's] criminal history of itself undermines his credit in his evidence,' the commission found.

Father Wilfred James Baker, once a priest at the Melbourne Catholic archdiocese, was jailed in 1999 for abusing children. The royal commission found that the senior administration of the Archdiocese of Melbourne, known as the 'curia', and which included Pell, knew in August 1996 that Baker would probably be charged in relation to an incident at Brighton in 1965. Pell and other senior officials were at the meeting where this was discussed, the commission found. 'Archbishop Pell had the authority to remove Father Baker,' the report said. 'Despite that knowledge, Archbishop Pell did not stand down Father Baker at that point in time.' Baker remained in his position at North Richmond – a parish with a primary school attached to it – until May 1997. A period of more than eleven years elapsed between the time that Father Baker was convicted of sexually abusing children and an application was made to have him reduced to the lay state. 'The delay was unacceptable,' the commission found.

In 2015, the commission heard that twenty people alleged that Father Nazareno Fasciale abused them between 1953 and 1985. Complaints were made to police in 1994, but he was not charged before he died in 1996. On 8 December 1993, the Melbourne Archdiocese Personnel Advisory Board (PAB), which responsible for appointing priests, met and carried a motion to accept Fasciale's resignation due to his poor health. Pell was among the senior officials who attended the meeting. 'We are satisfied that Father Fasciale did not resign solely because of his health,' the commission found. 'His resignation was also a result of complaints that he had sexually abused children in the 1950s and 1960s and because assurances had been given to the complainants that he would no longer minister.'

During the commission's hearings, Pell accepted the possibility that he was told of the complaints at or before the meeting. The commission found 'it was inconceivable that the true circumstances of Father Fasciale's resignation were not discussed, when so many senior priests were present with knowledge of complaints against him. Allowing Father Fasciale to resign ostensibly on health grounds was wrong.'

Then there were the findings relating to Father David Daniel, who resigned from the Melbourne archdiocese in 1995 on health grounds, when Pell was still a member of the PAB. Daniel was convicted of multiple child-sex offences in 2000, and died in 2014. The commission said:

> We are satisfied that the true reason for Father Daniel's resignation was the complaints against him of child sexual abuse and other sexual misconduct with adults. Bishop Pell probably knew about complaints of child sexual abuse against Father Daniel. Despite that knowledge, the PAB carried a motion to accept Father Daniel's resignation on the grounds proffered. We are satisfied that it was misleading and that all those present at the PAB meeting who knew of the true reason for the resignation and voted for the motion participated in an act that was misleading.

There have been prominent leaders – including Australian prime ministers, senior police force figures, and school principals – who have apologised profusely for the nation's failures to safeguard children. Even those who were not present at the time of the abuse have apologised. In October 2018, Australia's prime minister, Scott Morrison, formally and sincerely apologised on behalf of the government to victims of child sexual abuse.

'We believe you,' Morrison told more than 800 victims, survivors, and their families in Canberra who had come to watch from the parliament's Great Hall. He offered no excuses or denials:

> Today, we confront a question too horrible to ask, let alone answer. Why weren't the children of our nation loved, nurtured and protected? Why was their trust betrayed? ... [W]e must be so humble to fall before those who were forsaken and beg to them our apology ... A sorry from a nation that seeks to reach out in compassion into the darkness where you have lived for so long. Nothing we can do now will right the wrongs inflicted on our nation's children.

Politicians past and present cried as the apology was read. Perhaps some of them had been victims, or they were moved profoundly by the stories and experiences of those who had been. Some attendees wore badges bearing the names of loved ones who had been abused, but who had died or who could not attend. In a rare move, Question Time, which had been scheduled for that afternoon, was delayed a day at the request of survivors. Morrison continued:

> The crimes of ritual sexual abuse happened in schools, churches, youth groups, scout troops, orphanages, foster homes, sporting clubs, group homes, charities, and in family homes as well. It happened anywhere a predator thought they could get away with it, and the systems within these organisations allowed it to happen and turned a blind eye. It happened day after day, week after week, month after month, and decade after decade. Unrelenting torment. When a child spoke up, they weren't believed and the crimes continued with impunity. One survivor told me that when he told a teacher of his abuse, that teacher then became his next abuser. Trust broken. Innocence betrayed. Power and position exploited for evil dark crimes.

The apology was broadcast live by the ABC. Around the country, people wept.

If these same stories moved Pell to the same extent, he never conveyed it. He never accompanied victims to court, stood shoulder-to-shoulder with them throughout the royal commission hearings, or gave any indication that he had read the commission's findings or was interested in its research. After spending time in prison, facing questioning and a public backlash upon fronting the royal commission years before, and despite the commission making damning findings about his actions, Pell appeared largely unmoved.

His response to the commission's findings was the same as ever. Cold. Dismissive. Resolute. Tone-deaf. And, most of all, disingenuous. Little seemed to have changed from when he stood before the royal commission in 2016 and, before survivors of abuse from Ballarat, told the commission that Ridsdale's abusing was 'a sad story, and it wasn't of much interest to me'.

Following the release of the commission's redacted sections, Pell issued a statement saying he was 'surprised by some of the views of the Royal Commission about his actions. These views are not supported by evidence.' He maintained that he did not know of Ridsdale's abusing children at the time, and that this was not the reason for him being moved between parishes. He also said that a meeting he had with a delegation from Doveton parish in 1989 about Father Peter Searson did not mention sexual assaults, and nor did the delegation ask Pell to remove Searson. The statement was short. There was no acknowledgement of survivors, or any apology for having failed to do more, even in retrospect.

At the time of writing, the Vatican has remained silent on the findings.

In May 2020, the *Herald Sun*, the same newspaper that first broke the story of Pell's charges, reported that Pell is being investigated by police over an incident in the 1970s, when he was a priest in Ballarat. The report did not suggest the allegation was true, and Pell has always vehemently denied all allegations of sexual abuse against him. A Victoria Police spokesman said, 'Victoria Police will not be providing any comment in relation to these allegations.' The Vatican has made no comment on the matter.

In the meantime, in May 2020, a man came forward to tell me that he, too, had been molested by Pell at a swimming pool in Ballarat. He had been a student at St Patrick's Primary School, in Drummond Street, Ballarat, from Grade 3 to Grade 6. After completing his lower-school education, he went to St Patrick's College, a Catholic secondary school for boys in Ballarat.

'In Grade 3, I remember we had swimming lessons with our teacher,' he told me. 'They were on a regular basis, but I cannot recall how regularly. We had the lessons at the pool on Camp and Field Streets, the old YMCA near the old police station. We did not have lessons anywhere else.

'Our teacher would supervise the lesson. She would sit on a seat in the far corner, and issue directions and supervise from there. She never went into the pool, and remained dressed in her regular clothes. We did not have formal lesson as such. It was mainly free recreational swimming, and usually at the end we would have a few races among us all. There were about 25 kids in our class. There were no other children ever at the pool. It was a closed session.

'I cannot recall there being a swimming teacher or any other adults present except for my teacher and, on some occasions, George Pell. Our family were very Catholic. We went to the North Ballarat St Columba's Church almost every Sunday. We also had church sessions with the school during the week. If we did not attend St Columba's on a Sunday, we would attend a Sunday service at St Patrick's Cathedral in Ballarat. This occurred about once per month.

'I had seen George Pell many times before seeing him at the pool. He was a very high-profile and senior Church figure in Ballarat. He was an acquaintance of my mother, and we would often see him around town, and Mum would often engage in conversation with him or about him. I remember George in the pool with us children during swimming lessons on at least two occasions. I distinctly remember thinking, *George is at the pool again.*

'On one occasion, when I was in Year 3, I recall George Pell being in the pool playing with all of the children.

'I recall he was throwing all the kids in various ways. He was pushing them up from their behind, or pushing them forward from their crotch area, so they would fall into the water backward. George was in the pool with us.

'George threw us in the air. Lots of us were thrown. He would at times place his hand on our buttocks and hurl us across the water face forward. He would also throw us backwards in a similar way, with his hand over our genital area. He did this to me and others, although I have no recollection of who particularly, other than myself. In both cases, his other hand would be on the shoulder or armpit area. It was an uncomfortable thing at the time – not physically hurting, but uncomfortable. I have no recollection of George putting his hand inside my swimmers.'

The man emailed the Ballarat police station with details of his memories in March 2019. By this point, the Swimmers' trial had already been dropped by prosecutors. But the man had been living overseas. He did not report earlier because he had been living overseas for much of his adult life.

In October 2019, an officer from Taskforce SANO contacted the man by phone and said there was no evidence of any criminal threshold having been crossed. 'He said my evidence was two years too late,' the man told me. 'Since the convictions against Pell were reported in the Australian press, I have struggled significantly with my memories. In 2019, I had formal counselling sessions through my employer. The focus of these sessions has been Pell and the abuse in Ballarat centered around the Catholic Church. I have found this time to be difficult with significant mood swings, inability to concentrate, and not being able to function in my work. On one occasion, I had to leave work as I was too upset about all this to function. These feelings have carried through into 2020.' He told me he had 'no doubt' about his identification of Pell in the swimming pool. 'I knew him well, and he knew me and my family,' he said.

In June 2020, I contacted Victoria Police about the man's allegations. They confirmed the man's complaint, and told me in a statement: 'Investigations into reports of sexual assault are complex and sensitive. Where a matter is reported to police, an initial assessment takes place and a determination is made as to whether a formal investigation will commence. Some of the considerations are establishing that an offence has been committed or whether a matter is within the statute of limitations.'

What we do know about Pell, among all of the unproven allegations and his acquittal, is that he had occupied senior positions and was present in key parishes where abuse was rife. He knew about the abuse. He may not have been the only one who knew, or even the most senior person who did. No one should be convicted of crimes they did not commit, and no one should be made to take the fall for the actions of others. But Pell was no scapegoat. When it came to child sexual abuse by clergy, he could have and should have done more. And his failure to do so left countless lives shattered.

Clare Linane, from Ballarat, has been living with the aftermath of child sexual abuse for more than a decade. Linane's husband, brother, and cousin were all abused when they were children between 1973 and 1974 by Father Edward 'Ted' Dowlan.

'Pell knew in 1973,' Linane told me once the redacted pages had been made public. 'My husband, Peter, was abused in 1974. I want to stand in front of George Pell and scream at him, "Why didn't you help those little boys?"'

On Pell's statement about the findings, Linane said, 'Pell might be surprised about the findings, but none of us are surprised by Pell's response.

'He is a sad man, and he is not of much interest to us.'

CHAPTER THIRTEEN

Victims

'A key challenge for the commission has been the lack of research on institutional child sexual abuse to date. There has been no large-scale, cross-jurisdiction focus on the topic.'
– Justice Jennifer Coate, former child sexual abuse royal commissioner

Georgie Burg says when she thinks about the man who raped her, John Aitchison, she imagines a predatory animal watching wildlife at dusk.

In April 2018, Aitchison, then 67, was found guilty of five charges of rape and eight acts of indecency against Burg when she was 13 years old. The former Anglican priest was sentenced to nine years in jail, having already served prison time twice for child abuse that occurred in the United Kingdom, Victoria, New South Wales, and the Australian Capital Territory. Though young, Burg was already a talented violinist when Aitchison began sexually abusing her in Canberra in the 1980s. She had dreams of becoming a musician. The first rape took place in the pews of All Saints Anglican church in Ainslie after she had finished violin practice. The second occurred in a nearby church hall. Aitchison went on to abuse and rape Burg multiple times over the years, including at the church and in her mother's home.

Remarkably, an investigation I conducted for *Guardian Australia* revealed that the Uniting Church allowed Aitchison to deliver a sermon in Sydney in 2016, when Aitchison was a known and convicted paedophile, and the church then posted his sermon online for the world to read. The church said it felt comfortable hosting and promoting Aitchison because he had signed a piece of paper promising that he would not harm more children. The video of Aitchison delivering the sermon at the Pitt Street church was available on YouTube until April 2019.

The church also promoted Aitchison's involvement in a church event while he was on trial in 2018 for abusing Burg and facing further serious child-abuse charges, removing his name from the line-up only when he was convicted.

The event was a 'Behind the Scenes Organ Tour' scheduled for 6 May 2018, and was described as 'child friendly'. This was after the five-year inquiry into institutional responses to child sexual abuse by the royal commission, after a global reckoning with abuse, after public anger that so many people were failed by institutions for so long, and despite Aitchison's criminal history. Still, the church promoted Burg's abuser.

'My memory of the first rape is that while Aitchison was watching me play my violin, he was also looking for an opportunity and weighing the risks of attacking me,' Burg told me. 'He knew the movements of the "church ladies", he predicted what would happen and when. In some ways, watching wildlife at dusk is a good analogy. Aitchison had the same way of standing on the edge of things, watching us kids and then, without warning, he'd move like a kangaroo, but one that was more like a predator.

'What characterised both rapes were speed, opportunity, and an arrogance that, because he was a priest who was often around musical children, there was no reason for any other adults around to be particularly watchful. Those two rapes were over quickly – the first happened with my mother actually outside the church waiting in the car for me.

'What I think people miss in cases like Aitchison's and Pell's is that those who are claiming impossibility don't seem to have knowledge of what it was like to be a child musician and within a church setting. We were very, very musical children, and treated as though we were simply mini adults. In my experience, it was quite common for anyone who had a solo to be pulled aside at various points to "run" the solo. You could be pulled aside into really any area without any warning. It was also common for a soloist to be paired with an organist to "run" the solo before performances – in Aitchison's case, this allowed him plenty of opportunities to abuse kids, sometimes in open sight.'

Burg gave up music, despite her talent being so promising that she could have made it her career.

'Knowing what the supervision of child choirs was like, I find it completely believable that Pell was able to abuse the boys in the sacristy,' she told me. 'As the musical children at the centre of all this, we were extraordinarily talented, and this was what made us attractive in church settings. We knew we were there to play and shut up.'

One of the defence's arguments in Pell's case that Burg found hard to accept was that Pell would have to have been mad to take the risk of abusing the choirboys. But he was not insane, the defence team argued. Why would he take such a risk, knowing there were other people around who might walk in at any time?

'Because they can,' Burg says bluntly. 'Because they are every bit as dangerous as sharks. They're unpredictable, they were able to do whatever they wanted, and knew that no one would hold them accountable. Because they were powerful, it was a game. They found it satisfying in some sick, twisted way.'

A recurrent theme from the thousands of stories told to Australia's child sexual abuse royal commission is that abuses took place everywhere that adults were. Often, adults in charge and close to clergy turned a blind eye. Other times, adults simply weren't paying attention. Around these godly figures, they did not think they needed to.

'When adults are busy gossiping and being sociable, they're not looking at kids, and they're not looking at who is looking after those kids,' Burg said.

'Paedophiles know this. Look at Jimmy Savile in England, who was raping hundreds of kids – look at the Louis Theroux documentary about him. You've got Savile openly harassing BBC female journalists, and not even the camera crew says anything. This is how it happens. And this is why anyone who says, "It couldn't have happened," or "There were some problems, but it's all in the past," or 'Our child-safe policies are watertight" is guaranteeing that child abuse will continue.

'If you're determined not to look, you open up a space for a paedophile to step in – they see the arrogant entitlement in those statements; they know how dangerous it is, and they're ready to abuse the next generation.'

Men like Aitchison also knew that even if they were caught, no one was going to report them.

'These are intelligent, articulate, highly educated men,' Burg said. 'They hold multiple degrees – they're absolutely idolised. They can talk their way out of anything – being a kid on the receiving end of a mind like that, I've spent my life feeling really stupid, because they're fantastic at justifying and going on the attack if they ever feel caught out.

'The reality is that everyone covers for men like Aitchison. They're "valuable" to society. They're sent overseas on scholarships. They hold Order of Australia medals, and stand in front of hundreds of people talking about how they know better. Having spent four years end-to-end to jail Aitchison, I lost my job simply because I told my manager that there was an upcoming trial for Aitchison. That's how enormous the loyalty is to the churches. I haven't worked since. So you tell me – what happens to victims who speak out against these men? Will Pell's complainant be able to stay employed if his employer finds out?

'We know we aren't believed, even when we prove it in a court of law. We know that for the rest of our lives we get to be seen as "troublemakers" who are dangerous to employ because we're perceived as "litigious". We're expected to lose everyone we love, to lose our health, our sanity.

'Meanwhile? Our perpetrators are promoted, encouraged, supported, and lauded as heroes. Frankly, having lost my mother to suicide because of this, it really is surprising to me that more survivors haven't taken their own lives.

'If society hates you, what's the point?'

Coming forward to report abuse is complicated. A review of the empirical literature examining the impact of child sexual abuse on interpersonal functioning, led by Ramona Alaggia from the University of Toronto and published in 2017, examined factors that facilitated or presented a barrier to the disclosure of child sexual abuse. The abuse was still occurring at troubling rates, with the highest global rates found for girls in Australia/New Zealand (21.5 per cent) and for boys in Africa (19.3 per cent). According to the research, published in the journal *Trauma, Violence and Abuse*, 'These findings point to the incongruence between the low number of official reports of child sexual abuse to authorities and the high rates reported in prevalence studies.' The paper referred to a meta-analysis of 217 child sexual abuse studies published between 1980 and 2008, which revealed that rates of child sexual abuse were more than 30 times greater in studies where people self-reported abuse, compared to statistics from official reports to police and other protective services.

So why don't more children disclose the fact that they have suffered, even after they become adults? The study found there were far more barriers preventing children from disclosing than supports in place to help, encourage, and enable them to feel safe enough to tell someone. Environment, age, and cultural factors all played a part.

Alaggia's analysis found that disclosure is often a process, not a single event. People may disclose their abuse directly or indirectly, using different language at different times, omitting certain details, testing the responses of different people. They may disclose through diary entries or imagery. Different factors may trigger a move towards disclosure. For example, some victims are confronted with the trauma of their abuse when they have their own children. Or memories of their abuse might surface when their children turn the same age as they were when they were abused. Seeing themselves in their child at the same age may also prompt them to comprehend just how small and innocent they too would have been at that age, and help them to appreciate that the abuse could not possibly have been their fault.

The relationship to the perpetrator also played a role in disclosure, Alaggia found. Disclosure was much more difficult when the victim lived with their perpetrator, or when the perpetrator was close to the family, such as a family friend, relative, or respected community member.

In terms of environmental factors, one study revealed that neighbourhood/community conditions can hinder disclosure when there is lack of school involvement in providing a supportive environment, such as in following up on troubling student behaviour. Additionally, a child victim's anticipation of a negative response to disclosure, especially that they may not be believed by others outside their family such as neighbours or other community members, has shown to deter disclosure.

With children and youth under the age of 18, sexual abuse was more likely to be detected, for example by witnesses, teachers, or health-care providers, than disclosed, the research found. The legal system had been slow to implement the latest findings around disclosure and child sexual abuse, which meant that too many victims were still disadvantaged in legal proceedings. 'There are still a substantial number of children and youth who are subjected to sexual abuse, despite preventative efforts,' Alaggia concluded. 'Just as concerning is the fact that many victims continue to suffer in silence as evidenced by the high numbers of delayed disclosure. These hidden cases should not be overlooked, and these victims should not be forgotten.'

It turns out that it is a destructive myth that child sexual abuse is something that adults should move past and forget about because it might have happened decades prior. This belief implies that victims have a choice in terms of their suffering and recovery from abuse. It implies that trauma is a process that survivors of abuse can always predict or control.

Not all victims are the same in terms of the impact of the abuse on them. The strength of support systems, including family and friends, is frequently found to be central in assisting survivors of abuse to cope. It can also be difficult to identify the impact of child sexual abuse when children may have also suffered other kinds of neglect, hardship, and abuse, such as family violence and poverty. Often, the most vulnerable children are targeted by abusers because of their disadvantage, and these are the children who often have the least resources and support available to them, both immediately and in the long term.

An Australian study involving 1,991 twin pairs found that in twins where one had been sexually abused and the other had not, the abused twin had significantly higher rates of major depression and attempted suicide, even after controlling for other factors such as disadvantaged background. The study, led by Elliot Nelson from the Washington University School of Medicine, found that conduct disorder, alcohol dependence, nicotine dependence, social anxiety, rape as an adult, and divorce were also more common in the twin who was sexually abused as a child. Nelson also found that a history of child sexual abuse was a significant risk factor for later illicit drug use, across all drug classes.

Meanwhile, a study from the University of Arkansas published in 2000 examined the impact of child sexual abuse on adult interpersonal relationships. The investigators found that the trauma of child sexual abuse had implications for interpersonal functioning beyond that of the intimacy and sexual functioning between partners. Survivors often had fears about becoming a parent because of worries that they could not keep their children safe, feeling inadequate compared with their partner. They reported feeling less confident and less in control of their family dynamic and role. The investigators also noted that there are some survivors of child sexual abuse who report few adverse outcomes at all.

'Researchers have been very involved in the documentation of the type and magnitude of difficulties, yet we know very little about survivors who are functioning at higher levels,' the paper concluded. 'Although the study of the negative after-effects of child sexual abuse is very important, it is equally important to know what may counter the negative effects. This area of research would have great implications for clinicians in terms of planning interventions that may assist survivors in coping better with the impacts.'

The impact on family members of survivors of abuse is also profound, with these people often referred to as 'secondary victims'. Shireen Gunn is the manager of the Centre Against Sexual Assault in Ballarat. As well as working with primary victims, the centre also engages with family members of those who were abused. Disclosure often comes as a relief to them, she said.

'For many family members of survivors, especially the children of parents who have been abused, everything suddenly makes sense to them once the victim discloses that abuse,' Gunn told me. 'Suddenly, certain aspects of their childhood or behaviours from their parent start to make sense – it helps them to make sense of their experience. The other response from secondary victims is, of course, anger. They want to do something to hold their family member's perpetrator to account. But it's very important that the victim or survivor have control over what happens, if and when they take action or go to police.'

There is little research on the impact of sexual assault on secondary victims, according to the Australian Institute of Family Studies.

'To the extent that secondary victims are considered in the literature, the focus is usually on the manner in which their response to the victim/survivor's experiences helps or hinders the primary victim's recovery,' the institute said. 'This is an important concern. Higher levels of unsupportive behaviour by family members has been found to be more likely for sexual assault victims than for victims of non-sexual assaults.' But few studies had examined the trauma experienced by someone finding out a family member had been sexually abused.

I interviewed the family members of Georgie Burg, who, despite her own trauma, has become a strong and powerful advocate for abuse survivors. Her husband, Phil, and their children told me they have learned more about Burg's abuse as the years have gone by, sometimes accidentally, such as when she talks in her sleep or has nightmares. Or sometimes by necessity, as the calls she received from detectives while she was going through the process of taking her perpetrator to court required an explanation. Her son learned about the abuse of his mother just before Christmas when he was in Year 10, just after he had finished his exams. His parents had been talking to detectives and representatives from the Anglican church, and they decided it was time he knew what was going on. He was angered most by the fact that no one had helped his mother when she was a child. And he was saddened he could not take away her pain.

'It's almost worse, not helping when you can see something is wrong,' he told me. 'I'm a firm believer that if you see or know about something wrong, you have to do something. If you hide something like this happening to someone it's wrong. They [the church] should also know that the effect isn't just on that one person. It's like a web. Like a spider that keeps on building its web, things like this just keep building.'

He told me he felt angry that he could not always talk about the problem with friends or adults who 'think the world is safe and simple'. 'But it's not. Because sometimes I come home, and I've got Mum going through this. And it's painful at times.'

Some researchers have been exploring the potential of restorative justice, where victims can meet their perpetrators, or someone connected to their abuse, such as a family member who did not report it, and talk about how they have been affected. The sessions are moderated and voluntary for all sides, and driven by the wishes of the victim. Victims usually seek different resolutions from restorative justice, but they can range from recognition of what happened to them to an apology. Restorative justice programs are intended to provide an alternative to going through the courts, a process that can often be drawn-out and traumatising for victims. But experts in legal reform and abuse have warned that, if the programs aren't run carefully, these programs can cause harm, and even in a well-run restorative justice program, victims and survivors risk being retraumatised if they do not get the resolution they seek. While restorative justice is not new, it is rarely used in sexual assault cases because of their complexity, a demand for hard-justice approaches to dealing with perpetrators, and the potential for victims to be traumatised.

Anne Cossins, an associate professor in law at the University of New South Wales and an Australian legal-reform expert in the area of sexual assault, said restorative justice programs for sexual assault victims could be fraught. The limited evidence available suggests the only cases that benefit from going to restorative justice are historical sexual abuse cases, she said, after the victim had undergone counselling. 'But even then there can be a power imbalance between the perpetrator and the victim, if the victim still isn't coping, and then the process may bring their trauma back,' Cossins said. 'I worry about the retraumatisation of victims in that process and whether the people running the program would be appropriately qualified to deal with that type of distress. We know the most common cause of post-traumatic stress is sexual assault. There are a lot of myths around restorative justice, that it brings the victims closure and that the offender apologises and says he will never do it again. But you don't always get that outcome, and just because someone admits guilt, it doesn't mean they are sincere.'

But Associate Professor Bebe Loff, director of the Michael Kirby Centre for Public Health & Human Rights at Monash University, said alternatives to courts were needed. 'No one is happy about how victims of sexual assault are dealt with at the moment,' she said. 'We will never have a criminal prosecution system that will satisfactorily deal with most of these cases. Crimes need to be proven beyond reasonable doubt, and when you are talking about acts of sexual assault, it really is a challenge for the court to be able to ensure somehow that enough evidence can be produced to convince anybody that this was a crime.' The criminal justice system was set up that way for extremely good reason, Loff said – to prevent an innocent person being convicted.

'But if one is thinking about how to support victims in a way that doesn't mess up the criminal justice system while also providing a criminal justice response, you must be prepared to explore more creative approaches.'

In 2015, some adult victims of sexual assault were given the opportunity to face their perpetrators and describe the impact of the attack on their lives as part of the pilot of a world-first restorative justice program in Victoria. The program had the backing of senior police, psychiatrists, and sexual assault organisations, and was run by the South Eastern Centre Against Sexual Assault (SECASA) and evaluated by academics at Monash University. Among the letters of support for the program was one from the president of the Victorian Court of Appeal, Justice Chris Maxwell. In his letter, he wrote that there was 'an urgent need for restorative justice alternatives to the criminal justice system for victims of sexual violence', and that the importance of the pilot 'cannot be overstated'. 'It has the potential to transform the way we respond to sexual violence,' he wrote.

Carolyn Worth is the manager of SECASA, and headed the pilot program. She ensured that survivors and victims of sexual assault faced their perpetrator or the person they wanted to speak with in a supportive environment, with staff trained in facilitating restorative justice sessions. All participants were given written information about the process and its risks, including potential legal risks, and the trained facilitators were cognisant of the potential for manipulative or grooming behaviour on the part of the perpetrator.

Loff and her colleagues reviewed the pilot, and provided their findings in a report to the Criminology Research Advisory Council. They emphasised that restorative justice, 'when applied to sexual and family violence, cannot have as its primary aim the restoration of mutually respectful, equal relationships'. Closure was not the motivation for the survivor/victim taking part, and often harm was too complex to be 'repaired' simply through a restorative justice session. Eight survivor/victims and four people responsible for harming them agreed to participate in the study of the pilot, so Loff and her colleagues emphasised that, as with much research into restorative justice, small case numbers make it difficult to draw strong conclusions. But for the survivor/victims involved, being heard and having harms acknowledged were their strongest motivations to participate in the program. 'Securing particular outcomes was less of a motivation for participation,' the analysis, published in 2019, found.

> One finding that does emerge strongly, though not unconditionally, is that all participants believe that a process similar to the one they experienced should be made available to survivors/victims and the persons who have harmed them,' the analysis found. 'Another finding made here on the basis of limited data, but reinforced by other studies, is that restorative justice for entrenched and longstanding family violence should be approached with extreme caution.

Dr Judy Courtin, a lawyer representing victims of institutional sex abuse, published research in 2015 titled *Sexual Assault and the Catholic Church: are victims finding justice?* Her seminal research interviewed 70 people from Victoria and New South Wales, including 52 victims of abuse within the church and 18 immediate family members of those victims, and they were asked about their experiences with civil litigation, criminal prosecutions, and the Catholic Church's internal complaints processes. The central point of Courtin's research was to answer the question: what did justice look like for these people? What exactly did it mean? Their perpetrator acknowledging the harm? Seeing their perpetrator jailed? Compensation?

Her research found that in order to achieve justice, victims needed to be able to tell their story and also to feel that senior figures in the institution where the abuse occurred were held to account.

'Victims want to tell their own truth, but they want an equal exchange of the truth from the hierarchy about what happened,' she said. In fact, even more than individual perpetrators being prosecuted, she said, victims overwhelmingly told her that they wanted the hierarchy of the Catholic Church and its institutions, who often knew about the abuse but covered it up and allowed it to continue, to be held to account.

'Accountability of the hierarchy means criminal accountability for the crime of concealment,' Courtin said. 'We don't have one criminal conviction in Australia against members of the hierarchy of the Catholic Church who have taken part in concealing abuse that occurred. And those who are overseas enjoy impunity.'

The family members of victims said admission of guilt by the perpetrator was important to them.

'But an even bigger concern I found from them was their anger at the ongoing way the Church concealed the crimes, and a need for those people to also be held to account,' Courtin said.

'They felt that those who knew about paedophiles and yet kept quiet fundamentally enabled the activities of paedophiles. They protected them, they covered up their crimes, and they were often not held to account, and that's something that really upsets secondary victims. That maybe their family member wouldn't have been abused if those who knew had spoken up.'

CHAPTER FOURTEEN

Perpetrators

'I am fearful that some of the intent of the reforms of the royal
commission will get lost in the intergovernmental committee
work and that we'll see a tick-the-box approach where
something is done – but it doesn't speak to the intent of the
recommendation and it doesn't change the lives of children.'
– Leah Bromfield, co-director, Australian Centre
for Child Protection, University of South Australia

Melbourne-based forensic psychologist and associate professor Troy
McEwan did not read much of the coverage of Pell's trials, and
for good reason. If Pell were convicted and ordered to undergo
psychological counselling, there was a chance that McEwan would
have been the person assigned to him. She maintains this policy
with most cases; she'd rather learn about an offender's situation if
they are assigned to her as a case, not through the media. She treats
stalkers, sex offenders, and other people with problematic antisocial
behaviours.

In November 2013, the Victorian parliament's Inquiry into the
Handling of Child Abuse by Religious and Other Non-government
Organisations tabled its *Betrayal of Trust* report to government. As a
result, sweeping reforms were introduced to make organisations safer
for children and to increase the responsibility of those organisations
to uphold their duty of care.

McEwan said the reforms, while needed and welcome, had an adverse impact on self-reporters to Forensicare, also known as the Victorian Institute of Forensic Mental Health, the leading provider of forensic mental-health services in Victoria.

'We used to have a small but consistent group of self-referrers to our service. Probably around 10 per cent of our clients had self-referred,' she said.

'The introduction of the betrayal-of-trust legislation has essentially stopped that. People can still self-refer, but if they tell us about any sort of behaviour such as looking at child exploitation material online, we have to report them to police. We are obliged to report them. My personal view is it's not a sensible approach. Of course, we have always had an ethical obligation to report to police if there is imminent risk to a child. But what this legislation means now is people who are acknowledging what they're doing is not right and seeking help are in a position where they might have to put themselves in a very risky situation. This is often exacerbated by the fact that, by the time people came to us, they had often tried to see other clinicians and had a negative response. We are very limited in terms of assistance to those people now, which I think is sad. If you have people thinking these thoughts about children, wouldn't you want to know, and to help them?'

The criminal system alone was not a deterrent for some kinds of sex offenders, McEwan said. 'Obviously, you need a legal response. But it may not fix the desire to perpetrate. It's not a deterrent necessarily. If you think about why people engage in harmful sexual behaviour, there are various reasons.'

A simplistic way of breaking it down is to divide perpetrators into three groups, she said. The first are those who have a sexual orientation towards and desire for children, and who then choose to act on it. Then there are those who are sexually attracted to certain behaviours, such as sadism, and who find vulnerable targets to fulfil this attraction, whether they are children or adults. Finally, there are those who are sexually attracted to adults but are sexually frustrated, so they abuse children because it's easy to do so – a cowardly and criminal way to respond to their frustration.

This last group, McEwan said, are often rule violators in other parts of their lives, too.

'Their attitude is, *I want this thing, so I will get it.* They're much more opportunistic. The estimates are that they make up at least half the people engaging in sexual abuse of children. The vast majority of child offenders in the criminal justice system are not paedophiles in a diagnostic sense. People generally call them paedophiles, but it's wrong. Most men who have contact with prepubescent children are not paedophilic. They'll have sex with adults, and fantasise about that. But they want to have sex. And the child is an easy way to achieve that, in the same way other criminals might think, *I need money, so I'll break that window and steal that money.*'

There are varying numbers cited about what percentage of the population meets the diagnostic criteria for paedophilia, McEwan said – but, on the data available, it is greater than the incidence of schizophrenia, which affects about 1 per cent of the population. Clinical and forensic psychologist Dr Michael Seto wrote in a paper on paedophilia for the *Annual Review of Clinical Psychology* that the prevalence in the general population is unknown because large-scale epidemiological surveys are lacking.

> Much smaller surveys of convenience samples suggest that the upper limit for the prevalence of pedophilia is around 5%, as almost all of these surveys have shown that 3% to 9% of male respondents acknowledge sexual fantasies or sexual contact involving prepubescent children … Some pedophiles have not had any known sexual contact with children, and perhaps half of sex offenders against children would not meet diagnostic criteria for pedophilia.

No matter which group the perpetrator fell into, it depended on the individual person as to whether they would take the risk of offending. Like anyone in society, those considering abusing children possessed various levels of self-control or the ability to think through and recognise the consequences of their behaviour. Many stories in the media may have created a myth that all child sexual abuse involves some level of grooming, McEwan said.

'I can see why the media focuses on these cases, as they are often the more serious, prolonged cases, and it freaks out parents, because adults are often fooled by these perpetrators as well.' The child sexual abuse royal commission heard, for example, that perpetrators often cultivated friendships with the victims' parents, siblings, guardians, teachers, and other adults in their lives.

'But you don't need grooming to engage in sexual activity with children,' McEwan said. 'It depends on why you're engaging in that sexual activity and what your goal is. Someone who wants to sexually abuse a child, who is otherwise a very well-adapted person, they're smart and functioning in society, some of those people will never act on their interest in children and will just deal with it.

'Some people, however, will say to themselves, *I have this interest and I'm a person who is capable and smart*, and they will apply this capability to abuse children. If they make the choice to act on it, they use their skills to do so and to avoid getting caught. They're the same skills that enabled them to be a respected, well-regarded person in society.

'How the offence is carried out will be very different depending on the person. The well-respected smart person may offend very differently from the highly impulsive, antisocial person who has a drug problem. Because all the skills they bring to their offending are different. That's why there are so many maladapted people in prison. They're the people who get caught.'

She said the research into sex-offender treatment programs shows that those who go through a program staffed by qualified professionals do reduce their risk of reoffending. Sex-offender recidivism rates are quite low – around 15 per cent of people convicted of sexual offending are charged with a further offence. The general reoffending rate for all crimes, by comparison, is around 40–50 per cent.

'Sexual deviance is a significant risk factor for reoffending,' McEwan said. 'So paedophilia is one of those risk factors. Or it could be fetishism or sadism. The combination of sexual deviance and anti-sociality are the two biggest risk factors for reoffending.'

During treatment sessions, psychologists and psychiatrists try to assess when an offender is more likely to engage in criminal behaviours and then come up with strategies to deal with those situations.

'You can't change a sexual orientation – it would be like changing being heterosexual,' McEwan said. 'But you have to convince them not to act on it and find other ways of dealing with it. That's legitimately a tough thing to come to terms with. But most will not act on it because they are morally decent people who won't do it for the same reason they won't break into a house or knock an old lady over. So for people with a sexual deviance and who are abnormally aroused, thinking about it all the time, medication may help. And then it's about working individually with the person. If they've never acted on it – say, they have self-referred because they've thought about a child sexually and they're distressed by those thoughts – we talk about what went on when they had that thought. Was it fleeting, is there a genuine orientation and, if there is, are there other interests we can focus on and divert them to? We will talk about risky behaviours and what behaviours, for example on the internet, aren't helpful.'

An uncomfortable aspect of criminals who have been charged

with sexually abusing children is that those perpetrators have often been victims of physical, sexual, and emotional abuse themselves, McEwan said. Of course, being a victim of abuse does not mean that someone will go on to become an abuser themselves. But it is a reality that many in the criminal justice system were harmed when they were children, whether emotionally, physically or sexually.

This means acknowledging uncomfortable realities such as the fact that a small percentage of victims do become perpetrators. To treat offenders and help keep the community safe, McEwan's job is to understand the whole story, and that requires being interested in and empathetic about the perpetrator's past.

'It's my job to try to understand this person and what they did,' she said. 'Understanding is not excusing. That's a simplistic argument, and not a sensible one. My job is to help, whether it's the perpetrator or the court, understand why this might be happening so there is an opportunity to intervene effectively so that it doesn't happen again. Coming to that with an attitude of blame and punishment is not my job. They do need to be punished, of course, but it's not my role. I have to view them neutrally. I can't view them as someone who isn't deserving of help.'

This did not mean she liked them as a person, or even that she felt safe with them or that she could help them. 'But that doesn't mean someone else might not have the skills to help them. They've done awful things. But they're no less human, and I have to fundamentally treat them as such.

'Now, I completely understand people who are victims might not want to do that; they are not in a position to think that way, and that's fine. As a society, however, dehumanising people for anything is not a good idea. and that applies to sexual offenders as well.'

In their book, *Childhood Sexual Abuse: an evidence based perspective*, published in 1999, David M. Fergusson and Paul E.

Mullen wrote that up to 30 per cent of children experience child sexual abuse, and between 5 and 10 per cent of those experience severe abuse. In a separate study, the foundation professor of forensic behavioural science and director of Swinburne University's Centre for Forensic Behavioural Science, Professor James Ogloff, linked cases of children who were medically confirmed to have been sexually abused in Australia to police databases. (It should be noted than in most cases of child sexual abuse, there is no medical evidence of the crime.) Ogloff and his colleagues wanted to determine whether child sexual abuse victims were at increased risk of offending. Their sample of 2,759 child sexual abuse victims found they were almost five times more likely than the general population to be charged with offences, with the strongest associations found for sexual and violent offences. They were also more likely to have been victims of crime, particularly crimes of a sexual or violent nature. 'As expected, male child sexual abuse victims were largely responsible for the increased rate of sexual offences, in particular those boys abused at 12 years or older,' the study found. 'Given that almost one in 10 boys who were sexually abused in this age group subsequently were convicted of a sexual offence, sexual victimisation may be an important risk factor for this population (but not for females).'

Leonie Sheedy is the CEO of the Care Leavers Australasia Network, which supports survivors of abuse in children's homes and orphanages under the state's care. She told me that no matter what a survivor has done in their life, including committing crimes, 'we always must remember the first crime was committed on them as a child. I care about the little child.' But she is also sick of ignorance about victims and perpetrators, saying that too many people still believe that all victims of child sexual abuse are destined to commit crimes themselves, despite the research which shows that while some do, most do not.

Sheedy, who has her own horrific story of abuse while an orphan in the Catholic Sisters of Mercy St Catherine's Children's home in Geelong, Victoria, describes how as a child in state care she and so many other children were 'waiting for someone to hug us, waiting for someone to love us'.

'But no one ever did,' she said.

For those who have ever cared for or loved a child, the thought of them being deprived of simple acts of affection like a hug for years on end is heartbreaking. Numerous studies have now shown the importance of touch to child development, and developmental delay is common in those children who don't receive it. Such children are even more prone to illnesses, such as infections. In my time covering abuse, I would go on to hear countless stories of children deprived of the most basic acts of kindness and love.

Sheedy has spent almost two decades travelling all over the country supporting care-leavers as they disclose their abuse, often for the first time decades after it occurred, many of them on their deathbeds. She helps them with the often difficult task of tracking down their long-lost records from libraries, orphanages that have since shut down, and government departments, piecing together their childhoods. She assists them in facing court, or with applying for redress and compensation. She listens to people who still haven't disclosed their abuse to their own families, and those who have attempted suicide. She shows empathy towards people whose experiences as wards of the state have led them to drugs, crime, and prison.

She told me of a particular prisoner who wrote to her organisation wanting help to recover his ward-of-the-state records. Sheedy knew little about him, his history, and whether or not he was abused while in state care. But she managed to recover his files, and brought them to him in prison. Before meeting inmates, prison visitors are required to lock away all of their possessions, including their wallets, mobile phones, and keys. With no phone to distract her while waiting, Sheedy grew restless. So she did something she usually never does. She opened his ward-of-the-state file, and read the first 10 pages.

'And I saw right there, on top of one of the pages, that when he was a child he had been placed by the state into a residence with a known paedophile,' Sheedy said. 'He was a known abuser at the time, and they sent him there anyway.'

Once she had handed over his file, Sheedy confessed to the inmate that she had read some of it, and asked the prisoner if he would like a hug.

'He told me: "That's the first hug I've had since I was seven years old."' He was, by this point, 38 years old.

What I learned through around seven years of reporting on historical child sexual abuse is that a significant part of the population has been deprived of affection, safety, and love because of the actions of people in institutions where paedophiles were protected, harboured, and given unfettered access to children. These children were ignored, unseen, and unheard. If they were not physically, emotionally, or sexually abused themselves, their parents or grandparents likely were if they spent any time in certain religious institutions or orphanages.

These were pervasive crimes, often committed out in the open without fear of accountability by perpetrators. In too many institutions, these incidents of crime and cruelty were not rare, but the norm. Sometimes it has felt to me as though an entire generation has been harmed by abuse, provoking an epidemic of trauma. The intergenerational and vicarious trauma, too, is significant: children confused as to why their parents abuse substances or are incapable of showing affection: partners grappling with their partner's problems around intimacy and sex; family members angry and heartbroken when they learn, if they learn, of their loved one's abuse; victims who become self-destructive and who sometimes take drugs and commit crimes; and victims who are traumatised when they have children of their own.

I gave Sheedy a call in the weeks after Cardinal George Pell's appeal hearing as we waited for Victoria's Supreme Court to give a date for the appellate judges' decision as to whether he would be acquitted or his conviction would be upheld. I brought up the story of the prisoner she had told me about a couple of years earlier. After we hung up, she emailed me a letter she received from the prisoner in the weeks after she handed him his ward-of-the-state files. He gave her permission to share his letter with me, which reveals he was abused in multiple ways by multiple people after he became a ward of the state at the age of nine.

In the letter, he also recalls the hug he received from Sheedy during her visit, which he describes as a 'cuddle'.

He wrote that he felt, 'for the first time in a long time, someone cared about me'.

Sheedy told me, 'Touch is a really important thing. My youngest daughter taught me how to accept a hug. It took three kids for me to learn that. I remember in the orphanage I used to love hair-washing day. The nuns took us from the trough, they would turn us around, and lean our heads on their chest to dry our hair. I used to look forward to that. To that safe touch.'

In his letter to Sheedy, sent from a New South Wales prison in June 2015, the man wrote, 'I am serving an 18-year sentence for a guilty plea to murder.

'I did murder a paedophile, who took advantage of me at a vulnerable time of my life. I do realise that I went too far, and lost control, that is why I pleaded guilty to murder and I deserved the punishment that I received.'

He described being placed in numerous government homes throughout his childhood, running away from them, and being brought back to them each time by police.

'There was nothing called love in these homes,' he wrote. 'One day I ran from one of these homes, I went to Surfers Paradise in Queensland.

'I was 15 years old and I hitch-hiked and a bloke picked me up, over a three-day period he drugged me, tied me up and raped me repeatedly. I managed to run away to a hotel receptionist where I told them I had just been raped for the last three days. This bloke pleaded guilty to raping me and received 500 hours' community service while I suffered the effects of coming down from being drugged, my body was sore from where he tied me up and raped me.'

From there, he became homeless. His family, who had already disowned him, wanted even less to do with him after being told about the rape. He began to rob and cheat people, and did not trust anyone. 'I started to go to juvenile prisons, then gaol itself, now I am in prison for murdering a paedophile. If anyone would like to write to me, it would be much appreciated, as I don't receive much letters.'

The last Sheedy heard, he had been transferred to another prison – she does not know where – and she has not heard from him again.

I have often found myself wondering at what point society stops caring about child victims of crime. Is it when they turn into difficult teenagers, lashing out because of their abuse? Is it when initial efforts to help them fail? By January 2017, Victoria's youth justice system was front-page news. Detainees at the Parkville and Malmsbury youth justice centres were frequently rioting, assaulting staff and damaging property. In February 2017, teenage inmates who had been moved to a wing of the Barwon adult prison after rioting in Parkville several months earlier once again began to rampage. It took four hours for juvenile-detention officers to bring them under control. The state's media began reporting on the 'youth justice crisis', with many news headlines referring to the teenagers as 'thugs', and commentators calling for more punitive punishments. They caused millions of dollars in damages, ripping out fencing, forcing evacuations, and injuring staff. There were calls for the youth affairs minister at the time, Jenny Mikakos, to stand down.

The way the rioting was reported by some tabloid media made it clear that many in society had lost hope in these kids. At what point did these teenagers go from being youths who had been abused, and whom society had failed, to thugs who deserved harsh punishments and no sympathy or, at least, understanding? A long-term staff member at Parkville told me at the time that the teenagers responsible for leading the rioting had 'endured every kind of abuse you can imagine. If people knew what had been done to them, they would cry.'

I was unable to report these abuses due to a risk of identifying the victims and because of their age, and also because my source would not go on the record for fear of losing his job.

In 2016, the Human Rights Law Centre successfully argued before the Supreme Court that detaining children in an adult prison environment breached their human rights. The court heard that children were handcuffed during limited periods of release from their cells for exercise, and were placed in continuous isolation and restrained. When he handed down his findings in May 2017, Justice John Dixon found that, due to the nature of the environment of an adult prison, the children risked developing depression, anxiety, cognitive problems, and paranoia, and their existing mental-health problems risked being exacerbated. The 'extensive incidence of isolation by lockdown for substantial periods of the day, extending up to 23 hours, in cells designed for occupation by adult men' was also in breach of their human rights, he found. He added that the prison placed 'limitations on the developmental needs of detainees, specifically their physical, social, emotional, intellectual, and spiritual needs, that were affected by the use of Grevillea [a unti within Barwon Prison] as a youth justice precinct'. Mikakos responded to the ruling by saying, 'I make no apology for the fact we took the steps necessary to keep the community safe.'

These comments particularly struck me because the child sexual abuse royal commission was a mere seven months from delivering its final report to the attorney-general after five years of hearing horrific stories of children being abused and neglected in institutions. How could society be so appalled by the stories coming from the commission while simultaneously calling for children who had endured similar abuses to be punitively punished and locked away, against all the best evidence about youth rehabilitation? How rehabilitative can a punishment like jail be, when these youth have been punished in every way imaginable for their whole lives?

I would never argue that youth who commit serious crimes should not face consequences, but research has found that interventions are only effective when the trauma that drives the young person's behaviour is addressed, and when the punishment does no further harm to the child. That's what is really needed to keep society safe in future, and to prevent further crimes. Somehow, recognising this evidence and best practice is seen by some sectors of the media and public as being 'soft on crime'. Focusing simply on maximum security and punishment is also a waste of money. It doesn't rehabilitate youth or empower them to become productive members of society. It does, however, feed into populist arguments around law and order, even though, in the long term, community safety is only served by addressing the causes of crime. To change young people's behaviour, you need to build relationships and get to know what's going on in their lives. That's not soft. It's what the evidence shows.

Not all abused children become criminals. But most children, and indeed many adults, who come into contact with the justice system have been abused. To ignore this is to accept these abuses. While most people agree that the abuses uncovered by the child sexual abuse royal commission were unacceptable, there is still significant support for 'tough on crime' approaches to youth offenders, even though these approaches have been shown time and time again to fail. What these kids need is for people to believe in, and have high expectations for, their futures.

Most child sexual abuse – about 85 per cent – occurs in homes, perpetrated by family members and other people close to and known to victims. But, as Australian child-protection organisation Bravehearts points out, adolescents in institutional care have a higher lifetime prevalence of sexual victimisation than other children. There are certain conditions that, if present in an institution, significantly increases the risk to children and adolescents.

The child sexual abuse royal commission's final report found that an overwhelming amount of the institutional abuse reported to the commission occurred in faith-based institutions. Almost 2,500 survivors told the commission about sexual abuse in an institution managed by the Catholic Church, representing 61.8 per cent of all survivors who reported sexual abuse in a religious institution. The report said:

> In many religious institutions, the power afforded to people in religious ministry and the misplaced trust of parents combined with aspects of the institutional culture, practices and attitudes to create risks for children. Alleged perpetrators often continued to have access to children even when religious leaders knew they posed a danger.

We heard that alleged perpetrators were often transferred to other locations but they were rarely reported to police. The failure to understand that the sexual abuse of a child was a crime with profound impacts for the victim, and not a mere moral failure capable of correction by contrition and penance (a view expressed in the past by a number of religious leaders) is almost incomprehensible.

The royal commission also found that the strategies that perpetrators used in religious institutions were influenced by the institutional culture, such as how 'closed' the institution was to the rest of the public and how strongly it was governed by rules and procedures that did not provide transparency or review.

'Children are more likely to be abused in institutional contexts where the community has an unquestioning respect for the authority of an institution,' its final report said.

> Within institutional contexts, adult perpetrators held a range of positions. They used their role, their power and the trust bestowed upon them to access children and sexually abuse them. We heard that some adult perpetrators sexually abused a child once, while others did so repeatedly.
>
> It appears that some candidates for leadership positions have been selected on the basis of their adherence to specific aspects of church doctrine and their commitment to the defence and promotion of the institutional Catholic Church, rather than on their capacity for leadership.

It called for the Australian Catholic Bishops' Conference – the national episcopal conference of the Catholic bishops of Australia – to conduct a national review of the governance and management structures of dioceses and parishes, including in relation to issues of transparency, accountability, and consultation, and the participation of lay men and lay women. The selection criteria for employing bishops should be published, including their credentials relating to the promotion of child safety, and churches should 'establish a transparent process for appointing bishops which includes the direct participation of lay people'.

It found that Catholic schools in the Archdiocese of Melbourne had a 'dysfunctional' employment structure, in which the parish priest was the employer of the school principal and school staff for parish schools.

Questions have been asked over the years about how the vow of celibacy taken by clergy is associated with child sexual abuse. But the idea that celibacy somehow causes perpetrators in religious institutions to sexually assault children has at times been overstated. The child sexual abuse royal commission, having heard evidence from researchers, psychologists, victims, and other experts, found that celibacy alone was not a direct cause of child sexual abuse. Rather, it was a contributing factor that, when combined with other risk factors such as a lack of oversight and accountability, and a reverence towards clergy, contributed to an environment that allowed abuse to thrive. In its final report, the commission said:

> [B]ased on research we conclude that there is an elevated risk of child sexual abuse where compulsorily celibate male clergy or religious have privileged access to children in certain types of Catholic institutions, including schools, residential institutions and parishes. For many Catholic clergy and religious, celibacy is implicated in emotional isolation, loneliness, depression and mental illness. Compulsory celibacy may also have contributed to various forms of psychosexual dysfunction, including

psychosexual immaturity, which pose an ongoing risk to the safety of children. For many clergy and religious, celibacy is an unattainable ideal that leads to clergy and religious living double lives, and contributes to a culture of secrecy and hypocrisy.

The commission recommended that the Australian Catholic Bishops' Conference request that the Holy See consider scrapping compulsory celibacy for diocesan clergy. The commission also found that the inadequacy of canon law – that is, the rules that govern a Catholic organisation – contributed to the failure of the Catholic Church to protect children and to report or punish perpetrators within church institutions. The commission urged the conference to ask the Vatican to reform canon law by removing provisions that 'prevent, hinder or discourage compliance with mandatory reporting laws by bishops or religious superiors'.

'We recommend that canon law be amended so that the "pontifical secret" does not apply to any aspect of allegations or canonical disciplinary processes relating to child sexual abuse,' the report said.

In 2017, the then archbishop of the Archdiocese of Melbourne, Denis Hart, responded by saying that the seal of the confessional was 'inviolable' and 'can't be broken'. He said if someone confessed to abusing children, he would encourage them to admit to their crimes outside the confessional so that it could be reported to police. But he would not report those crimes himself.

'I would feel terribly conflicted, and I would try even harder to get that person outside confessional, but I cannot break the seal,' he said. 'The penalty for any priest breaking the seal is excommunication.'

Hart said that the commission 'hasn't damaged the credibility of the Church'. He angered many abuse survivors and advocates when he said he would risk going to jail rather than report allegations of child sexual abuse raised during confession. He said that he did not expect canon law to change, and that there was 'real value' in celibacy.

The Catholic archbishop of Sydney, Anthony Fisher, similarly dismissed calls to change confession. Changing mandatory reporting of abuse that came to light through confession was 'a distraction', he said.

'While we are yet to study what the commission has had to say about that, I think everyone understands that this Catholic and orthodox practice of confession is always confidential,' he said. 'Any proposal to stop the practice of confession in Australia would be a real hurt to all Catholics and Orthodox Christians.'

On celibacy rules, he said, 'We know very well that institutions who have celibate clergy and institutions that don't have celibate clergy both face these problems. We know very well that this happens in families that are certainly not observing celibacy.'

Five years of commission work and research were dismissed before the archbishops even had time to read the commission's full findings and the research that had informed it.

In May 2017, the findings were published from three research reports ordered by the commission on the topic of child-safe institutions. The reports examined key elements of child-safe organisations; the safety of young people in residential care; and abuse in the context of disability. A key challenge for the commission in conducting its inquiry was the lack of research on institutional child sexual abuse. There had been no large-scale, cross-jurisdiction focus on the topic. To address this, almost 100 research projects were commissioned, involving 40 universities and research centres around the world.

As part of that work, researchers from the Institute of Child Protection Studies at the Australian Catholic University, Professor Morag McArthur and Dr Tim Moore, received ethics approval to interview 27 children and young people living in residential care in Australia. These comprise group homes for children and young people who are temporarily unable to live with family or foster carers, often through no fault of their own. For example, there may not be enough foster carers to take them on, or, if there are enough, carers may not be willing to take on older teenagers, preferring young children.

The researchers asked the children in residential care about what they thought might prevent sexual abuse, what helped them to feel safe, how well their concerns were responded to, and what could be done to increase their safety. 'Residential care felt most safe when it was home-like: where young people felt welcome, where things felt "normal" and where adults looked out for them,' the researchers found.

> Participants stressed the importance of stability and predictability in residential care: where children and young people knew what was going to happen, where they felt that they knew their peers and how to manage their behaviours and where tensions could be resolved. Due to its highly chaotic and ever-changing nature, many characterised residential care as being unsafe.

The researchers found that the application of routines and fair rules, and being given an opportunity to have a say and a sense of control, also helped children feel safe. They found that much of the existing research relied heavily on the views of residential-care staff and clinicians and on documents, but failed to consider the experiences of children.

'People are very worried about the vulnerabilities of children, and that involving them might upset and retraumatise them,' Professor McArthur told me.

'They also question children's capacity to be engaged in these discussions. But children are capable, they want to participate, and they are agents who are active in their own lives. If we don't understand how children see and experience the world, we won't respond adequately, and that means we can't keep them safe.'

For a long time, society has been familiar with the mantra 'Children should be seen and not heard.' It is evident, now, how dangerous this thinking is.

The royal commission had previously found that although only 4.7 per cent of children who did not live at home were in residential care as of June 2014, 33 per cent of child sexual abuse reports related to children in such care.

Research was also commissioned about the prevalence and prevention of sexual abuse of children with disabilities in institutions. The research was led by Professor Gwynnyth Llewellyn from the University of Sydney's Faculty of Health Sciences, and it, too, highlighted the absence of child perspectives and ideas.

'Segregation and exclusion in closed institutional contexts away from public scrutiny leaves children with disability at heightened risk of violence and harm including sexual abuse,' her report found. 'Further, when children with disability are stereotyped as dependent and passive and unable to "speak up", they are at heightened vulnerability to being segregated, abused, overlooked and not heard.'

Llewellyn told a symposium organised by the child sexual abuse royal commission in May 2017 that data about the extent of the abuse was woeful.

'Right now, the abuse of children with disability in Australia is not being measured, and what is not being measured cannot be counted,' Llewellyn said. 'What cannot be counted cannot be monitored or evaluated.'

Her study found that while there were many existing studies describing the issue of sexual abuse of children with disabilities, such studies could not produce evidence-based solutions. They could only propose solutions, she said.

'There was much less research using study designs which test interventions or solutions or evaluate policy initiatives,' her report said. 'In other words, study designs that allow us to know what works, and ideally, for whom and under what conditions. Research that can determine what works and in which settings is urgently needed.'

Llewellyn's report also warned against thinking about children with disabilities as a special, distinct group. Doing so implied that responsibility for special groups fell outside mainstream services, and that those services could therefore be 'relieved' of their responsibilities to those children.

The research undertaken for the child sexual abuse royal commission revealed that abuse of children is still occurring in institutions. Many of the failures identified by the commission that occurred historically in religious institutions – such as little accountability and oversight, a lack of child-safety policies, and a failure to respect and listen to children – are still pervasive in institutions tasked with caring for children today. They are not issues unique to clergy.

The royal commission identified 10 elements that were critical to making an institution safe for children. These comprised:

1. Child safety being embedded in institutional leadership, governance, and culture.
2. Children participating in decisions affecting them and being taken seriously.
3. Families and communities being informed and involved.

4. Equity being upheld, and diverse needs taken into account.
5. People working with children being suitable and supported.
6. Processes to respond to complaints of child sexual abuse being child focused.
7. Staff being equipped with the knowledge, skills, and awareness to keep children safe through continual education and training.
8. Maintaining physical and online environments that minimised the opportunity for abuse to occur.
9. Continuously reviewing and improving the implementation of the Child Safe Standards.
10. Documenting the institution's child-safe policies and procedures.

To check the veracity and feasibility of implementing these standards, the commission asked the University of New South Wales's Social Policy Research Centre and Parent-Child Research Clinic to obtain independent feedback on the 10 elements from a panel of 40 Australian and international independent experts.

This research, led by Dr Kylie Valentine, asked the experts how relevant, reliable, and achievable the child-safe elements identified by the royal commission were.

The research found a high level of support for the elements if they were implemented well, but concerns were also raised about the level of resourcing needed to implement them.

'They support mandatory and comprehensive implementation, but with the recognition ... that some organisations that provide very important services to children and their families – for example, sport and recreation clubs and childcare centres – will in fact be poorly resourced and not able to support implementation themselves,' the report found.

One of the unique aspects of the child sexual abuse royal commission was that it wanted to hear from all victims and survivors of abuse, whether they were in prison, infirm, or on their deathbeds. In situations where people were unable to come to commissioners, the commissioners went to them. Over the five years of the inquiry, commission officers visited 713 institutional child-abuse survivors in correctional centres across Australia. This prison population represented 10.4 per cent of all survivors who told their stories to the commission. On average, survivors in prison were 11 years old when they were first sexually abused in an institution, although many said they experienced physical and sexual abuse prior to this, often within the family.

The royal commission's final report found:

The majority of survivors in prison described non-penetrative contact sexual abuse (65.4 per cent) and/or sexual abuse with penetration (59.2 per cent).

Almost one in four (24.0 per cent) said their privacy was violated, often by being watched while in the shower or being subjected to unnecessary strip searches in youth detention. Many also experienced other abuse alongside the sexual abuse, such as physical (72.3 per cent) and/or emotional abuse (72.1 per cent). More than one-quarter of survivors in prison (28.3 per cent) said they were sexually abused by custodial staff, including in youth detention settings, and one in five (19.3 per cent) said they were abused by a person in religious ministry.

Almost one-third of those interviewed in prison disclosed their sexual abuse for the first time when speaking to a commissioner.

It is not the job of victims of crime to be empathetic to these prisoners. It would be a tough task to ask a victim of a serious crime such as murder, rape, or child sexual abuse to care about the circumstances and history of their abuser. But someone has to. Including politicians, researchers and journalists.

'I think family violence suffers from same issue, where the complexities of the issue are discarded for the political argument or the politically correct argument,' Associate Professor McEwan told me. 'As a scientist, that drives me batty, of course. I'm interested in the complexity of the thing. And there must be a science or social-science discussion around complex issues. These areas have a lot of "Can't say"s. That's always an indication there's a political discourse going on. Because in science you can say anything. As soon as you say, "We can't ask that question," unless there's an ethical reason, the only reason is it must be political.'

McEwan said that while she had no research to back it up, in her clinical experience she found that people who had been convicted but had denied the offence were trying to hold onto an idea of themselves as a good, respectable person.

'They don't see themselves as an offender, and to accept they did it would shake their fundamental belief of themselves,' she said. 'My guess is people who deny having offended do so because they have a concept of themselves outside of the offence, such as "I'm a good dad" or "I'm a teacher" or "I am liked by my friends", and they're protecting that. If they admit to this thing they've done, they don't believe that those two things – being a criminal and also being a good dad, for example – can sit together.'

What I have learned through covering the royal commission and the Pell case, trawling through research into abuse and violence, and talking to various experts is that people whom society perceive as being 'good', 'admirable', and 'respectable' can and do commit crimes. Accepting this has proven difficult for society, including the media, which has struggled to tell such conflicting narratives about perpetrators in a way that is accurate while also being respectful to victims. Accolades do not justify or excuse abuse, but may explain why abusers went undetected for so long, or, if detected, were excused and celebrated regardless.

And it explains why, despite all of his failures to report and act on child sexual abuse, George Pell is living quietly in Sydney, still a priest, and still a cardinal.

Author's note

Some people will have wanted me to give my opinion in this book about Pell's guilt or innocence, and on whether the courts got it right or wrong. But that's not what this book is about. It is about more than the trials of one man, Cardinal George Pell. It is about the circumstances which lead to children being abused. It is about the evidence, uncovered by researchers, court cases, and Australia's royal commission into child sexual abuse within institutions. It is about the ways that the media and society respond to crimes against and involving children, and the ways the narrative changes depending on who it is that is accused. It is about the complexities of justice.

Most of this book was written in a mere six months, after I had sat through months of courtroom testimony about Cardinal Pell, but also after years of researching and writing about child sexual abuse more generally. I believe I am the only journalist to have covered Cardinal Pell's appearances at the child sexual abuse royal commission, as well as the entirety of his committal hearing, mistrial, retrial, and appeals. I want to share what I have learned, including the facts as they unfolded. I want readers to have as much evidence as possible before them as they consider the Pell trials. And I want any response to his conviction and appeals to be, at the very least, informed by the evidence.

I faced many difficulties in writing this book. For a start, transcripts of the committal hearing, mistrial, and retrial could only be viewed in person in the courts. In order to check anything in the transcripts – a quote, a date, the spelling of a name, or the order of witnesses – I and other journalists had to set up a time to go into the Magistrates' or County Court. Journalists are highly experienced in dealing with sensitive documents, so it was hard to understand why we were only allowed to read transcripts in person under the watchful eye of the court staff, but not digitally via a secure hard drive.

As it happens, the courts are inconsistent in terms of how they provide transcripts and in what format. At the County Court in Melbourne, the court staff trusted the journalists attending the trial enough not to sit with us for days on end when we needed to review transcripts. At the Magistrates' Court, however, a court officer watched over us the entire time. It was insulting, although I do not blame the court officers, who were just doing their jobs. The mistrial and retrial documents were only made available in printed form, so we could not conduct any digital word searches. We had to flick through pages across five volumes of folders more than three inches thick. At least the committal transcripts were digital, but we were only able to view them on a court computer, not our own.

Sometimes there were distractions. In the County Court, for example, as I went through the folders of transcripts, I would hear conversations from the adjacent meeting rooms, and people leaving the courtrooms across the corridor wailing and in tears, perhaps because someone they cared about had been convicted or they had faced a trying cross-examination. We were not allowed to leave the documents unattended. We needed permission to leave for the toilet; even ducking out for lunch or a coffee required coordinating with the court staff. For all these reasons, and more, I will not miss the tiny room on level four of the County Court where I was locked away for weeks, poring over paper documents; or the Magistrates'

Court, where I was watched over as I transferred notes and quotes from the court computer to my own by laboriously typing out what I needed. If courts want to ensure accuracy and truth-telling by reporters, it is hard to understand why they do not make access to the evidence as easy as possible.

The Supreme Court, by contrast, provided journalists with digital transcripts almost immediately and streamed the appeal with only a slight delay, so that suppressed information could be blocked if a lawyer, for example, accidentally named one of the alleged victims. In the case of the trial transcripts, some statements, at times, were attributed to the wrong barrister. Only journalists who were in the room would have been able to identify these errors. All the more reason for those journalists, at the very least, to be given easier access.

The other difficulty I have faced is that hardly anyone was prepared to speak on the record. While I am grateful for the background information that sources provided me with, people were reluctant for me to quote them on even the most mundane, non-controversial matters. Some of the most well-informed and best-placed people to speak about the case generally refused to do so publicly. This left a vacuum that less-informed commentators and conspiracy theorists rushed to fill.

There was, therefore, a double urgency to this book: the backlash to Pell's initial conviction and subsequent acquittal was immediate and swift. Globally, opinion pieces were written as to why Pell must have been innocent and why the jurors must have got it wrong, and these were aired and published before the appeals process could conclude. Conspiracy theories emerged about unnecessary suppressions of the case, and comments were made that Pell was receiving special treatment. (In the case of access to the court transcripts, I agree.) These articles and comments came from people who were not at the trial, and who could not have accessed the transcripts. The timeframe in which this book was written means it necessarily leaves out some aspects of the royal commission and Pell trials. I have also aimed to include some of the best research into perpetrators, survivors, and institutional abuse. However, these topics merit entire books in and of themselves. It has not been possible to incorporate every finding, but I hope readers will nonetheless come away with a stronger understanding of child sexual abuse, how it occurs, and its impact.

I also wrote this book amidst personal struggles. In November 2019, the foster baby I had cared for over a period of one-and-a-half years was taken out of the foster system and placed in a permanent home, and I found myself grappling with the reality that I would never see her again. In December, I had a serious accident, falling from a height of three metres, shattering both bones in my lower leg and seriously injuring my elbow. I underwent a painful surgery. As I write this, I am still unable to walk.

But this book is informed by years of reporting on child sexual abuse. It is fuelled by an interest in evidence-based research and science, and an understanding that everyone involved in reporting on this case should take an opportunity to reflect on and question what they could have done better. I ask myself this daily. I also firmly believe that journalists should not be advocates for any group or cause. The truth should speak for itself. Revealing the truth is the best way to spark reform and long-lasting change. And so, I wrote this book.

It has been written with children past, present, and future, and the need to protect them, at the forefront of my mind. I hope that by sharing what I have learned, children can be better understood and protected, and, most importantly, believed, seen, valued, and heard. Achieving this relies on society valuing children and having high expectations for them and their futures, no matter their past or where they have come from.

Acknowledgements

I would like to thank Henry Rosenbloom at Scribe for his support and patience while I embarked on my first book. Thank you for taking a chance on me and for giving me this opportunity; I don't take it for granted. To Benython Oldfield from Zeitgeist Agency, thank you for taking me on and navigating me through this process when it was clear I had no idea what I was doing; you have been so generous and kind. To Emily Maguire, your mentorship and urging me onwards got me through this. The literary scene and up-and-coming authors are so lucky to have you. Your feedback, advice, support, and understanding kept me going when I believed I could no longer cope. I could not have done this without you.

To Tim Lucas and the staff at Buildkite, thank you for giving me an office to work from, and for your friendship, support, and laughter, making this process so much less lonely. You made me feel part of the team. I am so grateful. To Miles Martignoni, thank you for being an unwavering friend. To David Marr, thank you for encouraging me, for the debates, for the phone calls, and for the Nandos.

To *Guardian Australia*, thank you for trusting me to cover this story. It has been one of the greatest and most gruelling learning opportunities of my career. To Lenore Taylor and all of the news editors, desk editors, subeditors, reporters, and staff at *Guardian Australia*, thank you for your patience with me, for your support, and for helping me to navigate a difficult story. To the reporters from other news organisations who covered the majority of the Pell case, thank you for understanding what this whole process has been like when no one else could. I am grateful to have worked alongside and to have learned from such brilliant people. In particular, thank you to Emma Younger, Shannon Deery, Adam Cooper, Karen Sweeney, Tessa Akerman, Robb M. Stewart and Sonali Paul for the reporting you do and for answering my dozens of questions about the court process. Thank you to Lucie Morris-Marr especially, for assuring me that there is light at the end of the tunnel, and for persisting on this story with courage. Your strength inspired me constantly.

To Emily Dowling, I would not be here without you. Your support and encouragement has been above and beyond. I can never thank you enough for what you do and your excellence at it.

To the sources I cannot name but who guided and encouraged me through this process and gave me impeccable information and advice, thank you for trusting me. You know who you are. Here's to getting that steak.

Thank you to Benjamin Law, Jess Hill, Gay Alcorn, and other authors and journalists who answered my questions, helped me learn about the book-writing process, and provided encouragement.

To Jessica – I hope you are safe forevermore. I wish I could tell you how happy you made my life. I miss you every day. This book was written with children like you in my heart.

Thank you to my friends who believed in me and who supported me and put up with me through the good times and bad – in particular, Ri Liu, Dr Kate O'Halloran, Dr Sarah Michael, Associate Professor Alice Motion, Saffron Howden, Lucy Barton, Ryan Verner, Freddy Ras, Olivia Latrache, Gideon Meyerowitz-Katz, and Ben Beccari. To the court media officers who helped with questions and logistics, thank you, and in particular thank you to Ed Gardiner for your professionalism and lugging of transcripts back and forth. To those who gave me their time to be interviewed for this book, especially those who did so despite great personal trauma and pain, thank you. To all of those who supported this book, thank you for backing journalism and authors. Your belief in me has at times been overwhelming, and it means so much.

Joint trials or separate trials?

According to the Australian Law Reform Commission, there are multiple factors that may lead to multiple trials being ordered, but the two most common are 'charges where evidence in relation to one count is not admissible in relation to another, but is prejudicial; and where the charges are for sexual offences'.

'When deciding whether to order joint or separate trials, a trial judge needs to determine whether each complainant's evidence will be cross-admissible,' the commission states. 'A possibility of prejudice to defendants is recognised to arise from joint trials, because jurors might use evidence relating to an offence charged in one count to decide that the person has also committed a different offence, even though there may be insufficient evidence to support a conviction for the second offence.' It is commonly believed that jurors will 'assume that past behaviour is an accurate guide to contemporary conduct, and knowledge of other misconduct may cause the jury to be biased against the accused'.

In other words, if jurors consider multiple charges relating to offences against multiple victims in the one trial, it may give them the impression that the case against the accused is stronger than it actually is, leading to what is known as 'accumulation prejudice'. There can also be concern that jurors may conflate evidence between different charges and events, especially in complex cases. But the most current research suggests that so long as certain mechanisms are put in place, the assumption that jurors are incapable of considering high-profile cases fairly is wrong.

A thorough empirical study of this subject has been conducted by forensic psychologist and lawyer Professor Jane Goodman-Delahunty; professor of law and criminology, and pre-eminent Australian expert on legal reform in the area of sexual assault, Anne Cossins; and research associate Natalie Martschuk. Their research, published in May 2016 as 'Jury Reasoning in Joint and Separate Trials of Institutional Child Sexual Abuse', aimed to test the theory that joint trials were less favourable to defendants than separate trials. The researchers recruited 1,029 jury-eligible Australians, who were then allocated to one of 90 mock juries. The jurors included 580 women and 449 men aged between 18 and 82. The mock jurors were randomly assigned to one of 10 trials, which varied from 45 to 110 minutes in length, and they watched a realistic video simulation of a child sexual assault trial in which the defendant faced either two or six charges relating to institutional child sexual abuse.

The juries were allocated one of four types of trial: a separate trial with an adult male complainant with moderately strong evidence; a separate trial with an adult male complainant with moderately strong evidence and in which relationship evidence about the defendant's previous but uncharged sexual acts and grooming behaviours was presented to the jurors; a separate trial with an adult male complainant with moderately strong evidence in which tendency evidence from two prosecution witnesses was admitted; and a joint trial involving the same defendant and three adult male complainants, who gave weak, strong, and moderately strong evidence, respectively.

All of the juries were presented with the same core evidence.

However, the directions given to the juries by the judge varied across the trials. Juries were given:

- Standard jury directions; or
- Standard jury directions plus a context evidence direction, whereby the judge told jurors that they could use evidence showing that the charged acts were part of an ongoing history and relationship between the defendant and the complainant for context to help them better understand the charges, but could not use that relationship as evidence of the defendant's tendency to have a sexual interest in or assault children; or
- Standard jury directions, plus a context evidence direction, plus a question trail which highlighted the important legal questions that should be considered and a set of logically ordered propositions relating to the issues in the case; or
- Standard jury directions plus a direction about the character, reputation, or conduct of a person – in other words the tendency that a person has or had to act in a particular way, or to have a particular state of mind'; or
- Standard jury directions plus a tendency evidence direction with a question trail.

The researchers specifically looked for instances of verdicts driven by inter-case conflation of the evidence, reasoning by accumulation prejudice, or character prejudice. They found that across the four different types of trials, no convictions were made on those bases, and few mock juror comments suggested they were motivated by emotional, superficial, or impressionistic considerations.

They found that all of the mock juries, no matter the trial type or directions given, were capable of distinguishing between the individual charges and the facts and strength of evidence relating to those charges. They also found that the perceived credibility of the complainant predicted the culpability of the defendant. The results provided little indication of mock juries being susceptible to bias against the defendant or flawed reasoning when all charges were considered within one trial rather than split into separate trials. 'Even if there was such an effect, there was no evidence that decisions to convict were the result of impermissible propensity reasoning,' the study found. 'Given that the verdicts were not based on impermissible reasoning, there was no evidence of unfair prejudice to the defendant.'

Jury trials or judge-only trials?

The thinking behind allowing or preferring judge-only trials is that a judge, with all of their experience, is more capable of casting aside prejudices and making a fair and balanced decision. Jurors may have little legal experience, and therefore a judge may be better able to apply areas of law in complex cases. Judges also deliver their reasons for a decision, whereas the deliberations of a jury are kept secret. The community may feel more confident about a judge's decision in controversial cases for these reasons. While jurors are capable of casting prejudices aside – even in the age of social media – when given strong and clear directions by the judge, it is believed there are some cases where publicity is so heavy that casting prejudices aside becomes impossible for someone who is not legally trained.

However, there are measures available to courts to mitigate this risk, such as delaying proceedings through what is known as a 'stay' until publicity fades. The courts also have the option of implementing a permanent stay of proceedings – which means the case will never be tried and the charges are dropped because of the impossibility of a fair trial and an inevitable abuse of process. But permanent stays are not ideal, as they deny the community and the complainant an opportunity for justice.

In 2008, a notorious convicted paedophile, Dennis Ferguson, was facing additional child sexual abuse charges. At the time, he was already in jail, serving a 14-year sentence for previous child sexual abuse crimes. A district judge in Queensland ordered a permanent stay of the new charges against Ferguson, saying that pretrial publicity and Ferguson's previous, widely reported convictions meant he would not get a fair trial. However, the state prosecutors appealed the decision, and the stay was overturned by the Court of Appeal, which found that the district court judge had failed to consider implementing numerous measures that could mitigate the risk of an unfair trial, such as strong judge directions, staying the trial for a few months, or issuing a suppression order. The Queensland attorney-general at the time, Kerry Shine, told reporters that the Court of Appeal decision revealed that 'an accused person can receive a fair trial with a properly directed jury, that juries can arrive at intelligent decisions on the evidence put before them and only the evidence put before them'.

There is also little empirical research to support claims that judges are more capable than jurors of making a non-prejudicial decision, even in complex high-profile cases. A paper from the University of Sydney Law school, led by Rebecca McEwen and published in 2018, described how, despite a view that judge-only trials were preferable in cases of significant prejudicial publicity, there was a lack of supporting evidence for this belief.

In his 1982 High Court judgment in the case of Victoria v the Australian Building, Construction, Employees' and Builders Labourers' Federation, Justice Anthony Mason stated, 'Obviously judges are more capable than jurors of putting aside prejudicial matter, including public prejudice. Objectivity and independence are the qualities which judges are expected to bring to judicial determination.' But McEwen and her colleagues found this belief worthy of interrogation. They cited research into juries that suggested judges were no more immune to inadmissible evidence and prejudicial publicity than jurors. 'Existing research suggests that while judges may have an advantage in dealing with technical legal questions, they face very similar problems to jurors when dealing with inadmissible evidence or prejudicial publicity,' the paper said. It concluded there was a 'pressing need to more thoroughly interrogate the principles underpinning the preference for trial by judge alone on the basis of prejudicial publicity'.

'The danger is that the assumption that a trial by judge alone is an adequate response to the problem of prejudicial publicity may stymie efforts to evaluate the true impact of such publicity and the best ways to ensure a finder of fact (judicial or lay) is able to make an impartial decision. That, in turn, risks undermining the integrity of the criminal justice system.'

The importance and value of the jury system is a fundamental pillar of Australia's legal system. In a jury trial, the jurors alone are the deciders of the facts of the case. They then apply the relevant areas of the law, outlined by the judge, to those facts. The role of the judge in a jury trial is to provide instructions about the relevant areas of law that apply to the case, summarise the case fairly, give instructions about standards of proof, and give instructions about particular kinds of evidence. The judge also rules on evidentiary and procedural matters, such as the admissibility of evidence, or resolves concerns of the defence and prosecution; this is done when jurors are not in the room. The judge also helps the jurors to understand their role.

Importantly, 12 people with varied life experiences come together to decide a verdict, making it less likely that any one person's biases or prejudices will be given more weight than others. It is also arguable that jurors are more representative of the community and community views than a single judge, whose privilege and power might afford them a unique, but not necessarily representative, perspective. Jurors must discuss and debate the facts of the case, and take turns in putting forward their views. If a trial is run procedurally soundly, and strong directions are given by a judge, jurors are capable of reaching sound verdicts. To suggest there is something dangerously fallible about the jury system in the absence of any significant procedural unfairness is to suggest that the entire criminal legal system is fundamentally flawed. It would be to suggest that every single jury trial may have been better or differently decided by a judge alone. Numerous judges themselves have spoken of their belief in the jury system. In the High Court judgment of Gilbert v The Queen [2000], Justice Michael McHugh said: 'Put bluntly, unless we act on the assumption that criminal juries act on the evidence and in accordance with the directions of the trial judge, there is no point in having criminal jury trials.'

Far from having superior knowledge to assist them in determining the facts of a case, judges have been known to make statements in their decisions in child sexual abuse and sexual assault cases that are not informed by evidence at all. A judge commented during a sexual assault hearing in the District Court of New South Wales that ended in April 1995: 'If events such as these occur one expects some complaint to be made and that such a complaint is made within a reasonably early stage of the events themselves. Take, for example, an allegation that someone was raped and the complaint is made a year later. That, in the eyes of everybody, would cast some suspicion on the acceptability of the allegation.' In fact, extensive research now shows that numerous barriers prevent victims from coming forward, often for decades. Many never disclose their abuse at all.

The High Court's judgment in Longman v The Queen [1989] stated: '[E]xperience has shown that human recollection, and particularly the recollection of events occurring in childhood, is frequently erroneous and liable to distortion by reason of various factors.' However, research commissioned by the child sexual abuse royal commission found that police, judicial officers, legal professionals, and juries held misconceptions about the role of memory. They found that police often sought specific details about the scene of the offence from child-abuse victims, which few victims were able to provide. Inconsistencies in memory and reminiscences was also a problem, with details that victims provided in statements to police often differing from the details they provided at a later date, such as when they gave evidence in court at trial. However, the researchers found that, in reality, 'memory is less like a digital recording of a concert that sounds the same each time you play it back, and more like an improvisational performance based on a common theme. It can differ each time it's played back, and those differences can accumulate over time.' These differences did not mean that the overall theme or event did not happen or that a complainant had lied about it.

'Research has shown that many people believe that a more vivid memory of an event is an indicator of memory accuracy, even for childhood memories,' the review, led by psychologist and lawyer Jane Goodman-Delahunty, found. 'However ... detailed and vivid memories are rare, and vividness is not a predictor of accuracy.'

In the case of R v Henry & Manning (1969), Lord Justice Salmon described how 'in cases of alleged sexual offences it is really dangerous to convict on the evidence of the woman or girl alone'. 'This is dangerous because human experience has shown that in these cases girls and women do sometimes tell an entirely false story which is very easy to fabricate, but extremely difficult to refute. Such stories are fabricated for all sorts of reasons, which I need not enumerate, and sometimes for no reason at all,' he said. Yet numerous studies have since shown that sexual assaults are in fact under-reported and that false reports are rare. The chair of Australia's child sexual abuse royal commission, Justice Peter McClellan, said there was evidence that judges and lawyers fare no better than lay people in their ability to detect deception.

At the Supreme Court of New South Wales annual conference in September 2015, McClellan quoted a judgment from the former NSW chief justice Jim Spigelman that read, 'Many judges share a conventional wisdom about human behaviour, which may represent the limitations of their background. This has been shown to be so in sexual assault cases.

'Legislative intervention was required to overcome the tendency of male judges to treat sexual assault complainants as prone to be unreliable ... There is a substantial body of psychological research indicating that children, even very young children, give reliable evidence.'

Index

60 Minutes (TV program), 28
7.30 Report (TV program), 2, 9, 17

AAP, 211
Abbott, Tony, 9, 32, 290
ABC, 2, 9, 17, 33, 35, 41, 211, 280, 285, 326, 346
accumulation prejudice, 399, 401
acquittal, 320–350
adult prisons, 376–377
The Age, 211, 280
Aitchison, John, 351–355, 359–360
Alaggia, Ramona, 355–357
alibi evidence, 101, 193, 304
All Saints Anglican Church, Ainslie, 351
Annual Review of Clinical Psychology, 367–368
appeals
    see High Court appeal; Victorian Court of Appeal
Australian Catholic Bishops' Conference, 24, 379–381
Australian Catholic University, 290–291
Australian Centre for Child Protection, 365
Australian Institute of Family Studies, 359

Australian Law Reform Commission, 399
Australian Parliament, apology by prime minister, 344–346
Australian Rules Football, 85
The Australian, 280
Azzopardi direction, 155, 188–189

Baker, Father Wilfred James, 343
Ball, Richard, 27–28, 47–49
Ballarat cinema, rape allegation, 16–17
Ballarat Survivors Group, 23, 50–54, 64–68
Barwon Prison, 329, 333, 376
Basha hearings, 119–123, 125–126, 145
Batty, Luke, 25
Batty, Rosie, 26
BBC, 354
Beach Inquiry, 315
Beazley, Kim, 295
Bega school girl murders, 72
'Behind the Scenes Organ Tour', 352
Bell, Justice Virginia, 324, 326
Benedict XVI, Pope, 34
Best, Robert, 53
Betrayal of Trust report, 365–366

beyond reasonable doubt, 218,
   336–337, 361
   at committal, 5, 7
   directions to juries, 82–83,
      190–192, 271–272
   High Court appeal, 321, 323,
      331–332, 334
   Supreme Court appeal, 303–304,
      313
Boas, Gideon, 8, 337–338
Bolt, Andrew, 64, 291–292, 294–295,
   333
Bonomy, Robert, choirboy, evidence
   in Cathedral trials, 130, 241
Bourke, John, 16–17
Boyce, Chris, 300, 306–310, 324
Bravehearts, 378
Brennan, Father Frank, 250, 293
Broken Rites, 45
Bromfield, Leah, 365
Burg, Georgie, 351–355, 359–360
Burg, Phil, 359

Cardinal (Milligan), 77
Care Leavers Australasian Network
   (CLAN), 60, 371
Carelink, 27–28, 40, 47
Carleton, Richard, 28
Cash, Sean, 45
Cathedral mistrial, 71–95
   see also charges; committal hearing;
      the complainant; second alleged
      choirboy victim
   arraignment, 76, 155, 303
   defence process, 112, 119,
      120–121, 122, 124, 268
   defence's closing address, 171–190
   defence's opening address, 89,
      91–95
   defendant not called, 140, 155
   directions hearings, 21, 73–74,
      89–90, 98–101, 104–105, 106,
      137, 154–158, 188–190, 214
   evidence
      see names of witnesses

jury selection, 74–84
mistrial declared, 195
not guilty plea, 20, 76, 99,
   141–143, 190–191
prosecution's closing address,
   153–154, 158–171, 172, 175,
   179–180
prosecution's opening address,
   84–91, 92, 95
separate trials, 99–100
Cathedral retrial, 208–243, 210–211,
   244–275
   see also charges
   defence's closing address, 265–271
   defendant not called to stand, 316
   evidence
      see names of witnesses
   guilty, 272–274, 276, 298, 316
   Kidd's closing address, 274
   not guilty plea, 214
   prosecution's closing address,
      254–265
Catholic Cathedral College, East
   Melbourne, 198
Catholic Church, 76–77, 214,
   219–220
   see also Melbourne Response;
      names of popes; Towards Healing
   Archdiocese of Melbourne, 8–9,
      25, 40, 42, 50, 139, 343, 380
   Archdiocese of Sydney, 38–39, 75
   Australian Catholic Bishops'
      Conference, 24, 379–382
   celibacy, 380–381, 382
   clericalism, 69–70
   concealment of abuse, 364
   confidentiality of confession,
      381–382
   culture of secrecy, 69–70
   moving abusers policy, 51, 60,
      62–63, 339–340
   royal commission, 24–29, 31,
      35–40
      Ballarat, 50–58
      Melbourne Response, 40–50

Sexual Assault and the Catholic Church (Courtin), 363–364
Vatican, 3–4, 55, 58, 218–219, 250, 312, 333, 335, 381
Catholic Church Insurance, 38
Catholic Education Office, 340–341
Catholic Regional College, Noorat, 59
The Catholic Weekly, 290
celibacy, 380–381, 382
Centre Against Sexual Assault, Ballarat, 358–359
Centre for Forensic Behavioural Science, Swinburne University, 371
charges, 1, 3, 6–9, 11
	Cathedral mistrial, 73–74, 76–77, 79, 87, 91, 100, 113, 115, 141–142, 148, 153, 157–158, 166–170, 178–179, 193
	Cathedral retrial, 215–216, 219–220, 254, 258, 265, 273, 276, 277, 288
	committal, 17–22, 39
child abuse royal commission
	see Royal Commission into Institutional Responses to Child Sexual Abuse
child development, and touch, 372–373
child sex offenders, 365–389
	and celibacy, 380–381, 382
	in criminal justice system, 367
	grooming behaviours, 69, 368
	groupings, 366–368
	in institutions, 365–366, 378–379
	known to families, 378
	media coverage, 365, 368
	paedophilia, 367–368
	in prisons, 387
	recidivism rates, 369, 371
	risk factors, 369, 380–381
	self-referrers, 366, 369–370
	sex abuse victims, 371–375
	and sexual deviance, 369–370
	treatment programs, 369–370
	ways of offending, 368–369
child sexual abuse, 49, 92, 299, 351–364, 371
	see also Melbourne Response; Royal Commission into Institutional Responses to Child Sexual Abuse; Towards Healing
	apologies to victims, 31, 295, 344–346, 360
	in Catholic Church, 36, 38–40, 50, 342, 347–350, 378–380
	change in law, 180
	children with disabilities, 382–385
	and closure, 362–363
	concealment, 342, 364
	and crime, 375–376, 377
	disclosure by children, 355–357
	effect on adult relationships, 358–360
	evidence and memory, 103–105
	in institutions, 365–366, 378–379
	known to offenders, 356, 378
	murder of paedophiles, 374–375
	as perpetrators, 371–375
	a process not single event, 356
	in religious institutions, 25, 39, 39–40, 68–70, 373, 378–382, 385
		see also Catholic Church
	restorative-justice, 360–361, 362–364
	retraumatisation, 361
	Royal Commission lessons, 388–389
	secondary victims, 358–359, 364
	trauma, 357, 359, 360–361, 373–374, 377
	twin study, 357–358
	victim-advocacy groups, 45
	wards-of-the-state, 373–374
	in youth justice systems, 375–377
	and youth rehabilitation, 377–378
Child Sexual Abuse (Fergusson and Mullen), 370–371
children with disabilities, 382–385

choir procession
  Cathedral mistrial, 86, 88, 90,
    92, 109–110, 113, 118–121,
    130–132, 136–139, 143,
    161–162, 176, 240
  Cathedral retrial, 216, 224–226,
    234, 239–241, 252–256,
    259–262
choirboys, 307
  see also the complainant; second
    alleged choirboy victim
  evidence in Cathedral trials,
    118–119, 125–126, 129–130,
    134–136, 149, 163, 222,
    239–242, 253–254, 256
Christchurch mosque shootings, 297
Christian Brothers' Education, 198
Clarke, Peter, 327
clericalism, 69–70
Close Encounters of the Third Kind
  (film), 16
Coleridge, Archbishop Mark,
  124–125
College of Consultors, 51, 54, 61–62
'Come Home Cardinal Pell'
  (Minchin, song), 57, 178, 218
committal hearing, 5, 327, 392
  and Basha hearings, 119–120
  charges, 9, 17–20
  evidence, 11–14, 18, 114, 134,
    148, 151, 155, 187
  findings, 18–19
  media constraints, 4–5, 7–12, 17,
    21–22
  process, 5–7
  role of magistrate, 11–12
  suppression orders, 1–3, 8–10,
    21–22
  swimming pool allegations, 9,
    10–11, 16, 17–20
compensation, 25, 31–32, 40, 42,
  44–46
Compensation Panel, 40, 46
the complainant
  anonymity, 102–103

charges, 20–21
delay in complaining, 100–101
disclosure, 103–107, 205–207
evidence in mistrial, 99, 102,
  116, 117, 132–134, 139, 140,
  147–153, 159–162, 164–168,
  178–185, 187–188, 191–192
evidence in retrial, 209, 212–213,
  215–216, 257–258, 260,
  262–268, 273, 293, 299
friendship with second deceased
  victim, 197–198, 202, 204
High Court appeal, 320–321,
  322–326, 330–333, 401–402
second incident, 87–88, 148,
  169–171, 179, 182, 189–190,
  216, 236, 257, 304
statements, 289–290, 334–335
Victorian appeal, 300–302, 304,
  306–308, 310–313
concentration-camp survivors, 182,
  184–185
Connor, Jeffrey, altar server
  diary, 121, 122, 137–138, 146,
    161, 163, 179, 186, 248–249,
    251, 259
  evidence in Cathedral mistrial,
    138, 146–147, 161, 163, 179,
    186
  evidence in Cathedral retrial,
    251–252, 259, 332
  and McGlone, 245, 247–248
conservative politicians and
  commentators, 294–296
conspiracy theories, 393–394
Cooper, Adam, 211
Cossins, Anne, 361, 400
County Court of Victoria, 40, 71–73,
  75, 213, 276, 392
Court of Appeal of the Supreme
  Court of Victoria
  see Victorian Court of Appeal
Courtin, Dr Judy, 1, 363–364
Covid-19, 327–328
Cox, Geoffrey, organist, 137, 261

evidence in Cathedral mistrial, 88–89, 111–112, 155, 162–163

evidence in Cathedral retrial, 216, 225–227

Craven, Greg, 290–291

Crikey, 280

Criminology Research Advisory Council, 362

crowdfunding campaign, 61, 67

culture wars, 294, 296

The Daily Telegraph, 292

Daniel, Father David, 344

Dearing, David, choirboy, evidence in Cathedral trials, 118–119, 125, 163, 239–241

Dearing, Rodney, choir member, 118–119

evidence in Cathedral trials, 125, 241

deceased second choirboy

see second alleged choirboy victim

deeds of release, 32, 44

Deery, Shannon, 211

Derrij, Farris, choirboy, evidence in Cathedral trials, 125–126, 239

Devine, Miranda, 292

Dignan, Damian, 9

directions hearings

Azzopardi direction, 188–189

Cathedral mistrial, 21, 73–74, 81–83, 89–91, 95, 98–101, 104–105, 106, 137, 154–157, 190–192

Cathedral retrial, 211, 271–274, 281, 283

Jury Directions Act 2015, 99, 155

jury v. judge-only trials, 403–406

Markuleski direction, 99

standard jury directions, 403

District Court of New South Wales, Cathedral retrial, 406

Dixon, Justice John, 376–377

the dock, 115, 117, 172–173, 251

Dowlan, Brother Edward, 53, 64–65, 342–343, 349–350

Doyle, Christopher, choirboy, evidence in Cathedral trials, 138, 242

DPP [Department of Public Prosecutions] v George Pell, 76, 85, 213

Dutton, Peter, 113

Edenhope, Vic., 54

Egan, Father Brendan, 251

elections, 26, 295

Ellis, Angela, 90, 111, 223, 225, 272

'Empirical Guidance on the Effects of Child Sexual Abuse on Memory and Cognition' (Royal Commission), 105

Eureka pool, Ballarat, 2–3, 9, 16–20, 283–284

evidence

see the complainant; names of witnesses; second alleged choirboy victim

Evidence Act, 21, 104–105, 151

Facebook, 81

fair trial, 8–9, 74, 79, 80, 120, 281, 403–404

Fairfax media, 9

family violence, 26, 362–363, 388

Fasciale, Father Nazareno, 343–344

Feast of Christ the King, 249

Ferguson, Chief Justice Anne, 298–303, 306, 310–311

Ferguson, Dennis, 404

Ferguson, Sarah, 285, 326–327

Fergusson, David M., 370–371

Finnigan, Peter, choir marshal, 92, 109, 111, 118, 135, 137, 139, 256

evidence in Cathedral trials, 112, 114–115, 117, 216, 228–230, 261, 332

Fischer, Tim, 250

Fisher, Archbishop Anthony, 41–42, 382

Ford, Stuart, choirboy, evidence in Cathedral trials, 130–131, 241–242

Forensicare, 366

Foster, Aimee, 41
Foster, Anthony, 31–35, 47, 50
    applications for compensation,
        31–32
    evidence to royal commission, 41
    meeting with Pell, 27–30
    push for royal commission, 26,
        30–33
    Rome experience, 67–68
    settlement with Catholic Church, 32
Foster, Chrissie, 47
    applications for compensation,
        31–32
    attends retrial, 251, 311
    on dismissal of appeal, 311–312
    evidence to royal commission, 31,
        41–42
    evidence to Victorian parliamentary
        inquiry, 29
    meeting with Pell, 27–30
    push for royal commission, 26,
        30–33
    Rome experience, 67–68
    settlement with Catholic Church, 32
Foster, Emma, 27–29, 31, 41–42, 311
Foster, Katie, 27, 31, 41, 311
Fox, Peter, 26
Francis, Pope, 3, 35, 60, 64, 312, 335
Furness, Gail, 37–38, 45–49, 61–64

Galbally, Paul, 248
Gargasoulas, James, 214
Gibson, Mark
    appeal, 307–308, 309
    Cathedral mistrial, 108, 110, 111,
        121–129, 185, 194
        Azzopardi direction, 188–189
        closing address, 153–154,
            158–171, 172, 175, 179–180
        directions hearing, 104–106
        examination of Reed, 146–149,
            151–154
        examination of witnesses,
            116–119, 125–126, 131–
            132, 134, 138, 145–147

        opening address, 84–91, 92, 95
        and Portelli, 123, 124–129,
            134, 177
    Cathedral retrial
        closing address, 213, 236,
            254–265
        examination of Reed, 254–255
        examination of witness-
            es, 223–225, 230–236,
            245–250
        opening address, 213,
            214–218
        and Portelli, 238, 241
    prosecution's closing address,
        Cathedral retrial, 254–265
    relation with journalists, 113,
        211–212, 313
    style, 84–85, 158–159, 307, 308
Gilbert v The Queen [2000], 406
Gillard, Julia, 26, 32–33, 298, 336
GoFundMe, 23, 67
Goodman-Delahunty, Jane, 400,
    407
goods and services tax (GST), 295
Google, 80–81
grooming behaviours, 42, 58, 69, 91,
    93, 152, 177, 368
Guardian Australia, 25, 61, 66, 225,
    293–294, 328–329, 338–339,
    351–352
The Guardian, 211
Gunn, Shireen, 358–359

Hart, Archbishop Denis, 8–9, 130,
    381–382
hearsay, 12–13, 90–91, 153, 197
Hell on the Way to Heaven (Foster), 26
Henderson, Gerard, 294
The Herald Sun, 57, 211, 280, 282,
    294–295, 346–347
Hersbach, Paul, 42–45
Hickie, Ian, 49
High Court appeal, 236, 312,
    320–321
    acquittal, 320–350, 333

court set-up, 322, 327–328
defence arguments, 320–324
effect of Covid-19, 327–328
judgment, 328–333
jury v. judge-only trials, 404–407
media, 322, 328–329, 355
other cases, 404–407
prosecution arguments, 324–326
release of Pell, 333–334
Richter's interview, 317–318
statements on decision
    complainant, 334–335
    Gillard, 336
    Vatican, 335
Hilton Rome airport hotel, 140
Hotel Quirinale, Rome, 61
Howard, John, 32, 290, 295–296
Human Rights Law Centre, 376

Independent Commissioners, 42, 43,
    45, 80, 404
Institute of Child Protection Studies,
    Australian Catholic University,
    382–384
internet, 35, 41, 80–81, 300, 308, 370
Ireland, 26

joint trials, 21–22
    v. separate trials, 399–402
journalists
    see media
Judd, Kerri, 300, 324–326
judge-only trials, v. jury trials, 5–6, 7,
    74, 283, 403–408
Judicial College of Victoria, 120
juries, 173–174, 256–257
    acquittal, 321–324
    appeal, 301–309, 311, 316–318
    Azzopardi direction, 188–189
    Cathedral mistrial, 117–118
        Azzopardi direction, 155
        Basha hearings, 119–123
        deliberations, 193–194
        directions, 79–84, 91, 95,
           99–103, 137, 157, 301

evidence ends, 149–156
interaction with counsel and
    solicitors, 97–98
leave applications, 107–108, 180
mistrial declared, 195–196
omission of information to
    jury, 103–104
Pell's robes, 94, 128, 168–169
pressured by Richter, 183–185
questions, 98, 112–113,
    180–181
selection, 74–84
split, 194, 286–287
tour of Cathedral, 96–97
Cathedral retrial, 298, 337–339
balloting out, 265–266
directions, 89, 97–98,
    222–223, 271–272, 274,
    277, 291, 293
jury's tour of Cathedral, 222
proposed animation, 269
selection, 213–214, 270–271
verdict, 272–274, 276, 298, 316
changes to Jury Directions Act,
    99–100
hung, 209
Jury Reasoning in Joint and Separate
    Trials of Institutional Child Sexual
    Abuse, 401–402
jury trials or judge-only trials,
    403–408
mock jurors, 337, 400–402
risk of prejudice, 7–10, 21, 58,
    73–74, 80, 91, 173, 218, 285,
    399
Jury Directions Act 2015, 99–100, 155
Jury Reasoning in Joint and Separate
    Trials of Institutional Child Sexual
    Abuse (Delahunty, Cossins, and
    Martschuk), 400
jury trials, v. judge-only trials, 5–6, 7,
    74, 283, 403–408

Kairos, 114, 139–140, 179
Kaufmann, Dr Leah, 291

Keneally, Kristina, 65–66
Kennedy, Paul, 26, 33
Kidd, Judge Peter Barrington, 21, 313, 318
  background, 71–73
  Cathedral mistrial, 121, 122, 124–125, 168
    admissibility of May's evidence, 132–134, 137
    Azzopardi direction, 155, 188–189
    and Connor, 138
    directions to jury, 95, 97–98, 99–101, 137, 154–156, 157–158, 190–193
    discussions with Richter, 135–136, 148–150, 156, 171–172, 182–184
    examination of choirboys, 146–148
    jurors' questions, 112–113, 180–181
    jurors' tour of Cathedral, 97–98
    jury deliberations, 193–196
    jury empanelment, 73–83
    leave to jurors, 106–107, 180
    and media, 174
    refuses questioning on complainant's counselling, 150–152
    road map for jurors, 155–156
    ruling on cross-examination, 90–92
    ruling on McCarthy, 152–153
    ruling on application on Potter, 116–118
  Cathedral retrial, 231, 248–249, 264
    directions to jury, 213–214, 222–223, 235–236, 242–243, 271–272, 273, 274, 291–293
    discussion with Richter, 226–228
    and media, 276–278, 279
    ruling on swimming pool charges, 284–285
    ruling on video animation, 269, 303
    sentencing, 287–289, 300
    suppression orders, 276–278, 280–284, 285
    closing address, Cathedral retrial, 274
Kiefel, Chief Justice, Susan, 321, 325–326, 328–329
Kirchengast, Dr Tyrone, 337

La Greca, Andrew, choirboy, evidence in Cathedral trials, 132, 134–136, 253–254
Lake Boga, Vic., 19–20, 284–285
Lateline (TV program), 41
Law Council of Australia, 99
Lee, Katrina, 11, 75, 84, 113, 285–286
Levey, Paul, 23, 53–54, 58–61, 63, 67
Liberal Party of Australia, 296
Linane, Clare, 349–350
Linane, Peter, 349–350
Little, Archbishop Frank, 246
live-streaming, 35, 41, 300, 322, 393
Llewellyn, Gwynnyth, 384–385
Loff, Bebe, 361–363

Macquarie Media, 280
Magistrates Court of Victoria, 4, 392
Mallesons, 71
Mallinson, John Whalley, director of music and organist, 88–89
  evidence in Cathedral mistrials, 108–111, 163–164
  evidence in Cathedral retrial, 216, 223–226
Malmsbury youth justice centre, 375–376
The Markuleski direction, 99–100
Marr, David, 34, 58, 293–296
Martignoni, Miles, 294
Martschuk, Natalie, 400
Mason, Justice Anthony, 404–405

Mathews, Ben, 336–337
Maxwell, Justice Chris, 298–299, 303–309, 311, 362
May, John, sacramental wine maker, evidence in Cathedral trials, 132–134, 137, 145–146, 226
Mayes, David, choirboy, evidence in Cathedral trials, 138–139, 252–253
McArthur, Morag, 382–384
McCarthy, Monsignor William, 117, 152–153, 193, 224
McClellan, Justice Peter, 144, 408
    issue of video-link evidence by Pell, 54–57
    media briefing, 23–25, 34
    questions Pell, 36, 47, 61–65
McEwan, Troy, 365–370, 388
McEwen, Rebecca, 404–405
McGlone, Daniel, altar server, evidence in Cathedral retrial, 222, 244–250, 258–259, 262, 318, 332
McHugh, Justice Michael, 406
media, 211–212
    see also suppression orders
    briefing by Justice Peter McClellan, 23–25, 34
    Cathedral mistrial, 76, 78–81, 80, 82, 84, 107–108, 113–114, 138, 140, 144–145, 154, 171–172, 174, 194, 195, 286–287
    Cathedral retrial, 208–212, 250–251, 272–273
    child sexual abuse, 368, 388–394
    committal, 3–5, 8–12, 10, 17, 21–22
    conviction, 276–283, 291–293
    High Court appeal, 322, 324, 328–329
    Pell's press conference, 66–67
    responses to acquittal, 333–339
    royal commission, 36, 50, 58, 66–67, 68, 314
    youth justice crisis, 376–377
meet-and-greets, 246–247, 252, 255, 256, 262–263, 266, 303–305, 323–326, 332
Melbourne Archdiocese Personnel Advisory Board, 343
Melbourne Assessment Prison, West Melbourne, 301
Melbourne Remand Centre, 286
Melbourne Response
    appointment of Ball, 27–28, 47–49
    compensation, 24, 30–32, 40–46
    components, 42
    established by Pell, 24, 30, 35, 37, 92–93, 110
    and the Fosters, 26–28, 30–35, 41–42
    independent commissioners, 40, 42, 43, 45–46
    key components, 40, 42
    and royal commission, 33, 37, 40–50
Michael Kirby Centre for Public Health & Human Rights, 361
Mikakos, Jenny, 376–377
Miller, Senior Constable Rodney, 72
Milligan, Louise, 2–3, 17–18, 77
Minchin, Tim, 57, 178, 218–219
mock cross-examination, 85
mock jurors, 337, 400–402
Monash University, 361–362
Moore, Dr Tim, 382–384
Morris-Marr, Lucie, 1, 57–58
Morrison, Scott, 113, 344–346
Mortimer, John, 189
Mortlake parish, 51, 53–54, 59–60, 340
Mueller, Carl, choirboy, evidence in Cathedral trials, 123, 222
Mulkearns, Bishop Ronald, 53–54, 60–62, 340–342
Mullen, Paul E., 371
murder, 374–375
Myers, Allan, 54–55

Nangle, Brother Paul, 342
Nathan, Anthony, choirboy, evidence in Cathedral trials, 131, 240

National Pastoral Institute, Elsternwick, 59
National Tertiary Education Union, 291
Nelson, Elliot, 358
Nenna, Damian, choirboy, evidence in Cathedral mistrial, 126
Newcastle Herald, 26
News Ltd, 1, 64, 280, 291, 294, 296
The New Daily, 211
Nine News, 280

O'Brien, Peter, 6–7, 338–339
O'Callaghan, Peter, 43–45
Occam's razor, 189
O'Donnell, Father Kevin, 27–28, 30–31, 311
O'Dwyer, Paul, 56–57
Office of Public Prosecutions Victoria, 148, 300, 324, 334
   DPP v George Pell, 76, 85, 213
Ogloff, James, 371
O'Hanlon, Christopher, choirboy, evidence in Cathedral mistrial, 122, 123

Parissi, Luciano, choirboy, evidence in Cathedral trials, 130, 240–241
Parkville youth justice centre, 375–376
Patton, Shane, 1
Pell, Cardinal George
   see also Melbourne Response
   appointed Cardinal, 29
   conservative support, 294–296
   health, 54–57, 83–84, 273, 287, 301
   political role, 295–296
   press conferences, 3
   prominence in Catholic Church, 3, 25, 29, 33, 35, 44, 64, 73, 91, 104, 113, 177–178, 220, 270, 272, 311–312
permanent stays, 403–404
perpetrators
   see child sex offenders

Phillip Island, Vic., sexual abuse allegations, 29
physical distancing, 328–329
police
   see Victoria Police
The Pope
   see names of popes
Portelli, Monsignor Charles, master of ceremonies, 224–225, 318
   evidence in Cathedral mistrial, 88–89, 126–129, 153, 161, 163–164, 176–177, 186–187
   evidence in Cathedral retrial, 213, 216–217, 236–239, 245, 259, 262, 270, 303–304, 323–326
   reliability, 323, 325–326
   role and procedures, 116, 123–125, 176–177, 186–187, 229–233, 332
   smoker, 125, 126, 127, 129, 177, 264, 266
Porteous, Archbishop Julian, 9
Porter, Christian, 339
Potter, Max, sacristan, 90, 217
   evidence in Cathedral mistrial, 88–89, 115–118, 133–134, 164
   evidence in Cathedral retrial, 230–236, 262, 332
   reliability, 117–118, 133–134, 234–236
   role and procedures, 111, 115–116, 127, 152–153, 163–165, 186–187, 224–225, 247, 252
PowerPoint presentation, 268, 286
powers of discovery, 35, 40
presumption of innocence, 9, 189, 300
The Prince (Marr), 34, 294
Private Media, 280
psychiatry, 12, 28, 31, 47, 49
psychological counselling, 150–151, 365

Quinn, Aidan, choirboy, evidence in Cathedral trials, 132, 222

R v Henry & Manning [1969], 407
rape, 16–17, 27, 30, 91, 142, 153,
    157, 158, 181, 251, 268, 289, 311,
    351–353, 359–360, 375, 406
'The Reckoning' (podcast), 294
Reddit (website), 296–297
Reed, Detective Sergeant Chris, 247, 320
    evidence in Cathedral trials, 75,
        117–118, 139–142, 147–153,
        253–254
    interview with Pell, 141–143, 219
    interview with Potter, 117–118,
        232–233
restorative-justice programs, 360–363
Reuters, 84, 211
Revelation (documentary series), 285,
    326–327
Richter, Robert, 131–140
    absent, 168
    appeal, 300, 306–307, 330–331
    Azzopardi direction, 155
    Cathedral mistrial, 83–85, 156
        closing address, 133, 171–191,
            265–271
        complainant's counselling,
            151–152
        cross-examination, 109–115,
            118–120, 120–124,
            128–129
        and deliberations, 193–194
        evidence ends, 144–156
        examination of choirboys,
            131–132, 134–136, 137,
            138–139
        examination of complainant,
            165–167, 169, 257
        examination of Reed, 147–153
        examination of wine supplier,
            145–146
        jury interaction with legal
            teams, 97–98
        objection to Gibson's leave,
            153–154
        opening address, 91–95
        Pell not called, 140

    reprimanded by Kidd,
        183–185
    reprimanded for shouting, 136
    Cathedral retrial, 217, 241,
        254–255, 264, 286–287
        cross-examination of Potter,
            234–236
        evidence of Portelli, 236–237,
            239
        examination of choirboys, 239,
            246, 249–250, 253, 307
        examinations, 225–231
        exchange with Kidd, 226–228
        his case to lose, 209–210
        objection, 231–232
        opening address, 218–222
        relation with journalists,
            211–212
        on suppression order, 282
        verdict shock, 272–273
    committal hearing, 10–17, 19,
        162, 327
    interview, 313–319
    sentencing argument, 289–290
    style, 10, 11–12, 84–85, 159, 171
    video animation, 313
Ridsdale, Gerald, 13, 50–54, 58–63,
    66, 294–295, 314, 339–340
robes, 311
    complainant's evidence, 106,
        165–167
    Gibson's argument, 168–169
    jury examination, 83–84, 324
    manoeuvrability, 221, 306
    Portelli's evidence, 127–128, 163–
        164, 176, 217, 236–237, 324
    Potter's evidence, 233–234
    Richter's argument, 93–94, 120,
        122, 134–135, 187
Royal Commission into Institutional
Responses to Child Sexual Abuse,
    23–70, 144, 157, 208, 244, 351,
    353–354, 365, 368, 408
    apology by prime minister,
        344–346

culture of Catholic Church, 68–70
evidence of Hersbach, 42–44, 45
evidence of Levey, 58–59, 61
final report, 100, 378–380,
    380–381, 387
and the Fosters, 26–35, 41–42
hearings on Ballarat, 50–68
hearings on Melbourne Response,
    40–50
informal media briefing, 23–25, 34
Markuleski direction, 99–100
ordered by Gillard, 298, 336
Pell's appearances
    commission findings, 339–344
    evidence from Rome, 54–57,
        60–61, 67–68, 71
    first, 35–39
    second, 44–49
    statement on findings, 346
    third, 50–54, 61, 62–63
    video-link evidence, 44–45,
        54–57, 58, 140–141, 219
podcast, 294
recommendations on Catholic
    Church, 379–382
research reports
    child safety elements, 385–386
    children with disabilities,
        384–385
    effects on memory and
        cognition, 105
    residential care requirements,
        382–384
Richter's comments, 314
scope, 25, 35, 220
Rubeo, Father Victor, 42–44
Rudd, Kevin, 32
Rumpole of the Bailey (TV program), 189

sacramental wine, 87–88, 90,
    117–118, 132–134, 145–146, 164,
    217, 226
Sacred Heart Parish, Oakleigh, 41
Sacred Heart Primary School,
    Oakleigh, 27, 41

Salmon, Lord Justice, 407
Savile, Jimmy, 354
schizophrenia, 367
search warrants, 139–140
Searson, Father Peter, 341, 346
second alleged choirboy victim, 87,
    103, 136, 139, 157, 181, 254, 265,
    276, 312
    death, 95, 103, 137, 201
    father's evidence, 12–13, 197–207
sentencing, 287–290, 299
separate trials, v. joint trials, 21–22,
    399–402
Seto, Dr Michael, 367–368
Sexual Assault and the Catholic Church
    (Courtin), 363–364
sexual deviance, 369
Shann, Ruth, 112, 119, 130, 133,
    168, 240, 248, 272, 300
Sheedy, Leonie, 60, 371–375
Sheridan, Paul, detective
    superintendent, 141
Shine, Kerry, 404
Silk, Sergeant Gary, 72
Sisters of Mercy, 372
Sky News, 294
Smee, Ben, 328–329
South Eastern Centre Against Sexual
    Assault & Family Violence (Secasa),
    362
Southwell, Judge Alec, 29, 34
Spotlight (film), 91
St Alipius boys' school, Ballarat, 2–3,
    51, 66
St Alipius presbytery, Ballarat East, 62
St Catherine's Children's Home,
    Geelong, 372
St Columba's Church, North Ballarat,
    347
St Joseph's Boys Home, Ballarat, 17, 19
St Kevin's College, Toorak, 86, 88,
    104, 118, 198–199, 201–202, 216,
    252, 308
St Patrick's Cathedral, Ballarat, 347
St Patrick's Cathedral, Melbourne,

12–13, 84–86, 96–97, 108–109,
110, 111, 112, 116, 145
see also Cathedral mistrial; Cathedral retrial
appellate judges' tour, 302
archbishop's sacristy, 86, 126,
163, 170, 231, 234, 245,
255–256, 262, 263, 307, 331
choir, 198
choirboy tour, 307
dates of alleged abuses, 219
dates of Pell masses, 91, 121, 122,
123, 124, 125, 139–140, 161,
224–225, 238, 251, 258–259,
304, 305
jury tour, 97–99
layout, 111, 113, 125, 127
priests' sacristy, 86, 88, 90, 93,
108, 113, 127, 163–164, 165,
170, 215, 216, 226, 245–246,
249, 250, 253, 262, 263–265,
268, 307, 326, 332
restoration work, 223, 307
walk-through with May, 140
St Patrick's College, Ballarat, 342, 347
St Patrick's Primary School, Ballarat,
347
State Court of Bosnia-Herzegovina, 72
suicide, 27, 31, 41, 52, 355, 357,
358, 372
suppression orders, 8–10, 21–22,
208–209, 273, 275, 276–283,
285–286, 291, 296, 393
Supreme Court appeal
see Victorian Court of Appeal
Supreme Court of New South Wales,
408
Sweeney, Karen, 211
Swimmers' trial, 21, 406–408
delayed, 209–212
dropped, 284–285, 348
Eureka pool, Ballarat, allegations,
2–3, 9, 16–20, 19–20, 283–284
Lake Boga, Vic., allegations,
19–20, 284–285

suppression order, 273, 277, 279,
283
swimming pool charges, 284
YMCA swimming pool, Ballarat,
allegations, 326–327, 347–349
Swinburne University, 371
Sydney Morning Herald, 18, 34

Taskforce Sano, 1, 58, 205, 327,
348–349
tendency and coincidence evidence,
72, 284–285
terrorism, Christchurch mosque
shootings, 297
Theological College, 124
Theroux, Louis, 354
Thomas, Aaron, choirboy, evidence in
Cathedral trials, 136–137, 242
tobacco industry, 300
Torquay Life Saving Club, sexual
exposure allegations, 1–2
touch, 372–373
Towards Healing, 24, 35, 37
transcripts, 102–103, 114, 134, 145,
156, 161, 221, 291, 293, 311, 321,
325, 392–394
Trauma, Violence and Abuse, 355
Turnbull, Malcolm, 113
Twitter, 277–278, 280, 285, 286,335
Tyack, Les, 1–2

umpiring, and the law, 85
United States, 26, 82
Uniting Church, 351–352
University of Arkansas, 358
University of New South Wales, 361, 386
University of South Australia, 365
University of Sydney, 384, 404
University of Toronto, 355

Valdi Room, 68
Valentine, Dr Kylie, 386
Vatican, 3–4, 55, 58, 218–219, 250,
312, 333, 335, 381
Victoria, 74, 82, 362

Victoria Police, 1, 5, 60, 158, 247, 312, 318, 320, 342, 346–347
  Beach Inquiry, 315
  concealment of crimes in Ballarat, 206–207
  evidence of Detective Sergeant Chris Reed, 75, 117–118, 139–143, 147–153, 253–254
  interview with Pell, 140–142, 178–179, 219, 254, 265
  interview with Potter, 117–118, 232–233
  Pell's police statement, 141, 258–259
  police investigation, 147–150
  search warrants, 139–140
  Taskforce Sano, 1, 58, 205, 327, 348–349
  video of Rome police interview with Pell, Cathedral mistrial, 140–142
  walk-through St Patrick's Cathedral with May, 140
Victoria v Australian Building, Construction, Employees' and Builders Labourers' Federation [1982], 404
Victorian Bar News, 71–72
Victorian Court of Appeal, 235–236, 274, 298–319, 300, 301, 317, 321, 325, 338, 362, 393, 404
  appeal dismissed, 298–299, 310
  appeal process, 299–302
  courtrooms, 78–79
  defence arguments, 309–310, 311, 312
  dissenting judgment, 312, 330–332
  grounds, 303
  prosecution arguments, 303–305, 307–309, 310, 324
  role of appellate judges, 302
  video animation, 303, 313
Victorian Institute of Forensic Mental Health, 366

Victorian Parliamentary Inquiry into the Handling of Child Abuse by Religious and other Non-Government Organisations, 29, 32–33, 205, 365–366
video animation, 269, 303, 313
video-links, 123–124, 223, 242, 330, 336, 352
  appellate courts, 300, 309, 320–321, 325, 330
  complainant, 99, 103, 212–213, 215, 302–303
  jury selection, 73, 75, 214
  Pell, 41, 44, 54–58, 219, 254, 303, 313, 333

Wainer, Dr Bertram, 315
Waks, Manny, 96
Walker, Bret, 299–301, 303–306, 309, 311, 313, 317, 320–324, 326
Waller, Vivian, 101–103, 207, 312, 334
Waller Legal, 101
Wallington, Belinda, 11–12, 15, 17–21
The Wall Street Journal, 84
war crimes, 72
ward-of-the-state files, 373–374
Washington University School of Medicine, 358
Weinberg, Justice Mark, 298–299, 303, 308–309
  dissenting Victorian appeal judgment, 311–313, 330–331
Welch, Martin, choirboy, evidence in Cathedral mistrial, 120–121, 123
White Cliffs, NSW, 59
Wikipedia, 229, 282
Wilson, Archbishop Philip, 342
wine
  see sacramental wine
witness support dogs, 11
witness support staff, 10
witnesses
  see evidence

word-on-word cases, 99
Worth, Carolyn, 362

YMCA swimming pool, Ballarat,
    326–327, 347–349
Younger, Emma, 211